Strategic Market Analysis

EUR/USD INTERBANK MARKET AS DIVERSIFIED ORGANIZATION

Georgette Boele, Ph.D.

Library of Congress Control Number: 2002093484

Copyright © 2002 by Georgette Boele

Published by Alan Guinn

All rights reserved.

Reproduction or translation of any part of this work beyond that permitted by Section 107 or 108 of the 1976 United States Copyright Act without the permission of the copyright owner and publisher is unlawful. Requests for permission or further information should be addressed to Alan Guinn, 3 Lincoln Avenue East, Massapequa, NY 11758 (Alan@AlanGuinn.com.)

This publication is designed to provide accurate and authoritative information in regards to the subject matter covered. It is sold with the understanding that neither the author nor the publisher is engaged in rendering legal, accounting, or other professional service. If legal advice or other expert assistance is required, the services of a competent professional person should be sought.

ISBN: 0-9712707-1-6

Printed in United States of America and United Kingdom

Cover and book design: Ed Schultheis
Art and typesetting: Bob Klei, RWK Graphics

PREFACE

Strategic Market Analysis was the title of my Ph.D. Dissertation.

Within this project I have developed the rationale and linkage to combine two of my passions: Strategic Management & Organization, and Financial Markets.

I have used the specialty of Strategic Management & Organization as an analysis tool (with Financial Markets as the organization) to uncover the links between Financial Markets (my other specialty).

This analysis is necessary to fully understand the influence of the following markets on the EUR/USD Interbank Market:

- FX Option Market
- Commodity (Oil & Gold) Market
- Equity Market
- International Debt Market
- Short-Term Interest Rate Market

Each one of these markets can be the dominating force at any given time; however, a dominant position is never fixed, nor should it be assumed. It represents a continuous force game between these market variables.

In stating the obvious, it's clear that none of the market forces mentioned can beat the constant and powerful force of Market Psychology.

FOREWORD

Foreign exchange markets have frequently been described as having a chaotic behaviour. This is particularly evident when it is punctuated by major crises that have considerable consequences for the underlying nations, by disturbing the natural flows of real exchanges due to modified competitiveness or at the extreme by annihilating the reserve function of a currency. Contrary to a common understanding, the recent aggregation of old EU currencies into the Euro has, however, not simplified the degree of complexity of the determination of the Euro /USD parity. The reduction of currencies and its simplification to a single currency zone have happened in a context of a quasi-exponential growth of the instruments, options swap and new debt markets. These create new crossroads that may imply directly or indirectly foreign exchange trans-actions beyond the over-simplistic influences of the traditional economic variables and/or trading behaviours that can influence a parity. The lesson of recent history is that the Euro has not only to gain the hearts of the 360 million of Europeans who are effective users of this brand new currency, but also to gain market share and recognition among the financial actors that dominate the sub segments of the global financial markets. Within a context of interconnectivity of some actors, but also of segmented behaviours of others, foreign market efficiency is seriously limited by what Herbert Simon defined as "bounded rationality". The chaos must be organised in order to become intelligible.

It is at this level where the work of Georgette Boele has found its *reason d'être* and its originality. Beyond the mere description of the current complexity and the various market influences at stake, in the options, commodity, debt, money and equity markets, it provides a frame of analysis based on the organisation theory to explain the complex causalities between the influencing factors. By looking at the forex market as an organisation, it enables the analysis in terms of structure but also in terms of behaviour of the decision makers. Actors decide with different and sometime divergent strategic goals. Think of how a day trader that woke up one business day to benefit from intraday fluctuations can in the same moment collide with the long-term utility function of a central bank. The main benefit of this thesis is to integrate two dominant schools of thought: the competitive strategy approach and the strategic organisation theory and to apply their respective methodologies to define the Forex market in an unexpected manner. The result is a compilation of sub-markets influences that make the global financial markets. It highlights the growing influence of the option market in changing the risk level of the market and the new signalling function of the derivative markets to observe expected market trends by participants. It also helps to clarify the reliability level of dominant variables. For instance, the hierarchy of variables will change considerably in a growth or recessionary context. Traditional economic variables lose weight before the complex and sometimes subliminal influences of market psychology and the mere source of flows between two asset classes.

The review of the mental underpinning behaviours of individual traders is reviewed diligently, describing the fallacies of certain tricks as influential as long as they are used by a significant number of actors. The effects of the personalisation of the trading can lead to egregious behaviours. When aggregated it becomes waves of speculation.

Once the last page of this work is turned, it is already time to look for future research and promising applications of the frame defined by Georgette Boele to the central banks' behaviour.

Since the invention of philosophy, knowledge jumps by a succession of surprises. Thales in ancient Greece lamented on the inescapable nature of change as the ultimate certainty. Fortunately, psychology has taught us that our degree of openness reduces the negative perception of change. Georgette Boele, through her remarkable work, provides the reader a wide tool kit to observe change and opens the way for new possible monitoring, helpful for both the practitioners and the curious mind.

Geneva, April 10th, 2002

> Didier Duret
> Head of Product Development
> Private Clients Europe 2
> ABN AMRO Bank Switzerland

CONTENTS

ACKNOWLEDGEMENTS   x

Chapter 1   1
STRATEGIC MANAGEMENT AND ORGANIZATION
    1.1   Strategic Management   2
    1.2   The basis of my research   4
          Summary 1   12
          References   13

Chapter 2   14
FOREIGN EXCHANGE
EUR/USD INTERBANK MARKET AS DIVERSIFIED ORGANIZATION
    2.1   Introduction   15
    2.2   History   16
    2.3   EUR/USD Interbank Market   19
    2.4   Configuration approach   25
    2.5   Entrepreneurial & cognitive approach   28
    2.6   Design approach I: Business Plan   31
    2.7   Design approach II: SWOT Analysis   45
    2.8   Positioning approach I: Elements of industry structure   52
    2.9   Positioning approach II: Concept of industry evolution   53
          Summary 2   55
          References   57

Chapter 3   58
BEHAVIORAL FINANCE (COGNITIVE APPROACH) &
MARKET PSYCHOLOGY (ORGANIZATIONAL CULTURE)
    3.1   Introduction   59
    3.2   Trading is taken personally   61
    3.3   Prospect theory   63
    3.4   Regret   68
    3.5   Cognitive dissonance   69
    3.6   Overconfidence   70
    3.7   Overreaction & underreaction   71
    3.8   Anchoring   73
    3.9   Mental compartments   74
    3.10   Disjunction effect   75
    3.11   Gambling behavior and speculation   76
    3.12   The irrelevance of history   77
    3.13   Magical thinking   78
    3.14   Conclusion   79
          Summary 3   80
          References   81

Chapter 4 — 82
FUNDAMENTAL ANALYSIS
TECHNO STRUCTURE (I) OF EUR/USD INTERBANK MARKET
ORGANIZATION

4.1	Introduction	83
4.2	Economic data US	88
4.3	Economic data Eurozone	104
4.4	US & Eurozone data compared	109
4.5	Market impact of economic data	118
4.6	Conclusion	129
	Summary 4	130
	References	131

Chapter 5 — 132
TECHNICAL ANALYSIS
TECHNO STRUCTURE (II) OF EUR/USD INTERBANK MARKET
ORGANIZATION

5.1	Introduction	133
5.2	Chart: Candlesticks	134
5.3	Trends	136
5.4	Trading ranges	137
5.5	Changing markets	138
5.6	Volume & open interest	139
	Summary 5	140
	References	141

Chapter 6 — 142
DIVISION I
FX OPTION MARKET

6.1	Introduction	143
6.2	Configuration approach	144
6.3	Entrepreneurial approach	146
6.4	Design approach I: Business Plan	147
6.5	Design approach II: SWOT Analysis	165
6.6	Positioning approach I	176
6.7	Positioning approach II	178
	Summary 6	180
	References	181

Chapter 7 — 182
DIVISION II
COMMODITY OIL & GOLD MARKET

	7.1	Introduction	183
	7.2	History	184
	7.3	Configuration approach	194
	7.4	Entrepreneurial & planning approach	196
	7.5	Design approach I: Business Plan	205
	7.6	Design approach II: SWOT Analysis	212
	7.7	Positioning approach I	220
	7.8	Positioning approach II	222
	7.9	Appendix A	223
		Summary 7	232
		References	233

Chapter 8 — 234
DIVISION III
EQUITY MARKET

	8.1	Introduction	235
	8.2	Configuration approach	236
	8.3	Entrepreneurial approach	238
	8.4	Design approach I: Business Plan	239
	8.5	Design approach II: SWOT Analysis	261
	8.6	Positioning approach I	273
	8.7	Positioning approach II	275
		Summary 8	276
		References	277

Chapter 9 — 279
DIVISION IV
INTERNATIONAL DEBT MARKET

	9.1	Introduction	280
	9.2	Configuration approach	281
	9.3	Entrepreneurial approach	283
	9.4	Design approach I: Business Plan	284
	9.5	Design approach II: SWOT Analysis	306
	9.6	Positioning approach I	318
	9.7	Positioning approach II	320
		Summary 9	321
		References	322

Chapter 10			324
DIVISION V			
SHORT-TERM-INTEREST-RATE MARKET			
	10.1	Introduction	325
	10.2	Configuration approach	326
	10.3	Entrepreneurial approach	328
	10.4	Design approach I: Business Plan	329
	10.5	Design approach II: SWOT Analysis	343
	10.6	Positioning approach I	352
	10.7	Positioning approach II	354
		Summary 10	355
		References	359
GLOSSARY			360
INDEX			364

**This book is dedicated to:
Guus and Henny Boele**

ACKNOWLEDGEMENTS

I would like to thank the following people:

1. DUNCAN EDWARDS
   In my opinion, Duncan was one of the highest quality individuals in financial markets. He guided me in the traders' environment until his untimely death in November 1999. He also stimulated me to search for my own answers in financial markets. The ultimate result of my search is my Ph.D. and this book.
2. JONATHAN ROGERS
   In my opinion, he is one of the best trainers in financial markets. He has been a great coach, trainer and friend during the beginning stage of my Ph.D. and book.
3. ALAN GUINN
   He is a Consultant and Professor at Rushmore University. He has been a great advisor and friend during my Ph.D. work. We speak the same language, and understand the same concepts, which, I know from experience, is something to embrace.
4. RUSHMORE UNIVERSITY
   Rushmore University has created a unique team of professionals who speak the same language, and that is very difficult to find. From my top-sport experience I realize that finding professionals is one thing but finding a team of them who speak the same language, and function as a team, is another thing entirely. Other Universities may be able to compete, but they will lose the competition. The main winner will be the student, like supporters in the sports game.
5. CEES QUIRIJNS
   The specialty of my friend Cees is building trading models based on technical analysis. He is one of my best friends. He has supported and stimulated me through my business life. Further, he has provided me with excellent feedback on my Ph.D. work. The idea Market Psychology as Organizational Culture is the result of one of our brainstorm sessions. Further, he showed me the way to Behavioral Finance, and he advised me about the structure of Chapter 5 (trends, trading ranges, changing markets).
6. MY PARENTS GUUS AND HENNY BOELE
   My father has always been able to keep me sharp even when my battery was low. My mother always supported me with her great advice.

7. RENÉ KORSAAN
   A former colleague, we have stayed friends ever since.
8. GEMAYA DE RUIJTER
9. ALETTE CASSEE
   She gave me a chance to work in financial markets (one of my passions) by hiring me.
10. ABN AMRO BANK SWITZERLAND, GENEVA BRANCH.
    Since I started work in Geneva, I have felt like a fish in the water—very much at home. The positive working atmosphere has stimulated a large part of my Ph.D. work. I would like to thank especially: Fernanda Matos Dias, Herbert Meier, and Tineke Ritzema.
11. ABN AMRO BANK AMSTERDAM.
    All my colleagues on the following desks for the wonderful working relationship and the support:
    – Foreign Exchange Trading Desk (spot)
    – Foreign Exchange Option Marketing Desk
    – Foreign Exchange Option Trading Desk
    – Treasury Sales
    – Short-Term-Interest-Rate Trading desk

    Especially:
    Annelies Pruik, Claes von Holten Lindholm, Daan Horstman, Eric Wilde, Ernst van Gelderen, Greg O'Higgins, Henri Muijres, Claus Holst, Louk Nooij, Mark Holland, Philip Hardeveld, Simon Meijlink, Steve Ostendorf, Steven Wesiak, Wim Mesman.
12. All my other friends, family members and colleagues.

Chapter **1**
STRATEGIC MANAGEMENT AND ORGANIZATION

CHAPTER 1

1.1 STRATEGIC MANAGEMENT

As the reader will find out soon, I share many concepts with Mintzberg. It took a while to enter his world with my financial background. However, when I finally made the transition, it had wonderful outcomes as a result. It is clear how Strategic Management & Organization can be combined with financial markets. To make this clear, the wonderful book "Strategy Safari" by Henry Mintzberg, Bruce Ahlstrand and Joseph Lampel (1998) helped significantly. I will give an overview of what is described in the book to make my case, because it is the basis of the earlier mentioned combination. The reader will also find that I refer to principles written in this book in a creative way. I always try to combine things to come to something original. As my publisher and friend Alan Guinn used to say: "it is thinking out of the box". Whatever creative touch I give to these principles, I believe that this book as well as "Structures in Fives" by Henry Mintzberg is an absolute must read, not only by those interested in Strategic Management & Organization but also by those who try to analyze financial markets in a non-conventional way.

By Mintzberg, Ahlstrand and Lampel[1]
In the book Strategy Safari by Mintzberg, Ahlstrand and Lampel, ten different schools are presented. "These schools, together with the single adjective that seems best to capture each one's view of the strategy process, are listed below:

The Design School	strategy formation as a process of conception.
The Planning School	strategy formation as a formal process.
The Positioning School	strategy formation as an analytical process.
The Entrepreneurial School	strategy formation as a visionary process.
The Cognitive School	strategy formation as a mental process.
The Learning School	strategy formation as an emergent process.
The Power School	strategy formation as a process of negotiation.
The Cultural School	strategy formation as a collective process.
The Environmental School	strategy as a reactive process.
The Configuration School	strategy formation as a process of transformation"

---

[1] Mintzberg, H., B. Ahlstrand, J. Lampel, *STRATEGY SAFARI: The Complete Guide Through the Wilds of Strategic Management,* Copyright © 1998. Reprinted by permission of Pearson Education Ltd, 128 LongAcre, London WC2E 9AN

Five Ps for Strategy by Mintzberg, Ahlstrand and Lampel[2]
"The word strategy can be so influential. But what does it really mean? Ask someone to define strategy and you will likely be told that strategy is a *plan* – a direction, a guide or course of action into the future, a path to get from here to there. It turns out that strategy is one of those words that we inevitably define in one way yet often also use in another. Strategy is a *pattern*, that is, consistency in behavior over time. To others, strategy is a *position*, namely the locating of particular products in particular markets. To others, strategy is a *perspective*, namely an organization's fundamental way of doing things, for example, the McDonald's way. As perspective, strategy looks in – inside the organization, indeed, inside the heads of the strategists, but it also looks up – to the grand vision of the enterprise. Thus we have four different definitions of strategy. A fifth is in common usage too: strategy is a *ploy*, that is a specific "maneuver" intended to outwit an opponent or competitor".

"The strategy beast: areas of agreement (adapted from Chaffee, 1985:89-90)[3]

- Strategy concerns both the organization and environment
- The substance of strategy is complex.
- Strategy affects the overall welfare of the organization.
- Strategy involves issues of both content and process.
- Strategies are not purely deliberate.
- Strategies exist on different levels.
- Strategy involves various thought processes".

---

[2]Mintzberg, H., B. Ahlstrand, J. Lampel, *STRATEGY SAFARI: The Complete Guide Through the Wilds of Strategic Management,* Copyright © 1998. Reprinted by permission of Pearson Education Ltd, 128 LongAcre, London WC2E 9AN

[3]Mintzberg, H., B. Ahlstrand, J. Lampel, *STRATEGY SAFARI: The Complete Guide Through the Wilds of Strategic Management,* Copyright © 1998. Reprinted by permission of Pearson Education Ltd, 128 LongAcre, London WC2E 9AN

1.2 THE BASIS OF MY RESEARCH

In my research I combine the principles of strategic management of chapter 1.1 with financial markets. In fact, I use these principles as an analysis tool for financial markets. Analyzing financial markets is complex. They are uncertain, they are interlinked, and every player has a different view based on experience and knowledge, and these views are influenced by the positions of the players. My research is about the EUR/USD Interbank Market. This approach can also be used for the other financial markets such as the option market, commodity market, equity market, international debt market and short-term-interest-rate market. I have traded EUR/USD as a professional trader. EUR/USD has existed since the start of 1999 and is the most liquid currency pair. However, I found it difficult to trade because I couldn't find answers for its behavior. My analytical mind motivated me to search for these answers. The picture became clear for me when I combined strategic management & organization principles with financial markets, and in this case, the EUR/USD Interbank Market. I need six of the ten schools described earlier to come to the total analysis. These six schools will be outlined in the future six approaches. Further, I will explain the "why" of these six schools.

Configuration approach
The first school I will use is the configuration school. I define the EUR/USD Interbank Market as an organization which has a diversified configuration. In following chapters, the reader will find out why, but first let me offer some extra information about the different configurations. I will give a short overview of the five structures mentioned in the book "Structures In Fives: Designing Effective Organizations by Mintzberg. Further I will describe the machine, professional and diversified organization in more detail, because these configurations will be used in the following chapters. For more details I refer to "Structures In Fives: Designing Effective Organizations" by Henry Mintzberg.

Table 1.2.1 Summary of the five configurations[4]

Configuration	Coordination mechanism	Dominant part	Decentralization
Entrepreneurial	Direct supervision	Strategic Apex	Vertical and horizontal centralization
Machine	Standardization work processes	Techno Structure	Partial horizontal decentralization
Professional	Standardization skills	Operating Core	Vertical and horizontal decentralization
Diversified	Standardization output	Middle Line	Partial vertical decentralization
"Adhocracy"	Mutual adjustment	Support Staff	Selective decentralization

---

[4] Mintzberg, H., *STRUCTURES IN FIVES: Designing Effective Organizations*, Copyright © 1993. Reprinted by permission of Pearson Education, Inc., Upper Saddle River, New Jersey.

Machine configuration[5]

Table 1.2.2

Machine configuration	
Main coordination mechanism	Standardization of work process
Dominant organizational part	Techno Structure
Important design parameters	Formalization of behavior
	Vertical and horizontal task specialization
	Vertical centralization and partial horizontal centralization
Situation factors	Old, large
	Regulated
	Not-automatic technical system
	Simple and stable environment
	External control
	Not dependent on fashion.

The machine organization can be divided into the following organizational parts:
1. Strategic Apex
2. Middle Line
3. Operating Core
4. Techno Structure
5. Support Staff

Figure 1.2.1 Machine configuration[6]

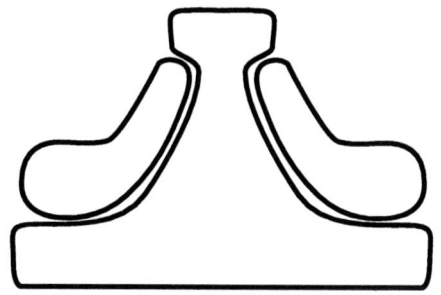

"The machine organization exists in a simple and stable environment. The working activities in this organization are routine, simple and are continually repeated. The processes are standardized. The problems that are popping up on the work floor are solved by standardization and checking of the different tasks. There is no room to solve the problems in an informal way.

Mintzberg, H., *STRUCTURES IN FIVES: Designing Effective Organizations*, Copyright © 1993. Reprinted by permission of Pearson Education, Inc., Upper Saddle River, New Jersey

---

[5]Mintzberg, H., *STRUCTURES IN FIVES: Designing Effective Organizations*, Copyright © 1993. Reprinted by permission of Pearson Education, Inc., Upper Saddle River, New Jersey.
[6]Mintzberg, H., *STRUCTURES IN FIVES: Designing Effective Organizations*, Copyright © 1993. Reprinted by permission of Pearson Education, Inc., Upper Saddle River, New Jersey.

The communication is vertical, from the leader to the Middle Line and from the Middle Line to the Operating Core, by detailed action plans. The Techno Structure and Support Staff are well developed. The staff analysts are responsible for the standardization and coordination of tasks and they have a lot of informal power. All the power is concentrated at the top, including the Strategic Thinking process. In the machine organization, strategy is defined as a plan and plans are the medium for communication and control. The machine organization is a configuration that has an obsession: control. The obsession for control shows that two things are very important. First, the organization tries to diminish all the uncertain variables, so that the organization has no problem at all. Second, the machine structure continuously creates new problems (for example, motivation problems). Control systems are needed to control these problems. The Strategic Apex invests a lot of time and energy in the structure to keep the organization together. However, it is the structure which is creating a lot of problems".

Division II, Commodity Market (chapter 7), has a Machine configuration.

Professional configuration[7]

Table 1.2.3

Professional configuration	
Main coordination mechanism	Standardization of skills
Dominant organizational part	Operating Core
Important design parameters	Training
	Horizontal task specialization
	Vertical and horizontal decentralization
Situation factors	Complex, stable environment
	Not-regulation, not highly technical system
	Dependent on fashion.

The professional organization can be divided into the following organizational parts:
1. Strategic Apex
2. Large Support Staff
3. Small Techno Structure
4. Large Operating Core (the professionals)

---

[7]Mintzberg, H., *STRUCTURES IN FIVES: Designing Effective Organizations,* Copyright © 1993. Reprinted by permission of Pearson Education, Inc., Upper Saddle River, New Jersey.

Figure 1.2.2: Professional configuration[8]

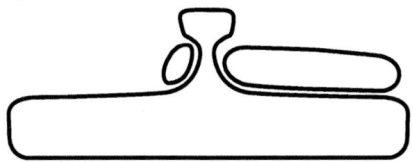

"The professional organization exists in a complex and stable environment. Examples of professional organizations are universities, hospitals and accountancy bureaus. The products and services offered by these organizations are complex.

Mintzberg, H., *STRUCTURES IN FIVES: Designing Effective Organizations,* Copyright © 1993. Reprinted by permission of Pearson Education, Inc., Upper Saddle River, New Jersey

In a professional organization the diagnosis is a fundamental task (different from the machine organization) but there is an exact description for the diagnosis (the stable environment). The organization is dependent on the skill of its professionals. So power is connected to skills. The professionals produce standard products and services, but to produce them a lot of training is necessary. The professionals are more or less independent, but working closely together on a client's case. The Operating Core has the key position in the professional organization. The professionals need a lot of support from staff colleagues, so that they don't have to think about the less interesting stuff. In the professional organization two hierarchies co-exist. Firstly, there is the democratic bottom-up hierarchy for the professionals, and secondly, there is the top-down machine hierarchy for the rest of the organization. The administrators are the ones who make the decisions. They have the indirect power because they are able to solve the communication distortions and other problems between the professionals. They are the intermediaries between the internal organization and the external stakeholders. So in fact the managers are professionals with extra tasks. The managers are allowed to stay as long as the professionals think that their interests are being well represented".

Division I, FX Option Market, has a Professional configuration

---

[8]Mintzberg, H., *STRUCTURES IN FIVES: Designing Effective Organizations,* Copyright © 1993. Reprinted by permission of Pearson Education, Inc., Upper Saddle River, New Jersey.

Diversified configuration

Table 1.2.4

Diversified configuration	
Main coordination mechanism	Standardization of output
Dominant organizational part	Middle line
Important design parameters	Division to market
	Systems for control of results
	Partial vertical decentralization
Situation factors	Diversified markets
	Old, large
	Dependent on fashion

The diversified organization can be divided into the following organizational parts:
1. Strategic Apex
2. Middle Line
3. Small Techno Structure
4. Support Staff
5. Operating Core

Figure 1.2.3: Diversified configuration[10]

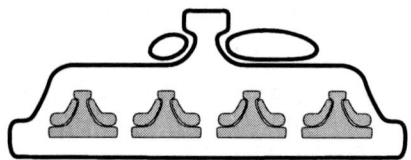

"The diversified organization consists of a collection of partial independent parts (=divisions) which are linked together by the central structure. The middle line and operating core can be divided into sub-organizations, which are defined for a specific market.

Mintzberg, H., *STRUCTURES IN FIVES: Designing Effective Organizations,* Copyright © 1993. Reprinted by permission of Pearson Education, Inc., Upper Saddle River, New Jersey

The sub-organizations also can be divided into Strategic Apex, Techno Structure, Support Staff, and Operating Core. The Strategic Apex of the organization is responsible for the strategy definition and for building the sub-organizations. The Strategic Apex is also responsible for the funding of the sub-organizations and service providing. The power is decentralized over the sub-organizations. However, inside the sub-organizations the power is centralized. The control of the sub-organizations is done by the definition of measurable targets to the sub-organizations. Strengths of the organization are: efficient usage of capital, diversification of risks and flexible organization strategy. However, this organization is focused on the short-term time frame and synergy is usually not the result".

---

[9]Mintzberg, H., *STRUCTURES IN FIVES: Designing Effective Organizations,* Copyright © 1993. Reprinted by permission of Pearson Education, Inc., Upper Saddle River, New Jersey.
[10]Mintzberg, H., *STRUCTURES IN FIVES: Designing Effective Organizations,* Copyright © 1993. Reprinted by permission of Pearson Education, Inc., Upper Saddle River, New Jersey.

The following organizations are diversified organizations:
- EUR/USD Interbank Market Organization (chapter 2)
- Equity Market Division (chapter 8)
- International Debt Market Division (chapter 9)
- Short-Term-Interest-Rate Market Division (chapter 10)

The Entrepreneurial approach

<u>The Entrepreneurial School by Mintzberg, Ahlstrand and Lampel</u>[11]
"This school focused the strategy formation process exclusively on the single leader, but it has also stressed the most innate of mental states and processes - intuition, judgment, wisdom, experience, insight. This promotes a view of strategy as perspective, associated with the image and sense of direction, namely vision".

In the EUR/USD Interbank Market Organization traders are the strategists of the organization. They take positions based on their intuition and views about the market. This way of decision making has Market Psychology as a result.

Cognitive approach

<u>The Cognitive School by Mintzberg, Ahlstrand and Lampel</u>[12]
"If we are really serious about understanding strategic vision as well as how strategies form under other circumstances, then we had better probe into the mind of the strategist. That is the job of the cognitive school: to get at what this process means in the sphere of human cognition, drawing especially on the field of cognitive psychology".

The cognitive approach is defined as Behavioral Finance to cope with Market Psychology, see chapter 3.

---

[11]Mintzberg, H., B. Ahlstrand, J. Lampel, *STRATEGY SAFARI: The complete guide through the wilds of strategic management,* Copyright © 1998. Reprinted by permission of Pearson Education Ltd, 128 LongAcre, London WC2E 9AN

[12]Mintzberg, H., B. Ahlstrand, J. Lampel, *STRATEGY SAFARI: The complete guide through the wilds of strategic management,* Copyright © 1998. Reprinted by permission of Pearson Education Ltd, 128 LongAcre, London WC2E 9AN

Design approach

<u>The Design School by Mintzberg, Ahlstrand and Lampel[13]</u>
"The design school proposes a model of strategy making that seeks to attain a match, or fit, between the internal capabilities and external possibilities" (SWOT Analysis). "Once alternative strategies have been determined, the next step is to evaluate them and chose the best one. Richard Rummelt (1997), a DBA from Havard General Management group, has perhaps provided the best framework for making this evaluation, in terms of a series of tests: consistency, consonance, advantage, feasibility".

First, let's look at Business Plans of the overall organization and the five divisions. These Business Plans will give an overview of the market within the organization or division. The goal is to make the reader understand how this market is working. For example Business Plan of Division I, FX Option Market, will first explain plain vanilla and exotic options. The variables in the FX option market will be described and explained. The marketing plan in the Business Plan is tight to the positioning approach. However, the rationale of the Business Plan is to be descriptive.

In most of the following chapters, we'll complete a strengths & weaknesses/opportunies & threats analysis (SWOT analysis) of the EUR/USD Interbank Market organization and of the five sub divisions. The SWOT analysis of the EUR/USD Interbank Market organization will define the best strategy to understand the movements in the EUR/USD Interbank Market, so that sales groups can improve their advice to their clients, the traders are able to recognize what is happening, and they know how to react. The SWOT analysis of the five divisions is built to analyze the influence of a certain division in the overall organization. In financial market terms: defining the influence of another financial market on the EUR/USD Interbank Market.

Planning approach

The planning approach is mainly used by strategists in Division II, Commodity Market, of the EUR/USD Interbank Market Organization.

---

[13]Mintzberg, H., B. Ahlstrand, J. Lampel, *STRATEGY SAFARI: The Complete Guide Through the Wilds of Strategic Management,* Copyright © 1998. Reprinted by permission of Pearson Education Ltd, 128 LongAcre, London WC2E 9AN

Positioning approach

The Design School by Mintzberg, Ahlstrand and Lampel[14]
"The position school, in contrast (to the planning and design school), argued that only a few key strategies – as positions in the economic marketplace – are desirable in any given industry: ones that can be defended against existing and future competitors".

Competitive Strategy by Michael E. Porter[15]
Michael Porter is an important name when talking about the positioning school. His elements of industry structure model and the concepts of industry evolution can be found in his book "Competitive Strategy, Techniques for Analyzing Industries and Competitors" (1980). I offer this as a highly recommended book that offers the reader additional insight.

According to Porter, the state of competition in an industry depends on five basic competitive forces. The collective strength of these forces determines the ultimate profit in the industry. The five forces are: potential entrants, intensity of rivalry among existing competitors, bargaining power of buyers, bargaining power of suppliers, and pressure from substitute products[16]. Structural analysis gives us a framework for understanding the competitive forces operating in an industry that are crucial to developing competitive strategy. The key question is: Are there any changes occurring that will affect each element of structure? The product life cycle hypothesis is that an industry passes through a number of phases: introduction, growth, maturity, and decline. As the industry goes through its life cycle, the nature of competition will shift. Important facets: buyers and buyer behavior, products and product change, marketing, manufacturing and distribution, R&D, foreign trade, overall strategy, competition, risk and margins and profits[17]. For more in depth information, see *Competitive Strategy* by Michael E. Porter.

I will translate the elements of industry structure model and the industry evolution process for the EUR/USD Interbank Market organization as well for the five divisions.

---

[14]Mintzberg, H., B. Ahlstrand, J. Lampel, *STRATEGY SAFARI: The Complete Guide Through the Wilds of Strategic Management*, Copyright © 1998. Reprinted by permission of Pearson Education Ltd, 128 LongAcre, London WC2E 9AN

[15]COMPETITIVE STRATEGY: Techniques for Analyzing Industries and Competitors by Michael E. Porter. Copyright © 1980, 1998 by The Free Press, an imprint of Simon & Schuster Adult Publishing Group. Reprinted with permission of the publisher.

[16]COMPETITIVE STRATEGY: Techniques for Analyzing Industries and Competitors by Michael E. Porter. Copyright © 1980, 1998 by The Free Press, an imprint of Simon & Schuster Adult Publishing Group. Reprinted with permission of the publisher.

[17]COMPETITIVE STRATEGY: Techniques for Analyzing Industries and Competitors by Michael E. Porter. Copyright © 1980, 1998 by The Free Press, an imprint of Simon & Schuster Adult Publishing Group. Reprinted with permission of the publisher.

SUMMARY 1

I've used six of the ten schools which are described by each view of the strategy process in "Strategy Safari" of Mintzberg, Ahlstand and Lampel (1998) to analyze the EUR/USD Interbank Market. These six schools (later called approaches) are:
- The Configuration School
- The Entrepreneurial School
- The Cognitive School
- The Design School
- The Planning School
- The Positioning School

These six schools are the basis of my research.

Chapter 2 on Foreign Exchange, will cope with the following subjects:
1. The Configuration approach and the EUR/USD Interbank Market.
2. The Entrepreneurial and Cognitive approach and the EUR/USD Interbank Market.
3. The Design approach and the EUR/USD Interbank Market.
4. The Positioning approach and the EUR/USD Interbank Market.

REFERENCES

Mintzberg, H., STRUCTURES IN FIVES: Designing Effective Organizations, Copyright © 1993. Reprinted by permission of Pearson Education, Inc., Upper Saddle River, New Jersey.

Mintzberg, H., B. Ahlstrand, J. Lampel, STRATEGY SAFARI: The complete guide through the wilds of strategic management, Copyright © 1998. Reprinted by permission of Pearson Education Ltd, 128 LongAcre, London WC2E 9AN

COMPETITIVE STRATEGY: Techniques for Analyzing Industries and Competitors by Michael E. Porter. Copyright © 1980, 1998 by The Free Press, an imprint of Simon & Schuster Adult Publishing Group. Reprinted with permission of the publisher.

Chapter **2**

FOREIGN EXCHANGE EUR/USD INTERBANK MARKET AS DIVERSIFIED ORGANIZATION

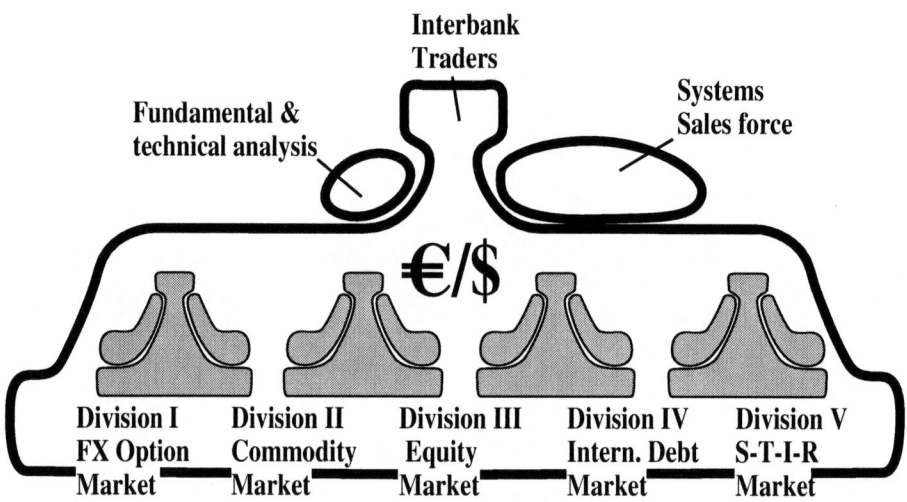

Only the picture not the text: Mintzberg, H., *STRUCTURES IN: Designing Effective Organizations*, Copyright © 1993. Reprinted by permission of Pearson Education, In., Upper Saddle River, New Jersey.

2.1 INTRODUCTION

This chapter will start with a brief overview of the history of the Snake, EMS and Maastricht Treaty, followed by an introduction to the EUR/USD market. The principles of the Strategic Management and Organization theory will be translated for the EUR/USD Interbank Market. The six schools mentioned in Chapter 1 will be the basis for the analysis of the EUR/USD Interbank Market. The configurational approach will explain that EUR/USD Interbank Market can be seen as a Diversified Organization. Business plan (design approach) will give an overview of the products, production and marketing of this organization. The Marketing plan can sometimes also be part of the positioning approach, however in business description is more an aim than positioning with respect to competitors. In the SWOT analysis the aim is to come to a framework that explains the movements in EUR/USD (product) or which type of EUR/USD we are dealing within a specific moment (Equity market EUR/USD or Commidity EUR/USD etc). The strengths will give the most important factors influencing the movement in EUR/USD and the weaknesses, the ones which have less or no influence. In the chapters 3, 6-10 the specific variables will be explained. The positioning approach will deal with the EUR/USD Interbank Market Organization within the industry and in which phase the industry currently resides.

2.2 HISTORY

Snake[1]

In 1972, European governments introduced the Snake or limited intervention scheme. The Snake is a system of exchange rate management. The participants pledged to maintain their currencies within a +/- 2.25% band against the other currencies within the system by means of a parity grid, based on central rates parities against the USD. The Central Banks of these countries intervened through the USD to maintain these bands. The Snake moved within a 4.5% band against the USD. The central bank of the currency under pressure was obliged to intervene and bring its currency back to safer territory within the band. The Snake was formally established in April 1972 and consisted of the original six members of the European and Economic Community (EEC): Belgium, France, Germany, Italy, Luxembourg and the Netherlands. Denmark, Ireland, Spain (1989) and the UK (1990) joined afterwards. The initial concept of the Snake was that it would reduce exchange rate fluctuations and enable manufacturers within the EEC to maintain a reasonable level of activity despite the vast fluctuations of the USD exchange rates.

EMS[2]

The European Monetary System (EMS) was launched on 13th March 1979 to replace the Snake and was more successful at enhancing trade. The EMS worked more successfully—partly, because the USD was not involved. Each country transfers part of its national reserves to a central fund for use in intervention and those national currencies are used for the intervention (not the USD). The EMS includes a mechanism for enabling currency adjustments to take place in an orderly way. The EMS also represents the initial phase of European integration within the monetary and economic fields. The original goals of the EMS were:

---

[1] European Communities, Economic and Monetary Union, from Rome to Maastricht, http://europa.eu.int
ACI Diploma, European Monetary System, Author: Bob Steiner, Markets International Ltd.
http://homepages.uel.ac.ul/K.Bain/ems.html
http://ebooks.whsmithonline.co.uk/ENCYCLOPEDIA, ERM and EMS

[2] European Communities, Economic and Monetary Union, from Rome to Maastricht, http://europa.eu.int
ACI Diploma, European Monetary System, Author: Bob Steiner, Markets International Ltd.
http://homepages.uel.ac.ul/K.Bain/ems.html
http://ebooks.whsmithonline.co.uk/ENCYCLOPEDIA, ERM and EMS

1. To facilitate exchange rate stability in order to foster monetary and price stability, as well as intra-European trade, and thereby to promote economic integration in the European Community.
2. To put the onus for correcting policies on governments asking for changes in parities.
3. To facilitate the eventual creation of a European currency to rival the USD in its global economic importance.

The Exchange Rate Mechanism (ERM) within the EMS is a parity grid system. The ERM is based on the European Currency Unit (ECU) instead of the USD (Snake). The ECU is the sum of fixed amounts of all the currencies within the EU, except the Austrian, Swedish and Finnish currencies. Each currency included in the EMS is assigned an ECU central rate. Sterling was assigned a notional rate. Central rates were expressed in terms of a given quantity of currency per ECU. The market rates of the ECU changed constantly as foreign exchange rates fluctuated.

The ECU central rates are used to obtain a bilateral central rate for each pair of currencies in the ERM. Taken together, these bilateral central rates made up the parity grid. All ERM currencies were obliged to stay in bands, which were 15% on either side of their bilateral central rates. Once a currency was in danger of breaching its bands, the EU governments concerned were obliged to do one of the following:

- Intervene directly in the foreign exchange market to strengthen or weaken the currency.
- Adjust economic policy to affect currency market perceptions.
- Revalue or devalue the central rates of some of the currencies.

In September 1992, market speculation was sufficient to force the Italian lira and GBP to leave the ERM. By August 1993, speculation forced a more general readjustment of the currencies. The EU had chosen to widen the ERM bands from +/- 2.25%, as they then were for most currencies, to +/- 15.0% for all currencies.

Maastricht Treaty[3]

The Maastricht Treaty of 1991 set out a three stage path towards monetary union. The first stage, already begun in mid-1990, involved the easing of restrictions on capital movements and closer economic policy coordination. The second stage started at the beginning of 1994, and established an European Monetary Institute (EMI) in Frankfurt to pave the way for transition to the final stage through closer alignment or convergence of economic policies and the economies of the member states The EMI is to be followed in the final stage by the establishment of a European Central Bank (ECB) that

---

[3] C. Enoch & Marc Quintyn, European Monetary Union: Operating Monetary Policy, International Monetary Fund
European Communities, Economic and Monetary Union, from Rome to Maastricht, http://europa.eu.int

will be responsible for monetary policy. The ECB has primary responsibility for maintaining price stability. Under monetary union, the ECB and the central banks of the member states will form the European System of Central Banks (ESCB) to take responsibility for a single monetary policy. However, the Maastricht Treaty defines only in general terms how the ECB should operate:
- There should be open markets with free competition;
- The ESCB cannot finance public deficits or buy governments securities in the primary markets;
- The execution of its operations should be decentralized so that recourse can be made to the National Central Banks (NCBs) "to the extent deemed possible and appropriate."

The third and final stage was the introduction of a single currency (Euro) at the beginning of 1999. Convergence criteria, which should have been met by the members, are:
1. INFLATION CRITERION
   Three countries with the lowest inflation against the headline CPI + 1.5%
2. INTEREST RATE CRITERION
   Long term government bond yields should be no more than 2.0% higher than the average of the long term interest rates of the same three countries as in the inflation criterion
3. EXCHANGE RATE CRITERION
   A country fulfills this criterion if its currency has participated in the exchange-rate mechanism (ERM) of the European Monetary System (EMS) for at least two years, while remaining within the +/- 2.25% fluctuation margin around its central rate.
4. FINANCE POLICY CRITERION
   The country's general government budget deficit should be no more than 3% of GDP. The country's total general government debt outstanding should be no more than 60% of GDP, or approaching that level satisfactorily.

2.3 EUR/USD INTERBANK MARKET

Introduction

A foreign exchange currency spot transaction is a purchase or sale of one currency for another currency, for delivery two working days after the dealing date. If the spot date falls on a public holiday in one or both of the centers of the two currencies involved, the next working day is taken as the value date. In the currency spot market, a variable number of units of one currency are quoted per one unit of another currency. When quoting against the USD, it is the practice in the professional interbank market to quote most currencies in terms of a varying number of units per 1 USD. Quoting the Euro against the USD is an exception to this general rule[4].

The Euro was launched in the professional interbank market on 1st January 1999. The currencies of the EMU members were fixed against the Euro.

Table 2.3.1

Currency	Code	EUR fixing rate
Deutsche Mark	DEM	1.955830
French Franc	FRF	6.559570
Dutch Guilder	NLG	2.203710
Italian Lira	ITL	1936.270
Portuguese Escudo	PTE	200.4820
Spanish Peseta	ESP	166.3860
Austrian Schilling	ATS	13.76030
Luxembourg Franc	LUF	40.33990
Belgium Franc	BEF	40.33990
Finnish Markka	FIM	5.945730
Irish Punt	IEP	0.787564
Greece Drachma (2001)	GRD	340.7500

Source: ECB

The Euro replaced these currencies in the professional market between banks and other professional market participants like hedge funds, financial institutions etc. The retail market still provides trading and prices in these European currencies. At the start of 2002, the introduction of Euro bank notes and coins replaced the local currencies.

The professional market started trading in Euros at the beginning of 1999. The EUR/USD replaced the most important currency pair of USD/DEM. Traders had to change their market view because the base currency in the currency pair was no longer the USD but the EUR.

---

[4] ACI Diploma, Foreign Exchange, Author: Bob Steiner, Markets International Ltd.

Table 2.3.2

Currency pair	Rate	Definition
USD/DEM	2.0110	1 USD is equivalent to 2.0110 DEM
EUR/USD	1.0280	1 EUR is equivalent to 1.0280 USD

Table 2.3.3: Basics

Terminology	Explanation
Pip	1/10000, 2.011**0**, 1.028**0**
"Big" figure	100 pips, 2.**01**10, 1.**02**80
Base currency	USD in USD/DEM
	EUR in EUR/USD
Quoted currency	DEM in USD/DEM
	USD in EUR/USD
Long	The trader bought the underlying
Short	The trader sold the underlying

Graph 2.3.1: payoffs of long (black) and short (grey) positions[5]

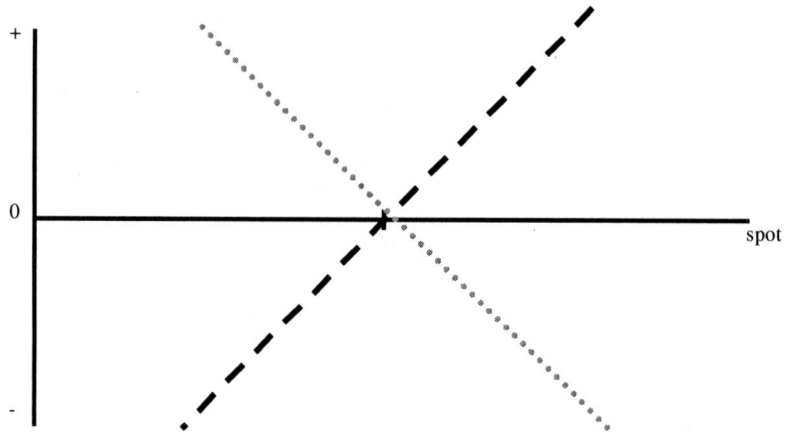

Traders are used to thinking in the base currency, in millions, in pips and figures (see table 2.3.3 for explanation). The introduction of the Euro was very confusing for a lot of experienced traders. The following examples will make this clearer.

When a trader is asked to give a price for 10 EUR/USD, his/her response is: 80-85 This means that the trader wants to buy at 80 (pips) and wants to sell at 85 (pips). The total quote should be familiar to the party who is asking, the full quote is 1.0280-85, 10 EUR/USD means 10 million EUR/USD.

---

[5]Wim Mesman, ABN AMRO FX Options Marketing Desk, presentation

Table 2.3.4

Trader	Other party	Result
80-85	says MINE	Trader sells 10 million EUR/USD at 1.0285
80-85	says YOURS	Trader buys 10 million EUR/USD at 1.0280

If the trader was quoting USD/DEM than he would sell 10 million USD/DEM in the first situation and buy 10 million USD/DEM in the second situation. So this is the opposite. The terms YOURS and MINE are always from the base currency point of view. A second confusion for traders was the reaction on economic data and rumors. The experienced traders were used to buying USD on US positive news and to selling on positive European news. The result of the introduction of the Euro was that traders had to react in the opposite way now.

Table 2.3.5

News/Rumor	EUR/USD	USD/DEM
Positive for US	USD stronger EUR/USD lower	USD stronger USD/DEM higher
Positive for Europe	EUR stronger EUR/USD higher	DEM stronger USD/DEM lower

Development of the EUR/USD Interbank Market

The expectations for the new currency were very high and within a short time it became clear that the introduction rate of around 1.1700 against the USD was far too ambitious. From the introduction at the beginning of 1999, EUR/USD went down in almost one straight line. Main reasons were:

1. MARKET PLAYERS WERE EXTREMELY POSITIVE ABOUT THE EUR (CHAPTER 3) AND WERE EXTREMELY LONG EUR.
   The market was extremely long EUR/USD from the start. Long means that they had already bought EUR/USD and, since everyone had more or less the same position, no new buyers entered the market. The weak side of the market was the existence of large long positions, so EUR/USD could only go down.
2. THE POSITIVE SENTIMENT TURNED INTO NEGATIVE SENTIMENT.
   From the start the positive sentiment changed quickly into a negative sentiment and this has been the most important reason for the movement in EUR/USD.
3. THE ECB HAD TO PROVE ITSELF AS A CENTRAL BANK.
   Market participants were not familiar with the central bank, the ECB. This was a new institution that had to be tested by the market. The credibility of the ECB was dependent on how the ECB would react to these market tests. The name of the ECB was harmed by conflicting comments of ECB members and members of the ESCB. Markets like consistency and that was one of the missing characteristics of the ECB in its first 1.5 years, especially when the EUR/USD came under more pressure.

4. A LACK OF ONE VIEW FROM EUROPEAN POLITICIANS.
   The short history of the EUR has shown us that the European politicians have had (sometimes still have) difficulties to show one public official view.
5. GROWTH DIFFERENTIAL IN FAVOR OF THE US (CHAPTER 4)
   In the meantime, the US economy had its best years ever. The US stock markets were making new highs; there were high non-inflationary growth numbers, low interest rates and high confidence in the economy. In Europe, France needed an interest rate hike to fight inflation while the economy in Germany needed the stimulation of low interest rates.
6. INCREASING DEMAND FOR LOWER STRIKES IN THE OPTION MARKET (CHAPTER 6).
7. RALLY IN OIL PRICE (CHAPTER 7).
8. HIGH DEMAND FOR USD OUT OF M&A ACTIVITY (CHAPTER 8).
   The US also attracted large direct investment flows from Europe, because European companies were buying US companies to expand their markets.
9. HIGHER RETURN ON US INVESTMENTS (CHAPTER 8).
10. MSCI ADJUSTMENT IN FAVOR OF THE USD (CHAPTER 8)
11. HIGHER DEMAND FOR USD DENOMINATED BOND ISSUES AND HIGHER RETURN ON USD DENOMINATED BONDS (CHAPTER 9).
12. US BOND MARKETS ARE MORE LIQUID AND HIGHER DEVELOPED (CHAPTER 9).
13. HIGHER DEMAND FOR USD DENOMINATED MONEY MARKET ISSUES (CHAPTER 10).
14. DECREASE IN US CP ISSUES AND US DEBT GROWTH (CHAPTER 10).

The result was that the EUR/USD dropped from around 1.1700 at the beginning of 1999 to a low of 0.8225 (26th October 2000), which was a disaster for the new currency. At the end of 2000 and the beginning of 2001 EUR/USD was saved by the economic turnaround in the US. It became clear that the US economy was sliding into a recession. EUR/USD rallied from the low of 0.8225 to a high of 0.9595 (5th of January 2001), before the correction started. EUR/USD moved in a downward sloping trend channel from the beginning of January until the 8th August 2001. The pair was close to a retest of 0.8225 on the 6th of July 2001 (0.8344). The weaker than expected US payrolls on that same day prevented this retest. Since then, the market variables have become more in favorable for EUR/USD: oil prices dropped and there was a higher demand for the EUR out of the Option Market. On the 8th of August, EUR/USD was near to breaking this downward sloping trend channel. The support came from an unexpected side. The US Beige Book reported that sustained weakness in the US manufacturing sector spilled over to the other businesses. The market was not prepared for this news and the US Beige Book of the 8th of August made a break of the trend channel a fact. EUR/USD surged to a high of 0.9239 (22nd of August) before retesting the breakout level (of 8th of August) On the 11th of September, EUR/USD made a low of 0.8947 before the news of the terrorist attacks on the US reached the market. That same day, EUR/USD closed 1.76% higher at 0.9140 (2.16% higher than the low). In the coming days EUR/USD would make a high of 0.9333 (17th of September). However, the price action following was disappointing. On the 12th of October, the EUR/USD was sold off due to the following reasons:
   – DISAPPOINTING RETURN ON SHORT USD POSITIONS.
   – MARKET WAS EXTREMELY SHORT USD.
   – USD SUPPORTIVE M&A ACTIVITY

- SELL-OFF IN GOLD AGAINST THE USD SUGGESTING THAT THE MARKETS COOLED DOWN (THIS STARTED ON THE 10TH OF OCTOBER).
- OIL COMING OFF THE LOWS.
- STRONG US EQUITIES
- ECB LEFT THE RATES UNCHANGED

Since the 11th September, the market is sensitive to rumors about further attacks and US data. Market participants have not been willing to take positions, market participants react on US data and rumors so the movements in the markets are shock wise. On the 16th of October, I drew the conclusion (in my daily report) that almost all the variables were positive for the EUR, but EUR/USD was not moving much higher. When the variables become less positive this could put EUR/USD under pressure.

The end of October 2001, market players realized that the problems (for example recession and terrorist attacks) were more widespread. The mixed US data avoided excessive positioning on one side. It kept the market players sharp, curious and wondering if they missed something. A global recession would not urge investors to switch out of USD into EUR because of the belief in the market that there is no global recovery without US recovery. At the end of November 2001, the focus was back on US data and the impact of the Enron story started to come through. In the beginning of January 2002, EUR/USD rallied to a high of 0.9065 supported by the introduction of the Euro coins and notes. What will the effect be if Eurozone citizens start trusting their new currency? It's like an inside-out process. First the citizens need to trust this new currency before the rest of the world can be convinced. Finally the ECB received credits from this introduction of the Euro coins and notes. EUR/USD came under pressure again after it failed to take out a key resistance at 0.9122. On the 28th of January EUR/USD made a low around 0.8567. On the 30th of January EUR/USD received support out of the option market. There was market talk about buying interest of EUR calls in the 6 and 12 months. One day later the bias for EUR puts disappeared signaling that the option market doesn't expect a test of lower levels. Beginning of February, US manufacturers complained again about the strong USD. Mid February market talks suggested that there was demand for EUR calls in the 1 month timeframe. In April CHF and Gold received support from increased tensions in the Middle East and fear about that the conflict might widen. USD/CHF and GBP/USD broke out of their channels signaling that EUR/USD should follow. EUR/USD took more time to break its downward sloping channel. The support received from the option market (demand for EUR calls) on 12th and 17th of April was an important contributor to the break of key resistant level 0.8880 on 17th of April 2002. By the end of April, there was again talk of demand of EUR calls with strikes above 0.9500 for the 6 and 12 months. Apart from the support out of the option market, the sentiment towards US in general was changing with as result USD weakness. Some of the reasons for this change were:
- Accountancy problems of US companies
- Chapter 11 of Enron and Global Crossing.

- Uncertainty about US company earnings[6], outlook and future demand.
- Talk about US companies losing contracts in the Middle East to European competitors.
- Steel boycott by the US[7].

The USD has been supported from safe haven flows in the past. However, when the tensions in the world increased (Argentina, Venezuela, Israel-Palestine, India-Pakistan, US-Iraq), the US story was adding to the uncertainty instead of reducing it. The result was the sell-off of the USD mainly against Gold, CHF (both favored when tensions arise in the world) and JPY. The switch into CHF and JPY was the same as after September 11, 2001 terrorists' attacks. USD/CHF has a high negative correlation with EUR/USD; so, a sharp down move in USD/CHF means automatically an up move in EUR/USD. EUR/USD received also important support from the rally in gold, which had a higher pace than the up move in the oil price. A flight into gold (hoarding) is usually a good indication for sentiment in the market. The demand of gold received an enormous boost from:

- Less hedging activity by gold miners[8].
- Uncertainty in the equity markets (accountancy problems, earnings uncertainty)[9].
- Israel-Palestine, India-Pakistan, US-Iraq.
- Lower USD (two way effect).
- People find no alternatives to cover the risk of erosion linked to inflation[10].

The negative sentiment had as result that players were looking for negative news out of US to sell-off the USD; from possible terrorist attacks in the US to sell-off of the US equities (neglecting the sell-off of European equities). The sell-off of the USD was mainly in US time after US data release. The market didn't take better US data into account at all, its only importance being the fact that it was released at all. The support from the option market and the negative US/USD sentiment caused a run-away market characterized by small corrections. EUR/USD rallied to a high of 0.9580 close to key resistance level 0.9595 and barrier level 0.9600 (according to market talk). In the current environment a test of this 0.9595 is just a matter of time. (20 June 2002)

---

[6]Rob Hayward, ABN AMRO Senior Foreign Exchange Strategist
[7]George Voutiritsas, Senior EUR/USD trader, ABN AMRO Chicago spot trading desk
[8]HBUR, gold desk
[9]HBUR, gold desk
[10]Didier Duret, Head of Product Development, Private Clients Europe 2, ABN AMRO Switzerland

2.4 CONFIGURATION APPROACH

The structure of an organization can be defined as the different ways in which work is divided into different tasks and how these tasks are coordinated. In the organization of the EUR/USD Interbank Market, the EUR/USD is the product. EUR/USD is the general product but can be divided into five different EUR/USD sub-products. The different EUR/USD sub-products are used in different markets. In fact the general EUR/USD is transformed into sub EUR/USD's to differentiate the product in the market to meet the needs of the clients. The organization of the EUR/USD Interbank Market is divided into five sub-organizations, each of which is defined for a specific market. Further, there are other tasks in the EUR/USD Interbank Market organization, which have an influence on the organization as a whole, and not only on the products of the organization. Management will give the total organization the positioning in the market. The organization needs to meet two fundamental constraints before it can talk about a structure: work divided into different tasks and coordination of the tasks.

First we will attempt to define the different tasks/parts of the organization in the EUR/USD Interbank Market. Then, we will define the coordination mechanism, the form of decentralization and the configuration.

Organizational parts
Strategic Apex
The EUR/USD interbank traders are responsible for the EUR/USD Interbank Market organization. They are the strategists of the organization.

Support Staff
This organizational part has the task of influencing the work of others in the organization. They train the people in the EUR/USD Interbank Market organization and keep the technology in the organization on the highest level. The technology (systems such as **Bloomberg, Dow Jones, Reuters, Telerate, booking systems and pricing systems**) is especially vital in this EUR/USD Interbank Market organization because the high-speed decision-making process done by the EUR/USD interbank traders is dependent on this technology. **Further, of significant importance are: the salespeople who match the clients and products.**

Techno Structure
The Techno Structure of the EUR/USD Interbank Market organization can be divided into:
1. Fundamental Analysis (Chapter 4)
2. Technical Analysis (Chapter 5)

Middle Line
The Middle Line of the EUR/USD Interbank Market organization can be divided into five sub-organizations, which are defined for specific markets: FX Option Market EUR/USD, Commodity Market EUR/USD, Equity Market EUR/USD, International Debt Market EUR/USD and Short-Term-Interest-Rate Market EUR/USD. The Middle Line managers are FX Option, Commodity, Equity, International Debt and Short-Term-Interest-Rate interbank traders. The sub-organizations can also be divided into the earlier mentioned organizational parts.

Operating Core
The operating core has four main functions:
1. Supply the general EUR/USD product for the production.
2. Transform the general EUR/USD product into the differentiated EUR/USD sub-products.
   - FX Option Market EUR/USD
   - Commodity Market EUR/USD
   - Equity Market EUR/USD
   - International Debt Market EUR/USD
   - Short-Term Interest-Rate EUR/USD
3. Distribute the differentiated EUR/USD sub-products
4. Provide direct support to input, transformation and output.

The operating core can also be divided into the five sub-organizations, which are defined under the Middle Line. In each of the sub-organizations the general EUR/USD product is transformed into one of the EUR/USD sub-products to give the clients the explanation of why the EUR/USD is behaving in that manner. I define five differentiated EUR/USD sub-products to explain the situation when the general EUR/USD is driven by one of these five markets. Every time, **one** of these five markets is the dominant force behind the movements in the EUR/USD, together with the culture of the organization (Market Psychology).

Culture
The culture of the total organization, and the different sub-organizations, is the Market Psychology of the different markets. Nothing beats Market Psychology (Chapter 3).

Coordination mechanism
The coordination mechanism used in the EUR/USD Interbank Market organization is the standardization of output. The general EUR/USD product (input) is transformed into five EUR/USD sub-products (output) to meet the needs of the clients. The focus of the sub-organizations/divisions is on the earlier defined markets. One of these specific markets will have the dominant influence on the EUR/USD interbank organization. One day the Equity Market EUR/USD is dominant and another day the FX Options EUR/USD is dominant. They interchange with each other and it is more or less impossible to know upfront which of the specific markets will be dominant.

Decentralization
The EUR/USD interbank traders are responsible for the strategy and building of the sub-organizations. The power is decentralized over the sub-organizations. However, the power is centralized **inside the sub-organizations.**

Configuration
The EUR/USD Interbank Market organization uses standardization of output as the coordination mechanism. Further, the Middle Line is the dominant force in the organization because it influences which of the EUR/USD sub-products is used by the EUR/USD Interbank Market organization in the market. The power is decentralized over the Middle Line (partial vertical decentralization). So the EUR/USD Interbank Market organization has a **Diversified Configuration.**
Outcome:

Table 2.4.1

EUR/USD Interbank Market organization	Definition
Strategic Apex	EUR/USD interbank traders
Techno Structure	Fundamental Analysis (Chapter 4) Technical Analysis (Chapter 5)
Support Staff	Technology (systems such as Bloomberg, Dow Jones, Reuters, Telerate, booking systems, pricing systems) Sales force, Training
Middle Line	FX Options traders Commodity traders Equity traders International Debt traders Short-Term-Interest-Rate traders
Operating Core	Division I, FX Options Market (chapter 6) Division II, Commodity Market (chapter 7) Division III, Equity Market (chapter 8) Division IV, International Debt Market (chapter 9) Division V, Short-Term-Interest-Rate Market (chapter 10)
Coordination mechanism	Standardization of output
Decentralization	Partial vertical decentralization
Configuration	Diversified organization
Culture	Market Psychology (Chapter 3)

2.5 ENTREPRENEURIAL & COGNITIVE APPROACH

The interbank EUR/USD traders are the people who make the decisions to take positions in EUR/USD. They can be seen as the strategists of the organization.

What kind of strategy process will they follow: entrepreneurial or cognitive approach?

Traders take a position on their feeling of the market. They usually say: don't think, just do. They fill more than ten hours per day reacting on their market based feelings. In fact this means that traders use the entrepreneurial approach. Rational thinking is more common in some trading professions, like derivative products, but trading (in most of the cases) may or may not be based on rational thinking (note Chapter 3 on Behavioral Finance). Currency markets are not difficult to understand from the product point of view, but they are difficult to follow from the pace point of view—the speed of the trades. Traders are dealing with a high-speed environment, however, the speed is continuously changing. It is possible to catch the speed for three hours and later lose it for the rest of the day (like a rhythm). EUR/USD is one of these high-speed markets. What makes this different is the short history and the numerous forces which are interacting in this market. EUR/USD seems like an easy liquid range trading market. In fact it is nothing at all like that. An extremely high level of complexity characterizes this market. EUR/USD is complex in terms of behavior. EUR/USD is highly linked with the earlier mentioned financial markets, because it is the most liquid currency pair in which to unwind unwanted positions. The links between EUR/USD and the other markets are not always obvious and, when they are uncovered, it becomes clear that the links are also linked to each other. The Equity market is linked with the International Debt market, the International Debt market with the Equity market, the Commodity Oil market and the Short-Term-Interest-Rate market. The dynamic and largely uncertain environment characterizes the financial markets. Further, the views about EUR/USD vary a lot, based on personal characteristics, loyalties, past experiences and circumstances of involvement of the market participants. The involvement of market participants is referring to the fact that their own positions can have influence on the view about EUR/USD (Cognitive Dissonance, see the Chapter on Behavioral Finance). The decision to enter a position is based on your view of the variables. The variables will never be all on the same side; it is always a trade-off between them, as is most of life.

EUR/USD interbank traders use the entrepreneurial approach. They are very creative, intuitive thinkers. Their actions are not based on formal or fixed rules. The only rules they have are some informal rules between traders and the rule to make money to survive. The rest of the rules are variable. The traders have the responsibility over their books to make money within a certain time frame. Competitive pricing is important to keep market share. Further, it is important to share market information with your colleagues. The amount of information shared may be limited by internal or external factors; i.e, how much you feel like—or want to—share.

Traders make the decisions to take positions based on their market experiences. They all have their own rigid view of how the world works and they are generally loathe to change this view, because it has made money before and it will make money in the future. Changing their view feels like selling yourself out. Traders are very flexible in reacting to changes in the market but rigid when it comes to changing their view of the market. Traders are prepared to make same wrong judgments over and over again, rather than changing their market behavior. Their strategies are not based on analysis but intuition, and are implemented right away.

The strategy is based on their experience and market information. The positions taken in the market are the result. They try to search for the weak side in the market by playing with positions and try to force the market if the weak side is found.

Table 2.5.1

Testing weak side of the market	Level
Overnight high and low	0.9200 and 0.9250
Start	0.9220
First move	0.9220 to 0.9250
Interbank party buys 10 mio	0.9270 (high)
Test of overnight high	Intraday stop losses around 0.9275-80
No break of overnight high Interbank party sell 10 mio	0.9255
Interbank party sells 10 mio.	0.9220
Interbank party sell another 10 mio around overnight low	0.9200
Test of overnight low	0.9180

The intraday stop losses are usually 25-30 pips away from the overnight high and low.

This search for the weak side in the market goes on as long as the overnight high and low are not taken out.

The market is moving in a range in the meantime. Many analysts, myself included, believe that the market is so large that traders are not able to move the market in liquid times. Illiquid markets on Friday afternoon, Monday morning and public holidays in one of the main centers (London, New York or Japan) are, of course, exceptions.

So, in financial markets, traders use the entrepreneurial approach to take decisions about their positions. This approach is responsible for the phenomenon of MARKET PSYCHOLOGY. To deal with Market Psychology as a result of the Entrepreneurial approach, another approach is needed, an approach that deals with the mental process of trading. This approach is called the Cognitive approach and this is equal to the study Behavioral Finance.

CHAPTER 2

The financial markets have been transformed to a very fast pace due to technology and the development of the derivatives markets. Before, the Entrepreneurial approach was enough to deal with financial markets, but to be able to follow the high pace of the market transformation, traders need more than this approach. They need the Configuration Approach (EUR/USD Interbank Market as Diversified Organization), Cognitive approach, Design approach (Business Plan & SWOT analysis), the Positioning approach (industry structure model and the concepts of industry evolution from Michael Porter).

Figure 2.5.1: Configuration/Design/Positioning for the EUR/USD Interbank Market

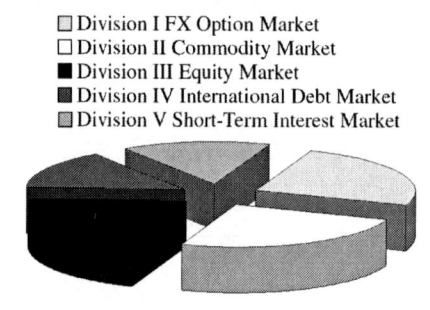

☐ Division I FX Option Market
☐ Division II Commodity Market
■ Division III Equity Market
■ Division IV International Debt Market
☐ Division V Short-Term Interest Market

Dealing with financial markets means using the following approaches:
    – Configuration
    – Entrepreneurial
    – Cognitive
    – Design
    – Planning
    – Positioning

The CECDPP approach

2.6 DESIGN APPROACH I: BUSINESS PLAN

Introduction

The Business Plan is the vision of the organization and consists of everything that is needed to arrive at:
A definition of the activities of the organization
Realistic goals
Communication of the goals and activities to the stakeholders and persons who are involved in the organization.
- Structure
- Definition of the risks involved

The strategy and outcome will be tested in the real situation. Any differences between the prognoses and the outcome will be analyzed. This analysis will try to find answers as to "why", so that the strategy can be adjusted to the current situation. A Business Plan can be divided into the following plans:
1. PRODUCT PLAN
   What product does the organization sell?
   What are the characteristics of these products?
2. PRODUCTION PLAN
   Description of the process.
   What is needed to sell these products?
3. MARKETING PLAN
   Clients?
   How large is the market?
   Competitors?

As we move forward, we will develop a Business Plan of the whole organization and of the different divisions.

Product plan

The organization sells two products:
1. DIRECT EUR/USD
2. INDIRECT EUR/USD

Traders can trade in the direct EUR/USD market and in the indirect EUR/USD market. The direct EUR/USD market means to buy EURs in exchange for USDs or sell EURs to buy USDs. The indirect EUR/USD market can only be explained by looking first to the other main currency markets. The other main currency markets we define are:
1. JPY MARKET
2. CHF MARKET
3. GBP MARKET

JPY market
Graph 2.6.1: EUR/USD versus USD/JPY (Daily data), Source Reuters

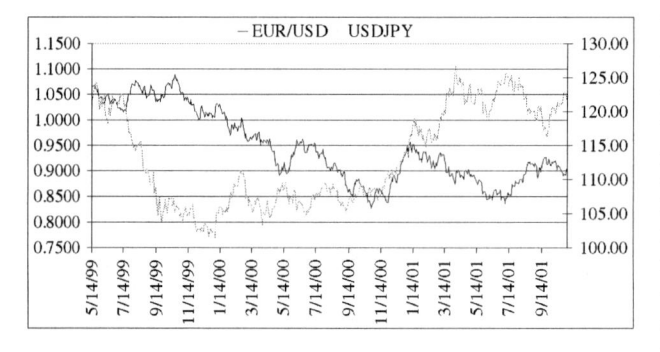

This market can be divided into EUR/JPY and USD/JPY and has an important local market. It is, for non-Japanese market participants, very difficult to understand this market and to receive important market signals on time. The Japanese exporters are some of the main players in the JPY market. They hedge their income in the EUR and the USD and they are very active in the currency interbank JPY market and the foreign exchange JPY Option Market. The Japanese life insurance companies and banks are also dominant players.

Graph 2.6.2: EUR/USD versus EUR/JPY (Daily data), Source: Reuters

CHF market

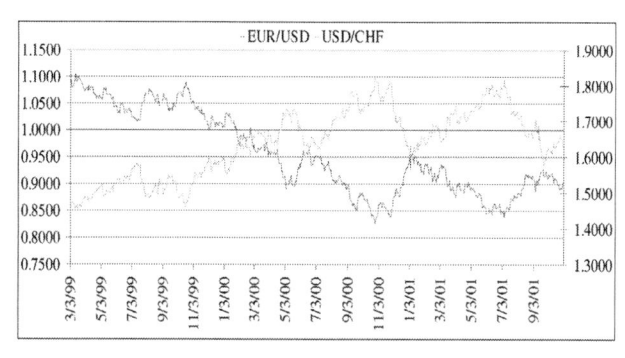

Graph 2.6.3: EUR/USD versus USD/CHF (Daily data), Source: Reuters

The CHF market can be divided into USD/CHF and EUR/CHF and also has an important local market. The main players in CHF market are Swiss banks. According to cover story "Forex transformed by mergers" in Euromoney of May 2001, UBS Warburg is the best in USD/CHF with a score of 229, Citigroup second with 185 points, Deutsche Bank third with 152 points and Credit Suisse First Boston fourth with 95 points. This market is easier for foreigners to understand than the JPY market, but it is still an insider market. The Swiss National Bank (SNB) is a dominant player in this market through its interest rate policy and gold sales (see Chapter 7 on commodity Oil and Gold).

Graph 2.6.4: EUR/USD versus EUR/CHF (Daily data), Source: Reuters

The interest rate policy has a high influence on and in EUR/CHF, while gold sales have their main influence on the USD/CHF. Gold is priced in USD. If the SNB sells gold out of their gold reserve it is actually selling USD/CHF. Further, CHF based funds and banks are also important players in this market. The USD/CHF market is, like the USD/JPY, a very technical driven market. There it is able to signal a change in market behavior. Since the USD/CHF is a much less liquid market than the EUR/USD, it is easier to notice turning points. I use the USD/CHF market as a leading indicator for the EUR/USD market. When the USD/CHF finishes its rally, it is an indication that the EUR/USD will probably reach its low very soon.

GBP market

Graph 2.6.5: EUR/USD versus GBP/USD (Daily data), Source Reuters

The GBP market can be divided into GBP/USD and EUR/GBP. The GBP has always received a lot support from the inclusion of, and impact derived from, Merger & Acquistitions. Further, the main drivers in this market are the interest rates differentials between the UK and the US and the UK and Europe.

Graph 2.6.6: EUR/USD versus GPB/USD (Daily data), Source: Reuters

In the JPY, the CHF or GBP market traders make or create an indirect EUR/USD position. The following table will illustrate this:

Table 2.6.1

Market	Buy EUR/USD	Sell EUR/USD
JPY market	Buy EUR/JPY	Sell EUR/JPY
	Sell USD/JPY	Buy USD/JPY
CHF market	Buy EUR/CHF	Sell EUR/CHF
	Sell USD/CHF	Buy USD/CHF
GBP market	Buy EUR/GBP	Sell EUR/GBP
	Buy GBP/USD	Sell GBP/USD

So when the trader needs to buy EUR/USD he buys EUR/JPY and sells USD/JPY.

Table 2.6.2

Buy EUR/JPY	Sell USD/JPY	Result
Buy EUR	Sell USD	Buy EUR/USD
Sell JPY	Buy JPY	No position in JPY

Traders are continuously arbitraging through the different markets. They will create an EUR/USD position via the indirect way if it is cheaper to do so or if they don't want to give clear signals to markets of what they are doing. Traders try to play the direct and indirect way if they are working large client orders. The flows of the JPY, CHF and GBP market all come together in the EUR/USD market. It is very difficult to see which currency pair is moving the EUR/USD market. **The EUR/USD is by far the most liquid currency market there is so the direct EUR/USD is more often used by the JPY, CHF or GBP markets than the other way around.**

Table 2.6.3

Currency pair	Correlation with EUR/USD based on daily data (Reuters)	Start	End
USD/CHF	-0.96	03/03/99	31/10/01
EUR/CHF	+0.83	07/04/99	31/10/01
GBP/USD	+0.93	26/03/99	31/10/01
EUR/GBP	+0.82	03/03/99	31/10/01
USD/JPY	-0.33	14/05/99	31/10/01
EUR/JPY	+0.74	03/03/99	31/10/01

Production plan

The Production plan describes everything that that is needed to sell the product direct EUR/USD and indirect EUR/USD. The traders are able to trade in EUR/USD when:

1. CLIENTS HAVE POSITIONS IN EUR AND USD.
   The traders are actually the market. They always have to provide the market with prices in EUR/USD. Clients involved in international trade between the US and Europe, and/or involved in direct investment in both countries, are exposed to currency risk. There are several forms of currency exposure: transaction exposure, economic exposure and translation exposure.
   • Transaction exposure is the currency exposure that results from a transaction done in the past.
   • Economic exposure is the currency exposure that has influence on the position of the client compared to its competitors.
   • Translating exposure is the currency exposure on the client's account.

   The client hedges mainly transaction exposure and economic exposure[11]. The hedge can be created by a natural hedge or a hedge executed in the currency markets. A natural hedge means that the (client) is funding in the same currency as the sales income, or is investing in the same currency as his main costs. A natural hedge can reduce the currency exposure for a great deal (long-term exposure) but in the end there is always some exposure left (short-term exposure). This short-term exposure can be hedged by making transactions in the EUR/USD currency market or FX Option Market.

   Examples of EUR/USD positions.
   European corporate sells products to the US but has it costs in EUR
   The European corporate is vulnerable for a higher EUR/USD rate, because it will decrease its revenues while its costs remain the same. A higher EUR/USD rate will have a negative influence on its profit.

   The US corporate wants to take over a European corporate.
   The US corporate is in negotiation to buy a European company. It will be vulnerable to a rise in the EUR/USD exchange rate, because that would increase its acquisition costs.

   Speculators or traders expect that the EUR will depreciate against the USD.
   They believe that the value of the EUR will decrease against the USD between now and 3 months time. They can initiate positions in several ways:

---

[11] ACI Diploma, Identifying, Measuring and Controlling Risk and Return, Author: Bob Steiner, Markets International Ltd.

- They sell the EUR/USD in the spot market and keep the position for three months.
- They sell the EUR/USD in the outright market with a value date three months later.
- They buy EURput/USDcall for three months.
- They sell EURcall/USDput for three months

An arbitrageur sees an opportunity in the indirect EUR/USD.
When an arbitrageur sees a mispricing between direct EUR/USD and indirect EUR/USD, he will sell the high EUR/USD and buy the low EUR/USD. The following example will make it clear.

EUR/CHF   1.5000-05
USD/CHF   1.6500-05
Direct EUR/USD 0.9100-05

Indirect EUR/USD
Bid   0.9088 (1.5000/1.6505)
Offer   0.9094 (1.5005/1.6500)

The arbitrageur will sell the direct EUR/USD at 0.9100 and will buy the indirect EUR/USD at 0.9094 (sell USD/CHF at 1.6500 and buy EUR/CHF at 1.5005)

2. CLIENTS NEED TO HEDGE THESE CURRENCY EXPOSURES.
   The European corporate (first example) can hedge its exposure in two ways:
   - It sells the USD with the same value date as its incoming USD revenues (outright transaction)
   - It protects its exposure by buying a EURcall/USDput with the same value date as its incoming USD revenues. The European corporate will pay a premium for this protection. It buys a right and not an obligation to sell its USD on the chosen value date and at the chosen strike price.
   - The US corporate (second example) that would like to acquire the European corporate can hedge its exposure by buying EURcall/USDput for the timeframe of the negotiation.

3. TRADERS (THE MARKET) ARE LINKED TO THEIR CLIENTS, BROKERS, COLLEAGUES, AND COMPETITORS.
   Traders need to be linked with the other market participants like brokers (voice brokers and Electronic Brokerage System = EBS), competitors and colleagues all over the world. The activities of the other market participants are the only way to liquidate their positions when they need to. Further, traders are highly dependent on their information systems like Reuters, Telerate, Dow Jones trade station and pricing systems.

4. THEIR INFORMATION SYSTEMS ARE ONLINE.
   If there are no information systems or they are not online, traders are blind in this market that is highly dependent on technology.

5. THEIR PRICING PROGRAMS ARE ONLINE.
   Without online pricing programs, the prices given by the traders are not correct.

Marketing plan

The marketing plan should answer the following questions:
1. WHO ARE THE CLIENTS?
2. WHAT IS THE SCALE OF THE MARKET?
3. WHO ARE THE MAIN COMPETITORS?
4. WHAT IS THE MARKET SHARE?

Clients
The clients are:
- FUNDS (HEDGE, BLACK BOX AND INVESTMENT FUNDS)
  Hedge funds, black box funds and investment funds can have portfolios in different financial products and in different currencies. They can have short-term speculative positions in different markets at the same time, based on all kinds of models. They can be highly leveraged and there is a need to act very quickly in the markets. Most of the time they are clients of several banks and the orders they leave in the market can have an enormous influence in the short-term intra day interbank markets.
- PENSION FUNDS AND INSURANCE COMPANIES
- Pension funds and insurance companies have longer-term time frames and market participants closely watch shifts in their portfolios, because these shifts will have a large influence on the longer-term trend of the EUR/USD currency market. These clients will not change their portfolio near lows or highs. They will enter the market if the direction of the EUR/USD is clearer.
- CORPORATES
  Corporates have EUR/USD exposure because of international trade or direct investment in the US by European corporates (or vice versa). They hedge their exposure. The levels of hedging depend on the decisions made by the management.
- CENTRAL BANKS
  Central banks enter the market to intervene in the EUR/USD market or to make commercial transactions.
- CURRENCY OPTION TRADERS, EQUITY TRADERS, MONEY MARKET TRADERS, INTERNATIONAL – DEBT MARKET, FUTURE MARKET TRADERS.
  They are hedging their EUR/USD currency exposure to make their books currency risk neutral.
- PRIVATE CLIENTS
  They take positions in the EUR/USD based on their view and the advice of their Treasury advisors. They give their relationship manager or their Treasury advisor the order to buy or to sell EUR/USD. These orders are transferred to the trading desk, where the orders are executed.

Market

The BIS Survey (BoE quarterly bulletin: winter 2001) of the global foreign exchange markets shows a decline of the average daily trading volume of 21% (spot and forward market) to $504 billion per day from $637 billion per day recorded in the previous survey in 1998. This fall has taken place against a backdrop of decreasing global foreign exchange activity, which declined by 19% over the same period to $1,210 billion from the record $1,490 billion in April 1998. The decline is said to be the result of the introduction of the Euro, greater efficiency as a result of the introduction of electronic brokerage, and consolidation in the banking system[12].

The breakdown indicates that most of the decline in volume was in the interbank market. This was down to $220 billion versus the $280 billion seen in 1998. Activity between banks and non-financial institutions slipped to $156 billion versus $241 billion. Trading between banks and financial institutions increased to $568 billion versus the $378 billion seen in 1998.

In terms of the main traded currency pairs, the data show that the EUR/USD accounted for 30% of total trading while the USD/JPY's share was 20% and the GBP/USD 11%. All the EUR trading accounted for 38% of total trading compared to the 53% that the 12 EUR currencies had commanded in 1998[13].

London remains the most dominant center with 31.1% of the volume. This is a fall from 32.5% in 1998. The US share of total trading volume was down to 15.7% versus 17.9% in 1998. Japan gained to 9.1% versus 6.9%. Germany took 5.4% of the market compared to 4.8%, and Australia took 3.2% versus 2.4% in 1998[14].

Since the introduction of the Electronic Brokerage System, the market has become more anonymous. Traders can leave their orders in this system without having information "slippage". Before, traders were mainly working with voice brokers and a personal relationship was often the basis for the working relationship between traders and brokers. Voice brokers always played an important role in delivering news and rumors. The newly introduced Electronic Brokerage System (EBS) doesn't fulfill either the news or rumor delivering process. So the actions of traders release less information when dealing with EBS than with voice brokers. Banks that need to work large orders will use the EBS more, because it takes longer before the other market participants see that the particular bank is working an order. Large investment banks use this way of trading the most, because they are less frequently in the market as interbank players than the other banks. When they need to do something, they want to stay anonymous as long as possible.

---

[12] S. Wharmby, The foreign exchange and over-the-counter derivatives markets in the United Kingdom. Bank of England Quarterly Bulletin: Winter 2001.
Tony Norfield and Rob Hayward, ABN AMRO Global FX Daily, 10 October 2001
[13] S. Wharmby, The foreign exchange and over-the-counter derivatives markets in the United Kingdom. Bank of England Quarterly Bulletin: Winter 2001.
Tony Norfield and Rob Hayward, ABN AMRO Global FX Daily, 10 October 2001
[14] S. Wharmby, The foreign exchange and over-the-counter derivatives markets in the United Kingdom. Bank of England Quarterly Bulletin: Winter 2001.
Tony Norfield and Rob Hayward, ABN AMRO Global FX Daily, 10 October 2001

All the large banks have trading desks to provide their clients with full service. Currency trading (also EUR/USD) is seen more as a service product than as a marginal product. Banks don't make money on the tiny spreads offered to their important clients, but they make money on the information that is given through trading with their important clients. They all want to have the hedge funds, black box funds, investment funds, pension funds, insurance companies, central banks and large corporates as their clients because of the information that is given to them by these clients. Small spreads and a good sales person are needed to keep these clients. These clients have accounts with several banks and they will only trade on the best price, the best advice and the best information. The banks also earn money by the larger spreads on the smaller amounts of their smaller clients.

Competitors and their market share[15]

Table 2.6.4: Euromoney Foreign Exchange results 2001 (May 2001)

2001	2000	Top firms	Estimated market share
1	3	Citigroup	9.74%
2	1	Deutsche Bank	9.08%
3	6	Goldman Sachs	7.09%
4	7	JP Morgan, merged with Chase 31 Dec 2000	5.22%
5	2	Chase Manhattan, merged with JP Morgan 31 Dec 2000.	4.69%
6	9	Credit Suisse First Boston	4.10%
7		UBS Warburg	3.55%
		Warburg Dillon Read ranked 4 and PaineWebber 79 in 2000.	
8	14	State Street Bank & Trust	2.99%
9	15	Bank of America	2.99%
10	10	Morgan Stanley Dean Witter	2.87%
11	12	Barclays Capital	2.46%
12	5	HSBC	2.44%
13	16	ABN AMRO	1.86%
14	48	BNP Paribas	1.81%
15	28	Bank of Nova Scotia	1.58%
16	26	CIBC Wood Gundy	1.55%
17	43	Bank of Montreal	1.52%
18	37	Toronto Dominion Bank	1.48%
19	8	Merrill Lynch	1.44%
20		Royal Bank of Scotland (Royal Bank of Scotland ranked 36, Natwest Global Financial Markets ranked 11 in 2000)	1.32%
21	21	Northern Trust	0.74%
22	31	Bank of Tokyo-Mitsubishi	0.72%
23	13	Royal Bank of Canada	0.71%
24	19	Credit Agricole Indosuez	0.67%
25	40	Dresdner Kleinwort Wasserstein	0.58%

---

[15]FOREX transformed by mergers, Euromoney, May 2001

In the last five years the number of players has reduced. Several names have combined altogether into a larger rival. The size of a player may not always be an advantage, as in FOREX the biggest players take a disproportionately large share. FOREX is, for the most part, a generic high volume, low margin business. FOREX was originally designed as a non-commission commission business, and the banks made their profits through the spread they charged clients. However, an important side effect of the consolidation is that the spreads are down nearly to zero. As spreads have tightened, it has become more difficult to make money through straightforward transactions or the everyday flow of business, other than by dealing with huge volumes.

Table 2.6.5: Source: Euromoney

2001	2000	Top firms	Estimated market share
Excluding institutional investors			
1	1	Citigroup	9.45%
2	2	Deutsche Bank	8.63%
3	9	Goldman Sachs	5.23%
Institutional investors only			
1	3	Citigroup	9.16%
2	1	Deutsche Bank	8.83%
3	5	Goldman Sachs	7.42%

Table 2.6.6: Source: Euromoney

2001	Most innovative	Key relationship banks	Key relationship banks (institutional investors only)	Key relationship banks (excl. instit.investors)	EUR/USD
1	Citigroup	Citigroup	Deutsche Bank	Citigroup	Deutsche Bank
2	Deutsche Bank	Deutsche Bank	Citigroup	Deutsche Bank	Citigroup
3	Goldman Sachs	HSBC	UBS Warburg	HSBC	Goldman Sachs

Table 2.6.7: Forwards and spot, Source: Euromoney

2001	Forwards under three years	Forwards over three years	Major currencies	Spot short-term strategy	Spot consistent pricing
1	Deutsche Bank	Deutsche Bank	Deutsche Bank	Citigroup	Citigroup
2	Citigroup	Citigroup	Citigroup	Deutsche Bank	Bank Deutsche
3	HSBC	HSBC	HSBC	HSBC	HSBC

Table 2.6.8: Options, Source: Euromoney

2001	Vanilla options	Exotic options	Trading strategies for options	Pricing options
1	Citigroup	Citigroup	Citigroup	Citigroup
2	Deutsche Bank	Deutsche Bank	Deutsche Bank	Deutsche Bank
3	UBS Warburg	UBS Warburg	Goldman Sachs	UBS Warburg

Table 2.6.9: Best research, Source: Euromoney

2001	Currency strategy	Economic	Short-term (0-3 months)	Long-term (over 3 months)	Options and Volatility
1	Citigroup	Citigroup	Citigroup	Deutsche Bank	Citigroup
2	Deutsche Bank	Deutsche Bank	Deutsche Bank	Citigroup	Deutsche Bank
3	Goldman Sachs	Goldman Sachs	HSBC	HSBC	UBS Warburg

Outcome of Business Plan

Table 2.6.10

Business Plan	Questions	Answers
Product plan	Products?	Direct EUR/USD
		Indirect EUR/USD
Production plan	What's needed?	Clients' positions
		Hedging
		Linked to other market participants, clients and colleagues.
		Online trading, information and pricing systems.
Marketing plan	Clients?	Funds, pension funds, insurance companies, CBs, corporates, private clients
	Scale of the market	Average daily net turnover of $504 billion.
	Competitors?	Citigroup, Deutsche Bank, Goldman Sachs etc.
	Market share?	9.74%, 9.08%, 7.09% etc.

The strategy that resulted from the Business Plan is the following:

To come to a better understanding of the product of the organization, utilize EUR/USD to provide the best service to your clients and differentiate from your competitors.

2.7　DESIGN APPROACH II: SWOT ANALYSIS

Introduction

Strategy can exist in several forms. The Strength Weakness Opportunity and Threat Analysis is based on strategy as a pattern. The decisions made in the organization and the goals that are defined and communicated are based on this pattern. The first step is to make an internal analysis, to obtain a definition of the strengths and weaknesses of the organization. The second step is to make the external analysis, to define the opportunities and threats of the organization. The final step is to combine the internal and external analyses to come up with solutions as to how to:

- MAXIMIZE THE STRENGTHS
- MINIMIZE THE WEAKNESSES
- IDENTIFY AND EXPLOIT THE OPPORTUNITIES
- TO DEFEND AGAINST INTERNAL AND EXTERNAL THREATS
- TO COME TO THE OPTIMAL MIX (STRATEGY) FOR THE ORGANIZATION

Strengths

The strengths of the EUR/USD interbank are in giving explanations about movements in the EUR/USD:

1. **MARKET PSYCHOLOGY** (SEE CHAPTER 3).
    - Trading is taken personally
    - Prospect theory
    - Regret
    - Cognitive dissonance
    - Overconfidence
    - Overreaction and underreaction
    - Anchoring
    - Mental compartments
    - Disjunction effect
    - Gambling behavior and speculation
    - The irrelevance of history
    - Magical thinking

2. **FX OPTION MARKET** (SEE CHAPTER 6)
    - Large expirations
    - Risk reversals
    - Volatilities
    - Barriers
    - Demand for OTM options
    - Hedging activity

    ☐ Large expires ☐ Risk Reversals ■ Volatilities
    ■ Barriers ▨ Demand OTM options ▨ Hedging activities

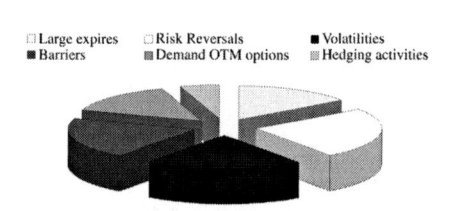

    Figure 2.7.1: FX Option Market

3. **COMMODITY MARKET** (SEE CHAPTER 7)
    - Oil as an explanation for EUR/USD weakness
    - Gold can play an important role in situations of uncertainty
    - Correlation between Gold/Bent and EUR/USD is 0.65

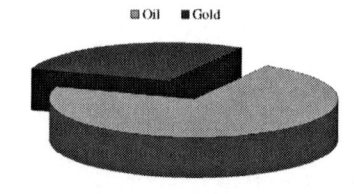

    ▨ Oil ■ Gold

    Figure 2.7.2: Commodity Market

4. **EQUITY MARKET** (SEE CHAPTER 8)
   – Higher return on US investments and higher US GDP
   – M&A activity
   – Merger arbitrage
   – MSCI adjustments
   – Higher USD turnover in the equity derivative market

   ☐ Return US investments & US GDP
   ■ M&A activity
   ■ Merger arbitrage
   ▨ MSCI adjustments
   ☐ USD turnover equity derivatives

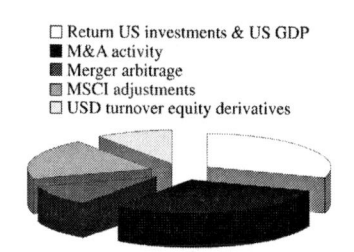

   Figure 2.7.3: Equity Market

5. **INTERNATIONAL DEBT MARKET** (SEE CHAPTER 9)
   – US Debt market offers better return
   – US Debt market is more highly developed
   – USD preferred as the currency denomination in issues
   – Market borrower driven
   – Increase USD turnover in the derivative market

   ☐ Higher US return
   ■ Development US Debt market
   ■ USD preferred in bond issues
   ▨ Market borrower driven
   ☐ Increase USD turnover derivative market

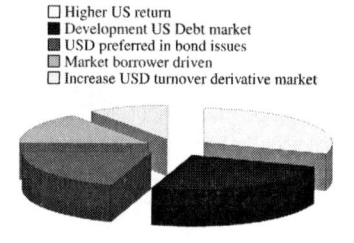

   Figure 2.7.4: International Debt Market

6. **SHORT-TERM-INTEREST-RATE MARKET** (SEE CHAPTER 10)
   – US Debt growth
   – Outstanding CP
   – 3 months interest rate spread
   – 3-months eurodollar future
   – 3-months euribor future

   ☐ US Debt growth
   ■ 3-months eurodollar future
   ☐ 3-months euribor future
   ■ Outstanding CP
   ▨ 3-months spread

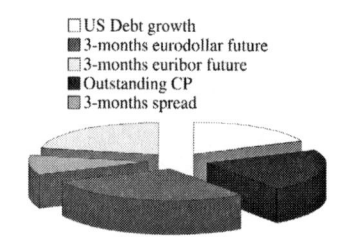

   Figure 2.7.5: Short-Term-Interest-Rate Market

Table 2.7.1: Correlations

	Correlation with EUR /USD	Start	Last date
Risk reversal * volatility	0.25	03 Jan 00	31 Oct 01
Gold/Brent	0.65	18 Jun 99	31 Oct 01
GDP US/Eurozone	-0.56	Q1 99	Q3 01
10 years interest rate spread	0.20	01 Jan 99	31 Oct 01
3-months eurodollar future	-0.45	20 Aug 99	31 Oct 01
3-months euribor future	-0.35	20 Aug 99	31 Oct 01
3-months interest rate spread	0.14	01 Jan 99	31 Oct 01
Outstanding US CP	-0.33	01 Jan 99	31 Oct 01

Figure 2.7.6: Correlation of the rational components

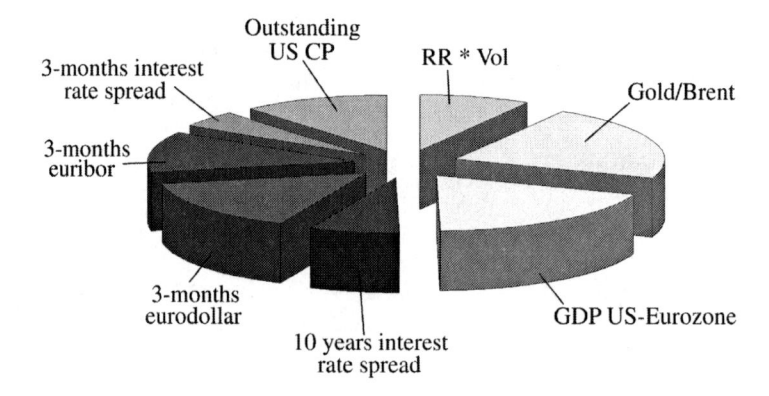

Figure 2.7.7: Strengths

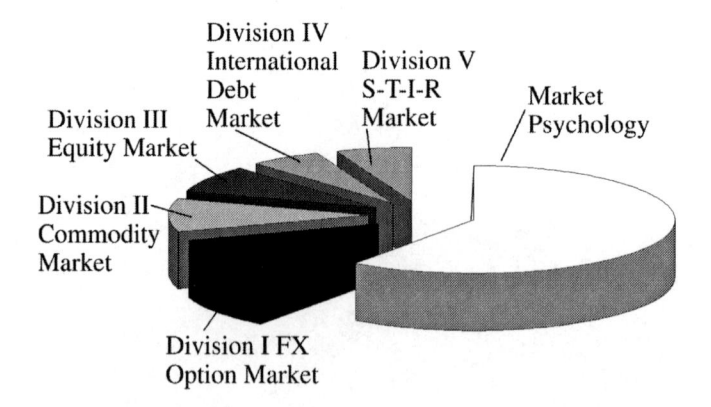

Weaknesses

The weaknesses of the EUR/USD interbank are:
1. MARKET PSYCHOLOGY (SEE CHAPTER 3)
   – Measurable?
2. FX OPTIONS MARKET (SEE CHAPTER 6)
   – Subjective
   – Measurable?
3. COMMODITY MARKET (SEE CHAPTER 7)
   – Gold correlation with EUR/USD is not stable.
4. EQUITY MARKET (SEE CHAPTER 8)
   – Lagging flow data
   – Stock indices
5. INTERNATIONAL DEBT MARKET (SEE CHAPTER 9)
   – Lagging flow data
6. SHORT-TERM-INTEREST-RATE (SEE CHAPTER 10)
   – Lagging flow data
   – Money Supply

Opportunities

The main opportunity is to create a strong European currency block against the USD block. European traders and market makers (and other stakeholders) have a long way to go to establish this stronger currency block; primarily, because European politicians and officials have to develop more of a "group" feeling. European politicians and officials need to be more consistent and single-minded. This is a time consuming process—which may, in fact, take years, but the result will be there, if only all the stakeholders invest sufficient time and delete the influence of ego. Hence, it offers a time consuming, but excellent opportunity for EUR.

Threats

From our studies and analysis, we are able to define two main threats. The first threat is a further concentration of the business so that, in the end, there is only one currency. Many financial traders believe that the concentration is limited to three currency blocks, the USD, the Euro and the JPY. The countries involved in these three currency blocks are significant players, no one of which offers all opportunities for the markets, but none seem to be prepared to give up all their history and culture for the sake of one worldwide currency. Enough countries worldwide will try to prevent the development towards one worldwide currency (for example the USD), because of the aforesaid issues. As is evidenced daily, not every country is pro US, so these countries will not accept the USD as the only currency worldwide. In the short-term, however, the USD will probably remain the most dominant currency block.

The second threat observed is that the JPY currency block will become more dominant than the Euro currency block. This development has much to do with the economic health and factual diminishing growth of, and diminishing lack of influence of Europe. This is not an immediate threat, because Japan has been faced with a low or no growth environment for almost ten years. It is evident to many that Japan is currently sliding into a recession again.

Outcome of the SWOT Analysis

Table 2.7.2 SWOT Analysis

Strengths	Weaknesses
Behavioral Finance (Chapter 3)	*Behavioral Finance:* measurable? (Chapter 3)
FX Options Market (Chapter 6): Large expirations Risk reversals Volatility Barriers Demand OTM options Hedging activity.	*FX Options Market (Chapter 6):* Subjective Measurable?
Commodity Market (Chapter 7): Oil as explanation for moves in EUR/USD Gold important in uncertain environment.	*Commodity Market* (Chapter 7): Gold correlation not stable
Equity Market (Chapter 8): Higher US return on investments & higher US GDP M&A activity Merger arbitrage MSCI adjustments USD turnover in equity derivatives	*Equity Market* (Chapter 8): Lagging flow data Stock indices
International Debt Market (Chapter 9): US Debt market offers better return US Debt market is higher developed. USD preferred in bond issues Market borrower driven Increase USD turnover derivative market	*International Debt Market* (Chapter 9): Lagging flow data
Short-Term-Interest-Rate Market (Chapter 10): US Debt growth Outstanding CP 3-months interest spread 3-months eurodollar future 3-months euribor future	*Short-Term-Interest-Rate Market* (Chapter 10): Lagging flow data Money Supply (M3)

Opportunities	Threats
Strong European currency block	One world-wide currency
	JPY currency block

To define the strategy for the organization as a pattern, we have to combine both the internal and external analyses. The outcome and strategy for the organization would be:
- Combine the cognitive (Behavioral Finance) and the configuration, design, planning and positioning approach to understand the product EUR/$ by uncovering the driving forces in the EUR/$ market.
- A strong European currency block is the main wish of the European politicians and officials. Speaking with one voice and full commitment are the necessary ingredients.
- One worldwide currency block is not an apparent threat, but competition from the JPY block may be.
- A development of a "we" feeling in Europe and improvement in the economic climate are the ways to improve the strength of EUR against this threat.

2.8 THE POSITIONING APPROACH I: ELEMENTS OF INDUSTRY STRUCTURE (M. Porter)

Potential entrants:
Online trading is a major potential entrant for the EUR/USD Interbank Market. It will be possible (in the future) to link these online trading sides automatically with trading systems such as Reuters dealing and Electronic Brokerage System (EBS). This will result in fewer traders and sales persons needed.

Intensity of rivalry among existing competitors:
Competitors are defined as the organizations in the Interbank Market with as products the other main currency pairs such as: EUR/GBP, GBP/USD, USD/JPY, EUR/JPY, EUR/CHF and USD/CHF. Preference of traders and investors can shift from one currency pair to another based on volatility, liquidity and other things.

Bargaining power of buyers:
The bargaining power of buyers is very high. The buyers in this market are the funds (investments, hedge, black box and pension funds), central banks, corporates and private clients. The first three buyer groups have a significant amount of power because they are clients with more banks. They trade with the bank which can offer the best price and the best service. **The task of the trader is to give the best prices (and market information/market view) and the task of the sales person is to differentiate the product from that of their competitors.**

Bargaining power of suppliers:
The suppliers in this market are the brokers (voice), the providers of the trading systems (EBS and Reuters Dealing), the providers of the information systems (Reuters, Telerate, Dow Jones, Bloomberg) and the providers of the pricing and booking systems (Fenics, OMR, Boss). The bargaining power of the suppliers has decreased in the last years and is less than the bargaining power of the buyers.

Pressure from substitute products:
The substitute products are the other main currency pairs: EUR/GBP, GBP/USD, USD/JPY, EUR/JPY, USD/CHF and EUR/CHF. EUR/USD is the most traded and liquid currency pair.

2.9 THE POSITIONING APPROACH II: CONCEPTS OF INDUSTRY EVOLUTION

This research is about defining the forces to understand the organization.
The industry evolution perspective is used to understand these forces and to be able to develop a competitive strategy. We believe that the EUR/USD Interbank Market Diversified Organization is in the maturity stage. The following analysis will explain why we hold that position. An overview of the other stages can be found in "Competitive Strategy" of Michael Porter (1980).

Buyer and Buyer Behavior
The EUR/USD is the most liquid currency pair in the currency markets. Buyers have a high power because they can shop several bank prices at the same time and trade with the bank which offers the best price. Buyers buy EUR/USD over and over again for speculative, hedging or commercial reasons.

Products and products change
The quality of the product EUR/USD is very high: high liquidity, small bid-offer spreads, quick prices and good information. Liquidity, bid-offer spreads, pricing and information are standardized. Sales people try to sell EUR/USD with views and information of the traders.

Marketing
There is market segmentation between professional parties and non professional clients. The first group has most of the power and can demand the highest quality. The second group is far less powerful and pays for the product EUR/USD and the quality is usually less. The packaging of EUR/USD with information and view of the traders is important to keep the clients satisfied. EUR/USD was launched as new product in an existing currency market.

Manufacturing and Distribution
There is an overcapacity of traders because EUR/USD replaced all these separate currencies. Before the introduction of the EUR 5-10 traders were needed while after introduction there exists a maximum two traders per time zone. From a cost cutting point of view (and increasing revenues), most of the trading desks are centralized in one large trading desk per time zone.

Overall Strategy
In Foreign Exchange, market shares are more or less set. However, to increase market share, buying another company or merging with another company is the theme.

Competition:
The competition among banks is high. In EUR/USD tight spreads are quoted. Some of the banks refocus on business other than Foreign Exchange. Sales persons try to differentiate their EUR/USD by selling it together with information and the views of the trader.

Margin and profits
The tight spreads mean that the prices are falling. It is almost impossible to make money on the spread. Foreign Exchange (as well EUR/USD) has become a service product, service needed to keep clients. There is an increased stability of market shares and price structures.

SUMMARY 2

The configurational, entrepreneurial, cognitive, design and positioning approach are used in the analysis.

EUR/USD Interbank Market is defined as an organization. The configuration of this organization is a Diversified Configuration. The Strategic Apex is the group of the EUR/USD interbank traders. The Techno Structure can be divided into fundamental and technical analysis. The systems (Reuters, Bloomberg, Dow Jones, Telerate etc) and the Sales Force form the Support Staff. The Middle Line is the group of traders of the five separate divisions:
- FX Option Market
- Commodity Market
- Equity Market
- International Debt Market
- Short-Term-Interest-Rate (S-T-I-R) Market

The Operating Core can also be divided into these five sub-organizations. In each of the sub-organizations the general EUR/USD product is transformed into one of the five EUR/USD sub-products.

Outcome Business Plan EUR/USD Interbank Market, table 2.6.10

Business Plan	Questions	Answers
Product plan	Products?	Direct EUR/USD
		Indirect EUR/USD
Production plan	What's needed?	Clients' positions
		Hedging
		Linked to other market participants, clients and colleagues.
		Online trading, information and pricing systems.
Marketing plan	Clients?	Funds, pension funds, insurance companies, CBs, corporates, private clients
	Scale of the market	Average daily net turnover of $504 billion.
	Competitors?	Citigroup, Deutsche Bank, Goldman Sachs etc.
	Market share?	9.74%, 9.08%, 7.09% etc.

Outcome of the SWOT Analysis EUR/USD Interbank Market, table 2.7.2

Strengths	Weaknesses
Behavioral Finance (Chapter 3)	*Behavioral Finance:* measurable? (Chapter 3)
FX Options Market (Chapter 6): **Large expirations** **Risk reversals** **Volatility** **Barriers** **Demand OTM options** **Hedging activity.**	*FX Options Market (Chapter 6):* Subjective Measurable?
Commodity Market (Chapter 7): **Oil as explanation for moves in EUR/USD** **Gold important in uncertain environment.**	*Commodity Market* (Chapter 7): Gold correlation not stable
Equity Market (Chapter 8): **Higher US return on investments & higher US GDP** **GDP** **M&A activity** **Merger arbitrage** **MSCI adjustments** **USD turnover in equity derivatives**	*Equity Market* (Chapter 8): Lagging flow data Stock indices
International Debt Market (Chapter 9): **US Debt market offers better return** **US Debt market is higher developed.** **USD preferred in bond issues** **Market borrower driven** **Increase USD turnover derivative market**	*International Debt Market* (Chapter 9): Lagging flow data
Short-Term-Interest-Rate Market (Chapter 10): **US Debt growth** **Outstanding CP** **3-months interest spread** **3-months eurodollar future** **3-months euribor future**	*Short-Term-Interest-Rate Market* (Chapter 10): Lagging flow data Money Supply (M3)

Opportunities	Threats
Strong European currency block	One world-wide currency
	JPY currency block

In Chapter 3 on Behavioral Finance, the following questions will be answered:
1. What is Behavioral Finance (Cognitive approach)?
2. What are the general principals which are prescribed in this area?
3. How does my personal experience influence the Behavioral Finance area?

REFERENCES

Enoch, C. and M. Quintyn. "European Monetary Union: Operating Monetary Policy", International Monetary Fund.
Euromoney. "Forex Transformed by Mergers", May 2001
European Communities. "Economic and Monetary Union: From Rome to Maastricht: a brief history of EMU.
Mintzberg, H., *STRUCTURES IN FIVES :Designing Effective Organizations,* Copyright © 1993. Reprinted by permission of Pearson Education, In., Upper Saddle River, New Jersey.
Mintzberg, H., B. Ahlstrand, J. Lampel, *STRATEGY SAFARI: The complete guide through the wilds of strategic management,* Copyright © 1998. Reprinted by permission of Pearson Education Ltd, 128 LongAcre, London WC2E 9AN
COMPETITIVE STRATEGY: Techniques for Analyzing Industries and Competitors by Michael E. Porter. Copyright © 1980, 1998 by The Free Press, an imprint of Simon & Schuster Adult Publishing Group. Reprinted with permission of the publisher.
Steiner, B. "European Monetary System" Markets International Ltd., ACI Diploma study material.
Steiner, B. "Foreign Exchange" Markets International Ltd., ACI Diploma study material.
Steiner, B. "Identifying, measuring and controlling risk and return" Markets International Ltd., ACI Diploma study material.
Wharmby, S. "The Foreign Exchange and Over-the-Counter Derivatives Markets in the United Kingdom", Bank of England Quarterly Bulletin, Winter 2001.

Chapter **3**

BEHAVIORAL FINANCE (COGNITIVE APPROACH) & MARKET PSYCHOLOGY (ORGANIZATIONAL CULTURE)

3.1 INTRODUCTION

A TRADER'S MIND

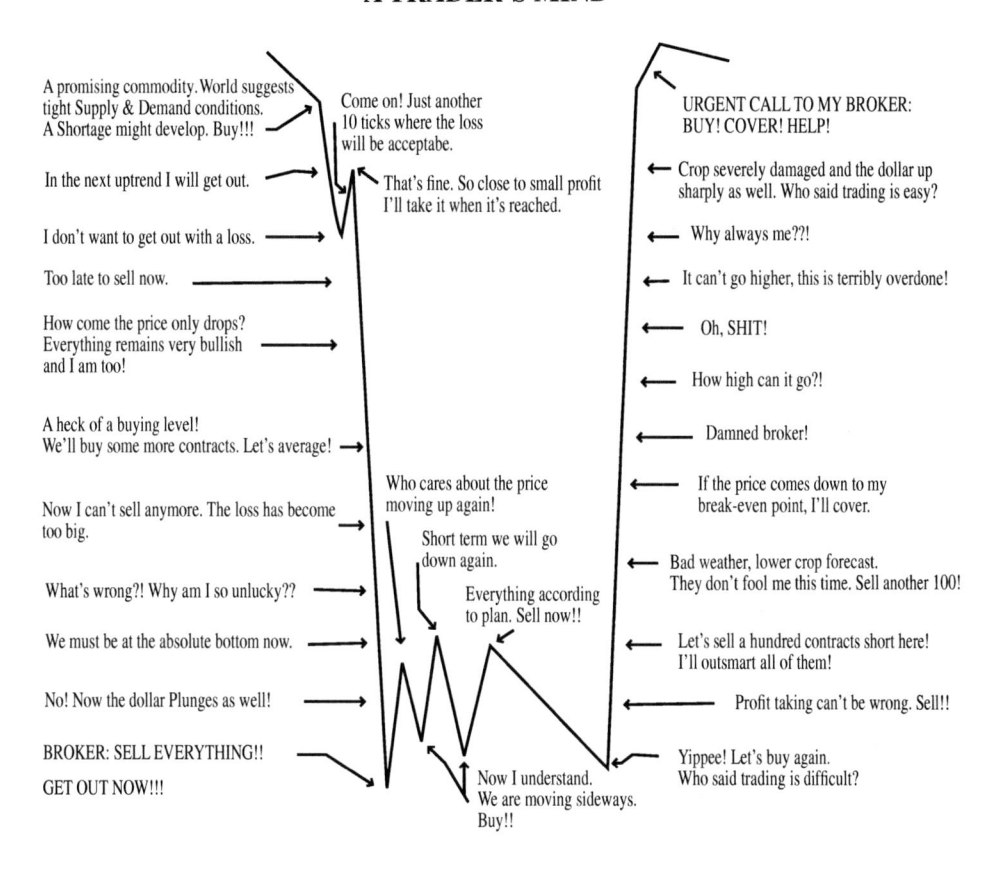

A promising commodity. World suggests tight Supply & Demand conditions. A Shortage might develop. Buy!!!

In the next uptrend I will get out.

I don't want to get out with a loss.

Too late to sell now.

How come the price only drops? Everything remains very bullish and I am too!

A heck of a buying level! We'll buy some more contracts. Let's average!

Now I can't sell anymore. The loss has become too big.

What's wrong?! Why am I so unlucky??

We must be at the absolute bottom now.

No! Now the dollar Plunges as well!

BROKER: SELL EVERYTHING!! GET OUT NOW!!!

Come on! Just another 10 ticks where the loss will be acceptabe.

That's fine. So close to small profit I'll take it when it's reached.

Who cares about the price moving up again!

Short term we will go down again.

Everything according to plan. Sell now!!

Now I understand. We are moving sideways. Buy!!

URGENT CALL TO MY BROKER: BUY! COVER! HELP!

Crop severely damaged and the dollar up sharply as well. Who said trading is easy?

Why always me??!

It can't go higher, this is terribly overdone!

Oh, SHIT!

How high can it go?!

Damned broker!

If the price comes down to my break-even point, I'll cover.

Bad weather, lower crop forecast. They don't fool me this time. Sell another 100!

Let's sell a hundred contracts short here! I'll outsmart all of them!

Profit taking can't be wrong. Sell!!

Yippee! Let's buy again. Who said trading is difficult?

Source: unknown

Traders are wired to the market[1].

In a very long study at a Boston financial company, researchers found that professional currency traders react to changing markets not just with their brains, but also subconsciously, with their whole bodies. As they sit at their desks moving millions of dollars through the financial system, their vital signs react almost instantaneously as prices dip and rise. **THEY ARE WIRED TO THE MARKET.**

Foreign currency traders are paid to act rationally – to ignore the waves of emotion that consume amateur investors. However, a strong emotional reaction is clear in regions far from the rational mind. Inexperienced traders react strongly. Experienced ones display more balance.

In chapter 1 the different schools were introduced. In chapter 2, I defined Market Psychology as the organizational culture. To understand and deal with this Market Psychology, Behavioral Finance or the cognitive approach is very important. In my dissertation, I'm a user of the results of research done in Behavioral Finance to understand and explain market behavior I've seen so far.

---

[1] Gareth Cook, *The Biology of "Irrational Exuberance"*. The Boston Globe, 10/23/2001

3.2 TRADING IS TAKEN PERSONALLY

Behavioral Finance investigates the cognitive factors and emotional issues that impact on the decision-making processes of individuals, groups and organizations. Behavioral Finance offers good explanations about what is going on in financial markets in terms of Market Psychology. However, we are obligated to add the fact that individuals in the trade take trading personally and this is the most important reason for the Market Psychology. During my time as a trader I continuously challenged myself on every mental aspect. These challenges were enormously direct and I couldn't walk away from them because of my very analytical nature. I simply refused to give up. The consequence was that I had to deal with personal challenges in a fast paced environment. The trigger for these mental confrontations was my experience "incurring" losses. This is common for every trader but the way that you deal with it determines whether you are suited for the job or not. For me it was a challenge to find out if I could handle it or not. I can proudly say that I handled it well. Some former colleagues, however, might possibly offer an opposing view.

Trading is a highly personal activity and the fact that people take it personally is the main reason for Market Psychology. Traders get paid to make money and the style they use is not important as long as they make a profit. Profit is the synonym for being a winner and loss for being a loser.

The experience of loss positions is vital for becoming a good trader. When you are in a loss period, every loss day decreases your confidence until there is not much left. Then you ask yourself why you do the job anyway. I call this the breakpoint in trading. Through this learning process, we learn that trading is **not** personal. The market does whatever it wants to do and your position is absolutely not important. Further, the market will occasionally test you, to see how strong your market perception is. For example, if I expected that the market would go up I started with a long position in the morning. During the day my position increased because of my market making responsibilities. Usually, important parties and information try to convince you that you are wrong. After I had liquidated my total position, the market moved as I had expected, only I was not in the position anymore to profit from it. Another aspect of trading is the relief when you finally make your first profit again after a loss period. This profit doesn't mean that the loss period is behind you. Usually you will get another loss period with a deeper trough than the first one before you really finish the loss period. So when you believe the worst is over it will start again.

Major trading lessons we must "take away" are:
1. It is not personal.
2. You can not influence the market.
3. There are no rules.
4. Sticking to your own rules is the only way to survive.
5. Trust your profits.
6. Be patient.

Trading remains personal for traders. People take trading personally and that's why we need Behavioral Finance to explain Market Psychology.

3.3 PROSPECT THEORY

The prospect theory explains the attitudes towards risk. Under the prospect theory (Kahneman and Tversky, 1979)[2], when faced with choices involving simple two and three outcome lotteries, people behave as if maximizing an "S"-shaped value function. This value function is similar to a standard utility function except that it is defined on gains and losses rather than on levels of wealth. The function is concave in the domain of gains and convex in the domain of losses. It is also deeper for losses than for gains, which implies that people are generally risk-averse. Critical to this value function is the reference point from which gains and losses are measured. A person who has not made peace with his losses is likely to accept gambles that would be unacceptable to him otherwise (Kahneman and Tversky, 1979)[3]. If the stock appreciates and the investor continues to use the purchase price as a reference point, the stock price will then be in a more concave, more risk-averse, part of the investor's value function. If the investor lowers her expectation of the stock's return, she will be likely to sell the stock. When the stock price declines, its price is in the convex risk-seeking part of the value function. The investor will continue to hold the stock even if its expected return falls lower than would have been necessary for her to justify the original purchase. Investors will be averse to selling a stock when the result would be a loss and thereby they reduce the supply of potential sellers, which could slow price decreases even more. Investors are more willing to sell the stock when it is in the money and thereby they increase the supply and slow further price increases[4].

So in fact there are two problems according to Kahneman and Tversky[5].
The first problem is risk avoidance. A subject is asked to respond on the following questions:
1. 50% chance of gaining $1,000.00
2. Sure gain of $500.00

The outcome is that 84% of the Kahneman and Tversky subjects chose the sure gain.

The second problem is risk seeking. A subject is asked again to respond on two questions:
1. 50% chance of losing $1,000.00
2. Sure loss of $500.00

In this case nearly 70% of the surveyed chose the risky alternative hoping thereby to avoid any loss whatever.

---

[2] D. Kahneman and A. Tversky, *Choices, Values and Frames*, Reprinted with the permission of Cambridge University Press, December 2000

[3] Terrance Odean, *Are investors reluctant to realize their losses?*, December 1997
D. Kahneman and A. Tversky, *Choices, Values and Frames*, Reprinted with the permission of Cambridge University Press, December 2000

[4] Terrance Odean, *Are investors reluctant to realize their losses?*, December 1997
D. Kahneman and A. Tversky, *Choices, Values and Frames*, Reprinted with the permission of Cambridge University Press, December 2000

[5] D. Kahneman and A. Tversky, *Choices, Values and Frames*, Reprinted with the permission of Cambridge University Press, December 2000

Further, there is an altitude of the surveyed towards small probabilities. According to Kahneman and Tversky (1979), people overestimate the value of small probabilities[6].

Disposition effect

The disposition effect is the tendency of investors to hold losing investments too long and sell winning investments too soon[7]. This effect predicts that, all-else being equal; gains are realized sooner than losses so that as trade holding time increases, the proportion of losses should increase as well[8]. The disposition effect says also that investors will generally trade less actively when their investments have lost money[9]. Further, the disposition effect is stock-specific; it predicts an increase in volume of winning stocks but not losing ones. Negative returns detract from overconfidence more than positive returns add to it[10].

Most investors treat the decision to buy a security quite differently from the decision to sell. Though the search for securities to sell is simple, in other respects the decision to sell a security is more complex than the decision to buy. When choosing securities to buy, an investor only needs to form expectations about the future performance of those securities. When choosing securities to sell, the investor will consider past as well as future performance. If the investor is rational he will want to balance the advantages or disadvantages of any tax losses or gains he realizes from a sale against the future returns he expects a security to earn. If an investor is psychologically motivated he may wish to avoid realizing losses and prefer to sell his winners[11].

Evidence is found that professional futures traders as a group hold losses significantly longer than gains (loss realization aversion). Gains are realized more quickly than losses regardless of the magnitude of the absolute gain. Traders hold on to losses with significantly greater position sizes and significantly greater mark-to market than for the gains that they hold. Traders pass up more opportunities to realize losses than gains, hold larger positions while holding losses and are exposed to bigger losses than potential gains[12].

---

[6]D. Kahneman and A. Tversky, *Choices, Values and Frames,* Reprinted with the permission of Cambridge University Press, December 2000

[7]Terrance Odean, *Are Investors Reluctant to Realize Their Losses?*, December 1997

[8]P.R. Locke & S.C. Mann, *Do Professional Traders Exhibit Loss Realization Aversion?* November 2000

[9]Brad. M. Barber & Terrance Odean, *The Courage of Misguided Convictions: the Trading Behavior of Individual Investors,* Financial Analyst Journal, Vol 55, Issue 6, 1999

[10]M. Statman & S. Thorley, *Investor Overconfidence and Trading Volume,* June 1999

[11]Brad. M. Barber & Terrance Odean, *The Courage of Misguided Convictions: the Trading Behavior of Individual Investors,* Financial Analyst Journal, Vol 55, Issue 6, 1999

[12]P.R. Locke & S.C. Mann, *Do Professional Traders Exhibit Loss Realization Aversion?* November 2000

Explanations for this investor behavior can be[13]:
1. Anticipation of changes in tax laws.
2. Desire to rebalance
3. Belief that the losers will bounce back. Investors expect the losers to outperform the winners in the future.
4. Attempt to limit transaction costs.
5. Belief that all stocks revert to the mean.

In experimental settings, Andreassen (1988) finds that subjects buy and sell stocks if they expect short-term mean reversion[14].

Personal experience

Frequently used trading techniques are averaging up and down. When traders are in a loss position they usually increase their position because of the higher likelihood of exiting the total position without loss. As a result, the position increase has a better average but a higher risk due to the larger position. The market usually moves in a trading range. Since most traders are range traders, this higher position risk is affordable because of the low probability that the price will break out of the range. I always tried to avoid averaging up and down because of the following reasons:
1. I'm a breakout trader and not a range trader.
2. Averaging up and down are trading strategies to "avoid" losses or to postpone losses in the case of a break.
3. I prefer to deal with the confrontation when it comes. You are not in charge of your position anymore because you hope that the market stays in the range.
4. You miss other trading opportunities.
5. If the range is broken the stop loss will hurt even more.

I always kept my stop losses close. However my major trading weakness was to let the profit run. So, I have cut my profit positions too quickly because I didn't have the patience to wait for higher profits. Impatience is a reflection of not trusting a situation when it is profitable, in fact, not trusting your own view (lacking confidence). Impatience can be solved by restoring your own confidence.

---

[13] Brad. M. Barber & Terrance Odean, *The Courage of Misguided Convictions: the Trading Behavior of Individual Investors*, Financial Analyst Journal, Vol 55, Issue 6, 1999
[14] Terrance Odean, *Are Investors Reluctant to Realize Their Losses?*, December 1997

Loss aversion

Investors dislike selling their shares at a loss. The investors will be risk averse in the domain of gains, but risk seeking in the domain of losses[15]. So loss aversion is an asymmetric attitude towards gains versus losses. Prospect theory conjectures that agents exhibit loss aversion, or greater sensitivity to losses than to gains. Loss aversion has important consequences for the economic theory. If people are loss averse, much of what we think we know about the economics of uncertainty may be incorrect. If Capital Asset Pricing Model (CAPM) is adjusted for loss aversion, this adjusted version specifies a higher risk premium for downside risk than upside risk. Loss aversion depends critically on the frequency with which investors monitor their returns and determine whether they have made losses or gains (investors' evaluation period). Empirical results demonstrate that both bonds and stocks appear to be priced more correctly by their downside betas than by their upside betas. Bonds have large downside betas relative to stocks, but their upside betas are similar to stock betas. Thus this loss aversion model provides an intuitive explanation for the equity premium. Bonds have low expected returns because they pay off well in bad states of the world. The downside risk of bonds is significantly less than their upside risk. A loss averse agent will prefer receiving $100 with certainty to receiving an equal chance to receive $200 or nothing. However, faced with the prospect of losing $100 with certainty, he will prefer a lottery with equal probability of either no loss or a loss of $200. A loss averse agent will be willing to make a bet double or nothing conditional on losing the first round of the betting, but he will not accept a second bet if he wins the first round[16].

Evidence shows that Chicago Board of Trade (CBOT) traders are highly loss-averse: they are far more likely to take on additional afternoon risk following morning losses than morning gains. A trader (according to a specific test) with morning losses has a 31.3% chance of taking above –average risk in the afternoon, compared to a trader who earns a profit in the morning who has only a 26.9% chance. Thus, a losing trader is 16% more likely to take above-average afternoon risk than a winning trader[17].

Loss is less painful to people when it comes after substantial earlier increases in wealth; known as the house money effect. There is evidence that, after a loss; people tend to shy away from risky bets that they might otherwise have taken, because losses over losses are more painful than on average. An informal interpretation is that in the aftermath of a painful loss, while the investor is still reeling from the shock, he is particularly sensitive to additional setbacks, increasing his risk aversion. After a fall in stock prices he becomes more wary of further losses and hence more risk averse. Loss aversion makes investors reluctant to invest in stocks even in the face of a sizable equity premium. Prior outcomes influence risky choices. Following a gain, people appear to be more risk seeking. It reflects the fact that a loss is less painful[18]

---

[15]Markku Kaustia, *Can Loss Aversion Move the Market? Evidence from IPO Trading Volume*, December 27, 2000
[16]Tyler G. Shumway, *Explaining Returns with Loss Aversion*, November 20, 1997
[17]Joshua D. Coval & Tyler G. Shumway, *Do Behavioral Biases Affect Prices?*, May 4, 2001

Personal experience

I experienced that it is easier to trade when you closed the day before with a profit. Every consecutive loss day-reduces your trading activity. However, on an intraday time frame I reacted differently. If I started with a good profit in the morning, I was reluctant to trade in the afternoon because I wanted to close the day with a profit. The change in trading behavior made sure that I would close the day without profit. As a market maker you can never step out of the market and the switch in my mind caused a lower reaction speed than was needed, so reduced the profit. When you start the day with a loss, you have more fighting power and alertness to reduce the loss and even turn it into a profit, because you don't want to close the day with a loss. In fact you are more aggressive. This aggressiveness will even be higher on Friday (last day of the week), last day of the month (double if that's also a Friday) and the last weeks of the year. On these days the profitable traders stay out of the market, while the other traders try to turn their losses into profits by taking higher risks. These days I experience lower liquidity, higher volatility and larger moves. The month December is characterized by low liquidity due to the fact that major players, who made money this year, closed their books. Only the players who still need to meet their targets will be active in the market.

---

[18] N. Barberis, M. Huang & T. Santos, *Prospect Theory and Asset Prices*, June 1999.

3.4 REGRET

According to Statman (2001)[19] hope and fear might be the strongest emotions that drive lottery buyers and stock traders, but regret is not far behind. Regret is the pain that we feel when we find, too late, that a different choice would have led to a better outcome. Aversion to the pain of regret affects our choices. Aversion to regret plays an important role in trading behavior as well. In particular it underlies the reluctance to realize losses, as described by Shefrin and Statman (1985).

According to Dodonova (2001)[20] regret theory assumes that people's utility depends on their wealth in the same way as conventional expected utility theory does. However, this theory also takes into account the fact that people, after making decisions under uncertainty, may feel regret if their decisions turn out to be the wrong ones even if the appeared correct with the information available ex ante.

Personal experience

Professional traders are mainly evaluated by how much money they make. Making money is the only way to survive. Especially intra day traders have a daily profit and loss responsibility. The competition between colleagues even puts more pressure on the individual traders. Taking a loss is a part of trading life; however losses are preferred to be small in size and low in frequency. Because of the ongoing pressure to make money and the competition pressure traders are afraid to miss the move. They feel the regret if a different decision had brought profit. Common sentences used are:
 – Why didn't I just follow my feeling?
 – I should have known better.

---

[19]M. Statman (2001), *Lotteryplayers/stock traders*, Financial Analysts Journal, January/February 2002
[20]A.R. Dodonova, *Applications of Regret Theory to Asset Pricing*, 2001

3.5 COGNITIVE DISSONANCE

The cognitive dissonance theory was first proposed by Leon Festinger in 1957 and is based on the principle that people prefer their cognitions, or beliefs to be consistent with each other and with their own behavior. Inconsistency, or dissonance, among their own ideas makes people uneasy enough to alter these ideas so that they will agree with each other. Alternatively, one can diffuse dissonance by reducing its importance; adding new information that gives more weight to one of the dissonant beliefs or appears to reconcile them[21].

Individuals are inclined to interpret new evidence in ways that confirm their pre-existing beliefs. They also tend to change their beliefs to enhance the desirability of their past actions[22]. There are two biases that are consistently observed in agents making decisions under uncertainty: cognitive dissonance and confirmatory bias. Confirmatory bias is identified with the phenomenon of people interpreting new evidence in ways that confirm their current beliefs. Cognitive dissonance is a broad bias, which asserts that after having chosen an action people tend to change their beliefs about the relative agreeableness of this action[23].

Personal experience

In financial markets, participants face an overkill of information. Every player can find information that confirms and that does not confirm a belief or position. Generally, players tend to use the information that confirms their belief or position. It is very difficult to take a neutral to new information because they are involved in the market. I experienced that it is easier to get a clear picture of the market when I didn't have a position (confirmatory basis). That probably explains why I have difficulty to accept someone who judges a trader's position without having the trading experience. It's much easier to stand aside and judge others than trying to stay neutral and have a clear view with a position. Further, I believe that the trading strategy averaging up or down can be explained from the cognitive dissonance point of view. Traders buy a certain currency because they believe it will go up. From the time they entered the positions it only went down. They buy some more because they have a very good average for the future up move. The following arguments are also used a lot:
- It's now too late too sell.
- The perfect buying level.
- As trader you need to know how it is to feel the pain of loss.

---

[21]The Gale Encyclopedia of Psychology
[22]L. Yariv, I'll See It When I Believe It - A Simple Model of Cognitive Consistency, Cowles Foundation Discussion Paper Number 1352, February 2002
[23]L. Yariv, I'll See It When I Believe It - A Simple Model of Cognitive Consistency, Cowles Foundation Discussion Paper Number 1352, February 2002

3.6 OVERCONFIDENCE

A simple and powerful explanation for high levels of trading on financial markets is overconfidence. Human beings are overconfident about their abilities, their knowledge and their future prospects. Overconfident investors trade more than rational investors, and doing so lowers their expected utilities. Overconfidence increases trading activity because it causes investors to be too certain about their own opinions, not giving the opinions of others sufficient consideration[24]. A trader's level of overconfidence changes dynamically with his successes and failures. A trader is not overconfident when he begins to trade. His expected overconfidence increases over his first several trading periods and then declines. Thus the greatest expected overconfidence in a trader's life span comes early in his career. An overconfident trader trades too aggressively and increases the expected market volume. Both volume and volatility increase with the degree of a trader's learning bias[25].

The effects of overconfidence[26]:
- Trading volume increases when price-takers, insiders, or market makers are overconfident.
- Overconfident traders can cause markets to under-react to the information of rational traders, leading to positive, serially correlated, returns.
- Overconfidence reduces a traders' expected utility.
- Overconfidence increases market depth
- Overconfident insiders improve price quality, but overconfident price-takers worsen it.
- Overconfident traders increase volatility, though overconfident market makers may dampen this effect.

The overconfidence effect is market wide and predicts an increase in volume of trading of all stocks, both winners and losers[27].

---

[24]Brad. M. Barber & Terrance Odean, *The Courage of Misguided Convictions: the Trading Behavior of Individual Investors*, Financial Analyst Journal, Vol 55, Issue 6, 1999

[25]Simon Gervais & Terrance Odean, *Learning to Be Overconfident*, Review of Financial Studies, Volume 14, No.1, Spring 2001, pp.1-27, Reprinted with the permission of Oxford University Press

[26]Terrance Odean, *Volume, Volatility, Price and Profit; When all Traders Are Above Average*, April 1998

[27]M. Statman & S. Thorley, *Investor Overconfidence and Trading Volume*, June 1999

3.7 OVERREACTION AND UNDERREACTION

According to the research done by Barberis, Shleifer and Vishny (1997)[28] underreaction can be described as the situation that news is incorporated only slowly into prices. Overreaction is the phenomena that securities that have had a long record of good news tend to become overpriced. So securities with strings of good performance get extremely high valuations on average return to the mean.

There are two important phenomena documented by psychologists: representativeness heuristic and conservatism. According to Kahneman and Tversky (1974) representativeness heuristic is the tendency of experimental subject to view events as typical or representative of some specific class and to ignore the laws of probability in the process. "People replace the laws of chance by heuristics, which sometimes yield reasonable estimates and quite often do not (Kahneman & Tversky 1974, pp.32)". People see patterns in random sequences. Locally a sample drawn from a random walk may not look at all like a random walk. Investors will try to infer the process too quickly, on a basis of too short a sample and hence make erroneous forecasts.

Conservatism is the tendency of slow updating of models in the face of new evidence (Edwards, 1968). The underreaction evidence is in particular consistent with conservatism.

Personal experience

<u>Underreaction to signals and US Beige Book and IMF report became the triggers (wake up call)</u>

On the 8th of August 2001, the US Beige Book reported that sustained weakness in the US manufacturing sector spilled over to other businesses. Outcome of the Beige Book:

- Retail sales generally remained weak in June and July.
- Manufacturing activity declined further in recent weeks.
- Loan demand was flat to down.
- Payroll report (65% of all jobs) has fallen in three of the past four months and annual growth is down to 0.5%.

The market was not positioned for this outcome and the Fed Beige Book gave an unexpected support to EUR/USD.

---

[28] N. Barberis, A. Shleifer and R.W. Vishny, *A model of investor sentiment,* February 1997
D. Kahneman, P. Slovic and A. Tversky, *Judgment Under Uncertainty: Heuristics and Biases,* Reprinted with the permission of Cambridge University Press, 1974.

On the 15th of August 2001, the IMF released the following text: "The size of US external current account deficit did not appear sustainable in the longer term and the IMF raised concerns that the USD might be at risk for a sharp depreciation, particularly if productivity performance proved disappointing. A sudden correction in the current account deficit was seen as possible having adverse effects on the US and the rest of the world economy". Usually IMF's reports do not have a large market influence, but this time the IMF's annual report on the US triggered a minor panic as it echoed the financial market's most primal fear. So market players over-react on information that is already known by market participants.

Overreaction in USD strength (or EUR weakness)

An example of overreaction is that on a certain point market players became so negative on EUR/USD that levels of 0.7000 and 0.7500 were seen as possible (October 2000). Around the same time the all time low was set.

3.8 ANCHORING[29]

It has been shown that the answers people give are influenced by the brackets shown on the questionnaire. In Psychology, we realize that given choices, people will normally make the choices offered—and not try to make "out of the box" decisions[30]. The tendency to be influenced by such suggestions is what psychologists call anchoring. Values in speculative markets are inherently ambiguous. There is no agreed-upon economic theory that would answer the question of how much a certain stock market is really worth. In the absence of any better information, past prices are likely to be important determinants of prices today. Anchoring affects valuations. A lot of economic phenomena are influenced by anchoring. The anchoring phenomenon would appear relevant to sticky prices. So long as past prices are taken, as suggestions of new prices, the new prices will tend to be close to the past prices[31].

Personal experience
Anchoring is an important part of equity markets due to large equity research departments. In currency markets I also experienced anchoring. This was the result of technical analysis. Traders buy close to important supports and sell close to important resistances. The effect is that the market will usually not take out important technical levels during the first test. The market follows what the psychology of the market sets. However, this can be changed by making people more aware of it and inviting more people who not think as market players.

---

[29]Reprinted from Handbook of Macroeconomics, Volume 1c, Robert J. Schiller, *Human Behavior and the Efficiency of the Financial System*, Chapter 20, Copyright © 1999, with permission from Elsevier Science.
[30]Alan Guinn
[31]Reprinted from Handbook of Macroeconomics, Volume 1c, Robert J. Schiller, *Human Behavior and the Efficiency of the Financial System*, Chapter 20, Copyright © 1999, with permission from Elsevier Science.

3.9 MENTAL COMPARTMENTS[32]

People may tend to place their investments into arbitrarily separate mental compartments, and react separately to the investments based on which compartment they are in. Shefrin and Statman (1994) have argued that individual investors think naturally in terms of having a "safe" part of their portfolio that is protected from the downside and a risky part that is designed for a chance of taking a risk. Another example of this is an investor's tendency to focus on and manage individual trades instead of the entire portfolio[33].

Personal experience

Unlike the equity markets where investors are looking at individual trades instead of the overall portfolio, interbank currency traders are less inclined to thinking in mental compartments. The main reason for this is that interbank currency traders are highly specialized and are responsible for a book. The following books can be defined:

EUR/USD	
JPY	EUR/JPY, USD/JPY, all the JPY crosses
GBP	EUR/GBP, GBP/USD all the GBP crosses
CHF	EUR/CHF, USD/CHF all the CHF crosses
AUD, NZD and CAD	EUR/AUD, AUD/USD, EUR/NZD, NZD/USD, USD/CAD
Scandies	EUR/DKK, USD/DKK, EUR/NOK, USD/NOK, EUR/SEK, USD/SEK, NOK/SEK, DKK/SEK, DKK/NOK

Emerging market currencies

Interbank currency traders try to make a profit by arbitraging between the different currency pairs in their book. For example, a CHF trader has positions in EUR/USD, EUR/CHF and USD/CHF but he looks at his overall position. In fact, concerning their own book, they are not thinking in mental compartments. They start thinking in mental compartments when they have positions in other than their own book. For example the JPY trader has a position in USD/CHF or GBP/USD based on his view of this other currency pair.

---

[32] Reprinted from Handbook of Macroeconomics, Volume 1c, Robert J. Schiller, *Human Behavior and the Efficiency of the Financial System*, Chapter 20, Copyright © 1999, with permission from Elsevier Science.
[33] Reprinted from Handbook of Macroeconomics, Volume 1c, Robert J. Schiller, *Human Behavior and the Efficiency of the Financial System*, Chapter 20, Copyright © 1999, with permission from Elsevier Science.

3.10   DISJUNCTION EFFECT[34]

The disjunction effect is a tendency for people to want to make decisions until information is revealed, even if the information is not really important for the decision and even if they would make the same decision regardless of the information. The disjunction effect can, in principle, explain why there is sometimes low volatility and a low volume of trade just before an important announcement is made, and higher volatility or volume of trade after the announcement is made[35].

Personal experience

The disjunction effect is mainly visible before the release of important US data like the Employment Report, retail sales, GDP, PPI and CPI and before the FOMC decisions. Two days prior to FOMC decisions, financial markets are very calm. The European mornings prior to important US data releases are also very calm. European markets are very dependent on US markets and players are unwilling to take significant positions before they have caught the feeling of the US markets. Most of the large currency moves appear in US time.

---

[29]Reprinted from Handbook of Macroeconomics, Volume 1c, Robert J. Schiller, *Human Behavior and the Efficiency of the Financial System,* Chapter 20, Copyright © 1999, with permission from Elsevier Science.

[35]Reprinted from Handbook of Macroeconomics, Volume 1c, Robert J. Schiller, *Human Behavior and the Efficiency of the Financial System,* Chapter 20, Copyright © 1999, with permission from Elsevier Science.

3.11 GAMBLING BEHAVIOR AND SPECULATION[36].

The tendency for people to gamble has provided a puzzle for the theory of human behavior under uncertainty, since it means that we must accommodate both risk-avoiding behavior with an apparently risk-loving behavior. Moreover, the gambling urge is compartmentalized in people's lives, and for each individual it only takes certain forms: people specialize in certain games. The favored forms of gambling tend to be associated with a **sort of ego involvement**: people may feel that they are especially good at games they favor or that they are especially lucky with these. The complexity of human behavior exemplified by the gambling phenomenon has to be taken into account in understanding the etiology of bubbles in speculative markets. Gamblers may have very rational expectations, at some level, for the likely outcome of their gambling, and yet have other feelings that drive their actual behavior. **The same people who are highly emotionally involved with the notion that the stock market will go up may give very sensible, unexciting, forecasts of the market if asked to make quantitative forecasts.**

---

[36]Reprinted from Handbook of Macroeconomics, Volume 1c, Robert J. Schiller, *Human Behavior and the Efficiency of the Financial System*, Chapter 20, Copyright © 1999, with permission from Elsevier Science.

3.12   THE IRRELEVANCE OF HISTORY[37]

One particular kind of overconfidence that appears to be common is a tendency to believe that history is irrelevant, not a guide to the future, and that the future must be judged afresh now using intuitive weighting of only the special factors we see now. This kind of overconfidence discourages people from taking lessons from past statistics; indeed most financial market participants virtually never study historical data for correlations or other such statistics[38].

One reason that people may think that history is irrelevant is a human tendency toward historical determinism, a tendency to think that historical events should have been known in advance. People may see history as relevant for the future only if they see the present circumstances as representative, in some details, of widely remembered past periods. Thus, for example, the public appears to have made much, just before the stock market crash of 1987, of similarities in that period to the period just before the stock market crash of 1929. Newspapers showed plots of stock prices before October 1929 superimposed on a plot of stock prices before October 1987, suggesting comparisons. In this way, historical events can be remembered and viewed as relevant, but there is not any systematic analysis of past data[39].

Personal experience

The historical statistical data are frequently used by strategists, analysts and economists in the area of equity markets and alternative strategies (hedge funds). Analysts also compared the equity markets before and during the Gulf War and the events of 11th September 2001. The research reports were based (in my opinion) on a systematic analysis of past data.

---

[37]Reprinted from Handbook of Macroeconomics, Volume 1c, Robert J. Schiller, *Human Behavior and the Efficiency of the Financial System,* Chapter 20, Copyright © 1999, with permission from Elsevier Science.
[38]Reprinted from Handbook of Macroeconomics, Volume 1c, Robert J. Schiller, *Human Behavior and the Efficiency of the Financial System,* Chapter 20, Copyright © 1999, with permission from Elsevier Science.
[39]Reprinted from Handbook of Macroeconomics, Volume 1c, Robert J. Schiller, *Human Behavior and the Efficiency of the Financial System,* Chapter 20, Copyright © 1999, with permission from Elsevier Science.

3.13 MAGICAL THINKING[40]

Arbitrary behaviors that are so generated are referred to by psychologists with the term "magical thinking". A wide variety of economic behaviors are likely to be generated in exactly the same way. Thus, for example, a firms' investment or management decisions, that happened to precede increases in sales or profits, may tend to be repeated, and if this happens in a period of rising profits the notion that these decisions were the cause of the sales or profit increase will be reinforced[41].

The tendency for speculative markets to respond to certain news variables may be generated analogously. The US stock market was often buoyed by the positive news about the economy, but in recent years it appears that there is a tendency to be moved in the opposite direction by such news. This new movement pattern for the stock market is sometimes justified in the media by a theory that the good news will cause the Federal Reserve to tighten the monetary policy and that then the higher interest rates will lower the stock market. But the whole belief could be the result of a chain of events that was set off by some initial chance movements of the stock markets. Because people believe these theories, they may then behave so that the stock price does indeed behave as hypothesized, so the initial correlations will persist later, and thereby reinforce the belief[42].

Personal experience

I believe that the market reaction on important figures depends on:
>   How much is priced in (expected by market participants)?
>   What is the market positioning?
>   What is the Positive or negative sentiment of market participants?

Usually, a few days before important figures, market players and analysts are making predictions about the upcoming data. If the majority of the players expect negative figures then you will see the sell-off before the figures are released. When the data are negative, as expected, you will see a correction of the first movement caused by profit-taking on outstanding positions.

---

[40]Reprinted from Handbook of Macroeconomics, Volume 1c, Robert J. Schiller, *Human Behavior and the Efficiency of the Financial System*, Chapter 20, Copyright © 1999, with permission from Elsevier Science.

[41]Reprinted from Handbook of Macroeconomics, Volume 1c, Robert J. Schiller, *Human Behavior and the Efficiency of the Financial System*, Chapter 20, Copyright © 1999, with permission from Elsevier Science.

[42]Reprinted from Handbook of Macroeconomics, Volume 1c, Robert J. Schiller, *Human Behavior and the Efficiency of the Financial System*, Chapter 20, Copyright © 1999, with permission from Elsevier Science.

3.14 CONCLUSION

Market Psychology is the most important facet of financial markets. It determines the market behavior of all markets; there is no exception. Market Psychology is the main driver of the EUR/USD Interbank Market organization as well as the main driver of all the separate divisions. Market Psychology is not easy to define. However, we should be able to read or feel it before we advise clients or enter a position. The main characteristic that trading is taken personally, which is explained by the general principles of Behavioral Finance. The main lesson I have learned from trading is that it is not personal, however many market participants take it personally. In fact financial markets together are one big ego business. I have shared an overview of most of the concepts of Behavioral Finance and my personal experience as professional trader and advisor.

SUMMARY 3

Behavioral Finance investigates the cognitive factors and emotional issues that impact on the decision-making processes of individuals, groups and organizations. Behavioral Finance gives good explanations about what is going on in financial markets in terms of Market Psychology. However, we are obligated to add the fact that people take trading personally and this is the most important reason for the Market Psychology

Some of the experiences I have gained as major trading lessons are:
1. Trading is not personal.
2. You can not influence the market.
3. There are no rules except for your own.
4. Sticking to your own rules is the best way to survive.
5. Trust your profits.
6. Be patient.

Trading remains personal for traders even if I'm convinced and others try to convince me that it is not. People take trading personally and that's why we need Behavioral Finance to explain market psychology.

In Chapter 4 on fundamental analysis, the following questions will be answered:
1. What is fundamental analysis and how does it apply?
2. In which categories can the indicators be divided?
3. What is the market influence of certain economic variables?

REFERENCES

Barber, B.M. and T. Odean (1999). "The courage of misguided convictions: the trading behavior of individual investors", Financial Analyst Journal, Vol 55, Issue 6, 1999

Barberis, N., M. Huang and T. Santos (1999). "Prospect Theory and Asset Prices".

Barberis, N., A. Shleifer and R.W. Vishny (1997). "A model of investor sentiment"

Cook, G. "The biology of irrational exuberance", The Boston Globe, 10/23/2001

Coval, J.D. and T. G. Shumway (2001). "Do behavioral Biases affect prices?"

Dodonova, A.R. (2001). "Applications of Regret Theory to Asset Pricing"

Gervais, S. and T. Odean (1997). "Learning to be overconfident", Review of Financial Studies, Volume 14, No.1, Spring 2001, pp.1-27, Reprinted with the permission of Oxford University Press.

Kahneman, D., P. Slovic and A. Tversky (1974). "Judgment Under Uncertainty: Heuristic and Biases", Reprinted with the permission of Cambridge University Press.

Kahneman, D. and A. Tversky (2000). "Choices, Values, and Frames", Reprinted with the permission of Cambridge University Press.

Kaustia, M. (2000). "Can loss aversion move the market? Evidence from IPO trading volume"

Locke, P.R. and S.C. Mann (2000). "Do professional traders exhibit loss realization aversion?"

Odean, T. (1997). "Are investors reluctant to realize their losses"

Odean, T. (1998). "Volume, Volatility, Price and Profit; When all traders are above average.

Reprinted from Handbook of Macroeconomics, Volume 1c, Schiller, R.J. "Human Behavior and the Efficiency of the Financial System", Chapter 20, Copyright © 1999, with permission from Elsevier Science.

Shumway, T. (1997). "Explaining returns with loss aversion".

Statman, M. (2001). " Lottery players/stock traders", Financial Analysts Journal, January/February 2002.

Statman, M and S. Thorley (1999). "Investor overconfidence and trading volume".

Yariv, L. "I'll See It When I Believe It - A Simple Model of Cognitive Consistency", Cowles Foundation Discussion Paper Number 1352, February 2002

Chapter **4**

FUNDAMENTAL ANALYSIS TECHNO STRUCTURE (I) OF EUR/USD INTERBANK MARKET ORGANIZATION

4.1 INTRODUCTION[1]

Economic indicators have become increasingly important to financial markets, and to the general public as a whole. They are now at the point almost everyone involved in markets needs to have some idea of what they mean. The link to the indicators is most clear-cut in the case of Fixed-Income markets, where news on growth and inflation directly affects expectations about monetary policy and about interest rate levels in general. The link between the indicators and other markets, for example, equities and currencies, is often more complex, since many more variables are involved and some of the links are channeled through the interest rate changes.

Indicators can be divided into two categories:
1. GROWTH INDICATORS
2. INFLATION INDICATORS

Growth indicators

GDP[2]

The gross domestic product (GDP), representing the market value of all goods and services produced in an economy, is the most important measure of aggregate economic activity provided within the national account. In general, GDP is published on a quarterly basis. The timing varies: United Kingdom and the US GDP reports are the first to come out, toward the end of the first month following the end of the quarter; many other countries report GDP with a two-month lag, and in some it is three months or even longer. There is a lot of variation in how accurately monthly date "previews" the GDP in different countries. In the US, market estimates of GDP generally fall into a narrow range and are fairly accurate, based on the main monthly indicators of consumer spending, business investment, inventory building and net trade.

In other countries, though, it is more difficult to estimate GDP from monthly reports (especially in Japan). In most European countries, overall GDP growth is measured using output data. They consider output data to be more accurate when it comes to estimating total GDP and measuring overall growth.

---

[1] JP Morgan, *Global Data Watch Handbook*, New York, January 1996
[2] JP Morgan, *Global Data Watch Handbook*, New York, January 1996

US GDP composition (% of nominal total), expenditure approach

Private consumption	**68**		
Private fixed investment	**14**		
Business fixed investment		10	
Producers durable equipment			7
Nonresidential construction			3
Residential investment		4	
Government purchases	**19**		
Federal		7	
Consumption			6
Investment			1
State and Local		12	
Consumption			9
Investment			3
Exports	**10**		
Imports (minus)	**12**		
Inventories	**1**		

Germany GDP composition (% of nominal total), expenditure approach

Private consumption	**55**	
Government consumption	**18**	
Investment	**19**	
Investment in machinery		7
Construction investment		12
Exports	**35**	
Imports (minus)	**29**	
Stockbuilding	**1**	

Composition GDP, output approach, %

Industry	36
Trade & communication	15
Services	34
Government, private households	14

GNP has only recently overtaken the GDP as the main measure used in most countries. GDP measures aggregate activity occurring within a country, while GNP measures aggregate output produced by factors owned by the country's residents. The difference is the net factor income from abroad, which is included in GNP and not in GDP.

Industrial production[3]
Industrial production is dominated by manufacturing activity, but in many countries it includes mining as well. The manufacturing data are used as a guide to the cycle. Manufacturing is the most cyclical component of activity, making is it disproportionately important to analysis of the short-term business trends. Also, since trade in manufacturing goods is sensitive to exchange rate movements and relative demand and price trends, this sector is a key to analyzing the transmission of business cycles around the globe.

The figures for manufacturing production, or industrial output as more broadly defined, are available monthly. Most countries survey manufacturers for their views on business conditions. The results of these surveys are important inputs for policy makers as well as market analysts for assessing the business cycle. Some surveys cover non-manufacturing as well as manufacturing. But, even so, the factory segment usually gets the most attention.

Retail sales[4]
The content and coverage of retail sales data can be very different across countries. The common thread is that they are indicators of consumer spending based on sales information collected from retailers. Consumer spending is the largest expenditure component in every country: it ranges from about 55% of GDP in Japan and Germany to 68% of the total in the US. It is less cyclical than other components, especially business and housing investments, but tracking it is still important because of its sheer size.

Indicators of investment and trade[5]
Investment activities, broadly defined to include construction and inventory accumulation as well as business equipment spending, are universally the most important drivers of fluctuations in growth. But the data used to track them are even more various than in the case of consumer spending. Housing starts, one of the most cyclical components of GDP, are carefully monitored in the US, Canada, Australia and Japan. In practice, survey data get a lot of weight when it comes to predicting investment behavior. International trade, particularly in manufactured goods, is a significant channel for transmitting growth fluctuations among all countries, although there is considerable variation in weight relative to GDP.

---

[3] JP Morgan, *Global Data Watch Handbook*, New York, January 1996
[4] JP Morgan, *Global Data Watch Handbook*, New York, January 1996
[5] JP Morgan, *Global Data Watch Handbook*, New York, January 1996

Inflation indicators

GDP deflator[6]

The GDP deflator is the broadest measure of inflation in the economy as a whole, just as GDP itself is the broadest measure of activity. However, the deflator is not the most accurate indicator in a short-term context, partly because it reflects not only price changes but also fluctuations in the composition of output. Also, because it is a strictly domestic measure, excluding import prices, the GDP deflator is an incomplete measure of price pressures, especially in the smaller more open economies. The fixed-weight indexes such as consumer and producer price indexes are generally the measures most closely followed by financial markets.

All countries publish measures of inflation at the producer or wholesale and retail levels, and measures of wage and labor cost inflation, that help to define the links between the two. Consumer price indexes are generally similar in construction and are based on a basket of goods and services consumed by an average household.

Producer and wholesale price indexes are among the most difficult indicators of all to use for cross-country comparisons. The measures vary widely in their coverage and construction.

Advance signals of inflation[7]

Business cycle analysts use reel economic data to assess changes in underlying inflation pressures before those appear in the actual inflation rates. In essence, this is a matter of assessing the degree of pressure on economic resources from ups and downs in resource utilization. The broadest measure of utilization, and one that is often used to predict inflation developments over substantial periods of time, is the GDP gap, the difference between total output and the economy's estimated potential. In practice it is not the most useful measure for short-term analysis, however, since the GDP measures are quarterly, and there is no consensus among economists about how to measure "potential" GDP.

The most common measures used are the unemployment rate, showing idle resources in the labor market, and factory utilization rates, giving a sense of pressure on manufacturing capacity. In the US, the unemployment rate has a reasonably good record of indicating pressure for wage increases, which in turn are the main determinant of consumer price inflation. Capacity utilization in industry is used to predict pressures on producer or wholesale prices. Again the relationship is well established in the US, with capacity utilization in manufacturing above 83% generally associated with upward pressure on the finished goods Producer Price Index (PPI). In Europe, direct measures of capacity utilization rates are not widely available on a monthly basis. The EU publishes a quarterly index, which provides some insight into cyclical pressure on prices. Outside the

---

[6] JP Morgan, *Global Data Watch Handbook*, New York, January 1996
[7] JP Morgan, *Global Data Watch Handbook*, New York, January 1996

US, PPI measures typically include intermediate and crude goods, whose price moves are often dominated by world commodity markets or exchange rate swings rather than domestic inflation pressures stemming from capacity constraints. But significant changes in utilization are still a clue to inflation.

CPIs and the cost of living[8]

Consumer price indexes are often viewed as "cost-of-living-indexes". In practice, CPIs almost inevitably overstate changes in the cost of living, reflecting a variety of upward biases. The main source of problems is that the CPI is always based on a fixed basket of goods and services, yet that basket quickly becomes less representative as consumers shift their spending patterns in response to prices changes and new products.

Monetary and fiscal aggregates[9]

Money aggregates were closely followed in the past years, when money growth targets were widely used to guide central bank monetary policy. However many countries have shifted away from monetary targeting. Central banks still pay enough attention to money supply to keep it in the limelight

Government financial positions are an important aspect of economy watching.

---

[8] JP Morgan, *Global Data Watch Handbook*, New York, January 1996
[9] JP Morgan, *Global Data Watch Handbook*, New York, January 1996

CHAPTER 4

4.2 ECONOMIC DATA US

Gross Domestic Product (GDP)[10]
Source   Bureau of Economic Analysis, Department of Commerce
Description   The main quarterly series is expenditure-based.
Timing   GDP is measured in current (nominal) and inflation-adjusted dollars. Advance report is issued around 25th of first month of the quarter. The data are revised in the preliminary report (one month later) and in the final report (two months later).
Seasonals   All data are seasonally adjusted. Focus is on change from previous quarter at an annual rate.
Revisions   Can be large, especially from the advance report to the preliminary report for a quarter.
Comments   Annual revision is usually made in July
Composition   Private consumption (68%), private fixed investments (14%), government purchases (19%)

Industrial production/capacity utilization[11]
Source   Federal Reserve Board
Description   Indexes of output and the rate of capacity utilization in the manufacturing, mining, and utilities industries. The report includes two sets of data, based on industry grouping (85½% manufacturing, 6¼% mining, and 7¾% utilities) and market grouping (46½% final products, 14½% intermediate products, 39% materials.
                Capacity utilization represents output as a percentage of capacity.
Timing   Measured monthly, released around the 15th of the following month.
Seasonals   Data are seasonally adjusted. Focus is on change from the previous month.
Revisions   Usually modest, extending back three months in each report.
Comments   Industrial production accounts for only ¼ of GDP but it is a highly cyclical part of the economy. The capacity utilization rate for manufacturing alone is more useful than the overall figure for signaling inflation pressure.

---

[10]JP Morgan, *Global Data Watch Handbook*, New York, January 1996
[11]JP Morgan, *Global Data Watch Handbook*, New York, January 1996

Index of leading economic indicators[12]
Source   The Conference Board
Description   A composite index of economic variables designed to signal turning points in the economy. The components are: factory workweek, initial jobless claims, new orders for consumer goods and materials, supplier deliveries component of national purchasing managers' survey, inflation-adjusted contracts and orders for plant and equipment, building permits, inflation-adjusted unfilled durable good orders, sensitive materials prices, stock prices (S&P 500), inflation-adjusted M2 and the expectations component of the University of Michigan confidence index.
Timing   Measured monthly and released around the end of the following month.
Seasonals   Data are seasonally adjusted. Focus is on change from previous month in the overall index.
Revisions   Minor
Comments   Three declines in a row are interpreted as signaling a recession. The index has its limitations; false signals are not uncommon.

National Purchasing Managers Survey (NAPM)[13]
Source   National Association of Purchasing Management.
Description   A survey of manufacturing activity. The purchasing managers' index, the highlight of the report, is a diffusion index based on an average of five components: new orders (30%), production (25%), employment (20%), supplier deliveries (15%), inventories (10%).
Timing   Monthly, reported on the first business day of the following month.
Seasonals   Data are seasonally adjusted. Focus is on the change from the previous month as well as the absolute levels.
Revisions   Only annual revision in January
Comments   The overall index is the key indication of manufacturing activity. Readings of 50 have been associated with manufacturing output growth of about 1% at an annual rate. On average, 49 has been the zero-growth point.

---

[12]JP Morgan, *Global Data Watch Handbook*, New York, January 1996
[13]JP Morgan, *Global Data Watch Handbook*, New York, January 1996

Chicago Purchasing Managers Survey[14]

Source	Purchasing Management Association of Chicago
Description	Broadly similar in structure to the national survey (with above 50 signaling expansion and below 50, contraction). The report includes an overall index with five sub-indexes (production, new orders, backlogs, employment and supplier deliveries) and a commodity price index (reflecting raw materials prices).
Timing	Released on the last business day of the reporting month. The final cutoff point for responses is typically the second week of the month (compared with the third week for the national survey).
Seasonals	Data are seasonally adjusted. Focus is on the change from the previous month.
Revisions	Annual revision in January.
Comments	The Chicago index is an imperfect indicator of what to expect in the national survey released one business day later. On average, the Chicago index correctly signals the direction of the national index about two-thirds of the time.

Philadelphia Federal Reserve Survey[15]

Source	Federal Reserve Bank of Philadelphia
Description	A survey of manufacturing in the Philadelphia Federal Reserve Bank district. The main indicator in the report is the current general activity index. Readings above zero imply expansion, and readings below zero imply contraction. The Philadelphia number is much more volatile than the purchasing managers' index. Along with the current general activity index, the most important parts of the report are the current month's indexes for prices paid and prices received and the six-month outlook index for general activity.
Timing	Released on the third Thursday of the reporting month. Most of the survey responses are actually from the prior month. The final cutoff point for responses is typically the first week of the month, compared with the second week for the Chicago survey and the third week for the NAPM.
Seasonals	The data are seasonally adjusted. Focus is on the change from the previous month with the current activity index and the two price indexes receiving the most attention.
Revisions	Annual revisions only.
Comments	The early release date reflects an early cutoff point for the survey responses, limiting its correlation with the national survey on a month-to-month basis.

---

[14] JP Morgan, *Global Data Watch Handbook*, New York, January 1996
[15] JP Morgan, *Global Data Watch Handbook*, New York, January 1996

Manufacturing and trade (M&T) inventories[16]

Source	Bureau of the Census, Department of Commerce
Description	The report includes inventories, sales, and the inventory-to-sales ratios of manufacturers, merchant wholesalers, and retailers.
Timing	Measured monthly, released around the middle of the second month following the reporting period.
Seasonals	The data are seasonally adjusted. Focus is on change from previous month in total inventories and the overall inventory-to-sales ratio.
Revisions	Modest
Comments	M&T inventories excluding the retail auto component are used by the Commerce Department to estimate non-farm inventories in the GDP accounts.

Employment report[17]

Source	Bureau of Labor Statistics, Department of Labor
Description	The report includes separate surveys of establishments and households. The establishment (payroll) survey records the number of employees on nonagricultural payrolls, the length of the average workweek; total hours worked and average hourly earnings.
Timing	Measured monthly and usually reported on the first Friday of the following month.
Seasonals	Data are seasonally adjusted. Focus is on change from the previous month.
Revisions	Can be large for the establishment survey.
Comments	The most important single report on economic activity. Contains extensive new information on the broad economy as well as on the individual sectors. Growth in hours worked provides an early signal on whether GDP is accelerating or decelerating in the current quarter. The annual revision to the establishment survey incorporates more complete information based on social insurance and tax record.

Jobless claims[18]

Source	Employment and Training administration, Department of Labor
Descriptions	Weekly figures on claims for unemployment benefits.
Timing	Reported weekly on Thursday with a 5-day lag for new claims and a 12-day lag for the number receiving benefits.
Seasonals	Data are seasonally adjusted. Focus is on the level relative to recent trend.
Revisions	Minor
Comments	Jobless claims are a key timely indicator of labor market conditions, especially at turning points. Their main value is in signaling a change in the trend.

---

[16]JP Morgan, *Global Data Watch Handbook*, New York, January 1996
[17]JP Morgan, *Global Data Watch Handbook*, New York, January 1996
[18]JP Morgan, *Global Data Watch Handbook*, New York, January 1996

Index of help-wanted advertising[19]
Source   Conference Board
Description   An index of the number of help-wanted ads placed in newspapers across the country.
Timing   Measured monthly, released with about a five-week lag.
Seasonals   The data are seasonally adjusted. Focus is on change from previous month
Revisions   Minor
Comments   The correlation between the index and employment growth on a month-to-month basis is poor.

Personal income and consumption[20]
Source   Bureau of Economic Analysis, Department of Commerce
Description   Individual's income and consumption are measured in the GDP accounts. Much of the data are available in inflation-adjusted as well as nominal dollars. The main components of personal income are wages and salaries, personal interest and dividends, proprietors' income, rental income of persons, other labor income and transfer payments. Consumption consists of purchases of goods and services. The report includes the personal saving rate, which is saving as a percentage of disposable income. Disposable income is personal income minus tax payments. Saving is calculated as a residual.
Timing   Measured monthly and released the end of the following month, one-day after the monthly update on GDP.
Seasonals   Data are seasonally adjusted. Focus is on change from the previous month in income; consumption and the saving rate.
Revisions   Can be large.
Comments   Consumption accounts for two-thirds of GDP, and income is the main determinant of consumption. The report provides limited new information.

---

[19] JP Morgan, *Global Data Watch Handbook*, New York, January 1996
[20] JP Morgan, *Global Data Watch Handbook*, New York, January 1996

Motor vehicle sales[21]

Source	Individual automakers; the Bureau of Economic Analysis provides seasonal factors
Description	Unit sales of new motor vehicles (including leases).
Timing	Measured monthly.
Seasonals	The data are seasonally adjusted.
Revisions	Annual revisions only.
Comments	Vehicle sales have the advantages of being reliable.

Retail sales[22]

Source	Bureau of Census, Department of Commerce
Description	Sales by retailers, including autos and non-auto goods. The data are classified by store type rather than actual products sold.
Timing	Measured monthly and released near the middle of the following month.
Seasonals	Data are seasonally adjusted. Focus is on the monthly change in total, especially in non-auto sales.
Revisions	Can be very large.
Comments	Retail sales account for about one-half of consumer spending and one-third of GDP. The latest data are reported in nominal terms only. Real data are reported with about a two-week lag, although it is possible to roughly estimate real figures once the CPI is available.

The Johnson Redbook[23]

Source	The Johnson Redbook Service
Description	A private survey of retailers, analogous to department stores in the retail sales report.
Timing	Reported weekly on Tuesday with a three-day lag.
Seasonals	Data are seasonally adjusted. Focus is on the monthly seasonally adjusted change.
Revisions	Revisions from the first week through month end can be substantial.
Comments	Good at signaling major changes in trend in spending. Can be extremely volatile.

---

[21] JP Morgan, *Global Data Watch Handbook*, New York, January 1996
[22] JP Morgan, *Global Data Watch Handbook*, New York, January 1996
[23] JP Morgan, *Global Data Watch Handbook*, New York, January 1996

Chain-store sales[24]
Sources   Various retail chains.
Description   Individual sales reports by retailers, reported as a change from a year ago.
Timing   Reported monthly, usually on the first Thursday of the following month.
Seasonals   The data are not adjusted. The focus is on the percent change from a year ago.
Revisions   Minor
Comments   The monthly correlation between chain store and retail sales is poor.

Fed Beige Book[25]
Source   Federal Reserve Districts
Description   Sum of commentary on current conditions by the Federal Reserve Districts. Beige Book is used as basis of discussion at the upcoming FOMC, which is two weeks after the release of Beige Book. Federal Reserve Bank gathers information on current economic conditions in its district through reports from Bank and Branch districts and interviews with key business contacts, economists, market experts and other sources. Beige Book summarizes this information by district and sector.
Timing   Released eight times per year.
                     2001:   January 17, March 7, May 2, June 13, August 8, September 19 November 28.
                     2000:   January 19, March 8, May 3, June 14, August 9, September 20, November 1, December 6.
                     1999:   January 20, March 17, May 5, June 16, August 11, September 22, November 3, December 8.

Consumer confidence[26]
Source   Two surveys, one from the Conference Board and one from the University of Michigan.
Description   Both are subdivided into current conditions and expectations components.
                     Both surveys are based on five questions, three of which are on expectations. The overall index is effectively an average of the five forces.
Timing   Both are measured monthly. The Conference Board index is usually released on the last Tuesday of the same month. The final University of Michigan reading is usually released on the last Friday of the same month.

---

[24]JP Morgan, *Global Data Watch Handbook*, New York, January 1996
[25]Bloomberg
[26]JP Morgan, *Global Data Watch Handbook*, New York, January 1996

Seasonals	The first is seasonally adjusted, the second not. Focus is on the monthly changes in the overall indexes.
Revisions	Minor for the first and updated between preliminary and final reading for the second.
Comments	Confidence is a useful, but unreliable, indicator of the trend in spending. Its greatest advantage is its timeliness.

Consumer credit[27]

Source	Federal Reserve Board
Description	Short- and intermediate-term installment credit used to finance personal consumption. The main components are auto credit, revolving credit, mobile home credit and other miscellaneous credit. The figures include newly incurred credit card debt, which is not accruing interest.
Timing	Measured monthly, usually released on the fifth working day of the second month following the reporting period.
Seasonals	The data are seasonally adjusted.
Revisions	Modest
Comments	Consumer credit is more useful as a tool for assessing household balance sheets than as an indicator or forecaster of economic activity on a month-to-month basis.

Durable goods orders[28]

Source	Bureau of Census, Department of Commerce
Description	Manufacturers' new orders, shipments, and unfilled orders for durable goods, all measured in current dollars. A durable good is defined as having a life expectancy of at least three years.
Timing	Measured monthly released around the 25th of the following month.
Seasonals	Data are seasonally adjusted. Focus is on change from previous month in orders.
Revisions	Revisions as well as additional details are released about one week later in the manufacturers' reports. Revisions are typically small relative to the volatility of the series.
Comments	The volatility of the report lessens its usefulness on a monthly basis. Over time the data are important, providing more of a sense of magnitude than the purchasing managers' data.

---

[27] JP Morgan, *Global Data Watch Handbook*, New York, January 1996
[28] JP Morgan, *Global Data Watch Handbook*, New York, January 1996

Manufacturers report[29]

Source	Bureau of the Census, Department of Commerce
Description	Manufacturers' new orders, shipments, unfilled orders, and inventories of durables and non-durable goods. The data are reported in current dollars.
Timing	Measured monthly, released around the end of the following month.
Seasonals	The data are seasonally adjusted. Main focus is on the change from the previous month in orders and inventories.
Revisions	Small relative to the volatility of the series.
Comments	Non-durables have less significance for the outlook than durables.

Investment plans survey[30]

Source	Bureau of Census, Department of Commerce
Description	A survey of actual and anticipated spending by non-farm businesses, including structures and equipment.
Timing	Reported in late February and late September.
Seasonals	Since the figures are annual totals, seasonal adjustment is not required.
Revisions	Can be substantial.
Comments	The survey was introduced in 1995.

Construction spending[31]

Source	Bureau of Census, Department of Commerce
Description	The value of construction is put in place.
Timing	Measured monthly, released early in the second month following the reporting period.
Seasonals	Data are seasonally adjusted. The reports highlight the change from the previous month in total nominal spending, although the real figures are more important.
Revisions	Can be large.
Comments	The report is important for adding up the construction components of current-quarter GDP.

Housing starts and permits[32]

Source	Bureau of Census, Department of Commerce
Description	Starts and permits of new housing units, including both single-family and multifamily units.
Timing	Measured monthly and released around the middle of the following month.

---

[29] JP Morgan, *Global Data Watch Handbook*, New York, January 1996
[30] JP Morgan, *Global Data Watch Handbook*, New York, January 1996
[31] JP Morgan, *Global Data Watch Handbook*, New York, January 1996
[32] JP Morgan, *Global Data Watch Handbook*, New York, January 1996

FUNDAMENTAL ANALYSIS

Seasonals   Data are seasonally adjusted. Focus is on change from the previous month
Revisions   Usually modest
Comments   New housing is only about 3% of GDP, but it is one of the most cyclical and interest-sensitive parts of the economy.

New home sales[33]
Source   Bureau of Census, Department of Commerce
Description   Sales of new single-family homes recorded at the time of the initial contract agreement. Sales are subdivided into four regions: Northeast, Midwest, South and West.
Timing   Measured monthly and released around the end of the following month.
Seasonals   Data are seasonally adjusted. Focus is on monthly change in total sales.
Revisions   Can be large.
Comments   Only about 2½% GDP, but single-family housing is a highly cyclical and interest-sensitive part of the economy.

Existing home sales[34]
Source   National Association of Realtors (NAR)
Description   A private report on sales of previously owned single-family homes.
Timing   Measured monthly and released near the end of the following month.
Seasonals   Data are seasonally adjusted. Focus is on the monthly change in total sales.
Revisions   Small relative to the volatility of the series.
Comments   Existing home sales are much less important than new home sales as an economic indicator. New and existing home sales tend to have similar trends, with the existing data lagging.

Homebuilders survey[35]
Source   National Association of Homebuilders (NAHB)
Description   A monthly private sector survey. The main indicator in the report is the housing market index, which is based on builders' perceptions of the market for new single-family housing.
Timing   Surveyed monthly, reported around the middle of the same month, usually the day before starts are released.
Seasonals   The data are seasonally adjusted. Focus is on the change in the housing market index.
Revisions   Minor
Comments   The attention paid to this survey is growing.

---

[33] JP Morgan, *Global Data Watch Handbook*, New York, January 1996
[34] JP Morgan, *Global Data Watch Handbook*, New York, January 1996
[35] JP Morgan, *Global Data Watch Handbook*, New York, January 1996

Mortgage applications[36]
Source   Mortgage Bankers Association (MBA)
Description   Indexes of applications for new mortgages.
Timing   Reported weekly on Thursday mornings covering the week that ended the prior Friday.
Seasonals   The data are seasonally adjusted.
Revisions   Minor
Comments   The purchase data are volatile from week to week, but the smoothed figures have shown a fairly strong correlation with homes sales, both new and existing, as would be expected. Few homes are bought with cash.

International trade[37]
Source   Bureau of Census, Department of Commerce
Description   Imports and exports of goods and services. Goods are classified to six main categories: food, feed, and beverage; industrial supplies and materials; non-automotive capital goods; automotive capital vehicles and parts; non-auto consumer goods and other. Services are classified according to travel; passenger fares; other transportation; royalties and license fees; direct defense expenditures; and other. The main goods categories are available in inflation-adjusted dollars.
Timing   Measured monthly and released around the middle of the second month following the reporting period.
Seasonals   Data are seasonally adjusted (regional data is not). Focus is on the monthly changes in total nominal exports, imports and the balance.
Revisions   Modest.
Comments   In general, high exports and high imports are interpreted as reflecting a strong economy. Exports and imports account for about 11% and 13% of GDP.

---

[36] JP Morgan, *Global Data Watch Handbook*, New York, January 1996
[37] JP Morgan, *Global Data Watch Handbook*, New York, January 1996

Current account (balance of payments)[38]
Source   Bureau of Economic Analysis, Department of Commerce
Description   The current account is the main focus, although the report also covers international capital flows. The current account balance is a broader measure of foreign transactions than the monthly international trade report, but is released quarterly and with a greater lag. The current account also includes investment income and nonmilitary unilateral transfers. Investment income covers earnings on direct and indirect investment and government debt. Unilateral transfers include official foreign aid and private remittances.
Timing   Measured quarterly, released about two and a half-months after the end of the quarter.
Seasonals   Data are seasonally adjusted. Focus is on quarterly change in the overall balance
Revisions   Modest.
Comments   The capital flows data would be of significant interest to the markets if they were available on a more timely basis.

Producer price index[39]
Source   Bureau of Labor statistics, Department of Labor
Description   A report on prices received by domestic producers. The report mainly reflects the output of the manufacturing sector. The report includes three sets of fixed-weight indexes: (a) stage of processing, (b) commodity group and (c) industry. The focus is almost exclusively on the stage of processing data, which in turn are divided into crude, intermediate and finished goods. Imported goods are excluded.
Timing   Measured monthly and released before the 15th of the following month.
Seasonals   Data are seasonally adjusted. Focus is on the monthly change, with total, core finished goods, core intermediate goods receiving the most attention.
Revisions   Minor.
Comments   The finished goods index is the most important indicator of domestic goods price inflation, with the core generally viewed as a better measure of the trend from month to month. Producer price inflation is only one of several factors that influence consumer price inflation.

---

[38] JP Morgan, *Global Data Watch Handbook*, New York, January 1996
[39] JP Morgan, *Global Data Watch Handbook*, New York, January 1996

Consumer price index[40]

Source	Bureau of Labor Statistics, Department of Labor
Description	A fixed-weight index of prices at the consumer level for a fixed basket of goods and services. The basket is re-weighted every ten years or so. The report is designed to measure prices paid by consumers
Timing	Measured monthly. The index measures prices on a full-month basis; the release date is just before the midpoint of the following month.
Seasonals	Data are seasonally adjusted. Focus is on the monthly change in total and core prices.
Revisions	Seasonal factors are re-estimated annually, with revisions incorporated in the January report.
Comments	A 10% drop in the value of the dollar on a trade-weighted basis adds about 0.5% to the CPI over the following year.

Employment cost index[41]

Source	Bureau of Labor Statistics, Department of Labor
Description	A fixed-weight index measuring employee compensation costs per hour in the private and state and local government sectors. Benefits account for account 30% of the index.
Timing	Data are quarterly, reflecting the pay periods including the 12th in March, June, September and December. Released around the 25th of the first month of the following quarter.
Seasonals	Data are seasonally adjusted. Focus on the change from a year ago.
Revision	Minor
Comments	It is a much more comprehensive and reliable measure of labor costs than the average hourly earnings in the employment report. Labor costs account for about two-thirds of all production costs in the economy.

---

[40] JP Morgan, *Global Data Watch Handbook*, New York, January 1996
[41] JP Morgan, *Global Data Watch Handbook*, New York, January 1996

CIBCR leading inflation index[42]

Source	Center for International Business Cycle Research (CIBCR), Colombia University
Description	An index of seven inflation related indicators.
Timing	Measured monthly, usually released on the first Friday of the following month.
Seasonals	The index includes both seasonally adjusted and not seasonally adjusted data.
Revisions	Can be large.
Comments	The index is a good summary measure of inflation pressures, particularly in the manufacturing sector.

Agricultural prices[43]

Source	Department of Agriculture
Description	A fixed-weighted index of the prices of farm products.
Timing	Measured monthly, released on the last business day of the same month.
Seasonals	The data are not seasonally adjusted.
Revisions	Can be large.
Comments	The reports do nor receive much attention, as major price swings are evident earlier in individual commodity markets.

Import and export prices[44]

Source	Bureau of Labor Statistics, Department of Labor
Description	Fixed-weight index of import and export prices. The data cover goods only.
Timing	Measured monthly, released near the end of the following month.
Seasonals	The data are not yet seasonally adjusted, putting the focus on the change of a year ago.
Revisions	Minor
Comments	Import prices reflect changes in the prices paid by the importers, which are not always passed on to domestic consumers. The report is a good indicator of imported price pressures.

---

[42] JP Morgan, *Global Data Watch Handbook*, New York, January 1996
[43] JP Morgan, *Global Data Watch Handbook*, New York, January 1996
[44] JP Morgan, *Global Data Watch Handbook*, New York, January 1996

Productivity and costs[45]
Source   Bureau of Labor Statistics, Department of Labor
Description   Indexes of output per hour, compensation per hour and labor cost per unit of output. The main data cover the non-farm business sector. Productivity is defined as total output divided by total hours worked. Unit labor costs are equal to total labor costs divided by total output.
Timing   Measured quarterly.
Seasonals   The data are seasonally adjusted. Focus is on the change from the previous quarter.
Revisions   Can be large, depending on revisions to GDP.
Comments   Quarterly readings can be highly volatile. Over time, unit labor costs are a major determinant of overall goods and services price inflation, as labor costs account for about two-thirds of all production costs.

Monetary aggregates[46]
Source   Federal Reserve Board
Description   Alternative measures of money supply.
                M1 includes currency, non-bank travelers' checks and demand and other checkable deposits.
                M2 includes M1 plus overnight repos, overnight Eurodollar deposits, general purpose and broker/dealer money market fund balances, money market deposit accounts and savings and small-time deposits.
                M3 includes M2 plus large time deposits, term repos, term Eurodollar deposits and institutional money-market mutual funds.
Timing   Reported weekly, with a ten-day lag.
Seasonals   Data are seasonally adjusted. Focus is on the weekly changes in M2.
Revisions   Can be large.
Comments   The monetary aggregates have faded in importance in recent years as their link with nominal GDP has broken down.

---

[45] JP Morgan, *Global Data Watch Handbook*, New York, January 1996
[46] JP Morgan, *Global Data Watch Handbook*, New York, January 1996

Federal budget[47]

Source	US Treasury
Description	A monthly statement of federal receipts and outlays. The deficit in the report is known as the unified budget deficit. The fiscal year runs from October through September.
Timing	Measured monthly released around the 15th working day of the following month.
Seasonals	Data are not seasonally adjusted. Focus is on the change in the balance from a year ago.
Revisions	Minor
Comments	The budget results determine the Treasury's financing need. The monthly budget numbers fluctuate significantly. An alternative measure of the federal deficit is published in the national income accounts (with quarterly GDP).

---

[47] JP Morgan, *Global Data Watch Handbook*, New York, January 1996

4.3 ECONOMIC DATA EUROZONE

Gross Domestic Product (GDP)[48]
Source   Eurostat
Description   The main quarterly series is output-based. GDP is measured in current (nominal) and constant prices.
Timing   Measured quarterly, 1st release with two-month lag, 2nd release and 3rd and final release with three and four months lag.
Seasonals   Data are seasonally adjusted according to national adjustment procedures. Focus is on change from the previous quarter at an annual rate.

Industrial production[49]
Source   Eurostat
Description   It is the aim of the production index to show the evolution of value added at factor cost at constant prices. Value added at factor cost can be calculated from turnover, plus or minus the change in stocks, minus purchases of goods and services, minus other taxes on products and taxes linked to production. In practice, the ideal production index can only be approximated using either input data or output data.
Timing   Measured monthly, released one and half months later.
Seasonals   Data are seasonally adjusted. Focus is on the change from the previous month.
Revisions   Based on the news of the prior month.

Retail sales[50]
Source   Eurostat
Description   Present sales of the following groups:
                food, beverages, tobacco
                non-food
                textiles, clothing, footwear
                household equipment
                Retail sales are measured in current and constant prices.
Timing   Measured monthly, released two months later.
Seasonals   Data are seasonally adjusted.
Revisions   Based on news of the prior month.

---

[48]European Communities, Eurostat
[49]European Communities, Eurostat
[50]ECB Monthly Bulletin

Producer Manufacturing Index (PMI)[51]

Source	Reuters
Description	The Reuters Eurozone Purchasing Managers' Index is modelled on the NAPM survey in the US and is based on data from eight Eurozone countries: Germany, France, Italy, Spain, the Netherlands, Greece and Ireland which collectively account for 92% of Eurozone manufacturing activity. The indices are compiled from survey data contributed by about 2,500 manufacturing companies in eight countries. A reading below 50 signals contraction and one over 50 signals growth.
Timing	Measured monthly, released the following month.
Seasonals	Data are seasonally adjusted
Comments	The Business Expectations index is unadjusted.

Unemployment rate[52]

Source	Eurostat
Description	The unemployment rates are calculated according to recommendations of the 13th international Conference of Labor Statisticians organized by the International Labor Office in 1982. Unemployed persons are those persons aged 15 years and over who: are without work, are available to start within the next two weeks, and have actively sought employment at some time during the previous four weeks.
Timing	Measured monthly, released with a one-month lag (beginning of October number of August).
Seasonals	Data are seasonally adjusted.

Trade balance[53]

Source	Eurostat
Description	The value of exports less the value of imports in the current month.
Timing	Measured monthly, released almost two months later
Seasonals	Data are not seasonally adjusted.

---

[51] Reuters PMI and www.reuters.com
[52] European Communities, Eurostat
[53] European Communities, Eurostat

CHAPTER 4

Balance of payments[54]
Source   ECB
Description   Current account plus capital account plus financial account. Current account can be divided into goods, services, income and current transfers. Financial account can be divided into direct investment, portfolio investment, financial derivatives, other investments and reserve assets.
Timing   Measured monthly, released almost two months later.
Seasonals   Data are seasonally adjusted
Revisions   Can be large.
Comments   The financial account provides information about the capital flows. However, this information would be more useful if it were available in a shorter time frame.

EU survey of business confidence[55]
Source   European Commission
Description   An additional early indicator for the state of the economy. Covers both manufacturing and the construction sector.
Timing   Measured monthly; released around the middle of the following month.
Seasonals   Data are seasonally adjusted. Focus is on the overall confidence indicator for manufacturing companies.
Revisions   Minor
Comments   Results often diverge considerably from the IFO survey report.

EU survey of consumer confidence[56]
Source   European Commission
Description   Measures consumer confidence as a composite index of households's assessment of their financial situation, employment conditions and general economic conditions.
Timing   Measured monthly, released around the middle of the following month.
Seasonals   Data are seasonally adjusted.
Revisions   Minor
Comment   A good indicator for the long-term trend in consumption.

---

[54]ECB, Balance of payments, comments consist my own opinion
[55]JP Morgan, *Global Data Watch Handbook*, New York, January 1996
[56]European Commission Directorate-General for Economic and Financial affairs, European Economy, Business and Consumer Survey Results, No 8/9 August/September 2001. European Communities

EU Economic Sentiment Indicator (ESIN)[57]

Source	European Commission
Description	ESIN provides a picture of economic activity about three months before GDP statistics become available. The survey results primarily reflect subjective interpretations of market conditions, which in turn are decisive for economic behavior. The components of the ESIN index (1995=100) are: Industrial confidence indicator (weight 33%), Consumer confidence indicator (33%), Construction confidence indicator (17%), Share price index (17%).
Timing	Measured monthly (August/September combined edition).
Revisions	Modifications are based on the results of recent work in Directorate-General for Economic and Financial Affairs and by experts at IFO.
Comments	Proven to be a good leading indicator of the objective economic situation.

Producer Price Index[58]

Source	Eurostat
Description	The index of producer prices shows the changes in the ex-works selling prices of all products sold on the domestic markets of the various countries. The EU indices refer to overall weighted price changes.
Timing	Measured monthly, released the following month.
Seasonals	Data are not seasonally adjusted.
Comments	Every price index gives an indication of the scarceness of resources. The Producer Price Index gives therefore a picture of adjustment processes and possible bottlenecks in different branches.

Harmonized Indices Consumer Prices (HICP)[59]

Source	Eurostat
Description	Harmonized Indices of Consumer Prices (HICPs) are designed for international comparisons of consumer price inflation. The HICPs are the result of the collaboration between Eurostat and National Statistical Institutes (NSIs) of Member States on harmonizing the different methods used to compile price indices. The harmonization process has resulted in an improved quality of the indices.
Timing	Measured monthly, released in the following month.
Seasonals	Data are not seasonally adjusted
Comments	HICPs are not intended to replace national Consumer Price Indices (CPIs).

---

[57] European Commission Directorate-General for Economic and Financial affairs, European Economy, Business and Consumer Survey Results, No 8/9 August/September 2001. European Communities
[58] European Communities, Eurostat
[59] European Communities, Eurostat

Monetary aggregates[60]

Source	ECB
Description	M1, M2 and M3. For a description of M1 and M2 see US monetary aggregates. The European Central Bank mainly watches M3. The components of M3 are: currency in circulation, overnight deposits, deposits with agreed maturity up to 2 years, deposits redeemable at notice of up to three months, repurchase agreements, money market fund shares/units and money market paper, debt securities issued with maturity up to 2 years.
Timing	Monthly, with a one-month time lag.
Seasonals	Data are seasonally adjusted. Focus is on the monthly changes in M3 especially.
Revisions	Can be large.
Comments	The focus is decreasing because of the large revisions.

German IFO survey of business[61]

Source	Institute of economic research (IFO)
Description	Offers reliable information on overall business sentiment and confidence in different business sectors.
Timing	Measured monthly.
Seasonals	Data are seasonally adjusted. Focus is on overall business confidence.
Revisions	Relatively large.
Comments	The most important early indicator for overall economic activity[62].

---

[60] ECB, Monetary developments in the Euro area
[61] JP Morgan, *Global Data Watch Handbook*, New York, January 1996
[62] Own view

4.4　US & EUROZONE DATA COMPARED

In this chapter the economic data of the US and Eurozone will be compared. Usually strong sustainable growth combined with low inflation and trade surplus should lead to a strong currency. However, the market impact of economic data depends mainly on market expectations. To protect yourself against surprises in economic data you need to do the following things:

1. Determine whether the current market environment is ruled by a positive or a negative sentiment regarding the currency.
2. Try to find out the positioning in the market. The net positioning in the futures market or repo rates can give a good reading of market positioning.
3. Ask yourself what kind of data impact will cause a squeeze of these positions?

The reader can find more about market sentiment and Market Psychology in Chapter 3 on Behavioral Finance.

US and Eurozone GDP compared

Table 4.4.1: GDP

Period	US GDP (chain yoy %)	Eurozone GDP constant	Difference	EUR/USD open	EUR/USD close
1999 Q1	4.0	2.0	2.0	1.1670	1.0765
1999 Q2	3.9	2.2	1.7	1.0771	1.0352
1999 Q3	4.0	2.8	1.2	1.0359	1.0682
1999 Q4	4.4	3.6	0.8	1.0676	1.0070
2000 Q1	4.2	3.6	0.6	1.0050	0.9560
2000 Q2	5.2	3.9	1.3	0.9560	0.9523
2000 Q3	4.4	3.2	1.2	0.9522	0.8837
2000 Q4	2.8	2.8	0.0	0.8840	0.9422
2001 Q1	2.5	2.5	0.0	0.9423	0.8774
2001 Q2	1.2	1.6	-0.4	0.8742	0.8495
2001 Q3	0.5	1.3	-0.8	0.8495	0.9098

Sources: Bloomberg, Reuters

Since the start of the Euro in 1999, the Eurozone GDP only exceeded the US GDP twice, in the second and third quarter of 2001. In all the other quarters, US GDP was superior (mainly up to the third quarter of 2000). The positive difference in GDP is in favor because the US can be seen as a support for the USD against the Euro.

Balance of payments and US and Eurozone trade balance compared

Table 4.4.2: Trade balance & balance of payments Eurozone

Period	US Trade balance in billion USD	Eurozone Trade balance in billion EUR	Eurozone balance of payments (current Balance) in billion EUR
January 1999	-15.5	-0.7	-8.6
February 1999	-18.9	3.9	0.1
March 1999	-18.4	5.5	4.3
April 1999	-18.7	4.2	2.4
May 1999	-20.9	1.3	-2.5
June 1999	-23.3	8.1	3.2
July 1999	-24.1	11.7	2.0
August 1999	-24.1	2.5	-3.0
September 1999	-23.5	1.4	-4.1
October 1999	-24.2	7.0	-2.1
November 1999	-25.5	3.1	-4.4
December 1999	-25.3	3.5	-5.5
January 2000	-26.4	-5.6	-10.2
February 2000	-29.5	-0.4	-2.5
March 2000	-31.5	3.8	1.7
April 2000	-29.4	0.1	-9.4
May 2000	-30.3	1.1	-4.7
June 2000	-31.0	2.7	-2.6
July 2000	-32.0	5.6	-5.1
August 2000	-30.8	-0.5	-6.7
September 2000	-34.5	-0.4	-5.4
October 2000	-34.0	1.8	-5.4
November 2000	-33.0	-0.3	-5.0
December 2000	-33.3	-0.6	-7.0
January 2001	-33.4	-5.9	-11.1
February 2001	-28.7	1.4	1.2
March 2001	-33.0	2.7	-0.6
April 2001	-31.8	-0.4	-6.7
May 2001	-28.9	2.9	-3.0
June 2001	-29.8	5.2	-1.6
July 2001	-30.2	8.5	-4.1
August 2001	-28.0	4.7	4.2
September 2001	-19.0	4.4	-1.3
October 2001	-29.4	7.6	

Source: Bloomberg

Fundamentally, the balance of payments must largely determine the ultimate fate of a currency. A substantial and persistent deficit results in an eventual devaluation of a country's currency[63]. From the inception of the Euro until now, the Eurozone has had a negative balance of payments. Many Foreign Exchange analysts use the negative balance of payments of the Eurozone as a main reason for the Euro weakness. The fact that

---

[63] ACI Diploma, *Economics and Forecasting,* Author: Bob Steiner, Markets International Ltd.

these data are lagging by two months (Eurozone) seems not to be important, because they use these data in their models and these models will give some forecasts. These data are very valuable but can, in my opinion, only be used to explain previous movements in EUR/USD. More details about the use of these data can be found in the Chapters on Equity, International Debt and Short-Term-Interest-Rate Markets.

Since 1999, the Eurozone trade balance has been mainly positive. In the same period, the US trade deficit has grown rapidly with a maximum absolute level of –$34.3 billion in September 2000 (101.76% higher than January 1999). Surprisingly, this huge trade deficit didn't hurt the USD up to now, because foreigners were willing to finance this deficit. Some of the factors that would lead them to be willing to do this are:
- The policy of European companies to try being present in the US market and
- European investors who overweight US equities and bonds because of higher returns (see chapter Equity and International Debt).
- A decrease in willingness would cause a sell off of the USD.

US & Eurozone industrial production, retail sales, NAPM and PMI compared

Table 4.4.3: Industrial Production, Retail Sales, NAPM and PMI

Period	US Industrial Production yoy % change	US Retail Sales yoy % change	US NAPM	Eurozone Industrial Production yoy % change	Eurozone close Retail Sales constant prices	Eurozone PMI
January 1999	3.1	6.9	49.9	1.6	2.1	48.00
February 1999	3.3	7.8	51.7	-0.2	1.6	49.23
March 1999	3.4	7.5	52.9	-0.4	3.0	50.13
April 1999	2.9	7.1	52.5	0.2	1.6	51.16
May 1999	3.1	7.6	54.4	-0.2	1.0	51.39
June 1999	3.9	7.0	56.7	1.4	3.6	52.52
July 1999	4.7	8.8	53.4	1.5	2.0	53.79
August 1999	3.2	10.2	54.7	3.4	2.2 5	4.42
September 1999	3.4	9.3	57.1	2.8	2.0	55.51
October 1999	3.6	8.1	56.9	3.7	3.6	57.14
November 1999	4.4	8.8	57.2	4.7	2.2	57.27
December 1999	5.1	9.7	57.6	5.2	2.7	57.43
January 2000	4.6	9.6	56.2	2.6	2.3	55.48
February 2000	5.0	10.0	56.4	5.4	3.7	57.00
March 2000	5.1	10.8	55.3	6.0	0.9	59.22
April 2000	5.6	8.9	54.7	6.6	3.9	60.59
May 2000	5.8	7.9	53.1	6.8	4.9	59.60
June 2000	6.1	8.1	52.1	5.1	1.5	59.48
July 2000	5.0	7.8	51.7	5.7	1.7	59.15
August 2000	4.6	6.5	49.9	6.8	1.7	58.54
September 2000	4.7	7.6	49.6	5.5	2.9	57.09
October 2000	3.5	6.8	48.3	3.9	1.6	55.65
November 2000	2.7	4.8	47.9	4.6	1.3	54.57
December 2000	1.6	3.1	44.3	7.1	1.7	53.41
January 2001	0.5	4.4	41.2	5.0	2.8	52.91
February 2001	-0.4	3.0	41.9	4.6	1.5	52.31
March 2001	-1.2	1.3	43.1	3.1	2.4	51.17
April 2001	-1.1	4.0	43.2	0.9	1.1	49.24
May 2001	-2.0	4.0	42.1	-0.1	0.2	48.50
June 2001	-3.3	3.5	44.7	1.8	1.7	47.84
July 2001	-3.2	3.2	43.6	-1.5	1.7	47.27
August 2001	-4.6	3.5	47.9	1.0	1.7	47.54
September 2001 -	5.4	0.1	47.0	-0.9	1.7	45.95
October 2001	-5.9	6.9	39.8	-2.7		42.90

Sources: Bloomberg, Reuters, NAPM, ECB Monthly Bulletin
Comment: Eurozone Industrial Production workday adjusted

In the period January 1999 until October 2001, the correlation between the Eurozone/US Industrial Production difference and the movements in EUR/USD is 0.25. The correlation between the US NAPM/Eurozone PMI and EUR/$ is –0,08.

US and Eurozone CPI and PPI compared

Table 4.4.4: CPI and PPI

Period	US CPI (all items) yoy % change	US PPI finished yoy % change	Eurozone CPI (HICP) yoy %	Eurozone PPI (ex cons) yoy % change
January 1999	0.8	1.7 / -2.5		0.8
February 1999	1.6	0.5	0.8	-2.5
March 1999	1.7	0.8	1.0	-2.2
April 1999	2.3	1.2	1.1	-1.7
May 1999	2.1	1.4	1.0	-1.5
June 1999	2.0	1.5	0.9	-1.2
July 1999	2.1	1.5	1.1	-0.5
August 1999	2.3	2.3	1.2	0.1
September 1999	2.6	3.1	1.2	0.7
October 1999	2.6	2.8	1.4	1.4
November 1999	2.6	3.1	1.5	2.1
December 1999	2.7	2.9	1.7	2.9
January 2000	2.7	2.5	1.9	3.9
February 2000	3.2	4.0	2.0	4.5
March 2000	3.8	4.3	2.1	4.9
April 2000	3.1	3.6	1.9	4.7
May 2000	3.2	3.7	1.9	5.4
June 2000	3.7	4.4	2.4	5.6
July 2000	3.7	4.3	2.3	5.6
August 2000	3.4	3.4	2.3	5.6
September 2000	3.5	3.5	2.8	6.3
October 2000	3.4	3.7	2.7	6.6
November 2000	3.4	3.8	2.9	6.4
December 2000	3.4	3.6	2.6	5.4
January 2001	3.7	4.8	2.4	4.8
February 2001	3.5	4.0	2.6	4.6
March 2001	2.9	3.0	2.6	4.2
April 2001	3.3	3.7	2.9	4.2
May 2001	3.6	3.9	3.4	3.4
June 2001	3.2	2.6	3.0	2.9
July 2001	2.7	1.4	2.8	1.9
August 2001	2.7	2.1	2.7	1.6
September 2001	2.6	1.6	2.5	0.7
October 2001	2.1	-0.4	2.4	-0.4

Source: Bloomberg

Since January 1999, the US CPI has exceeded the Eurozone HICP except for July & October 2001. The Eurozone HICP is used because the ECB watches this figure closely. Most interesting to see is the CPI or HICP relative to the GDP to judge if we are dealing with non-inflationary or inflationary growth.

Table 4.4.5: CPI/HICP relative to GDP

Period	Quarterly average US CPI	US GDP	CPI/GDP * 100%	Quarterly average Eurozone HICP	Eurozone GDP	CPI/GDP * 100%
1999Q1	1.67	4.0	41.75	0.87	2.0	43.50
1999 Q2	2.13	3.9	54.62	1.00	2.2	45.45
1999 Q3	2.33	4.0	58.25	1.17	2.8	41.79
1999 Q4	2.63	4.4	59.77	1.53	3.6	42.50
2000 Q1	3.23	4.2	76.90	2.00	3.6	55.56
2000 Q2	3.33	5.2	64.04	2.07	3.9	53.08
2000 Q3	3.53	4.4	80.23	2.47	3.2	77.19
2000 Q4	3.40	2.8	121.43	2.73	2.8	97.50
2001 Q1	3.37	2.5	134.80	2.53	2.5	101.20
2001 Q2	3.37	1.2	280.83	3.10	1.6	193.75
2001 Q3	2.67	0.5	534.00	2.67	1.3	205.38

Sources: see tables 4.4.1 and 4.4.4, own calculations.

For both the US CPI and the Eurozone HICP relative to GDP have increased over time and CPI/HICP became even larger than GDP in the fourth quarter of 2000 for the US and the third quarter of 2000 for the Eurozone. The main reason for this is the drop in US and Eurozone GDP instead of a large pickup in the CPI/HICP. The ECB has price stability as a main target and will closely watch the developments in HICP and M3. In the current economic environment of low growth and a lot of uncertainty, the Fed is focused on a growth stimulation policy.

US and Eurozone unemployment rate and M3 compared

Table 4.4.6: Unemployment rate and M3

Period	US Unemployment rate %	US Hourly earnings	US M3 yoy % change	Eurozone Unemployment rate %	Eurozone M3 yoy % change
January 1999	4.3	0.4	10.27	10.3	6.0
February 1999	4.1	0.2	10.42	10.3	5.3
March 1999	4.2	0.3	9.17	10.2	5.5
April 1999	4.4	0.3	9.93	10.1	5.3
May 1999	4.2	0.3	9.79	10.1	5.6
June 1999	4.3	0.4	9.59	9.9	5.6
July 1999	4.3	0.4	9.75	9.8	6.0
August 1999	4.2	0.2	9.80	9.8	5.8
September 1999	4.2	0.4	8.38	9.7	6.1
October 1999	4.1	0.2	8.16	9.6	5.8
November 1999	4.1	0.1	8.40	9.5	6.2
December 1999	4.1	0.4	8.73	9.4	6.1
January 2000	4.0	0.4	8.37	9.3	5.2
February 2000	4.1	0.4	7.91	9.2	6.2
March 2000	4.0	0.3	8.96	9.1	6.6
April 2000	4.0	0.3	9.17	9.0	6.7
May 2000	4.1	0.3	9.02	8.9	6.0
June 2000	4.0	0.4	9.21	8.9	5.3
July 2000	4.0	0.2	9.46	8.8	5.1
August 2000	4.1	0.4	10.04	8.7	5.5
September 2000	3.9	0.3	9.50	8.6	5.0
October 2000	3.9	0.4	10.00	8.6	4.9
November 2000	4.0	0.5	9.10	8.5	4.7
December 2000	4.0	0.4	8.90	8.5	4.9
January 2001	4.2	0.0	9.70	8.5	4.5
February 2001	4.2	0.6	10.20	8.4	4.4
March 2001	4.3	0.4	10.00	8.4	4.6
April 2001	4.5	0.3	10.90	8.4	4.8
May 2001	4.4	0.2	11.60	8.4	5.3
June 2001	4.5	0.5	12.00	8.4	6.3
July 2001	4.5	0.2	11.80	8.4	6.4
August 2001	4.9	0.4	10.90	8.3	6.6
September 2001	4.9	0.3	12.30	8.4	7.0
October 2001	5.4	0.1	12.90	8.4	7.3

Source: Bloomberg

The US M3 money supply has exceeded and still exceeds the Eurozone M3. An explanation for this difference is that the ECB is focused on price stability while the Fed is more focused on economic growth. The difference in M3 growth should be supportive for EUR against the USD. However, the unemployment rate is in favor of the USD. The US unemployment rate is approximately half of the unemployment rate of the Eurozone.

US and Eurozone confidence indicators compared

Table 4.4.7: Confidence (Conf.), Sentiment (Sent.) indicators

Period	US Michigan Cons. Sent.	US Chicago Cons. Conf.	Eurozone Cons. Conf.	Eurozone Business Conf.	German Business Sent.	Eurozone Econ. Sent.
January 1999	103.9	128.9	0	-8	91.1	101.1
February 1999	108.1	133.1	0	-11	89.9	100.7
March 1999	105.7	134.0	-1	-12	90.6	100.3
April 1999	104.6	135.5	-3	-11	90.0	100.7
May 1999	106.8	137.7	-4	-11	90.7	100.5
June 1999	107.3	139.0	-5	-9	93.1	100.5
July 1999	106.0	136.2	-3	-7	93.6	101.2
August 1999	104.5	136.0	-4	-7	95.1	101.0
September 1999	107.2	134.2	-4	-5	95.4	101.3
October 1999	103.2	130.5	-2	-3	96.1	101.8
November 1999	107.2	137.0	-1	-1	98.9	102.4
December 1999	105.4	141.7	-1	0	99.7	102.7
January 2000	112.0	144.7	-1	1	100.0	103.2
February 2000	111.3	140.8	0	3	100.9	103.3
March 2000	107.1	137.1	0	4	100.6	103.9
April 2000	109.2	137.7	0	5	101.2	104.0
May 2000	110.7	144.7	1	5	102.0	104.2
June 2000	106.4	139.2	-1	8	100.3	104.6
July 2000	108.3	143.0	0	7	98.9	104.2
August 2000	107.3	140.8	1	6	98.8	104.2
September 2000	106.8	142.5	-3	7	98.1	103.6
October 2000	105.8	135.8	-3	6	97.2	103.8
November 2000	107.6	132.6	-4	5	97.0	103.5
December 2000	98.4	128.6	-1	5	96.7	103.5
January 2001	94.7	115.7	-1	3	97.4	103.4
February 2001	90.6	109.2	-2	1	94.8	103.1
March 2001	91.5	116.9	-2	1	93.7	102.5
April 2001	88.4	109.9	0	-4	92.4	102.1
May 2001	92.0	116.1	-2	-5	90.8	101.7
June 2001	92.6	118.9	-3	-8	89.4	101.1
July 2001	92.4	116.3	-6	-10	89.7	100.7
August 2001	91.5	114.0	-8	-11	89.4	100.1
September 2001	81.8	97.0	-9	-13	85.0	100.1
October 2001	82.7	85.5	-10	-17	84.7	99.1

Source: Bloomberg

In the current market environment, with a lot of uncertainty, the focus is on consumer confidence in the US and German IFO business sentiment in the Eurozone. The confidence data are clearly under pressure for US and Eurozone. The influence on EUR/USD would depend on outcome versus expectations of the data.

4.5 MARKET IMPACT OF ECONOMIC DATA[64]

US GDP

Table 4.5.1: US GDP

Date	US GDP	Dow Jones*	Euro STOXX 50.	T-Bond Future	Bund Future*	EUR/$
30 Apr 99	4.5% Q1 1999 advance					0.47%
27 May 99	4.1% Q1 1999 preliminary	-2.20%	-2.17%	-0.48%		-0.20%
25 Jun 99	4.3% Q1 1999 final	0.26%	-0.60%	0.39%		0.24%
29 Jul 99	2.3% Q2 1999 advance	-0.75%	-2.75%	-0.30%		0.56%
26 Aug 99	1.8% Q2 1999 preliminary	-0.84%	-0.67%	-0.05%		0.26%
30 Sep 99	1.6% Q2 1999 final	0.87%	0.54%	0.57%		0.41%
28 Oct 99	4.8% Q3 1999 advance	2.19%	1.94%	1.02%	0.66%	-0.02%
24 Nov 99	5.5% Q3 1999 preliminary	0.09%	0.48%	0.07%	-0.47%	-0.92%
22 Dec 99	5.7% Q3 1999 final	0.21%	1.21%	0.03%	0.13%	0.14%
28 Jan 00	5.8% Q4 1999 advance	-3.13%	-0.54%	1.16%	0.43%	-1.32%
25 Feb 00	6.9% Q4 1999 preliminary	-2.24%	0.64%	-0.46%	-0.67%	-1.85%
30 Mar 00	7.3% Q4 1999 final	-0.56%	-2.12%	1.01%	0.50%	1.06%
27 Apr 00	5.4% Q1 2000 advance	-1.14%	-1.64%	-0.90%	-0.16%	-1.54%
25 May 00	5.4% Q1 2000 preliminary	-1.80%	0.79%	1.34%	0.53%	1.06%
29 Jun 00	5.5% Q1 2000 final	-1.13%	-3.18%	0.61%	0.28%	1.09%
28 Jul 00	5.2% Q2 2000 advance	-1.02%	-0.66%	-0.16%	-0.19%	-0.91%
25 Aug 00	5.3% Q2 2000 preliminary	0.09%	0.88%	0.12%	-0.10%	0.03%
28 Sep 00	5.6% Q2 2000 final	1.63%	-0.33%	-0.03%	0.24%	-0.45%
27 Oct 00	2.7% Q3 2000 advance	2.22%	0.58%	-0.09%	0.10%	1.05%
29 Nov 00	2.4% Q3 2000 preliminary	0.73%	0.60%	0.25%	0.01%	0.16%
21 Dec 00	2.2% Q3 2000 final	1.53%	-0.04%	0.24%	-0.38%	0.77%
31 Jan 01	1.4% Q4 2000 advance	-0.27%	1.09%	0.36%	0.09%	1.10%
28 Feb 01	1.1% Q4 2000 preliminary	-1.61%	-0.12%	0.03%	-0.11%	0.50%
29 Mar 01	1.0% Q4 2000 final	0.38%	0.68%	-0.12%	0.01%	-0.35%
27 Apr 01	2.0% Q1 2001 advance	1.30%	1.56%	-1.45%	-0.56%	-1.26%
25 May 01	1.3% Q1 2001 preliminary	-1.14%	-1.35%	-0.13%	-0.03%	0.47%
29 Jun 01	1.2% Q1 2001 final	-0.56%	1.76%	-0.78%	-0.31%	0.70%
27 Jul 01	0.7% Q2 2001 advance	-0.38%	1.65%	-0.03%	0.35%	0.00%
29 Aug 01	0.2% Q2 2001 preliminary	-1.26%	0.33%	0.60%	-0.07%	-0.41%
28 Sept 01	0.3% Q2 2001 final	1.67%	2.75%	0.15%	-0.08%	-0.70%
31 Oct 01	-0.4% Q3 2001 advance	-0.68%	2.00%	1.83%	0.15%	-0.54%

Sources: US Department of Commerce, Bloomberg, and Reuters
* Dow Jones future, T-bond and bund futures are the second contract.

---

[64] Similar approach as in the following paper, however different data used (open & close), R.C.Fair, *Shock Effects on Stocks, Bonds and Exchange Rates*, January 2001

The market reaction depends on whether the figure deviates from expectations. When the outcome is in line with expectations there will be no major market movements. Large movements occur when the outcome deviates from expectations. Better than expected US GDP figures should cause a rally in the stock markets, a selling wave in the bond markets and a sell off in EUR/USD.

US Trade Balance

Table 4.5.2: US Trade figures

Date	US International Trade in goods and services	Dow Jones*	Euro STOXX 50.	T-Bond Future	Bond Future	EUR/$
21 Jan 99	Trade deficit $15.5bn (Nov 98)					
19 Feb 99	Trade deficit $14.6bn (Dec 98)					
18 Mar 99	Trade deficit $15.5bn (Jan 99)					-0.10%
20 Apr 99	Trade deficit $18.9bn (Feb 99)					-0.33%
20 May 99	Trade deficit $18.4bn (Mar 99)		0.62%	-0.27%		-0.42%
17 Jun 99	Trade deficit $18.7bn (Apr 99)	0.74%	0.17%	1.28%		0.41%
20 Jul 99	Trade deficit $18.7bn (May 99)	-1.49%	-1.94%	0.51%		0.91%
19 Aug 99	Trade deficit $20.9bn (Jun 99)	0.27%	-1.24%	-0.33%		1.15%
21 Sep 99	Trade deficit $24.1bn (Jul 99)	-1.66%	-1.46%	-0.16%		1.27%
20 Oct 99	Trade deficit $23.6bn (Aug 99)	1.26%	0.8%	0.07%	-0.07%	-0.73%
18 Nov 99	Trade deficit $23.4bn (Sep 99)	1.29%	1.94%	-0.36%	-0.32%	-1.10%
16 Dec 99	Trade deficit $24.2bn (Oct 99)	0.24%	0.64%	-0.84%	-0.70%	0.90%
20 Jan 00	Trade deficit $25.5bn (Nov 99)	-1.68%	-0.54%	0.14%	0.45%	0.37%
18 Feb 00	Trade deficit $25.3bn (Dec 99)	-2.09%	-1.06%	0.67%	0.48%	-0.15%
21 Mar 00	Trade deficit $26.4bn (Jan 00)	1.92%	0.04%	0.26%	-0.06%	-0.95%
19 Apr 00	Trade deficit $29.5bn (Feb 00)	-0.97%	-0.89%	0.77%	0.05%	-0.50%
19 May 00	Trade deficit $31.5bn (Mar 00)	-0.79%	-3.07%	0.10%	0.26%	0.28%
20 Jun 00	Trade deficit $29.4bn (Apr 00)	-0.98%	0.69%	-0.16%	-0.06%	-0.24%
19 Jul 00	Trade deficit $30.3bn (May 00)-	-0.42%	-0.37%	0.06%	0.31%	-0.05%
18 Aug 00	Trade deficit $31.0bn (Jun 00)	-0.14%	-0.25%	0.28%	0.00%	-1.07%
20 Sep 00	Trade deficit $32.0bn (Jul 00)	-1.22%	-1.83%	-0.54%	0.08%	-0.24%
19 Oct 00	Trade deficit $30.8bn (Aug 00)	1.49%	3.82%	0.31%	0.04%	0.56%
21 Nov 00	Trade deficit $34.5bn (Sep 00)	0.38%	0.88%	0.09%	-0.12%	-0.95%
19 Dec 00	Trade deficit $34.0bn (Oct 00)	-0.82%	1.69%	-0.09%	-0.18%	-0.02%
19 Jan 01	Trade deficit $33.0bn (Nov 00)	-1.60%	-0.89%	-0.72%	-0.26%	-0.93%
21 Feb 01	Trade deficit $33.3bn (Dec 00)	-2.36%	-1.46%	-0.33%	-0.20%	-0.31%
20 Mar 01	Trade deficit $33.4bn (Jan 01)	-2.53%	1.52%	0.21%	-0.06%	1.12%
18 Apr 01	Trade deficit $28.7bn (Feb 01)	2.94%	3.02%	0.46%	0.03%	-0.14%
18 May 01	Trade deficit $33.0bn (Mar 01)	0.69%	1.07%	-0.03%	-0.13%	-0.17%
21 Jun 01	Trade deficit $31.5bn (Apr 01)	0.35%	-0.11%	0.22%	0.09%	-0.14%
19 Jul 01	Trade deficit $28.2bn (May 01)	0.88%	2.19%	-0.18%	-0.07%	-0.35%
17 Aug 01	Trade deficit $29.1bn (Jun 01)	-1.49%	-2.47%	0.87%	0.26%	0.71%
19 Sept 01	Trade deficit $29.2bn (Jul 01)	-2.35%	-2.55%	-0.09%	0.04%	-0.02%
19 Oct 01	Trade deficit $27.1bn (Aug 01)	0.07%	-1.45%	-0.65%	-0.15%	-0.47%

Sources: Bloomberg, Reuters
*Dow Jones future, T-bond and bund futures are the second contract.

A trade deficit indicates that US residents have a high demand for foreign currencies or foreign goods available and charged off in foreign currencies. Usually a permanent trade deficit will weaken the value of the currency. In the last two years the US trade deficit increased but it didn't stop the USD from getting stronger. The reasons for this will be discussed in the upcoming chapters. This situation can only exist if foreigners are ready to finance the deficit, which has been the case since the introduction of the EUR.

US Employment Report

Table 4.5.3: US unemployment rate & non-farm payrolls (NFP)

Date	US unemployment rate (1 month lag)	NFP	Dow Jones*	Euro STOXX 50	T-Bond Future	Bund Future	EUR/$
05 Feb 99	4.3%	145,000					
05 Mar 99	4.1%	433,000					0.29%
02 Apr 99	4.2%	167,000					0.07%
07 May 99	4.4%	261,000					-0.38%
04 Jun 99	4.2%	184,000	1.61%	0.48% -	0.03%		0.57%
02 Jul 99	4.3%	264,000	0.64%	0.53%	-0.65%		0.07%
06 Aug 99	4.3%	278,000	-0.42%	-0.52%	-1.11%		-0.22%
03 Sep 99	4.2%	206,000	1.05%	2.22%	1.13%		-0.66%
08 Oct 99	4.2%	186,000	1.13%	0.22%	-0.27%		-0.72%
05 Nov 99	4.1%	453,000	0.91%	0.49%	0.66%	0.53%	0.31%
03 Dec 99	4.1%	230,000	2.40%	2.39%	0.95%	0.53%	0.07%
07 Jan 00	4.1%	272,000	3.14%	3.23%	0.45%	0.63%	-0.34%
04 Feb 00	4.0%	303,000	-0.80%	0.52%	-0.30%	-0.92%	-0.82%
03 Mar 00	4.1%	175,000	2.02%	0.78%	0.43%	0.22%	-0.50%
07 Apr 00	4.0%	598,000	-0.21%	0.07%	1.15%	0.36%	-0.35%
05 May 00	4.0%	242,000	1.48%	0.54%	-0.70%	0.19%	0.66%
02 Jun 00	4.1%	226,000	1.10%	2.18%	0.23%	0.22%	1.62%
07 Jul 00	4.0%	60,000	1.32%	1.83%	0.39%	0.27%	-0.25%
04 Aug 00	4.0%	-70,000	0.37%	0.83%	0.22%	-0.10%	0.18%
01 Sep 00	4.1%	-62,000	0.00%	1.95%	0.12%	0.82%	1.24%
06 Oct 00	3.9%	209,000	-1.26%	-0.61%	0.67%	0.11%	-0.09%
03 Nov 00	3.9%	99,000	-0.38%	0.16%	-0.97%	-0.31%	0.96%
08 Dec 00	4.0%	134,000	-1.02%	-0.24%	-0.33%	-0.04%	-0.45%
05 Jan 01	4.0%	88,000	-2.72%	-0.28%	0.39%	0.05%	0.85%
02 Feb 01	4.2%	61,000	-1.35%	-0.99%	-0.06%	-0.08%	-0.23%
09 Mar 01	4.2%	167,000	-2.09%	-0.76%	-0.24%	-0.05%	0.05%
06 Apr 01	4.3%	59,000	-1.22%	-0.52%	0.88%	0.51%	0.80%
04 May 01	4.5%	-165,000	1.72%	0.48%	-0.76%	0.13%	0.36%
01 Jun 01	4.4%	41,000	0.91%	-0.30%	0.72%	0.58%	0.33%
06 Jul 01	4.5%	-99,000	-1.93%	-2.47%	0.19%	0.25%	1.24%
03 Aug 01	4.5%	18,000	-0.28%	-1.03%	0.06%	0.13%	0.11%
08 Sept 01	4.9%	-54,000	-2.39%	-	-	-	-0.32%
05 Oct 01	4.9%	-213,000	0.44%	-1.26%	-0.27%	0.04%	0.07%
02 Nov 01	5.4%	-415,000	0.98%	-0.33%	0.93%	-0.37%	0.04%

Sources: Bloomberg, Reuters
* Dow Jones future, T-bond and bund futures are the second contract.

A tight labor market in a high conjuncture is a signal for inflation. In this conjuncture the markets will not welcome a lower unemployment rate, higher non-farm payroll data and higher hourly earnings, because these data will increase the chance of higher interest rates. As a result, stock and bond markets would be sold off and, surprisingly, the USD as well. The USD would first weaken as a result of the asset sell off, while in the longer term the USD would strengthen as a result of the higher interest rate earned on the USD.

The market reaction will totally depend on the market sentiment. In an environment of increased uncertainty, the market would prefer to see the earlier mentioned data. A higher unemployment rate and lower non-farm payrolls would cause sell-off of the USD. However, the data shouldn't be too strong because otherwise the Fed would not have room to cut interest rates.

US Personal Income and Expenditure

Table 4.5.4: US Personal Income and Expenditure

Date	US Personal Income	US Personal Expenditure	Dow Jones*	Euro STOXX 50	T-Bond Future	Bund Future	EUR/$
01 Feb 99	0.5%	0.8%					
01 Mar 99	0.6%	0.3%					
01 Apr 99	0.5%	0.7%					0.20%
03 May 99	0.4%	0.4%					-0.22%
28 May 99	0.5%	0.4%	0.35%	1.10%	0.27%		0.06%
28 Jun 99	0.4%	0.6%	-0.62%	0.54%	0.80%		-0.62%
30 Jul 99	0.7%	0.3%	-1.46%	1.31%	-0.03%		-0.05%
27 Aug 99	0.2%	0.4%	-1.12%	0.78%	-0.78%		0.07%
01 Oct 99	0.5%	0.9%	-1.02%	-0.94%	-0.70%		0.39%
02 Nov 99	0.1%	0.4%	-0.79%	0.46%	0.40%	0.67%	0.00%
26 Nov 99	1.3%	0.6%	-0.94%	0.59%	0.00%	-0.52%	-0.15%
23 Dec 99	0.4%	0.5%	1.89%	2.10%	-0.48%	-0.01%	0.65%
31 Jan 00	0.3%	0.8%	2.14%	-0.70%	-0.44%	0.35%	-0.86%
28 Feb 00	0.7%	0.5%	1.41%	-1.12%	-0.53%	0.17%	-0.30%
31 Mar 00	0.4%	1.0%	-0.42%	0.32%	0.61%	-0.07%	-0.53%
28 Apr 00	0.7%	0.5%	-0.85%	0.81%	0.42%	0.19%	0.22%
26 May 00	0.7%	0.4%	-0.36%	1.49%	0.43%	0.23%	2.01%
30 Jun 00	0.4%	0.2%	0.33%	1.63%	-0.19%	-0.35%	0.18%
01 Aug 00	0.4%	0.5%	0.95%	-0.43%	0.22%	0.20%	-1.34%
28 Aug 00	0.3%	0.6%	0.47%	0.51%	-0.56%	-0.12%	-0.27%
29 Sep 00	0.4%	0.6%	-1.44%	-0.63%	0.06%	0.27%	0.52%
30 Oct 00	1.1%	0.8%	1.84%	0.14%	-0.09%	-0.18%	-0.11%
30 Nov 00	-0.2%	0.2%	-1.32%	-2.57%	0.58%	0.56%	1.75%
22 Dec 00	0.4%	0.3%	1.84%	1.01%	0.39%	0.03%	0.84%
01 Feb 01	0.4%	0.3%	1.38%	-1.31%	0.78%	-0.07%	0.19%
01 Mar 01	0.6%	0.7%	-0.05%	-0.54%	0.41%	-0.04%	0.64%
30 Mar 01	0.4%	0.3%	1.09%	0.46%	0.55%	0.23%	-0.66%
30 Apr 01	0.5%	0.3%	-1.14%	1.15%	0.22%	-0.19%	-0.39%
29 May 01	0.3%	0.4%	0.17%	-0.84%	-0.13%	0.26%	-0.51%
02 Jul 01	0.2%	0.5%	0.86%	1.61%	0.66%	0.00%	-0.26%
31 Jul 01	0.3%	0.4%	0.91%	1.02%	0.24%	0.12%	0.24%
30 Aug 01	0.5%	0.1%	-1.82%	-2.34%	-0.18%	0.18%	0.85%
01 Oct 01	0.0%	0.2%	0.18%	-2.64%	0.66%	0.27%	0.80%

Sources: US Department of Commerce, Reuters
* Dow Jones future, T-bond and bund futures are the second contract

The US consumer is the big motor behind the US economy. In times of uncertainty and possible recession, it is important that the consumer keeps spending to get the economy out of the difficult period. In current times, a high US Personal Expenditure is good for USD and good for the stock markets and not so good for the bond markets.

Monetary policy 1999

Table 4.5.5: Monetary Policy Fed & ECB in 1999

Date	Action	Dow Jones*	Euro STOXX	T-Bond Future 50	Bund Future	EUR/$
07 Jan 99	ECB Refinancing operations 3.0% Marginal lending rate 3.25% Deposit rate 2.75%					
21 Jan 99	ECB changed rates New rates: 3.0%, 4.5%,2.0%					
18 Feb 99	ECB, Rates unchanged					
04 Mar 99	ECB, Rates unchanged					-0.63%
31 Mar 99	ECB, Rates unchanged					0.47%
08 Apr 99	ECB cut rates New rates: 2.5%, 3.5%, 1.5%					-0.05%
22 Apr 99	ECB, Rates unchanged					0.60%
06 May 99	ECB, Rates unchanged					0.29%
18 May 99	Fed, Rates unchanged		0.21%	0.00%		0.14%
20 May 99	ECB, Rates unchanged		0.62%	-0.27%		-0.42%
02 Jun 99	ECB, Rates unchanged	-0.20%	0.20%	0.08%		-0.86%
17 Jun 99	ECB, Rates unchanged	0.74%	0.17%	1.28%		0.41%
30 Jun 99	Fed raised rates. NB** Fed. funds rate up 25bps to 5.0%	1.60%	-0.29%	0.90%		0.21%
01 Jul 99	ECB, Rates unchanged	0.99%	0.39%	-0.51%		-1.25%
15 Jul 99	ECB, Rates unchanged	-0.38%	1.06%	0.00%		-0.13%
29 Jul 99	ECB, Rates unchanged	-0.75%	-2.75%	-0.30%		0.56%
24 Aug 99	Fed raised rates by 25bps, NB** New rates: 5.25% and 4.75%	0.12%	0.57%	0.41%		0.48%
26 Aug 99	ECB, Rates unchanged	-0.84%	-0.67%	-0.05%		0.26%
09 Sep 99	ECB, Rates unchanged	0.22%	0.97%	-0.44%		-0.53%
23 Sep 99	ECB, Rates unchanged	-2.69%	0.49%	0.76%		0.69%
05 Oct 99	Fed, Rates unchanged, TB***	-0.18%	0.60%	-1.00%		0.03%
07 Oct 99	ECB, Rates unchanged	-0.49%	0.20%	0.10%		0.24%
21 Oct 99	ECB, Rates unchanged	-0.19%	-0.41%	-0.51%	0.22%	0.33%
04 Nov 99	ECB raised rates by 50bps New rates: 3.0%, 4.0%, 2.0%	0.47%	0.86%	0.40%	0.63%	-1.02%
16 Nov 99	Fed raised rates by 25bps, NB New rates: 5.5% and 5.0%	1.72%	0.78%	-0.49%	0.47% -	0.34%
18 Nov 99	ECB, Rates unchanged	1.29%	1.94%	-0.36%	-0.32%	-1.10%
02 Dec 99	ECB, Rates unchanged	0.22%	-0.47%	-0.30%	-0.64%	-0.72%
15 Dec 99	ECB, Rates unchanged	0.29%	-0.26%	-0.37%	0.29%	0.16%
21 Dec 99	Fed, Rates unchanged	0.80%	0.08%	-0.48%	-	-0.38%

Sources: Fed, ECB, and Reuters, * Dow Jones future, T-bond and bund futures are the second contract.
**NB = Neutral Bias, ***TB = Tightening Bias

Monetary policy in 2000

Table 4.5.6: Monetary Policy Fed & ECB in 2000

Date	Action	Dow Jones*	Euro STOXX	T-Bond Future 50	Bund Future	EUR/$
05 Jan 00	ECB, Rates unchanged	1.28%	-0.10%	-0.73%	-0.46%	0.20%
20 Jan 00	ECB, Rates unchanged	-1.68%	-0.54%	0.14%	0.45%	0.37%
02 Feb 00	Fed raised rates 25bps New rates: 5.75% and 5.25%	-0.54%	1.57%	0.64%	-0.16%	0.49%
03 Feb 00	ECB raised rates by 25bps New rates: 3.25%, 4.25%, 2.25%	0.63%	2.21%	0.07%	0.67%	1.43%
17 Feb 00	ECB, Rates unchanged	-1.04%	1.00%	0.54%	-0.02%	0.14%
02 Mar 00	ECB, Rates unchanged	0.05%	2.62%	0.36%	-0.12%	-0.92%
16 Mar 00	ECB raised rates by 25bps New rates: 3.5%, 4.5%, 2.5%	4.95%	0.91%	0.29%	0.40%	0.55%
21 Mar 00	Fed raised rates by 25bps New rates: 6.00% and 5.5%	1.92%	0.04%	0.26%	-0.06%	-0.95%
30 Mar 00	ECB, Rates unchanged	-0.56%	-2.12%	1.01%	0.50%	1.06%
13 Apr 00	ECB, Rates unchanged	-1.57%	1.99%	0.26%	0.05%	-0.67%
27 Apr 00	ECB raised rates by 25bps New rates: 3.75%, 4.75%, 2.75%	-1.14%	-1.64%	-0.90%	-0.16%	-1.54%
11 May 00	ECB, Rates unchanged	2.02%	2.97%	-0.13%	-0.64%	-0.23%
16 May 00	Fed raised rates by 50bps New rates: 6.50% and 6.0%	1.07%	1.80%	0.23%	0.20%	-0.75%
25 May 00	ECB, Rates unchanged	-1.80%	0.79%	1.34%	0.53%	1.06%
08 Jun 00	ECB raised rates by 50bps New rates: 4.25%, 5.25%, 3.25%	-1.13%	-0.37%	0.16%	-0.49%	-0.64%
21 Jun 00	ECB, Rates unchanged	0.61%	-1.00%	-0.71%	-0.27%	-1.03%
28 Jun 00	Fed, Rates unchanged	-0.02%	0.42%	-0.58%	-0.15%	-0.40%
06 Jul 00	ECB, Rates unchanged	-0.07%	-0.23%	-0.32%	-0.43%	-0.25%
20 Jul 00	ECB, Rates unchanged	1.63%	0.41%	1.52%	0.12%	0.90%
03 Aug 00	ECB, Rates unchanged	-0.14%	-1.83%	0.03%	-0.12%	-0.76%
22 Aug 00	Fed, Rates unchanged	0.50%	-0.09%	0.09%	0.19%	-0.57%
31 Aug 00	ECB raised rates by 25bps New rates: 4.5%, 5.5%, 3.5%	1.26%	0.18%	0.63%	-0.07%	-0.68%
14 Sep 00	ECB, Rates unchanged	-1.03%	0.89%	-0.84%	-0.22%	0.50%
03 Oct 00	Fed, Rates unchanged	-0.08%	0.89%	-0.29%	-0.15%	-0.22%
05 Oct 00	ECB raised rates by 25bps New rates: 4.75%, 5.75%, 3.75%	-0.39%	0.80%	0.26%	0.07%	-0.66%
19 Oct 00	ECB, Rates unchanged	1.49%	3.82%	0.31%	0.04%	0.56%
02 Nov 00	ECB, Rates unchanged	-0.41%	0.08%	-0.22%	-0.21%	-0.24%
15 Nov 00	Fed, Rates unchanged	-0.02%	0.62%	0.59%	-0.06%	-0.05%
16 Nov 00	ECB, Rates unchanged	-0.71%	-0.88%	0.12%	0.01%	-0.63%
30 Nov 00	ECB, Rates unchanged	-1.32%	-2.57%	0.58%	0.56%	1.75%
14 Dec 00	ECB, Rates unchanged	-1.36%	-1.52%	0.42%	0.07%	1.59%
19 Dec 00	Fed, Rates unchanged	-0.82%	1.69%	-0.09%	-0.18%	-0.02%

Sources: Fed, ECB, and Reuters
* Dow Jones future, T-bond and bund futures are the second contract

Monetary policy 2001

Table 4.5.7: Monetary Policy Fed & ECB in 2001

Date	Action	Dow Jones*	Euro STOXX	T-Bond Future 50	Bund Future	EUR/$
03 Jan 01	Fed cut rates by 50bps New rates: 6.00% and 5.75%+	2.38%	-0.43%	-1.91%	0.03%	-2.37%
04 Jan 01	ECB, Rates unchanged	-0.09%	1.98%	0.60%	0.36%	2.36%
18 Jan 01	ECB, Rates unchanged	-0.57%	-0.66%	0.27%	-0.06%	0.92%
31 Jan 01	Fed cut rates by 50bps New rates: 5.5% and 5.0%	-0.27%	1.09%	0.36%	0.09%	1.10%
01 Feb 01	ECB, Rates unchanged	1.38%	-1.31%	0.78%	-0.07%	0.19%
15 Feb 01	ECB, Rates unchanged	0.93%	0.87%	-0.51%	-0.27%	-1.47%
01 Mar 01	ECB, Rates unchanged	-0.05%	-0.54%	0.41%	-0.04%	0.64%
15 Mar 01	ECB, Rates unchanged	-0.45%	1.83%	-0.06%	0.05%	-1.48%
20 Mar 01	Fed cut rates by 50bps New rates: 5.0% and 4.5%	-2.53%	1.52%	0.21%	-0.06%	1.12%
29 Mar 01	ECB, Rates unchanged	0.38%	0.68%	-0.12%	-0.20%	-0.35%
11 Apr 01	ECB, Rates unchanged	-0.76%	0.69%	-0.16%	-0.50%	-0.08%
18 Apr.01	Fed cut rates by 50bps New rates: 4.5% and 4.0%	2.94%	3.02%	0.46%	0.03%	-0.14%
26 Apr 01	ECB, Rates unchanged	0.72%	0.87%	-0.06%	0.32%	0.60%
10 May 01	ECB cut rates by 25bps New rates: 4.5%, 5.5%, 3.5%	0.53%	2.37%	-0.62%	-0.17%	-0.56%
15 May 01	Fed cut rates by 50bps New rates are: 4.0% and 3.5%	0.23%	0.47%	-0.66%	0.07%	0.48%
23 May 01	ECB Rates unchanged	-1.33%	-0.95%	-0.13%	-0.28%	-1.06%
07 Jun 01	ECB, Rates unchanged	-0.04%	-0.16%	-0.65%	-0.35%	0.45%
21 Jun 01	ECB, Rates unchanged	0.35%	-0.11%	0.22%	0.09%	-0.14%
27 Jun 01	Fed cut rates by 25bps New rates: 3.75% and 3.25%	-0.20%	-0.47%	0.31%	0.09%	-0.57%
05 Jul 01	ECB, Rates unchanged	-0.82%	-0.13%	-0.53%	0.07%	-0.98%
19 Jul 01	ECB, Rates unchanged	0.88%	2.19%	-0.18%	-0.07%	-0.35%
02 Aug 01	ECB, Rates unchanged	0.28%	-0.74%	-0.30%	-0.32%	0.28%
21 Aug 01	Fed cut rates by 25bps New rates: 3.5% and 3.0%	-1.90%	0.52%	0.18%	-0.28%	0.39%
30 Aug 01	ECB cut rates by 25bps New rates: 4.25%, 5.25%, 3.25%	-1.82%	-2.34%	-0.18%	0.18%	0.85%
13 Sep 01	ECB, Rates unchanged	1.26%	1.03%	0.18%	-0.01%	0.44%
17 Sep 01	Fed cut rates by 50bps New rates: 3.0% and 2.5%	-0.84%		-0.68%		
17 Sep 01	ECB cut rates by 50bps New rates: 3.75%, 4.75%, 2.75%	3.86%		-0.47%	0.11%	
27 Sep 01	ECB, Rates unchanged	0.97%	1.65%	-0.06%	0.04%	-0.50%
02 Oct 01	Fed cut rates by 50bps New rates: 2.5% and 2.0%	1.48%	1.72%	0.42%	0.40%	0.21%
11 Oct 01	ECB, Rates unchanged	1.97%	0.78%	-0.74%	-0.09%	-0.92%
25 Oct 01	ECB, Rates unchanged	1.56%	-2.47%	0.50%	0.43%	-0.18%

Sources: Fed, ECB, and Reuters * Dow Jones future, T-bond and bund futures are the second contract
+ Board indicated that it stands ready to approve a further reduction of 25bps in discount rate to 5.50%

The pro-activity of a central bank is seen as more important than the actual decision. In the US, markets are confident that the Fed will do everything in its power to prevent a recession. After the inflation pressures cooled down (at the beginning of 2001) the Fed refocused on growth again. The uncertain environment was the main reason for the Fed to cut rates on the 3rd of January, 2001. This inter-meeting Fed rate cut was totally unexpected by the financial markets. As a result, the stock markets and the USD rallied. The bond market was sold off as players took their profit. They had already been expecting the rate cuts. From that time on, money market players priced in aggressive future rate cuts. Disappointed rate cuts (less than expected) caused a sell-off in the stock markets. The ECB is less pro-active than the Fed because ECB has an inflation target and the Fed more a growth target. ECB has not been willing to cut rates, because inflation in the Eurozone has been on the high side. However, money market players were pricing in aggressive rate cuts by the ECB as well. The EUR became vulnerable for every hold decision of the ECB. When they finally cut rates for the first time in 2001, it was taken as inconsequential by the market, because the inflation pressures didn't cool down.

The currency with the higher interest rate should be supported. However, in an environment with the probability of a recession, rate cuts are taken as positive by the market because they are seen as supportive of growth. In this case, the USD was supported, because the Fed took measures (rate cut) to boost domestic growth.

Week 2-6 July 2001
In the beginning of the week, market participants prepared themselves for data to be released that week. They tried to develop a feeling for what's going on in the market and take positions on this feeling or advise clients accordingly. The main focus is on data like GDP, German IFO and US employment report.
The data agenda for the week of 2-6 July 2001 was as follows:
Monday   US non-manufacturing NAPM
Tuesday   US factory orders
Wednesday   US off for Independence Day
Thursday   ECB meeting outcome
Friday   US Employment Report

EUR/USD started the week being under pressure. All the main currency pairs are close to important technical levels. The US non-manufacturing NAPM and US factory orders were better than expected, fueling a positive USD sentiment, and EUR/USD was coming under more pressure. Market participants increased their positions towards a better than expected outcome of the US Employment Report due on Friday. Any ECB decision on Thursday would hurt the EUR/USD for the following reasons:
– The lack of a rate cut was seen as negative for Eurozone growth.
– The rate cut was seen as inconsequential because the inflation pressures were still there (already there was a definitive lack of confidence).

On Thursday night the EUR/USD made a low of 0.8344 and rebounded to 0.8400 as the market awaited the US employment report (small short covering). A better set of data would make room for a retest of the all-time low and a worse set of data would have a rebound to the 0.8500 level as a result. The US employment report came out weaker than expected and the EUR/USD made a close around 0.8480 on the Friday night.

Before an important figure is released, the market is positioned and, and the market reaction to the release will depend on this positioning. When the market is very nervous, the release can have spikes in both directions before the real direction becomes clear. The first reaction after the data release is the result of the interpretation of the traders. The correction of this first move is the result of the interpretation of the economists. This second interpretation follows approximately one or two minutes after the data release.

4.6 CONCLUSION

Economic indicators have become increasingly important to financial markets, to the point that almost everyone involved in markets needs to understand what they mean. The impact of the economic indicators is most clear-cut in the case of Fixed-Income markets, where news on growth and inflation directly affects expectations about monetary policy and about interest rate levels more generally. The relation between the indicators and the other markets, for example equities and currencies, is often more complex, since many more variables are involved and part of the impact of economic indicator is channeled through the interest rate changes.

The market impact of economic data depends mainly on market expectations. To protect yourself against surprises in economic data you need to do the following things:
1. Determine whether the current market environment is ruled by a positive or a negative outlook.
2. Try to find out the positioning in the market. The net positioning in the futures market or repo rates can give a good reading of market positioning.
3. What kind of data will cause a squeeze of these positions?

Chapter (3), Behavioral Finance, will help the reader to read the Market Psychology.

SUMMARY 4

Indicators can be divided into two categories:
1. GROWTH INDICATORS
2. INFLATION INDICATORS

The market impact of economic data depends mainly on market expectations. To protect yourself against surprises in economic data you need to do the following things:

3. Determine whether the current market environment is ruled by a positive or a negative outlook.
4. Try to find out the positioning in the market. The net positioning in the futures market or repo rates can give a good reading of this market positioning.
5. What kind of data impact will cause a squeeze of these positions?

In Chapter 5 on technical analysis I will show the reader which technical analysis techniques I use and why.

REFERENCES

Fair, R.C. (Jan 2001) "Shock effects on stocks, bonds and exchange rates".
JP Morgan, "Global Data Watch Handbook", New York, January 1996
Steiner, B. "Economics and Forecasting", Markets International Ltd., ACI Diploma study material

Chapter **5**

TECHNICAL ANALYSIS TECHNO STRUCTURE (II) OF EUR/USD INTERBANK MARKET ORGANIZATION

5.1   INTRODUCTION

Technical analysis is widely used in financial markets. A chart gives a pictorial record of what has happened in the past. It shows how a market moves in terms of volatility and typical price increments. An important principle of technical analysis is that the current price already reflects all known factors[1].

In this chapter, I will not give an overview of technical analysis. Further, I will not tell the reader which techniques should be used. Reasons:

First of all, I'm not a technical analyst but I'm a user of technical analysis. Everyone has his or her own specialty.

Secondly, the chosen technique is very personal.

Third, there are very good books available in market about technical analysis. I prefer the following ones:

1. S. Nison, "Beyond Candlesticks", John Wiley & Sons, 1994
2. J.D Schwager, "A Complete Guide to the Futures Markets, John Wiley & Sons, 1984
3. J.J. Murphy, "Technical Analysis of the Financial Markets", New York Institute of Finance, 1999
4. M.J. Pring, "Technical Analysis Explained", McGraw- Hill Inc, 1992

The first title is my personal favorite, because I'm a user of Candlesticks as chart and this book instructs the reader about all the ins and outs about this type of chart. The other three titles will give the reader a complete overview of technical analysis and all the techniques used.

In chapter 5.2-5.6, I will show you which techniques I use and why.

---

[1] ACI Diploma, *Economics and Forecasting,* Author: Bob Steiner, Markets International Ltd.

5.2 CHART: CANDLESTICKS

Candlestick charts are constructed like the standard bar chart but with one additional concept. If the close differs from the opening price, a rectangle is created, centered on the high/low bar. If the close is lower than the opening price, the rectangle is filled or shaded in. If the close is higher than the opening level, then rectangle is left unfilled. This rectangle is called the real body[2].
The dark real bodies indicate that the close is lower than the opening and the white real bodies indicate that the close is higher than the opening.

Graph 5.2.1: EUR/USD Daily

Source: Reuters

I use candle charts because they give the best visualization of the market and its sentiment. Large real bodies show where the real weakness in the market was and where stop loss orders got hit. I find candlesticks very helpful when an important support or resistance is tested. A false break is when the body went through the technical level but corrected afterwards, leaving a hair or shadow behind. The real body is

---
[2] ACI Diploma, *Economics and Forecasting,* Author: Bob Steiner, Markets International Ltd.

back above the support level (below the resistance level) only the shadow is through the support or resistance level. In this situation a bar chart will show a break. I only consider a technical level as taken out when a large real body surpasses this level. See the large white body between 11-25 July 2001. A small real body signals that the market is more divided into two camps and no real body at all means that buyers and sellers keep each other in balance (i.e., there is doubt about the direction – see the two working days after 25 July 2001). This is my interpretation of the candle chart. If the reader is interested to know more about candlesticks, I would recommend the book "Beyond Candlesticks" by Nison.

5.3 TRENDS

Graph 5.3.1: EUR/USD Daily

Source: Reuters

EUR/USD is in a down trend, the two downward sloping trend channels show that. A trend channel is a trend line combined with a parallel line[3]. The trend channel in a bear market is the resistance line through the tops and in a bull market the support line though the bottoms[4]. When the support is taken out, this support becomes the new resistance. When the resistance is taken out this resistance becomes the new support. After a break of a technical level, the market tests this breakout level again (pullback). See in the above graph between 11-25 July 2001, the large white body is followed three days later by a pullback (small dark body with large shadow).

Further I utilize a simple moving average. In a downtrend, the moving average will be consistently above the price and in an uptrend, consistently below the price[5]. The crossing of the moving average line by the price therefore alerts the chartist to a change in nature of the trend[6]. For examples see the working day before 11 July 2001 and between 19 September – 3 October 2001. Moving averages can also be viewed in terms of providing support and resistance.

---

[3] Central Desk Technical Analysis, ABN AMRO, Presentation
[4] Central Desk Technical Analysis, ABN AMRO, Presentation
[5] ACI Diploma, *Economics and Forecasting,* Author: Bob Steiner, Markets International Ltd.
[6] ACI Diploma, *Economics and Forecasting,* Author: Bob Steiner, Markets International Ltd.

5.4 TRADING RANGES

Graph 5.4.1: EUR/CHF Weekly

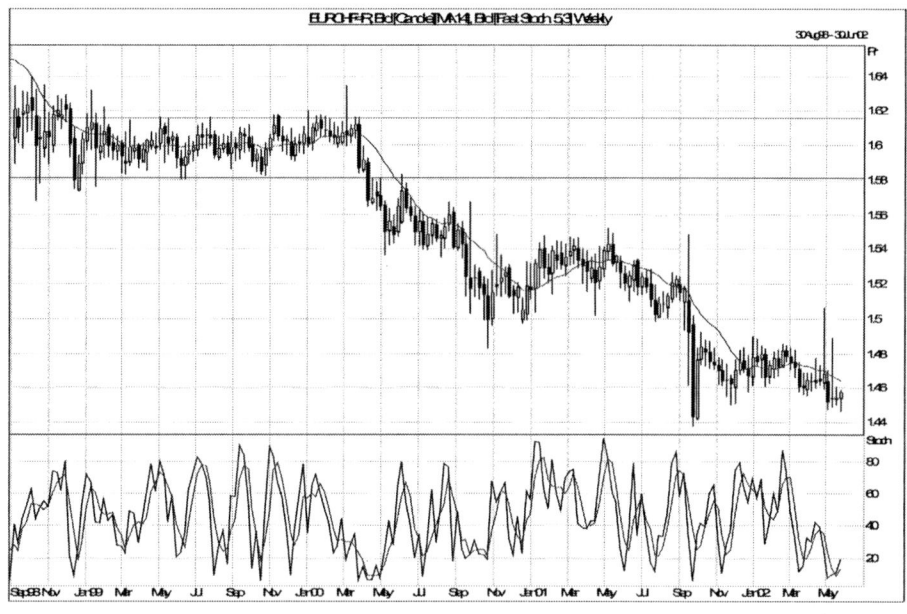

Source: Reuters

A trading range means that price action is between two horizontal lines of equal tops (upper band) and equal bottoms (lower band). In situations where a market is moving in ranges, I find the momentum indicator stochastics very useful. A momentum indicator measures the speed in prices to determine 'in advance' tops and bottoms[7]. For the rationale behind the stochastics see the books "A Complete Guide to the Futures Markets" of Schwager, "Technical Analysis of the Financial Markets" of Murphy and, "Technical Analysis Explained" of Pring.

This momentum indicator (stochastics) is plotted below the price graph. Crossings of both lines when coming out of overbought (horizontal line on 80) or oversold (horizontal line on 20) situations are important signals and therefore I watch them closely. When the lines are long in overbought or oversold situations this means that the market is trending.

---

[7] Central Desk Technical Analysis, ABN AMRO, Presentation

5.5 CHANGING MARKETS

Graph 5.5.1: EUR/USD Weekly

Source: Reuters

The changing market is the market between the trending market and the trading range. Two examples of changing markets are:
- Break of the downtrend on the 7th of January 2001
- Break of the triangle pattern on the 6th of May 2002.

In the case of changing markets I prefer to look at market patterns such as: triangles, spikes, reversal days, "V" tops and bottoms, double tops and bottoms, head and shoulders, rounded tops and bottoms and island reversals All these patterns are explained in the following books: "A Complete Guide to the Futures Markets" of Schwager, "Technical Analysis of the Financial Markets" of Murphy and, "Technical Analysis Explained" of Pring.

5.6 VOLUME AND OPEN INTEREST

Volume is the number of futures contracts traded during a given time period which is usually a day. Open interest is the number of unliquidated or open contracts in a given futures market. Open interest is the total number of outstanding longs or shorts. Volume and open interest can often give an indication to the future direction of the market[8].

Table 5.6.1[9]

Price	Volume	Open interest	Interpretation
Rising	**Rising**	**Rising**	**Market is strong**
Rising	Falling	Falling	Market is weakening
Falling	Rising	Rising	Market is weak
Falling	Falling	Falling	Market is strengthening

I use the open interest of the futures market as an indicator to estimate the weak side of the market. When there is a large open interest in outstanding long, then the downside is high. Reasons:
- Lack of new buyers.
- Weaker than expected fundamental data or a break of an important technical levels can cause a sharp move down due to large stop loss selling.

---

[8] ACI Diploma, *Economics and Forecasting*, Author: Bob Steiner, Markets International Ltd.
[9] ACI Diploma, *Economics and Forecasting*, Author: Bob Steiner, Markets International Ltd.

SUMMARY 5

As a practicing trader I use the following techniques (combined):
1. Chart:
   – Candlesticks
2. Trend following techniques:
   – Continuation patterns
   – Moving averages
3. Trading range techniques:
   – Stochastics
4. Changing market
   – Patterns
5. Open interest

Technical analysis is used in all the financial markets.

Chapter 6 on Division I (FX Option Market) will cope with the following subjects:
1. The Configuration approach and Division I.
2. The Entrepreneurial approach and Division I
3. The Design approach and Division I.
4. The Positioning approach and Division I.

REFERENCES

Steiner, B. "Economics and Forecasting", Markets International Ltd., ACI Diploma study material

RECOMMENDED BOOKS

Murphy, J.J. (1999). "Technical Analysis of the Financial Markets",
    New York Institute of Finance.
Nison, S. (1994). "Beyond Candlesticks" John Wiley & Sons
Pring, M.J. (1992). "Technical Analysis Explained", McGraw-Hill Inc.
Schwager, J.D. (1984). "A Complete Guide to the Futures Markets",
    John Wiley & Sons.

Chapter **6**

DIVISION I
FX OPTION MARKET

6.1 INTRODUCTION

Division I (FX Option Market) plays one of the major roles in the EUR/USD Interbank Market organization. The role is much larger than a lot of players can imagine, or give credit for. To understand the influence of the FX options on the EUR/USD Interbank Market, specialized knowledge is necessary (mathematics/econometrics and the terminology). The market players or insiders have the knowledge about the market; to translate this for the EUR/USD Interbank Market is not easy, because there are differentiated knowledge levels. (When moving from the FX Spot trading desk to the FX Options desk, one moves into an entirely different world.) The FX Option Market gives us reasons for movements/behavior in the spot market. So, Division I is very important in the EUR/USD Interbank Market organization.

Using a SWOT Analysis, we arrive at the following conclusions:
1. Large expirations support (support or resistance) a level in EUR/USD up to the expiration.
2. Risk reversals can be used as leading indicators when operating around extreme levels. They can also provide extremely important warning signals.
3. Higher volatilities are needed for the break of important levels and are perfect for use as warning signals.
4. Barriers tell you where to expect liquidity holes.
5. Demand of out-of-the-money options are good as leading indicators.
6. German firms tend to be more active in the derivative market from a hedging perspective.

We start this division with the Configuration approach, followed by the Entrepreneurial approach, the Design approach (I + II) and the Positioning approach (I + II). These approaches are explained in chapter 1 and 2.

6.2 CONFIGURATION APPROACH

The structure of an organization can be defined as the different ways in which work is divided into different tasks and how these tasks are coordinated. In the organization Division I, the main product is the FX Options. This is the general product, which can be divided into two sub-products: plain vanilla and exotics. To sell the different sub-products, knowledge is very important.

Organizational parts
Strategic Apex
The managers responsible for the trading desks including FX Option desk are responsible for this division. In practice the FX Option Market makers are the ones who have the real power and the managers are there, specifically, to solve problems between the professionals. The professionals are the real strategic thinkers in this division.

Support Staff
This organizational part has the task to influence the work of others in the organization. they accomplish this by training the personnel in Division I and making sure that the technology is updated so that the Strategic Apex receives live prices and news. Since the object is to get everyone on the same knowledge level and operate from this level, continuous building execution and training is necessary. Further, the **salespeople match the clients and products.**

Techno Structure
The Techno Structure of Division I is the same as for the total EUR/USD Interbank Market organization and can be divided into:
1. Fundamental Analysis
2. Technical Analysis
However, the Techno Structure will not play an important role in this division since the options specialists have the knowledge about the subject. The two specialties are usually not focused in detail around the derivative markets. The professionals develop their own skills.

Middle Line
There is no middle line.

Operating Core
The operating core is the group of professionals, the specialized option traders. The operating core has four main functions:
1. Supply the general FX Option Market product for the production.
2. Transform the general FX Option Market product into the differentiated sub-products.
3. Distribute the differentiated FX Option Market sub-products
4. Provide direct support to input, transformation and output.

Coordination mechanism
The coordination mechanism used in Division I is standardization of skills. Based on these skills, the professionals are able to sell the products.

Decentralization
The decisions are more or less made in the operating core. The professionals in the operating core coordinate their work through standardization of skills. Both are vertically and horizontally decentralized.

Configuration
Division I (FX Option Market) uses the standardization of skills as the coordination mechanism. Further, the Operating Core is the dominant force in the organization based on the high knowledge of the professionals concerning the products that are sold. The power is vertically and horizontally decentralized over the operating core. Division I has a **Professional Configuration** (see chapter 1).

Outcome

Table 6.2.1

Division I: FX Option Market	Definition
Strategic Apex	Option traders
Support Staff	Systems
	Sales force
Techno Structure	Fundamental analysis (Chapter 4)
	Technical analysis (Chapter 5)
Middle Line	-
Operating Core	Plain vanilla option traders
	Exotic option traders
Coordination mechanism	Standardization of skills
Decentralization	Vertically and horizontally decentralized
Configuration	Professional organization
Culture	Market Psychology (Chapter 3)

6.3 ENTREPRENEURIAL APPROACH

The strategists in this division are the professionals or the FX Option traders. They have the knowledge and background to make the decisions about their positions and how they want to price options. Their decisions are based on their view of the market. The following features add to the complexity of the job:
- Their view about the underlying currencies.
- Their view about the volatility in the currency spot market.
- The trader's need to know the levels of large expirations in the market.
- Their need to know the important levels in the Exotic Option Market and which player represents each side.
- An econometric or mathematical background necessary to understand and trade with the financial models and to understand the marketplace.

All these features will be explained within the product and production plan.

6.4 DESIGN APPROACH I: BUSINESS PLAN

Product plan

The products represented within Division I (FX Option Market):
Plain vanilla options
Exotic options

Plain vanilla option

Let's start at the beginning on options. What is an option? An FX Option gives the owner the **right but not the obligation** to exchange one pre-determined currency for another at a pre-determined exchange rate at a specific date in the future[1]. The buyer pays premium for acquisition of this right. In case its exercised, the option seller is obliged to exchange one pre-determined currency for another at the pre-determined. exchange rate.

Call option
A call option gives the holder the right to buy the underlying at a pre-determined exchange rate (strike = X) at a specific date in the future[2]. In FX options a call option on one currency is a put option on the other currency. For example:
EUR call/USD put — is a call on the EUR and at the same time, a put on the USD.

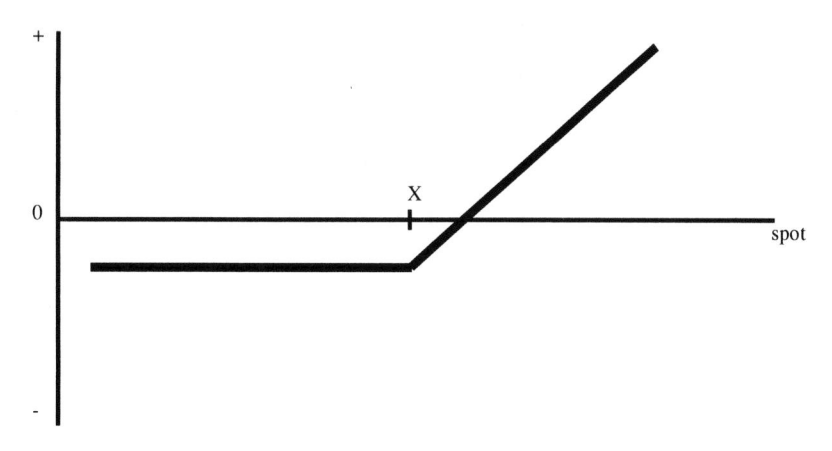

Graph 6.4.1: Payoff of long call option[3]

---
[1] Wim Mesman, ABN AMRO FX Options Marketing Desk, presentation
[2] Wim Mesman, ABN AMRO FX Options Marketing Desk, presentation
[3] Wim Mesman, ABN AMRO FX Options Marketing Desk, presentation

Graph 6.4.2: Payoff of short call option[4]

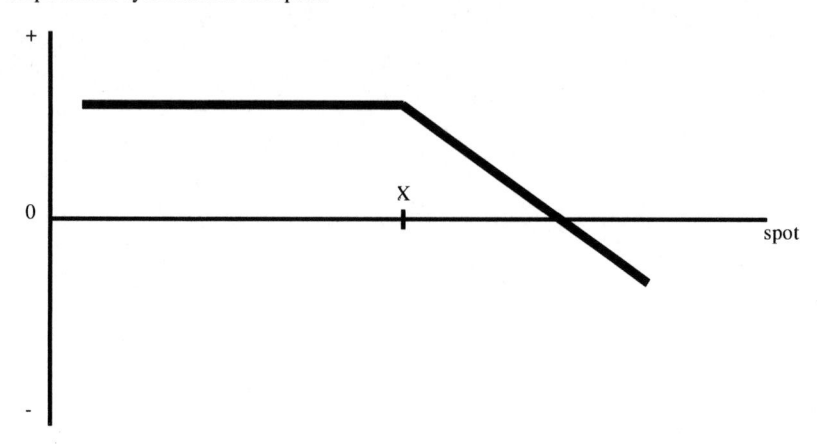

Put option
A put option gives its holder the right to sell the underlying at a pre-determined exchange rate (strike = X) at a specific date in the future[5]. In FX options a call option on one currency is a put option on the other currency. For example:
EUR put/USD call — is a put on the EUR and at the same time, a call on the USD

Graph 6.4.3: Payoff of long put option[6]

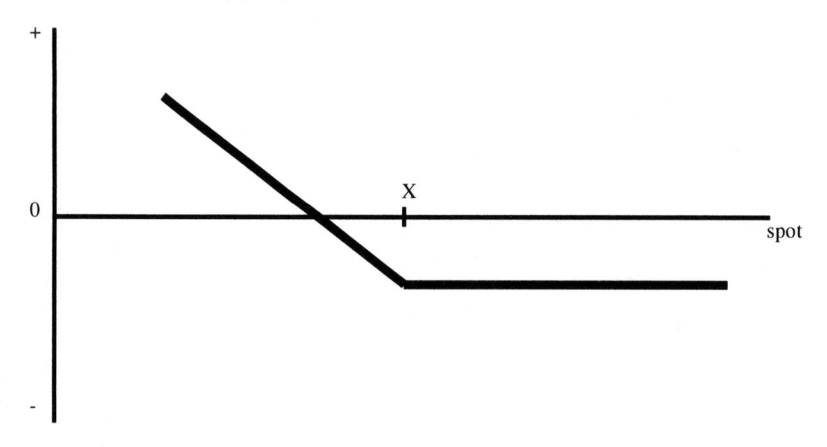

---
[4]Wim Mesman, ABN AMRO FX Options Marketing Desk, presentation
[5]Wim Mesman, ABN AMRO FX Options Marketing Desk, presentation
[6]Wim Mesman, ABN AMRO FX Options Marketing Desk, presentation

Graph 6.4.4: Payoff of short put option[7]

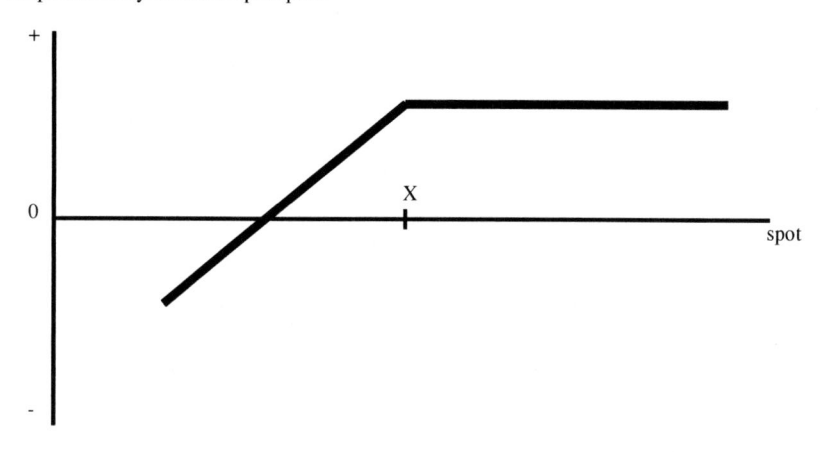

Option strategies
Covered calls and put[8]
To sell a call or a put without any underlying exposure is to write a *naked option*. A covered call or put arises when the writer has an offsetting position in the underlying; such as: a long position in the underlying to offset the selling of a call, or a short position in the underlying to offset the selling of a put. If that's not clear, look at it as the sale of a covered call or put can be used as yield enhancement, to increase income by receiving an option premium.

Graph 6.4.5: Covered call, long underlying (dashed line) + short call option (solid line)[9]

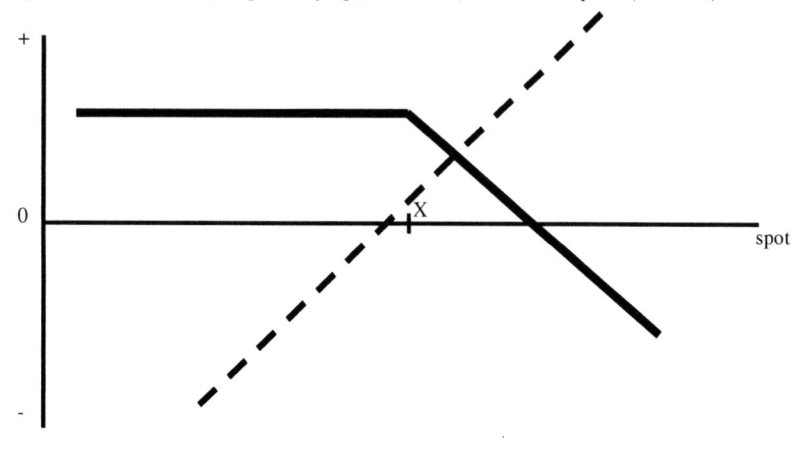

---
[7] Wim Mesman, ABN AMRO FX Options Marketing Desk, presentation
[8] ACI study material, *Options*, Author: Bob Steiner, Markets International Ltd.
[9] Wim Mesman, ABN AMRO FX Options Marketing Desk, presentation

Chapter 6

Spread[10]
Spreads involve the simultaneous purchase and sale of two different calls or two different puts. Let's look at several kinds.

A *long call spread* is the purchase of a call at one strike price, offset by the simultaneous sale of a call at another strike less in-the-money (or more out-of-the-money) than the first. This limits the potential gain if the underlying goes up, but the premium received from selling the second call partly finances the purchase of the first call. A call spread may be advantageous if the purchaser thinks there is only limited upside in the underlying purchase.

A *put spread* is similarly the simultaneous purchase of a put at one strike, offset by the simultaneous sale of a put less in the money than the first.
A *bull spread* is either the purchase of a call spread or the sale of a put spread.
A *bear spread* is either the sale of a call spread or the purchase of a put spread.
A *calendar spread* is the purchase of a call (or put) and the simultaneous sale of a call (or put) with the same strike but a different maturity. This is a volatility strategy. Also combinations of different strikes and different maturities are possible. Keep in mind the different types of spreads, as we will discuss them in several places throughout the book.

Straddle[11]
Straddle is the buy of both put and call at the same strike price. In return for paying two premiums, the buyer benefits if the underlying moves far enough in either direction. It is a trade, which expects increased volatility.

Graph 6.4.6: Long straddle, long call (black) + long put (grey) option[12]

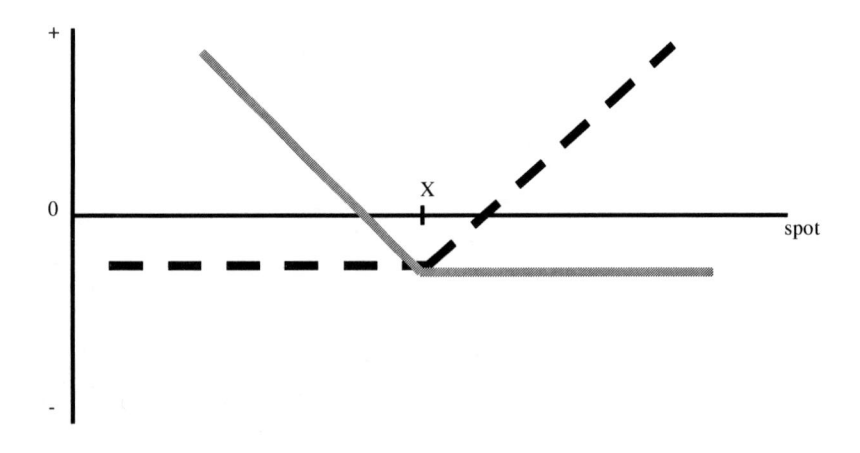

---

[10]ACI study material, *Options*, Author: Bob Steiner, Markets International Ltd.
[11]ACI study material, *Options*, Author: Bob Steiner, Markets International Ltd.
[12]Wim Mesman, ABN AMRO FX Options Marketing Desk, presentation

Strangle[13]
A strangle is similar to the straddle but the premiums are reduced by setting the two strikes apart, generally each strike will be out-of the money. Profits are only generated on a long strangle position if the underlying moves significantly.

Butterfly spread[14]
A butterfly spread is to purchase an out-of-the-money strangle and simultaneously sell an at-the-money straddle. This is equivalent to the purchase of a put spread and the simultaneous sale of a call spread. This strategy profits if the underlying remains stable, and has limited risk in the event of a large move in either direction. It is a volatility strategy and is considered to be directionally neutral.

Risk reversal
The risk reversal is an option strategy, in which you buy the call option and sell the put option or vice versa. This strategy is used by professional traders when it is expected that the preference will turn more in favor for the calls when the call is bought and the put is sold. Risk reversals are also used as zero-cost construction proposals for clients. One option is bought to hedge the client's position and the other option is sold to reduce the cost of the hedge. However, the client is giving up profit potential on his/her existing position. If the put option is bought and the call option is sold, the player expects that the preference in the market will change in favor for or more in favor for, puts.

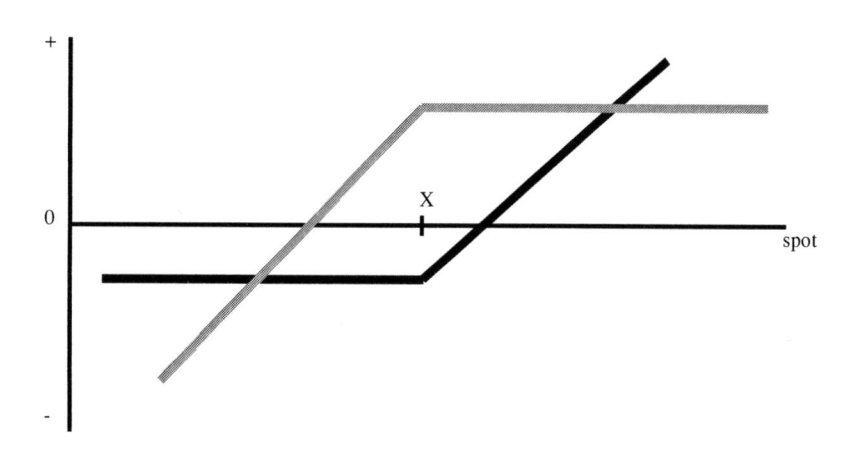

Graph 6.4.7: Risk reversal, long the call (black) + short the put (grey) option[15]

---

[13]ACI study material, *Options*, Author: Bob Steiner, Markets International Ltd.
[14]ACI study material, *Options*, Author: Bob Steiner, Markets International Ltd.
[15]Wim Mesman, ABN AMRO FX Options Marketing Desk, presentation

Exotic options

This product plan will not describe all the existing exotic options. The only exotic options which significantly influence EUR/USD movements in today's financial climate are:
- Barrier options
- Binary options (or digital options)

Barrier options
A barrier option is a general term for a family of path-dependent options, which are either canceled or activated if the underlying price reaches a pre-determined level. They are also known as *knock-out, knock-in* or *trigger options* and are usually straightforward European options until, or from the time the underlying reaches the barrier price[16]. Knock-in options become active if the underlying hits or crosses the barrier and knock-out options die if the underlying hits or crosses the barrier. There are four major types: up-and-out, up-and-in, down-and-out and down-and-in[17]. An option that dies in the money is called a reverse barrier, and the one that dies out-of-the-money is a regular barrier. A reverse barrier, also called nasty barrier, is difficult to hedge, a nice barrier is not. Most of the barrier options are American style options as far as the trigger concerns.

Graph 6.4.8: Knock-out call option[18]

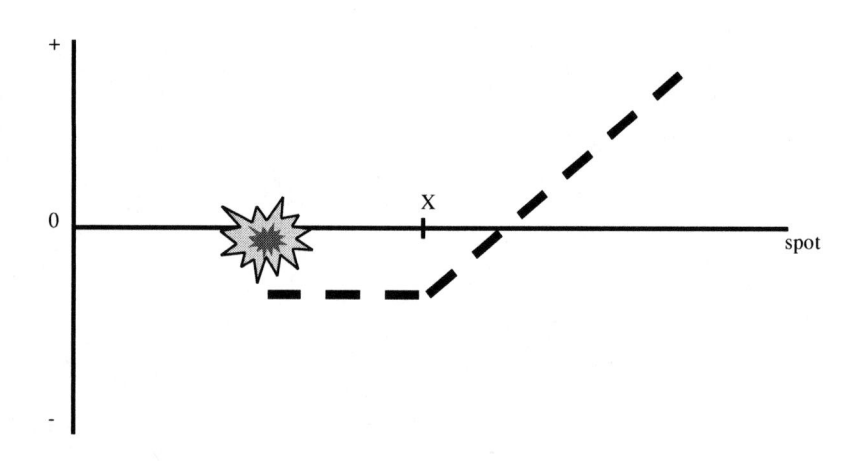

---

[16]ACI study material, *Options*, Author: Bob Steiner, Markets International Ltd.
[17]ACI study material, *Options*, Author: Bob Steiner, Markets International Ltd.
[18]Wim Mesman, ABN AMRO FX Options Marketing Desk, presentation

Graph 6.4.9: Reverse knock-out call option[19]

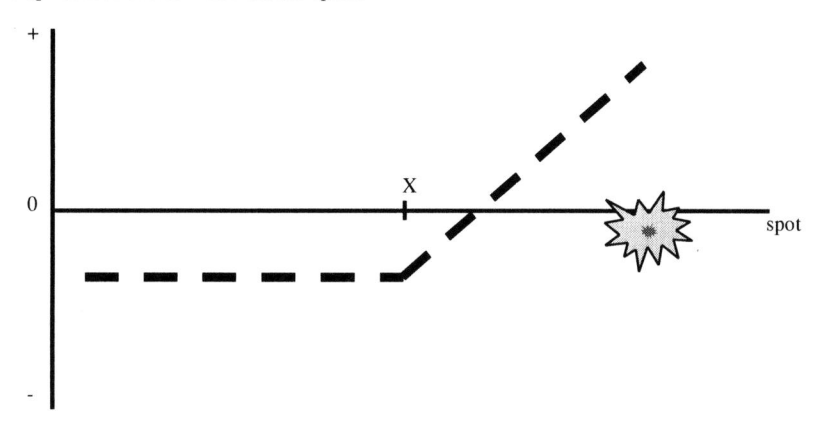

Binary options (or digital options)

A binary option has a discountinuous pay-out and pays out a fixed amount if the underlying reaches the strike. The two major forms are all-or-nothing and one-touch options. All-or-nothing options pay out a set amount if the underlying is above or below a certain point at expiry (digital option). One-touch options pay out a fixed amount if, at any time during the life of the option, the underlying reaches a certain point[20].

There are different types of touch options: one-touch, double touch, no-touch, double no-touch, touch and no-touch combined. Binary options are frequently combined with other instruments like deposits to create structured products.

---

[19]Wim Mesman, ABN AMRO FX Options Marketing Desk, presentation
[20]ACI study material, *Options*, Author: Bob Steiner, Markets International Ltd.

Production plan

The production plan describes everything that's needed to sell the products mentioned in product plan.
1. Strike
2. Expiration date
3. OTC/Exchange traded
4. Volatility
5. Intrinsic value
6. Extrinsic value
7. Pricing models
8. Greeks
9. Volatility smiles
10. Dynamic hedging

Strike[21]

The pre-determined exchange rate – at which the owner of the option can buy in case of a call option or sell in case of a put option – is the strike price or strike. The strike is the variable that is decided by the customer. An option is at-the-money (ATM = 50 delta), in the money (ITM, > 50 delta) or out-of-the-money (OTM, <50 delta) according to how its strike price compares with the current foreign exchange rate. An option is OTM if its strike price compares unfavorably (for the option holder) with the current foreign exchange rate. An option is ITM if its strike price compares favorably with the foreign exchange rate. An option is ATM if its strike price is the same as the current foreign exchange rate. These option explanations, ATM, ITM and OTM options are based on the spot level (for American style options). However, for European style options, the strike will be compared with the forward rate to decide if the option is ATM, ITM or OTM. An option will be exercised if it is ITM. An ATM option can also be exercised by the trader if this is more profitable to do so than buy or sell the position in the spot market (depending on the spread in the spot market).

Table 6.4.1

	Put	Call
Spot < Strike	ITM	OTM
Spot = Strike	ATM	ATM
Spot > Strike	OTM	ITM

Expiration date[22]
The expiration date is the date on which the option ends. An American option can be exercised at any time up to and including its expiration date. A European option can be exercised only on its expiration date. Most of the exchange traded options are American style and most of the OTC options are European style.

---
[21]Wim Mesman, FX Options Marketing Desk, presentation
[22]Wim Mesman, FX Options Marketing Desk, presentation

OTC or exchange traded[23]

The differerence between OTC options and those traded on an exchange is parallel to the difference between forwards (tailormade) and futures (standardized). In case of an exchange traded option, the underlying may be the corresponding futures contract or cash currency. Exchange traded options may be either European or American. On London International Financial Futures and Options Exchange (LIFFE), most options are American. On the IMM (Chicago Mercantile Exchange) the option buyer pays a premium up front as with an OTC option but pays no variation margin. However, on LIFFE the premium is effectively paid via the variation margin.

Volatility

Volatility measures the speed of the market by calculating the standard deviation of the return. Volatility is the standard deviation (σ) expressed as a percentage of spot on an annual basis[24].

Let's assume that EUR/$ spot rate is 0.9195
1 Week forward = 0.9200, Volatility = 14%
1σ = Fwd * vol annualized * $\sqrt{days/365}$ = 0.9200 * 14% * $\sqrt{7/365}$ = 0.0178
With a 68.3% certainty the €/$ range will be (1σ):   0.9022-0.9378
With a 95.4% certainty the range will be (2σ):   0.8844-0.9556

In the market there are two types of volatilities[25]:
– Historical volatility (actual)
– Implied volatility
    Traded in the inter-bank market
    Used to calculate option prices
    Given all other variables, it can be calculated back through the option pricing model

The higher the volatility the higher the probability that the option will end up in-the-money.

Table 6.4.2

Period	Volitility or Risk Reversal	Correlation with EUR/USD based on Reuters daily data
26/05/99-31/10/01	Volatility	-0.52
03/01/00-31/10/01	Risk Reversal	0.30
03/01/00-31/10/01	Volatility * Risk Reversal	0.26

---

[23]ACI Diploma, *Chapter Options*, Author: Bob Steiner, Markets International Ltd.
[24]Wim Mesman, FX Options Marketing Desk, presentation
[25]Wim Mesman, FX Options Marketing Desk, presentation

Graph 6.4.10: EUR/USD versus 1-month volatility * risk reversal

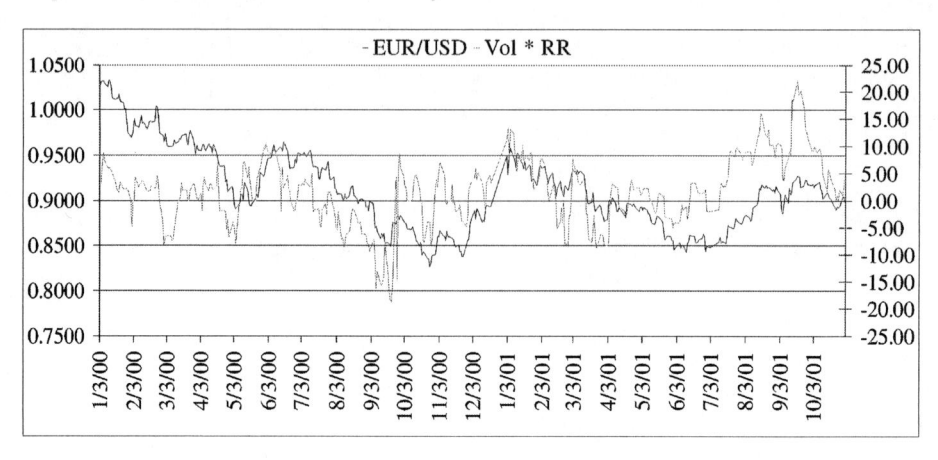

[Graph showing EUR/USD and Vol * RR from 1/3/00 to 10/3/01, with EUR/USD scale from 0.7500 to 1.0500 on the left axis and Vol * RR scale from -25.00 to 25.00 on the right axis]

Source: Reuters

Intrinsic value[26]
The intrinsic value is the difference between strike price and forward. This value can never be less than zero.

Extrinsic value[27]
The extrinsic value is the additional value above the intrinsic value (=optionality). This is depending on the time to maturity (time value) and the volatility.

Graph 6.4.11: Intrinsic and extrinsic value[28]

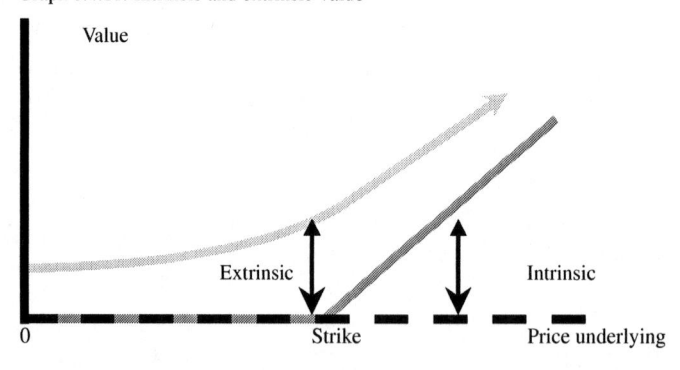

[Diagram showing Value on the y-axis, with curves illustrating Extrinsic value near the Strike point and Intrinsic value increasing with Price underlying]

---

[26] Wim Mesman, FX Options Marketing Desk, presentation
[27] Wim Mesman, FX Options Marketing Desk, presentation
[28] Wim Mesman, FX Options Marketing Desk, presentation

Pricing models

Black & Scholes

The most widely used pricing model for straightforward options was derived by Fischer Black and Myron Scholes and iis known as the Black-Scholes formula[29].

Figure 6.4.12: Black & Scholes[30]

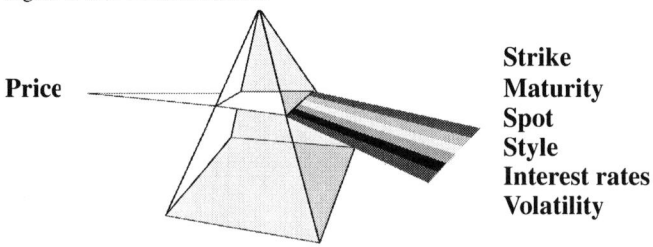

Price

**Strike
Maturity
Spot
Style
Interest rates
Volatility**

Black & Scholes formula uses the probability distribution of a given currency pair to price options on that currency. The returns of the assets follow a random walk; e.g., they are normally distributed. The 'forward price' is the mean of the distribution and asset prices are log-normally distributed; e.g., they cannot be negative[31]. Volatility and interest rates remain constant throughout the life of the option and there are no transaction costs[32].

Graph 6.4.13: Normal distribution[33]

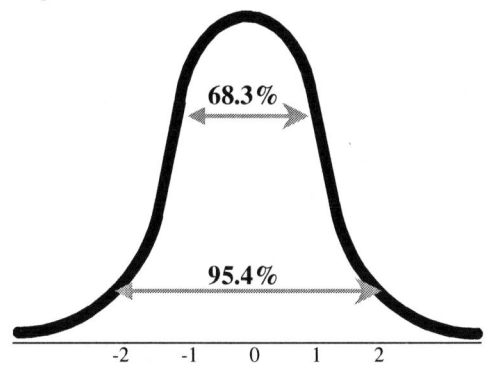

68.3%

95.4%

-2 -1 0 1 2

---

[29]ACI Diploma, *Chapter Options*, Author: Bob Steiner, Markets International Ltd.
[30]Wim Mesman, FX Options Marketing Desk, presentation
[31]Wim Mesman, FX Options Marketing Desk, presentation
[32]ACI Diploma, *Chapter Options*, Author: Bob Steiner, Markets International Ltd.
[33]Wim Mesman, FX Options Marketing Desk, presentation

The normal distribution is entirely characterized by its first two moments, the mean and the volatility. The moments of an option position represent the sensitivity to some order of change in the underlying security[34].

Binomial trees (Cox & Ross)[35]
One way of building a model for option pricing is to simplify the assumptions to the possibility that the price of something may move up a certain extent or down a certain extent in a particular time period.

Put/call relationship[36]
Call premium–put premium = (forward price – strike price) discounted to a present value.
Call premium–put premium = spot price - (strike price discounted to a present value)
Sell forward + buy call + sell put = 0
Buy forward = buy call + sell put
Sell forward = sell call + buy put

Synthetic forwards:
Buying a call and selling a put at the same strike creates a synthetic forward purchase and vice versa.

Buy call =	buy put + buy forward
Sell call =	sell put + sell forward
Buy put =	buy call + sell forward
Sell put =	sell call + buy forward

Greeks

Table 6.4.3[37]

Greeks	Explanation
Delta	Change in price of the option for a change in spot (1st moment of an option position)
Vega	Change in price of the option for a change in volatility
Gamma	Change in delta for a change in spot (2nd moment of an option position)
Theta	Time decay of the option
Phi & Rho	Interest rate sensitivity
dVega/dVol	Change in vega for a change in volatility
dVega/dSpot	Change in vega for a change in spot

---

[34]Taleb, Nassim, "DYNAMIC HEDGING: Managing Vanilla and Exotic Options", Copyright © 1997 by Nassim Taleb. Reprinted by permission of John Wiley & Sons, Inc.
[35]ACI Diploma, *Chapter Options*, Author: Bob Steiner, Markets International Ltd.
[36]ACI Diploma, *Chapter Options*, Author: Bob Steiner, Markets International Ltd.
[37]Wim Mesman, FX Options Marketing Desk, presentation

Delta[38]
- Long a Call
  - Delta is a positive number between 0 (OTM) and 100 (ITM)
  - Delta hedge is to sell underlying
- Short a Call
  - Delta is a negative number between 0 (OTM) and 100 (ITM)
  - Delta hedge is to buy underlying
- Long a Put
  - Delta is a negative number between 0 (OTM) and 100 (ITM)
  - Delta hedge is to buy underlying
- Short a Put
  - Delta is a positive number between 0 (OTM) and 100 (ITM)
  - Delta hedge is to sell underlying
- At maturity Delta is either 0 or (-)100

Vega[39]
Vega is positive when long an option (Call or Put).
Vega is almost 0 for short dated OTM or ITM options.
Vega is higher when:
- The option strike is near the forward.
- The maturity is long.
- Vega is linear for ATM option: same price increase for each increase in volatility

Vega decreases with passage of time.

Gamma[40]
Gamma is small for deep OTM or deep ITM options.
Gamma is positive for long option positions (Call or Put) and negative for short calls and short puts.
An option with a high gamma if difficult to delta hedge if the spot is volatile.

Theta[41]
Theta is negative for long option postions and positive for a short option position.
The more the market and strike prices diverge, the less effect time value has on an option's price. ATM options have the highest time time value and the highest theta.
Positive theta is generally associated with negative gamma.
Theta is higher when the volatility is higher.

---

[38] Wim Mesman, FX Options Marketing Desk, presentation
[39] Wim Mesman, FX Options Marketing Desk, presentation
[40] Wim Mesman, FX Options Marketing Desk, presentation
ACI Diploma, *Chapter Options*, Author: Bob Steiner, Markets International Ltd.
[41] Wim Mesman, FX Options Marketing Desk, presentation
ACI Diploma, *Chapter Options*, Author: Bob Steiner, Markets International Ltd.

Rho & Phi[42]
- Rho is the sensitiveness for domestic interest.
- Phi is the sensitiveness for foreign interest.
- Rho tends to increase with maturity.

dVega/dVol[43]
- The change in vega if volatility changes (also gamma of vega).
- When dVega/dVol is positive we get longer Vega if the volatility goes up and vice versa.

dVega/dSpot[44]
- The change in vega for a change in spot level.
- This is dependent on the direction of the risk reversal.

Volatility smiles[45]

The holes in the Black & Scholes formula are:
- Fat tails:
    - The tails of the actual distribution lay above the normal distribution.
    - This is the fourth moment, gamma of gamma[46].
    - The tails will represent the general pricing of the wings[47] (ITM and OTM optons).
- Skewed distribution
    - The implied skew will measure the degree of asymmetry of the distribution.
    - The skew is the delta of the gamma[48].

---

[42]Wim Mesman, FX Options Marketing Desk, presentation
[43]Wim Mesman, FX Options Marketing Desk, presentation
[44]Wim Mesman, FX Options Marketing Desk, presentation
[45]Wim Mesman, FX Options Marketing Desk, presentation
[46]Taleb, Nassim, "DYNAMIC HEDGING: Managing Vanilla and Exotic Options", Copyright © 1997 by Nassim Taleb. Reprinted by permission of John Wiley & Sons, Inc.
[47]Taleb, Nassim, "DYNAMIC HEDGING: Managing Vanilla and Exotic Options", Copyright © 1997 by Nassim Taleb. Reprinted by permission of John Wiley & Sons, Inc.
[48]Taleb, Nassim, "DYNAMIC HEDGING: Managing Vanilla and Exotic Options", Copyright © 1997 by Nassim Taleb. Reprinted by permission of John Wiley & Sons, Inc.

The volatility on Information Screens are annualised, implied and for at the money forward (ATMF) straddles. For different deltas, the market uses different volatilities.
- To deal with one of the holes in Black & Scholes (fat tails)
- To reflect the illiquidity in the market for low delta options
- The market has a memory

Usually a higher volatility is used for lower deltas. This is reflected in the 25 delta Strangles. Sometimes there is a bias for Calls (positive) or for Puts (negative). This is reflected in the 25 delta Risk Reversals.

Example:
ATMF volatility in €/$ 9.0%
Risk reversal   +1.50 (bias for calls)
Strangle   0.25

What is the volatility for 50 delta Call/Put?
50 delta Call/Put volatility = ATMF volatility = 9.0%
What is the volatility for 25 delta Call?
25 delta Call volatility = ATMF + Strangle + (RR/2)
= 9.0% + 0.25% + (1.5/2) = 10.0%
What is the volatility for 25 delta Put?
25 delta Put volatility = ATMF + Strangle - (RR/2)
= 9.0% + 0.25% - (1.5/2) = 8.5%

Dynamic hedging by Nassim Taleb[49] *(highly recommended, a favorite option book)*

Contamination (or Convexity) principle[50]
The fundamental principle of dynamic hedging and option trading is the contamination principle. Roughly defined it means that if there is a possible spot in time and space capable of bringing a profit, then the areas surrounding it need to account for that effect.

Liquidity and liquidity holes
The market is a large movie theater with a small door[51].
Liquidity in a market is defined by the ease with which an operator can enter and exit it for a given block of securities. Slippage is a practitioner's measurement for liquidity. A liquidity hole is a temporary event in the market that suspends the regular mechanism of equilibrium attainment[52].

---

[49]Taleb, Nassim, "DYNAMIC HEDGING: Managing Vanilla and Exotic Options", Copyright © 1997 by Nassim Taleb. Reprinted by permission of John Wiley & Sons, Inc.
[50]Taleb, Nassim, "DYNAMIC HEDGING: Managing Vanilla and Exotic Options", Copyright © 1997 by Nassim Taleb. Reprinted by permission of John Wiley & Sons, Inc.
[51]Taleb, Nassim, "DYNAMIC HEDGING: Managing Vanilla and Exotic Options", Copyright © 1997 by Nassim Taleb. Reprinted by permission of John Wiley & Sons, Inc.
[52]Taleb, Nassim, "DYNAMIC HEDGING: Managing Vanilla and Exotic Options", Copyright © 1997 by Nassim Taleb. Reprinted by permission of John Wiley & Sons, Inc.

Barrier options and binary options can be responsible for liquidity holes. Example: the following knock-out call is bought by option trader.

Currency pair	EUR/USD
Period	3 months
Strike	0.8500
Barrier/trigger	0.9000
Stop loss order	0.9000

To hedge this option the option trader needs to sell the currency spot depending on the options delta. When spot moves higher the option trader needs to hedge more (dynamic hedging) because the option becomes less OTM or more ITM. When spot hits the level of 0.9000, the option dies and the option trader has, all of sudden, a short position in the underlying. To unwind this position the option trader left a stop loss buy order with the currency trader for the amount of the total hedge. A concentration of barriers could have a concentration of stop losses in that area. The triggering of large stop losses linked to barriers can cause a liquidity hole

Sticky strikes[53]
Sticky strikes are strikes in which the buildup of a large open interest alters the behavior of the market around the strike price near expiration. As expiration nears, traders will need to buy all their deltas below and sell all of them above the strike, and the underlying will tend to stick around the strike.

Barriers[54]
Long the barrier means that the operator benefits from the hitting of the trigger. The delta of a barrier option is switching sign as the underlying price comes closer to the barrier level. This occurs because close to the barrier the option structure weakens and is dominated by the bet. Instability increases at the barrier and the delta on expiration day can reach the 2000 level.

---

[53]Taleb, Nassim, "DYNAMIC HEDGING: Managing Vanilla and Exotic Options", Copyright © 1997 by Nassim Taleb. Reprinted by permission of John Wiley & Sons, Inc.
[54]Taleb, Nassim, "DYNAMIC HEDGING: Managing Vanilla and Exotic Options", Copyright © 1997 by Nassim Taleb. Reprinted by permission of John Wiley & Sons, Inc.

Marketing plan

Clients[55]

Corporates, investors and fund managers
Investors and asset managers are on the buy side in this market. To lower their hedging costs they use exotic options. Exotic options are cheaper than plain vanilla options and are more tailormade. It is very important to match the clients risk profile with the appropriate strategy.

FX option traders
The traders are usually interested in collecting the option premiums.

Private clients
Private clients use mainly plain vanilla options as yield enhancement. However the price of the yield enhancement is unlimited currency market risk which can have unlimited loss potential as a result; or, can have limited profit potential (covered writing).

Hedge funds
Hedge funds use plain vanilla and exotic options for proprietary trading and position. They can be on both sides of the market based on their model/view.

---

[55] Wim Mesman, FX Options Marketing Desk, presentation

Outcome Business Plan

Table 6.4.4: Business Plan

Business Plan	Questions	Answers
Product plan	Products?	Plain vanilla options
		Exotic options
Production plan	What's needed?	Strike
		Expiration date
		OTC/Exchange traded
		Volatility
		Intrinsic value
		Extrinsic value
		Time value
		Pricing models
		Greeks
		Volatility smiles
		Dynamic hedging
Marketing plan	Clients?	Investors and asset managers, derivative dealers, non-dealers financials, non-financial institution, portfolio managers, hedge funds, private clients.
	Competitors?	Division II (Commodity Market)
		Division III (Equity Market)
		Division IV (International Debt Market)
		Division V (S-T-I-R Market)

Strategy:
Division I offers enormous possibilities to use options for hedging or speculation. To understand the different products, significant knowledge is needed.

6.5   DESIGN APPROACH II: SWOT ANALYSIS

FX Option market as driver of the EUR/USD Interbank Market

Strengths

The following features of the market are able to explain the movements in EUR/USD.
1. Volatilities
2. Large expirations
3. Risk reversals
4. Barriers
5. Demand for OTM options and Exotics
6. Hedging activity

Volatilities

Table 6.5.1: Volatility levels (1-month volatility)

Date	Volatility
29 Nov 1999	Vols moved sharply higher after Friday's action in EUR/USD, where a fresh low was set at 1.0073.
02 Dec 1999	Vols moved higher as spot moved towards lower territory.
03 Dec 1999	Vols jumped as spot touched sub-parity levels.
31 Jan 2000	1-month volatility jumped from 10.70 to 12.60 as spot made a new low of 0.9668.
25 Feb 2000	After lunch time there was a lot of demand for short-term volatilities in the broker market. The 1-month volatility surged higher from 11.65 to 12.20.
28 Feb 2000	In Asia time EUR/USD dropped to a low of 0.9390 and the 1-month volatility spiked to 15.25.
10 Apr 2000 04 May 2000	In this period the 1-month volatility moves up from 11.85 to 15.10. The high in spot was 0.9627 and the low 0.8844.
29 May 2000	Vols moved sharply higher as spot rallied through 0.9200 resistance. There were even 15.00 bids seen in the 1-month.
13 Jul 2000 22 Sep 2000	The 1-month volatility moved from 10.2 (13 Jul 2000) to a high of 16.2 on intervention day 22 Sep 2000.
17 Oct 2000 30 Oct 2000	The 1-month volatility moved from 14.70 to high of 16.40. In the meantime spot moved from high 0.8560 on 17 Oct 2000 to all time low of 0.8225 on 26 Oct 2000. The maximum 1-month risk reversal in this period was 0.50 for EUR puts
11 Sep 2001	The terrorist attacks caused high volatilities and a large spread. Further, the liquidity dried up.
17 Sep 2001	Volatilities headed higher as tension built up. Liquidity was scarce. The 1-month volatility spiked to 13.75-14.25 from 12.4–13.0. EUR/USD rallied to 0.9250.
18 Sep 2001	Volatilities on renewed intervention fears. The 1-month jumped from 14.4 to 14.7. Spot rallied to a high of 0.9335.

Source: Reuters, EUR/USD and volatility daily data

The behavior of the volatilities in the FX Option Market will give signals to the spot market. When the spot market is close to a technical resistance or support level the volatility will tell if the market is willing to try to break the level or not. To break a significant technical level, a higher volatility is necessary. The market volatility can turn out to be higher in down moves than in up movements. If EUR/USD is in a down move for quite a long time and the risk reversal is in favor for puts, than the volatilities will spike up when the market tries to move lower. A market correction opposite from the long-term trend will usually not be supported by higher volatilities as long as the market believes that the current trend is still valid. From 26 May 1999 up to now the low in 1-month volatility was 8.35, the high 16.40 and the average 11.88.

Large expirations (with New York cut, 10.00 a.m.)

Table 6.5.2: Large expirations[56]

Date	Large expiration	Open EUR/$	High EUR/$	Low EUR/$	Close EUR/$
29 Nov 1999	1.0200 good size	1.0153	1.0200	1.0034	1.0093
30 Nov 1999	1.0000	1.0094	1.0144	1.0040	1.0089
01 Dec 1999	1.0000 One Touch expiration 1,000 very good size	1.0091	1.0127	1.0042	1.0076
02 Dec 1999	1.0000 1 billion EUR	1.0081	1.0107	0.9995	1.0008
18 Feb 2000	0.9800 1 billion EUR	0.9877	0.9900	0.9804	0.9862
24 Feb 2000	0.9800 3 billion EUR	1.0034	1.0040	0.9886	0.9929
25 Feb 2000	0.9800 2.2 billion EUR	0.9926	0.9927	0.9720	0.9742
01 Mar 2000	0.9600 good size	0.9643	0.9767	0.9623	0.9734
03 Mar 2000	0.9600 good size 0.9650 good size	0.9645	0.9677	0.9585	0.9597
10 Mar 2000	0.9580 fair size 0.9680 fair size	0.9665	0.9685	0.9595	0.9628
30 Mar 2000	0.9600 good size 0.9600 small	0.9508	0.9621	0.9505	0.9609
05 Apr 2000	0.9600 small 0.9700 fair size	0.9612	0.9710	0.9590	0.9621
04 May 2000	0.8850 good size 0.8950 small	0.8954	0.8973	0.8844	0.8907
24 May 2000	0.9100 good size	0.9068	0.9127	0.9024	0.9030
25 May 2000	0.9000 good size	0.9029	0.9135	0.8974	0.9125
30 May 2000	0.9350 good size	0.9268	0.9410	0.9236	0.9298
02 Jun 2000	0.9500 good size	0.9312	0.9504	0.9292	0.9463
29 Jun 2000	0.9500 good size	0.9414	0.9536	0.9411	0.9517
24 Jul 2000	0.9325 good size	0.9360	0.9374	0.9307	0.9335
08 Aug 2001	0.8770/80 small 0.8800 good size	0.8776	0.8808	0.8733	0.8802
08 Aug 2001	Market talk of large expiration at 0.8750.	0.8776	0.8808	0.8733	0.8802
20 Aug 2001	0.9050 good size 0.9150 good size	0.9175	0.9202	0.9106	0.9145
24 Aug 2001	0.9150/60 modest size	0.9145	0.9164	0.9070	0.9148
11 Sep 2001	Large expirations around 0.9050 level.	0.8982	0.9169	0.8947	0.9140

Source: Reuters EUR/USD daily data

---

[56]ABN AMRO FX Options Marketing Desk, *FX Options Levels*

The last Friday of February 2000, options players reported a large expiration strike 0.9800 to roll off at 16.00 European time. The market started higher that day but a worse than expected Eurozone figure had put EUR/USD under pressure. After lunch time, there was a lot of demand for short-term volatilities and EUR puts in the broker market; this caused the risk reversals turning for puts. The 1-month volatilities spiked from 11.65 to 15.25. Large demand for short-dated volatilities is a signal that barriers are involved. The large expiration protected EUR/USD against going lower. At the time the expiration was rolled off, EUR/USD soon broke 0.9800 level the low at 0.9725. Market players were talking about the existence of a lot of barriers on the downside. However they wouldn't exist for long. The next Monday morning, in illiquid trade, EUR/USD was pushed, in one move, down to a low of 0.9390—crossing all the barriers in this move. When all other market players came in the market, the market was back around 0.9700 level. The rumor was that a party had interest to trigger the barrier of his/her knock-in put with a strike on a much higher level. This kind of market behavior is only possible in Friday afternoon/ evening trade and Monday early morning trade.

Risk reversals

Table 6.5.3: Risk Reversal information[57] Source: Reuters EUR/USD daily data

Date	Risk reversal	Open EUR/$	High EUR/$	Low EUR/$	Close EUR/$
29 Nov 1999	1-month risk reversal has moved in favor of puts EUR/USD calls.	1.0153	1.0200	1.0034	1.0093
01 Dec 1999	1-month risk reversals are heading more and more for puts. Even 3 months risk reversal is around puts EUR.	1.0091	1.0127	1.0042	1.0076
01 Feb 2000	1 month risk reversal moved to 0.40 for EUR puts, and also 3 months is for EUR puts.	0.9701	0.9780	0.9660	0.9721
25 Feb 2000	After lunch there was a lot of demand for EUR puts in the broker market causing the risk reversals turning for puts (0.25).	0.9926	0.9927	0.9720	0.9742
13 Mar 2000	1-month risk reversal flipped to calls EUR/USD puts.	0.9624	0.9728	0.9614	0.9645
20 Apr 2000	1-month risk reversal turned in favor for EUR puts again.	0.9401	0.9423	0.9346	0.9377
08 May 2000	1-month risk reversal flipped to calls EUR/USD puts.	0.8962	0.9045	0.8912	0.8973
31 May 2000	High in 1-month risk reversal of 0.75 for EUR calls.	0.9290	0.9382	0.9255	0.9377
20 Jun 2000	The 1-month risk reversal remained from 31 May-20 Jun 2000 between 0.40-0.75	0.9566	0.9621	0.9526	0.9543
21 Jun 2000	The 1-month risk reversal fell back to around 0.20 and the days later to around 0.0.	0.9540	0.9544	0.9428	0.9442
13 Jul 2000	The 1-month risk reversal turn in favor for EUR puts again.	0.9412	0.9424	0.9320	0.9370
21 Sep 2000	From 13 Jul 2000 the risk reversal moved more and more in favor for EUR put with a high on the 21 Sep 2000 of 1.25 for EUR puts.	0.8491	0.8615	0.8455	0.8614
22 Sep 2000	The 1-month risk reversal moved back to 0.30 for EUR calls as result of the intervention	0.8605	0.9022	0.8568	0.8758
29 Nov 2000	After being around par for some time the 1-month risk reversal moved in favor for EUR calls.	0.8560	0.8658	0.8552	0.8574
03 Jan 2001	The 1-month risk reversal around 0.90 for EUR calls.	0.9506	0.9570	0.9272	0.9281
13 Sep 2001	The 1-month risk reversal around 1.50 for EUR calls.	0.9067	0.9125	0.9044	0.9107
18 Sep 2001	The 1-month risk reversal around 1.60 for EUR calls.	0.9247	0.9282	0.9184	0.9273
19 Sep 2001	The 1-month risk reversal around 1.40 for EUR call. In the past two years previous extremes were near 1.00.	0.9268	0.9325	0.9223	0.9266

---

[57] ABN AMRO FX Options Marketing Desk, *FX Options Levels*

Up to now, a 1-month risk reversal of −1.25 or 1.60 could be seen as at extreme levels. Extreme risk reversal levels can provide the signal that the market will be close to a correction, since this extreme state does not last for long. Market participants need to be aware of the extreme levels of the risk reversal of the currency pair in order to be aware of the risk, and to protect them.

Barriers

Table 6.5.4: Barriers[58]. Source: Reuters EUR/USD daily data

Date	Barriers, exotic triggers	Open EUR/$	High EUR/$	Low EUR/$	Close EUR/$
30 Nov 1999	Some barriers around parity.	1.0094	1.0144	1.0040	1.0089
01 Dec 1999	1.0000 One Touch expiration	1.0091	1.0127	1.0042	1.0076
02 Dec 1999	Much talk in the market of players who are short triggers around 1.0000 and are likely to defend these triggers.	1.0081	1.0107	0.9995	1.0008
03 Dec 1999	Probably triggers are positioned at lower levels.	1.0015	1.0041	0.9987	1.0022
24 Jan 2000	Talk of a lot of barriers in region 0.9950 and lower combined with stop loss orders.	1.0021	1.0075	0.9995	1.0075
25 Jan 2000	Barriers 0.9950 and lower.	1.0073	1.0096	0.9985	1.0003
26 Jan 2000	Barriers 0.9950 and lower.	1.0010	1.0053	0.9989	1.0009
27 Jan 2000	Barriers 0.9950 and lower.	1.0015	1.0027	0.9866	0.9881
28 Jan 2000	Barriers 0.9950 and lower.	0.9875	0.9890	0.9733	0.9745
31 Jan 2000	Barriers 0.9950 and lower.	0.9777	0.9827	0.9668	0.9693
28 Feb 2000	Market cleared the barriers up to 0.9390.	0.9746	0.9746	0.9390	0.9717
20 Apr 2000	Rumors about a large trigger posted at 0.9350.	0.9401	0.9423	0.9346	0.9377
28 Apr 2000	Rumors about big size trigger at 0.9050.	0.9100	0.9140	0.9027	0.9120
01 May 2000	Probably another trigger at 0.9000.	0.9118	0.9171	0.9068	0.9157
21 Dec 2000	Option traders are reporting barriers at 0.9100.	0.9090	0.9172	0.9054	0.9160
08 Jan 2001	Rumors about big size barrier at 0.9600.	0.9574	0.9592	0.9463	0.9476
10 May 2001	Rumor of 0.8800 option protection.	0.8862	0.8921	0.8776	0.8812
12 Jun 2001	Rumor of 0.8400 option protection.	0.8434	0.8539	0.8412	0.8530
14 Aug 2001	Rumors about barriers around 0.9000.	0.8967	0.9036	0.8931	0.9029
23 Aug 2001	Barriers at 0.9250	0.9123	0.9167	0.9096	0.9150

In the period December 1999 – January 2000 EUR/USD touched the magic 1.000 parity level but there was no break. Option traders reported large stop loss orders as result of barrier positions below the parity. Option traders needed to buy spot on the way down until the barrier, and gave stop loss orders for the hedge amount to the spot traders in case the barrier level was taken out. The dynamic hedging of traders was damping the move down; slowing the speed. In fact the buying of the option traders were protecting the level. In this period the market came close to the parity level but, as was said before, there was no break. The market bounced back to 1.0400 level in January before taking a renewed test of the parity level at the end of January. The fourth time there was a break. The liquidity hole caused by the stop loss orders around 0.9950 accelerated the move and a low just below 0.9900 was set. In the coming two days the market reached a low of 0.9684 before back to 1.0080 the end of February. On 8th of January 2001, FX Option Market rumors about 0.9600 protected the barrier. The market tried four times to break this level but had no success. As result the other side of the market was tested.

---

[58]ABN AMRO FX Options Marketing Desk, *FX Options Levels*

Demand for OTM options and Exotics

Table 6.5.5: Option information[59]

Date	Demand	Open EUR/$	High EUR/$	Low EUR/$	Close EUR/$
19 Oct 2000	Investment banks and specialists demand for 1-3 month EUR calls. The low in this period was 0.8225 (26 Oct 2000) and the high 0.9592 (8 Jan 01).	0.8384	0.8452	0.8378	0.8431
27 Oct 2000	Big player has been spotted in the market rounding up short dated EUR calls.	0.8307	0.8441	0.8283	0.8394
18 Jul 2001	Some interest in the 1-month EUR calls.	0.8594	0.8742	0.8563	0.8734
19 Jul 2001	Decent demand for the 3-month EUR calls 0.8900 strike. Large demand to buy the 1-year EUR calls and sell the EUR puts.	0.8740	0.8789	0.8671	0.8709
23 Jul 2001	Decent demand for 3-month EUR call 0.8800 with knock-in 0.8590	0.8703	0.8720	0.8647	0.8689
25 Jul 2001	Buying interest for 1-month EUR call 0.8600 with knockout 0.8465 and 6-month EUR call 0.9000 with knockout 0.8470.	0.8732	0.8812	0.8712	0.8806
27 Jul 2001	Large demand for short dated EUR calls.	0.8774	0.8807	0.8721	0.8774
31 Jul 2001	Selected bids for upside strikes Some interest for 3-month one touch with strike 0.9700.	0.8740	0.8780	0.8718	0.8761
09 Aug 2001	Modest demand for 1-year EUR calls with strikes around parity.	0.8806	0.8941	0.8797	0.8922
13 Aug 2001	Demand for 0.9200 EUR calls in the 2-month and 3-month.	0.8930	0.9008	0.8918	0.8962
14 Aug 2001	Aggressive demand for 1-year EUR calls.	0.8967	0.9036	0.8931	0.9029
20 Aug 2001	Solid demand for EUR calls combined with knockouts	0.9175	0.9202	0.9106	0.9145

Source: Reuters EUR/USD daily data

On the 19th of October 2000, news came into the market that the investment banks and specialists with a 1-3 month time horizon had bought EUR calls that week. On 26th of October, EUR/USD hit an all time low of 0.8225 in very erratic trading. Major players had been spotted in the market, rounding up short dated EUR calls. This means that the party was canceling his short-term outstanding risk coming from call options sold before with a close expiration. Consequently, the party was expecting a sharp move up in price. In the period 27 October-31 October EUR/USD rebounded from 0.8225 to 0.8499.

---

[59] Koon How Heng, *ABN AMRO: An Option a Day report*

Hedging activity

In 1995, Bodnar and Gebhart completed significant research[60] about derivatives usage in risk management by US and German non-financial firms. German firms are more likely to use derivatives than US firms. This is true across all three classes of derivatives: foreign exchange, interest rate and commodity. The general pattern for usage across industry and size is very comparable, suggesting that the general tendency to use derivatives is driven by economic issues such as operational activities and firm characteristics. US firms and German firms indicate that they use derivatives mostly for risk management, differences appear in the primary goal of using derivatives. German firms are focusing more on managing accounting result whereas US firms are focused more on managing cash flows. German firms are more likely to incorporate their own market view on price movement when taking positions with derivatives.

Table 6.5.6

Sales groups	US			Germany		
	Number % of total	Yes % of N	No % of N	Number % of total	Yes % of N	No % of N
> DM10b	30 15.2%	27 90.0%	3 10.0%	36 28.6%	27 75.0%	9 25.0%
DM5b-DM10b	24 12.2%	19 72.9%	5 20.8%	18 14.3%	17 94.4%	1 5.6%
DM2,5b-DM5b	28 14.2%	16 57.1%	12 42.9%	24 19.0%	21 87.5%	3 12.5%
DM1b-DM2,5b	45 22.8%	29 64.4%	16 35.6%	25 19.8% 8	21 4.0%	4 16.0%
DM0,5b-DM1b	32 16.2%	14 43.8%	18 56.3%	11 8.7%	6 54.5%	5 45.5%
<DM0,5b	38 19.3%	7 18.4%	31 81.6%	12 9.5%	6 50.0%	6 50.0%

Source: see footnote 60

Most companies manage more than one price risk using derivatives, mostly a combination of FX derivatives and interest rate derivatives.

---

[60] G.M. Bodnar & G. Gebhardt, *Derivatives usage by Non-Financial Firms in the US and Germany*: A Comparative Survey, Journal of International Financial Management and Accounting, Vol. 10, No. 3, (1999)

Table 6.5.7: Exposures hedged with FX derivatives

	US		Germany	
Exposures	Frequently	Sometimes	Frequently	Sometimes
Contractual Commitments	50.6%	43.5%	77.2%	16.3%
Anticipated receivable/payable Pending commitments			29.3%	50.0%
Anticipated Transactions < 1yr	55.3%	36.5%	28.3%	41.3%
Anticipated Transactions > 1yr	11.8%	42.4%	6.5%	0.2%
Competitive Exposures	7.1%	16.5%	8.7%	14.1%
Foreign Repatriations	37.6%	37.6%	38.0%	37.0%
Translation of Foreign Accounts	15.3% 1	4.1%	5.4%	9.8%

Source: see footnote 60

Table 6.5.8: FX instrument choice by type of exposure

	US		Germany			
Exposures	Forward	Option	Forward	Option	Forward	Option
Contractual Commitments	82.5%	7.5%	7.5%	69.6%	47.8%	16.3%
Anticipated receivable/payable Pending commitments			20.7%	7.6%		5.4%
Anticipated Transactions < 1yr	60.0%	28.8%	5.0%	47.8%	20.7%	5.4%
Anticipated Transactions > 1yr	21.3%	31.3%	2.5%	23.9%	17.4%	3.3%
Competitive Exposures	5.0%	16.3%	2.5%	8.7%	5.4%	2.2%
Foreign Repatriations	82.5%	7.5%	7.5%	58.7%	4.3%	12.0%
Translation of Foreign Accounts	12.5%	11.3%	6.3%	3.3%	1.1%	3.3%

Source: See footnote 60

German firms use more derivatives for hedging purpose than US firms do. Since German firms need to hedge other than EUR exposures so they are partly responsible for the higher demand of USD derivatives.

Table 6.5.9: OTC FX derivatives market in billions of USD

	National Amounts			EUR/USD			
	USD	EUR	Delta	Open	High	Loss	Close
End June 1999	13,181	4,998	8,183	1,1850	1,1953	1,0254	1,0352
End Dec 1999	12,834	4,667	8,167	1,0359	1,0911	0,9986	1,0070
End June 2000	13,961	5,863	8,098	1,0050	1,0414	0,8843	0,9523
End Dec 2000	14,073	5,981	8,092	0,9522	0,9597	0,8225	0,9422

Source: BIS (2001a, 2001b)

The results of additional research (Guay, Kothari March 2001)[61] suggest that the magnitude of derivatives positions taken by most firms is economically small in relation to their typical risk exposures. Maintaining an economically smaller derivatives program is potentially consistent with:
1. Firms using derivatives to fine-tune their overall risk-management program that likely includes other means of hedging (operational hedges).
2. Firms making decentralized decisions on derivative use.

---

[61] W. Guay & S.P. Kothari, *How Much Do Firms Hedge with Derivatives*, March 2001

Weakness

These market events are chosen subjectively based on how I experienced it. Since I keep a daily logbook of things that happen in the market, I can find what happened on any specific day based on my experience. I realize that there also have been situations where these were not leading the movements in EUR/USD, however my experience in has been mainly positive.

Outcome SWOT Analysis

Table 6.5.10: SWOT Analysis

Strengths	Weaknesses
Large expirations	Subjective
Risk reversals	Measurable?
Volatilities	
Barriers	
Demand for OTM options	
Hedging activity	

Opportunities	Threats
More knowledge	

The strategy resulting from this SWOT Analysis is the following:
It is possible to find objective methods to measure trends and keep on working on personal expertise and knowledge.

6.6 POSITIONING APPROACH I

The positioning approach is taken from an unusual point of view. In this positioning approach, as well as the ones in the coming chapters, we have the following key question:

Is this division able to explain the movements in the EUR/USD Interbank Market and how is this compared to the competitors?

Potential entrants:
The potential entrants are low since almost all the financial markets are defined as a division in the EUR/USD Interbank Market Organization. The only market left is the real-estate market, including the funds operating in this market.

There is a large intensity of rivalry among existing competitors:
- Commodity Market Division
- Equity Market Division
- International Debt Market Division
- Short-Term-Interest-Rate Market Division

Division I (FX Option Market) plays one of the major roles in the EUR/USD Interbank Market organization. The role is much larger than a lot of players can imagine or give credit for. To understand the influence of the FX options on the EUR/USD interbank market, specialized knowledge is necessary (mathematics/econometrics and the terminology). The market players or insiders have the knowledge about the market but to translate this for the EUR/USD Interbank Market is not easy, because there are differentiated knowledge levels. The FX Option Market can give us reasons for movements/behavior in the spot market. So, Division I is very important in the EUR/USD Interbank Market organization.

Bargaining power of buyers:
The buyers are the funds, central banks, non FX option traders, corporates, investors and private clients. The buying power is dependent on the knowledge because the FX Option market is a very knowledge driven market. The information can only be picked up by the buyers who clearly understand the mathematics used in this market. The funds and central banks have the highest buying power, followed by non-FX option traders, corporates, investors and private clients.

Bargaining power of suppliers:
The suppliers in this market are the brokers (voice), the providers of the trading systems (EBS and Reuters Dealing), the providers of the information systems (Reuters, Telerate, Dow Jones, Bloomberg), the providers of the pricing and booking systems (Fenics, OMR, Boss) and providers of specialized courses and seminars.

Pressure from substitute products:
The substitute products are the products offered by the other divisions in the EUR/USD Interbank Market Organization.
- Commodities Oil and Gold
- Equity products
- International Debt Market products
- Short-Term-Interest-Rate Market products.

6.7 POSITIONING APPROACH II: CONCEPTS OF INDUSTRY EVOLUTION

In the industry of Division I (FX Option Market) the products are specialized and there are different levels of knowledge interacting with each other. It's necessary to understand all the levels of knowledge before it's clear what's driving this industry. The exotic option industry is in a growing stage and the plain vanilla option industry is close to a maturity stage. The FX Option Market is in a growth stage, because the real effects of this industry on the EUR/USD Interbank Market is not totally known by the EUR/USD traders. They are not yet familiar with all the aspects of this industry. When they start using the major features of this industry, then the transition to the mature stage will take place. For more details about the concepts of industry evolution, see "Competitive Strategy" of Michael Porter (1980).

Buyer and Buyer Behavior
The buyer group of options, mainly exotic options, is widening. The buyers need to have a system that can handle booking of such options, valuation and a good risk management needs to be in place. There can be differences in quality based on the knowledge of the customer.

Products and products change
There are plain vanilla and exotic options. Both products differentiate in technical and performance point of view. The quality is good and the products can be tailor-made to the client's needs.

Marketing
The marketing is done through FX Options Marketing desks. These desks provide quick and good pricing to the network.

Manufacturing and Distribution
There is still an under capacity of skilled people who have understanding of exotic options. The traders inform the sales persons about the variables in this market. However, there is still a language barrier. The plain vanilla options are widely understood, accepted and sold. Standardization is entering plain vanilla options.

R&D
R&D is building the knowledge from the FX traders, sales persons and the network.

Foreign Trade
There is an export of knowledge from the options traders to the rest of the market.

Overall Strategy
Marketing of options through a different desk than the option traders.

Competition
The competition is fierce in plain vanilla options but in exotic options, less, because more sophisticated risk management, systems, and traders are needed.

Margins and profits
The margin and profits in plain vanilla options are lower than in exotic options because plain vanilla options are more standardized.

SUMMARY 6

Outcome of the Business Plan Division I, FX Option Market, table 6.4.4

Business Plan	Questions	Answers
Product plan	Products?	Plain vanilla options
		Exotic options
Production plan	What's needed?	Strike
		Expiration date
		OTC/Exchange traded
		Volatility
		Intrinsic value
		Extrinsic value
		Pricing models
		Greeks
		Volatility smiles
		Dynamic hedging
Marketing plan Clients?	Clients?	Investors and asset managers, derivative dealers, non-dealers financials, non-financial institution, portfolio managers, hedge funds, private clients.
	Competitors?	Division II (Commodity Market)
		Division III (Equity Market)
		Division IV (International Debt Market)
		Division V (S-T-I-R Market)

Outcome of the SWOT Analysis Division I, table 6.5.10

Strengths	Weaknesses
Large expirations	Subjective
Risk reversals	Measurable?
Volatilities	
Barriers	
Demand for OTM options	
Hedging activity	

Opportunities	Threats
More knowledge	

Division I (FX Option Market) as a Professional Configuration.

Chapter 7 on Division II (Commodity Oil & Gold Market), will cope with the the following subjects:
1. The Configuration approach and Division II.
2. The Entrepreneurial, Planning approach and Division II.
3. The Design approach and Division II.
4. The Positioning approach and Division II.

REFERENCES

Bodnar, G.M. and G. Gebhardt (1999). "Derivative usage by Non-Financial Firms in the US and Germany: A Comparative Survey", Journal of International Financial Management and Accounting, Vol.10, No.3, pp53-87.

Guay, W. and S.P. Kothari (Mar 2001). "How much do firms hedge with derivatives"

Mintzberg, H., *STRUCTURES IN FIVES: Designing Effective Organizations*, Copyright © 1993. Reprinted by permission of Pearson Education, Inc., Upper Saddle River, New Jersey.

Mintzberg, H., B. Ahlstrand, J. Lampel, *STRATEGY SAFARI: The Complete Guide Through the Wilds of Strategic Management,* Copyright © 1998. Reprinted by permission of Pearson Education Ltd, 128 LongAcre, London WC2E 9AN

COMPETITIVE STRATEGY: Techniques for Analyzing Industries and Competitors by Michael E. Porter. Copyright © 1980, 1998 by The Free Press, an imprint of Simon & Schuster Adult Publishing Group. Reprinted with permission of the publisher.

Steiner, B. "Chapter Options", Markets International Ltd. ACI Diploma study material.

Taleb, Nassim, "DYNAMIC HEDGING: Managing Vanilla and Exotic Options", Copyright © 1997 by Nassim Taleb. Reprinted by permissions of John Wiley & Sons, Inc.

Chapter **7**

DIVISION II
COMMODITY OIL &
GOLD MARKET

7.1 INTRODUCTION

Division II (Commodity Market) played an important role in the downtrend of EUR/USD from January 1999 until the end of 2001. This division is focused on oil and gold. Oil will prove to have an important effect on the movements in EUR/USD and gold always had a historical relationship with the dollar. Division II is one of the five market divisions in the EUR/USD interbank diversified organization. The first division is the FX Option Market, because of its large influence on EUR/USD. Another reason to put Division I (FX Option Market) in the first place is the important influence of options in the other divisions. The Commodity Market is put as second division, because its influence on the moves in the EUR/USD is high and its influence is longer term than the influence of the third division: Equity Market. The Equity Market has been dominant in the first 1½ years of the existence of the EUR (see Chapter 8).

In the SWOT Analysis and the Organization Structure the following conclusions can be found:
1. Oil has been a major driver for the EUR/USD weakness.
2. Gold can play an important role in situations of uncertainty.
3. The Commodity market division has a Machine configuration.

We start this division with the Configuration approach, followed by the Entrepreneurial approach, the Design approach (I + II) and the Positioning approach (I + II). These approaches are explained in chapter 1 and 2.

CHAPTER 7

7.2 HISTORY

Oil

World Oil Market and Oil Price Chronologies: 1970 – 2000, Source: www.eia.doe.gov

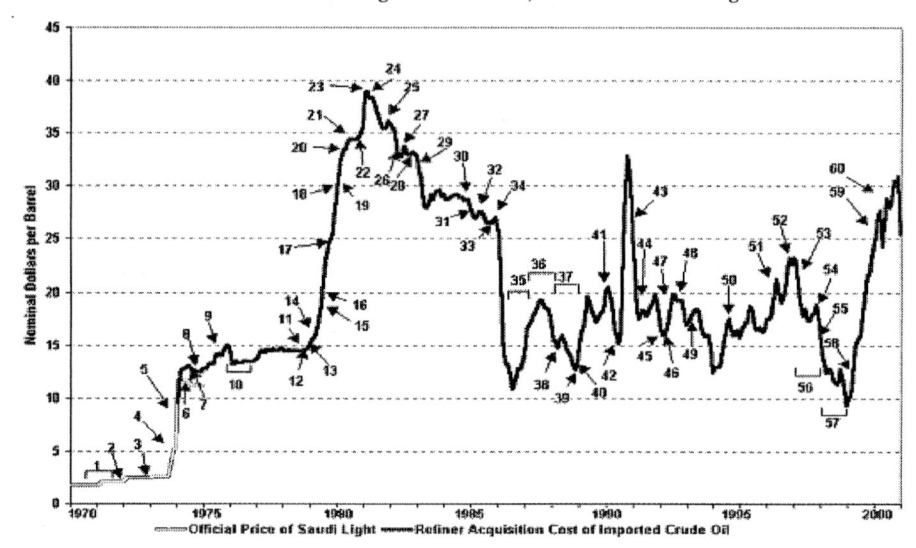

Table 7.2.1, Source: www.eia.doe.gov

No.	What happened?
1	OPEC (Organization of Petroleum Exporting Countries, founded September 1960) begins to assert power; raise tax rate & posted prices
2	OPEC begins nationalization process; raises prices in response to falling US dollar.
3	Negotiations for gradual transfer of ownership of western assets in OPEC countries
4	Oil embargo begins (October 19-20, 1973)
5	OPEC freezes posted prices; US begins mandatory oil allocation
6	Oil embargo ends (March 18, 1974)
7	Saudis increase tax rates and royalties
8	US crude oil entitlements program begins
9	OPEC announces 15% revenue increase effective October 1, 1975
10	Official Saudi Light price held constant for 1976
11	Iranian oil production hits a 27-year low
12	OPEC decides on 14.5% price increase for 1979
13	Iranian revolution; Shah deposed
14	OPEC raises prices 14.5% on April 1, 1979
15	US phased price decontrol begins
16	OPEC raises prices 15%
17	Iran takes hostages; President Carter halts imports from Iran; Iran cancels US contracts; Non-OPEC output hits 17.0 million b/d
18	Saudis raise marker crude price from 19$/bbl to 26$/bbl
19	Windfall Profits Tax enacted

No.	What happened?
20	Kuwait, Iran, and Libya production cuts drop OPEC oil production to 27 million b/d
21	Saudi Light raised to $28/bbl
22	Saudi Light raised to $34/bbl
23	First major fighting in Iran-Iraq War
24	President Reagan abolishes remaining price and allocation controls
25	Spot prices dominate official OPEC prices
26	US boycotts Libyan crude; OPEC plans 18 million b/d output
27	Syria cuts off Iraqi pipeline
28	Libya initiates discounts; Non-OPEC output reaches 20 million b/d; OPEC output drops to 15 million b/d
29	OPEC cuts prices by $5/bbl and agrees to 17.5 million b/d output
30	Norway, United Kingdom, and Nigeria cut prices
31	OPEC accord cuts Saudi Light price to $28/bbl
32	OPEC output falls to 13.7 million b/d
33	Saudis link to spot price and begin to raise output
34	OPEC output reaches 18 million b/d
35	Wide use of netback pricing
36	Wide use of fixed prices
37	Wide use of formula pricing
38	OPEC/Non-OPEC meeting failure
39	OPEC production accord; Fulmar/Brent production outages in the North Sea
40	Exxon's Valdez tanker spills 11 million gallons of crude oil
41	OPEC raises production ceiling to 19.5 million b/d
42	Iraq invades Kuwait
43	Operation Desert Storm begins; 17.3 million barrels of SPR crude oil sales is awarded
44	Persian Gulf war ends
45	Dissolution of Soviet Union; Last Kuwaiti oil fire is extinguished on November 6, 1991
46	UN sanctions threatened against Libya
47	Saudi Arabia agrees to support OPEC price increase
48	OPEC production reaches 25.3 million b/d, the highest in over a decade
49	Kuwait boosts production by 560,000 b/d in defiance of OPEC quota
50	Nigerian oil workers' strike
51	Extremely cold weather in the US and Europe
52	U.S. launches cruise missile attacks into southern Iraq following an Iraqi-supported invasion of Kurdish safe haven areas in northern Iraq.
53	Iraq begins exporting oil under United Nations Security Council Resolution 986.
54	Prices rise as Iraq's refusal to allow United Nations weapons inspectors into "sensitive" sites raises tensions in the oil-rich Middle East.
55	OPEC raises its production ceiling by 2.5 million barrels per day to 27.5 million barrels per day. This is the first increase in 4 years.
56	World oil supply increases by 2.25 million barrels per day in 1997, the largest annual increases since 1988.
57	Oil prices continue to plummet as increased production from Iraq coincides with no growth in Asian oil demand due to the Asian economic crisis and increases in world oil inventories following two unusually warm winters.
58	OPEC pledges additional production cuts for the third time since March 1998. Total pledged cuts amount to about 4.3 million barrels per day.
59	Oil prices tripled between January 1999 and September 2000 due to strong world oil demand, OPEC oil production cutbacks, and other factors, including weather and low oil stock levels.
60	President Clinton authorizes the release of 30 million barrels of oil from the Strategic Petroleum Reserve (SPR) over 30 days to bolster oil supplies, particularly heating oil in the Northeast.

Table 7.2.2, Source: www.eia.doe.gov (for more details 1999-2001 see appendix A)

2001	Sources include Dow Jones (DJ), New York Times (NYT), Wall Street Journal (WSJ), the Washington Post (WP), World Markets Online (WMO), Oil Daily (OD), Los Angeles Times (LAT).
Jan 11	Crude oil prices rise sharply on indications that the OPEC will cut output quotas at its next meeting scheduled for January 17th in Vienna. The NYMEX contract for February crude closes $29.48 per barrel, up $1.84 or about 7%. (DJ)
Jan 17	OPEC agreed to cut production quotas by 1.5 million bbl/d February 1, 2001. (NYT, WP) California utilities impose rolling blackouts on large portions of the State, as demand for electricity exceeds available supplies (DJ, LAT, WSJ).
Feb 14	Kuwait's Prime Minister appoints Adel-al Subeih as Minister of Petroleum (DJ).
Feb 16	US and British aircraft strike Iraqi air defence targets near Bagdad (DJ).
Mar 4	Tests in recent days confirm the world's largest oil find in three decades in the Kashagan field in the Caspian Sea (WSJ).
Mar 15	The world's largest oil rig, located 80 miles offshore Brazil and operated by the Brazilian state oil company Petrobras, suffers three explotions (WSJ).
Mar 17	OPEC agreed to cut production quotas by 1 million bbl/d, effective April 1, 2001
Mar 21	BP and ENI agree to build a $2.5 billion gas liquefaction plant in Egypt with the Egyptian Petroleum Corp (WSJ).
Mar 28	Oil workers in Venezuela, the world's third largest oil exporter, begin a strike (Reuters).
Mar 28	Crude oil prices drop after the US Department of Energy reports a sharp increase in US crude inventories (WSJ).
Apr 10	E.ON AG of Germany announces plan to take over Powergen PLC of the UK in a $7.4 billion deal that would create the world's second largest electricity provider (WSJ).
Apr 10	The front month gasoline futures price rises 3.4% to its highest level since June 2000, following a fire that shut down El Paso Energy's Coastal Refinery in Aruba (WSJ).
Apr 12	ExxonMobil Corp. announces that it has made a major oil discovery in Indonesia (DJ).
Apr 12	Data released by the International Energy Agency show that the OPEC continued to produce oil above its target level in March (DJ).
Apr 17	Chevron announces that oil reserves in the Tengiz field are about 368 million barrels according to its latest estimates. This is more than double previous estimates (WMO).
Apr 19	US President Bush states publicly that the US government has no intention of removing economic sanctions on Iran and Libya (WP).
Apr 23	The Australian Government rejects Royal Dutch/Shell Group's planned takeover of Woodside Petroleum Ltd, Australia's largest energy company (WSJ).
Apr 27	Saudi Arabian Energy Minister Ali al-Naimi meets a number of senior US officials (WMO, Reuters).
May 3	ExxonMobil announces that it has made a major oil discovery offshore Angola (WMO).
May 16	Norwegian Oil Minister Olav Akselsen announces that Norway's oil production has plateaued and that there are no plans to raise or lower in concert with OPEC (Reuters).
May 17	President Bush issues the administration's new energy policy (LT, WP, WSJ). BP and Shell say that they will build a $150 million, 100-mile natural gas pipeline in the Gulf of Mexico WSJ).
May 18	Saudi Arabia selects the eight companies to take part in its "Gas Initiative", three core venture gas projects that have an anticipated worth of $25 billion. They are: Core Venture1: ExxonMobil, Shell, BP and Philips; Venture 2: ExxonMobil, Occidental and Enron; Venture 3: Shell, TotalFinaElf and Conoco (WMO).
May 21	The price of Brent futures crude oil for delivery in early June peaks at $29.68 per barrel, the highest in a year. This comes as concern increases over US gasoline supplies, heightening Israeli-Palestinian tensions, a possible Iraqi halt in oil exports and OPEC statements to the effect that a production quota increase in June is unlikely (WMO).

	The Enron Corporation's power generating venture in India, the Dabhol Power Company, serves formal notice that it will terminate its power supply contract and pull out
May 23	Shell announces that it has discovered a huge reserve of oil in Oil Mining Lease 118 off-shore Nigeria (WMO).
May 30	Iraqi Oil Minister Amir Mohammad Rasheed signs an oil and gas cooperation agreement with his Algerian counterpart (WMO).
May 31	The US and Britain win Security Council approval of a one-month extension of the UN oil-for-food program (WSJ).
June 3	Iraq announces that it will halt crude exports in response to a UN Security Council resolution that extends the oil-for-food program by only one month, instead of the normal six-month period (NYT).
June 5	OPEC held its 115th extraordinary meeting to review the state of world oil markets, leaving quotas unchanged.
June 16	The Iraqi Trade Minister, Mohammed Mehdi Saleh, states that Iraqi crude oil exports will not resume as long as the US-British changes to the memoranum governing the oil-for-food program are being considered (AP).
June 19	Administrative workers for Shell in Nigeria go on strike (Reuters).
June 27	Crude oil and gasoline futures on the NYMEX collapse to their lowest level in over a year. This comes in the wake of reports that inventories are steady or rising for gasoline and crude oil (DJ)
July 2	The UN Security Council, facing almost certain Russian veto, agrees to postpone indefinitely a vote on the US-led package for Iraq, despite support by the four council members. Instead it will extend the program that allows Iraq to export oil and import food and other commodities under UN supervision (WP).
July 3	OPEC agrees to maintain current production quotas (WP).
July 11	Iraq resumes oil exports. The oil-for-food program will be extended for five months (NYT).
July 16	BP agrees to buy a 51% stake in German energy conglomerate E.On's Veba Oel petroleum station and oil unit in a deal valuing the business about $5.56 billion (DJ).
July 18	Crude oil futures fall to their lowest level in 14 months after data from the Energy Information Administration and the American Petroleum Institute show larger-than expected build in crude oil stocks (DJ).
July 25	OPEC agree to cut crude oil production quotas by about 4% (DJ).
Aug 2	Crude oil futures prices for September delivery on NYMEX rise $0.94 to $27.71 per barrel, their highest level in sic weeks. This comes after a July 31 report by American Petroleum Institute showing a decline in US petroleum inventories for the first time in more than a month (WSJ).
Aug 8	The Energy Information Administration announces that petroleum demand in July is the second highest July figure ever recorded (DJ).
Aug 10	The US and Great Britain reject a proposal by UN Secretary General Kofi Annan to permit the Iraqi government to use $1 billion per year to fund Infrastructure improvements and to increase oil production capacity (WMO).
Aug 13	Iraqi Vice-President Ramadan announces that Syria will soon hire contractors to build a new oil pipeline stretching from the Iraqi boarder to Syria (DJ).
	BP signs an agreement with Algerian state oil and gas company Sonatrach for the development of the 7.1-trillion-cubic-foot in Salah natural gas field (WMO).
Aug 24	The US decides to support a modified British proposal to tighten procedures for pricing Iraqi crude oil (WP).
Sep 3	Libya's Foreign Minister announces that US companies will be given one year to resume oil operations in the country before Libya decides whether their licenses should be revoked and given to other firms (Reuters).

Sep 5	The NYMEX begins trading of 14-day Brent futures contracts, which had previously been traded on the International Petroleum Exchange in London. The price of Brent crude is an important international benchmark used in pricing formulas for up to two-thrids of the world's crude oil (DJ).
Sep 7	The US Fedral Trade Commission approves Chevron's bid to buy Texaco (DJ).
Sep 11	Terrorist attacks in the US.
Sep 13	Relative calm returns to world oil markets as US retail gasoline prices return to normal levels and Brent futures fall back to $28.02 per barrel for October delivery after spiking to above $31.00 in the aftermath of the September 11 attacks (WMO).
Sep 17	Philips completes its $7.36 billion stock acquisition of Tosco, after getting approval from the US Federal Trade Commission (WSJ, LAT).
Sep 20	Iraq accuse Kuwait of excessive extraction of the joint al-Ratqa border oilfield (Reuters). PG&E, California's largest utility, files its bankruptcy plans (NYT).
Sep 24	Crude oil and petroleum products futures fall to their lowest levelin nearly two years amid fears that a recession will reduce energy demand. Over the past six trading sessions crude oil and gasoline futures have fallen more than 26% and heating oil futures have fallen nearly 29%.
Oct 4	The US EIA releases its Winter Fuels Outlook 2001/2002, which predicts lower gasoline, heating fuel, and electricity costs for this winter as compared with the previous one (NYT).
Oct 7	Air raids by the US and its coalition partner, Great Britain, begin against Taliban and al-Qaeda targets in Afganistan (Reuters).
Oct 8	Enron agrees to sell its Portland General Electric to Northwest Natural Gas for $1.88 billion in cash and stock (DJ).
Oct 9	Royal Dutch/Shell announces that it will acquire Texaco's interests in two US refining ventures, Motiva Enterprises and Equilon Enterprises, for $2.1 billion in cash, $1.4 billion in debt, and $300 million in pension liabilities (DJ).
Oct 9	The US House of Representatives pass a measure urging the Bush administration to pump more oil into the Strategic Petroleum Reserve (AP).
Oct 18	Crude Oil for November delivery falls to its lowest level since August 1999 on the New York Mercantile Exchange (NYMEX). Poor economic prospects in the next few months, and OPEC's inability to respond so far are seen as factors contributing to the sliding prices of crude oil (Oil Daily).
Oct 22	OPEC announces that its 10 members with output restrictions implemented only 539,000 barrels per day of a promised one million cut in September (Reuetrs).
Oct 28	Mexican President Vicente Fox states that Mexico would not cut or freeze Pemex's crude output for now (Reuters).
Oct 31	OPEC President Chakib Khelil states that OPEC oil producers are prepared to cut supply to get weak oil prices back up to the group's $25-per-barrel target price.

Gold by Green[1]

Prior to 1850, gold was not just a precious metal but a genuinely rare one. In the period 1855-1890, countries like Great Britain, Germany and France, which had a large stock of gold, switched to the gold standard. Many other countries also adopted the gold standard in the 1870s, so that the value of their currencies was fixed against a common standard: gold. The US and Australia remained the main suppliers throughout this period.

The private sector remains predominant almost to the end of the 19th century. In 1895, of the 6,100 metric tonnes (m.t.) of monetary stock, central banks held around 2,750 m.t., but by 1905 the balance had swung in favor of central banks, which then had 4,710 m.t. of the monetary stock against private holding of 3,916 m.t. Thereafter, the central banks consolidated as prime holders of gold. The new supplies from South African discoveries aided the switch from private to government hands. South Africa helped to lift production to over 200 m.t. a year after 1890 and the other discoveries pushed it beyond 350 m.t. by the late 1890s. In the new century, output approached 700 m.t. annually by 1914. Close to 60% of this gold went into monetary stocks. One incentive was the widening of the gold standard club in the 1890s. Russia joined in 1893, Japan in 1897, India in 1898 and finally the US in 1900. In practical terms, central bank stocks rose by 70% during the 1890s. The gold standard had international as well as domestic aspects. It implied that nations settled balance of payment differences with each other in gold. Many smaller nations, while having domestic gold circulation, did not bother to keep gold itself in reserve, but held sterling balances, which were considered as being as good as gold. The Bank of England itself still kept a remarkably small reserve of under 200 m.t. in 1900.

The gold standard was suspended in 1914, with the outbreak of the Great War. The lesson of war was that governments wanted gold firmly in their own hands, not those of their citizens. In the aftermath of war, it was the dollar, not sterling, that became the world's most powerful currency as the center of economic power shifted from Britain to the US. The London gold price continued to be quoted in sterling for another 50 years, but that depended on the sterling-dollar exchange rate. This was clear evidence that two hundred years of a stable sterling price for gold was at an end. It was not realistic to expect Britain to go back to the gold bullion standard in 1925 at the old price. Sterling was trapped in an unrealistic exchange rate. By 1930 the French and Americans held virtually 60% of all the official gold stocks. In that same period, gold production was down 75% since 1914. In the end Britain suspended the gold standard so that the Bank of England did not have to sell gold at a fixed, statutory price. The result was that people in Europe became distrustful of paper money so they began collecting gold. The gold was bought through fear; fear of devaluation, fear of war.

---

[1] T. Green, *Central Banks Gold Reserves*, World Gold Council, www.gold.org

The destiny of monetary gold, for the next twenty or more years, now rested with the US. The US pre-eminent position as the holder of gold in the immediate post-war years (after World War II) was a clear reflection of its unique economic power. After the war, the Bretton Woods Agreement emerged from the International Monetary Fund (IMF) and Financial Conference of the United and Associated Nations in July 1944.

Table 7.2.3, Source: World Gold Council

		Gold and the International Monetary System, a chronology
1717		In UK Sir Isaac Newton (Master of the Mint) gives guinea statutory valuation of 21sh (shillings). Mint price of gold 77sh 10_d per standard ounce. UK Gold Standard Commences.
1797		Napoleonic Wars. Bank of England suspends gold payments.
1816		UK Coinage Act (Post-Napoleonic Wars). Sovereign the standard unit @ one standard. Ounce of gold (11/12 fine) = 77sh 10_d.
1844		Bank of England obliged to buy gold @ 77sh 9d.
1870-1900		All major countries, other than China, switch to the gold standard, linking their currencies to gold. Bimetallism is abandoned.
1913		Federal Reserve Act establishes US system of reserve banks. At least 40% of note issue to be backed by gold.
1917	1 Sept	US prohibits gold exports.
1919	1 Apr	UK prohibits gold exports without official permission. UK now off Gold Standard. June US gold exports permitted again.
12 Sept		London Gold Fixing established
1925	28 Apr	UK returns to Gold Standards at pre-War parity of $4.86 = GBP 1
	May	Gold Standard Act. Currency convertible at 77sh 10_ d per standard ounce. But only in amounts of 400 oz. Export of gold again permitted.
1931	Sept	UK abandons Gold Standard
1933	20 Apr	US convertibility suspended. Export all transactions and holding of gold forbidden.
1934	31 Jan	Presidential Proclamation makes dollar again convertible to gold (new price $35/oz)
1936	Sept	Tripartite Agreement. US, UK and France willing to buy and sell gold freely with each other in exchange for own currency.
1939	3 Sept	London gold market closed on outbreak of war.
1944	July	Bretton Woods Conference sets basis of post-war monetary system. USD to maintain $35 = 1 oz gold conversion rate (see Chapter 6).
1945	27 Dec	IMF Articles of Agreement effective.
1954	22 Mar	London gold market re-opens after WOII.
1961	1 Nov	Gold Pool established (members Belgium, France, Germany, Italy, Netherlands, Switzerland, UK and Federal Reserve Bank of NY. Members would sell (and later buy) gold in the London market to maintain price close to par in that market.
1967	18 Nov	Sterling devaluated from $2.80 to $2.40. This leads to pressure on dollar and hence to substantial buying of gold.
1968	15 Mar	London market closed at request of US government.
	17 Mar	Gold Pool abolished and 2-tier market created.
	31 Mar	First amendment to IMF articles agreed. A new reserve asset (SDR).

		Gold and the International Monetary System, a chronology
1971	15 Aug	USD convertibility to gold suspended.
	18 Dec	Smithsonian Agreement
1972	8 May	USD devalues to $38/fine oz
1973	12 Feb	US proposes further devaluation to $42.22/fine oz
	2-18 March	Major central banks suspend dealing in foreign exchange markets.
	19 Mar	Most major countries adopt floating exchange rate regime.
	13 Nov	2-tier gold market formally abandoned.
1975	1 Jan	US abolish restrictions on citizen buying, selling or owning gold.
	Jan	First US gold auction
	30 June	Second US gold auction.
	31 Aug	Group of 10 major industrial countries and Switzerland agree that there would be no attempt to peg price of gold and that total stock held by IMF and the monetary authorities of the G10 countries would not be increased.
1976	2 June	First IMF gold auction.
1978	1 Apr	2nd Amendment to IMF Articles of Agreement comes into effect. Gold's formal role in international monetary system disappears.
	23 May	US gold auctions resume.
1979	13 Mar	European Monetary System established
	Nov	Final US gold auction.
1980	7 May	Last of 45 IMF gold auctions.
1982	Mar	US Gold Commission reports to Congress.
1985	22 Sept	Plaza Agreement on currencies. See Chapter 6.
1987	21 Feb	Louvre Accord on currencies. (21-22 Feb).
1992	7 Feb	Treaty on European Union signed at Maastricht.
1998	1-2 May	Austria, Belgium, Finland, France, Germany, Ireland, Italy, Luxembourg, Netherlands, Portugal and Spain confirmed as participants in EMU scheduled to start in January 1999.
	7 July	The Governing Council of The European Central Bank decides that 15% of its initial reserves of 39.5 billion Euro, due to be transferred to it on the first day of 1999, will consist of gold.

Table 7.2.4, Source: World Gold Council

	Events 1999
Jan 1-5	Euro ushers in ESCB as world's biggest gold holder. Revaluation gains for national central banks
Feb 9	German government drops opposition to IMF gold sales
Mar 3	UK support for additional help for poor countries' debt relief including IMF gold sales
Mar 4	Potential Swiss gold sales first quarter of 2000 by the very earliest.
Mar 8	Russia's gold reserves rising.
Mar 11	No gold sales from Romania
Mar 15	Chirac and Clinton support IMF gold sales (Mar 16)
Mar 17	South Africa warns on gold sales
Mar 29	Switzerland wants IMF gold sales capped at 5mn oz (156 tonnes).
Apr 6	ECB revalues gold holdings
Apr 9	More Canadian gold sales
Apr 19	Swiss approve constitutional changes.
Apr 21	Russian central bank allowed dealing directly with gold producers.
May 7	UK shocks gold market with sale plan for 415 tonnes.
	Canadians sell more gold
June 14	Financial Times World Gold Conference.
June 18	G7 finance ministers reach initial agreement on proposals for IMF gold sales to HIPC scheme.
June 22	IMF gold sales considered by the US Senate Banking Committee.
July 1	Legislation to veto proposed IMF gold sales introduced to US Congress.
July 6	Bank of England auctions 25 tonnes of UK gold reserves.
July 28	Mining countries call for moratorium on central bank sales of gold.
Aug 5	Canada's central bank sells 2.5 tonnes of gold in July.
Aug 9	IMF considering alternatives to gold sales.
Sept 3	Canada's central bank sells 5.3 tonnes of gold in August.
Sept 10	IMF new proposal on the table to aid heavily indebted poor countries.
Sept 21	UK holds second gold auction.
Sept 26	15 European central banks agree to limit gold sales over the next five years (The Washington Agreement).
Sept 28	Japan central bank reaffirms its commitment to gold.
Oct 5	Canada's central bank sells 4.2 tonnes of gold in September.
Oct 21	Kuwait plans to deposit entire gold reserve with Bank of England for gold leasing.
Nov 25	Jordan sells half its gold reserve.
Nov 29	Third UK gold auction.
Dec 6	Dutch central bank announces sale of 300 tonnes.
Dec 14	Dutch sell first 3.5 tonnes.

Table 7.2.5: EU Changes in Gold Reserves, 1 January 1999[2]

	Former gold holdings, tonnes	Gold returned from EMI, tonnes	Gold transferred to ECB, tonnes	Remaining gold holdings, tones
EMI	2,712	-2,712	0	0
ECB			747	747
EMU participants				
Austria	369	61	-22	408
Belgium	237	59	-27	269
Finland	50	12	-13	49
France	2,547	637	-159	3,024
Germany	2,960	740	-232	3,469
Ireland	11	3	-8	6
Italy	2,074	519	-141	2,452
Luxembourg	7	2	-1	8
Netherlands	842	210	-41	1,012
Portugal	500	125	-18	607
Spain	486	122	-84	524
Total	**10,084**	**2,490**	**-747**	**12,574**
Non-participants				
Denmark	53	13	N/A	67
Greece	113	28	N/A	141
Sweden	147	37	N/A	184
UK	572	143	N/A	716
Total	**885**	**221**	**N/A**	**1,106**
Total EU 13,	**681**	**0**	**0**	**13,681**

Source: World Gold Council

Table 7.2.6: Major Gold Holdings (July 2001)

Country	Tonnes	Gold as a % of total reserves
US	8,137	56.2%
Switzerland	2,305	39.1%
UK	396	7.8%
ECB	767	15.0%
Germany	3,460	36.6%
France	3,025	41.8%
Italy	2,305	39.1%
Netherlands	908	46.3%
Portugal	607	37.4%
Spain	523	13.0%
Austria	347	20.2%
Belgium	258	18.0%
Greece	123	15.9%
Finland	49	5.1%
Ireland	5	0.9%
Luxembourg	2	17.7%

Source: World Gold Council

---

[2] World Gold Council, www.gold.org

7.3 CONFIGURATION APPROACH

The structure of an organization can be defined as the different ways in which work is divided into different tasks and how those tasks are coordinated. In the organization Division II (Commodity Market) the main product is commodity. We divide it into two sub-products: oil and gold.

Organizational parts
Strategic Apex
The commodity traders, central banks and producers are responsible for Division II. They are the strategists of the organization.

Support Staff
The organizational part has the task of influencing the work of others in the organization. This is accomplished by training the people in Division II (Commodity Market) and making sure that the technology is updated so that the Strategic Apex receives live prices and news. Further, the **salespeople match the clients and products.**

Techno Structure
The Techno Structure of Division II is the same as for the total EUR/USD Interbank Market organization and can be divided into:
1. Fundamental Analysis (Chapter 4)
2. Technical Analysis (Chapter 5)

Division II uses a combination of both specialties.

Middle Line
The middle line of Division II is the group of other traders in this division; i.e., the futures and options.

Operating Core
The operating core has four main functions:
1. Supply the general Commodity Market product for the production.
2. Transform the general Commodity Market product into the differentiated sub-products: oil and gold.
3. Distribute oil and gold.
4. Provide direct support to input, transformation and output.

Coordination mechanism
The coordination mechanism used in Division II (Commodity Market) is the standardization of working processes. The analysts in the Techno Structure will analyze the market up side down and, at the time news comes out, they will give the traders direct input of the translation in the market. The time frame of producers is longer than that of traders so they will have the time to look at any new developments.

Decentralization
In the Commodity Market, traders and producers have the formal power and the analysts have power in terms of the translation of market events. There is partial horizontal decentralization.

Configuration
Division II (Commodity Market) uses standardization of working processes as the coordination mechanism. The Techno Structure is the dominant force in the organization because it is able to translate the events happening in the market. The power is partially decentralized to the Techno Structure. So Division II (Commodity Market) has a **Machine Configuration (see chapter 1 for the picture).**

Outcome

Table 7.3.1

Division II: Commodity Market	Definition
Strategic Apex	Commodity Market traders and producers
Support Staff	System
	Sales force
Techno Structure	Fundamental Analysis (Chapter 4)
	Technical Analysis (Chapter 5)
Middle Line	Futures traders
	Option traders
	Bullion banks
Operating Core	Oil market
	Gold market
Coordination mechanism	Standardization of working processes
Decentralization	Partial horizontal decentralization
Configuration	Machine organization
Culture	Market Psychology (Chapter 3)

7.4 ENTREPRENEURIAL AND PLANNING APPROACH

In Division II, commodity suppliers, central banks and traders are the strategic thinkers (Commodity Market). The suppliers are likely to make decisions based on planning. The decisions of central banks to reduce their stock are most likely based on planning; however, the timing is more based on the Entrepreneurial approach. The traders take their decisions about the position and pricing based on the Entrepreneurial approach, and based on their view on the market. The traders will always show a two-way price while the suppliers will not. The suppliers are: the OPEC members, non-OPEC members (Oil) and API, gold producers and the central banks that are selling a part of their gold reserves (gold).

Oil by Energy Information Administration

Producers

Table 7.4.1: Top World Oil Producers, 2000

Country	Production estimate (million bbl/d)
Saudi Arabia	9.12
United States	9.08 (5.83 of which was crude oil)
Russia	6.71
Iran	3.81
Mexico	3.48
Norway	3.32
China	3.25
Venezuela	3.14
United Kingdom	2.75
Canada	2.74
Iraq	2.59
United Arab Emirates	2.51
Kuwait	2.25
Nigeria	2.15
Indonesia	1.56
Brazil	1.54
Libya	1.47
Algeria	1.43

Source: www.eia.doe.gov
OPEC members are bold

OPEC members are Saudia Arabia, Iran, Venezuela, UAE, Iraq, Nigeria, Kuwait, Libya, Indonesia, Algeria and Qatar

Table 7.4.2: Top World Oil Net Exporters, 2000

Country	Production estimate (million bbl/d)
Saudi Arabia	7.84
Russia	4.31
Norway	3.11
Venezuela	2.66
Iran	2.59
United Arab Emirates	2.18
Iraq	2.09
Kuwait	2.05
Nigeria	1.86
Mexico	1.44
Libya	1.29
Algeria	1.22
United Kingdom	1.06

Source: www.eia.doe.gov
OPEC members are bold

In 2001, OPEC had a market share of 39.4%; in 2002, 38.2%. The market share is and power of OPEC is reduced because of competition with Russia and Norway. Venezuela, OPEC's only American member, has ranked consistently in the last several years as one of the four top sources of U.S. oil imports (along with Canada, Mexico, and Saudi Arabia).

Graph 7.4.1: OPEC Market Share[3]

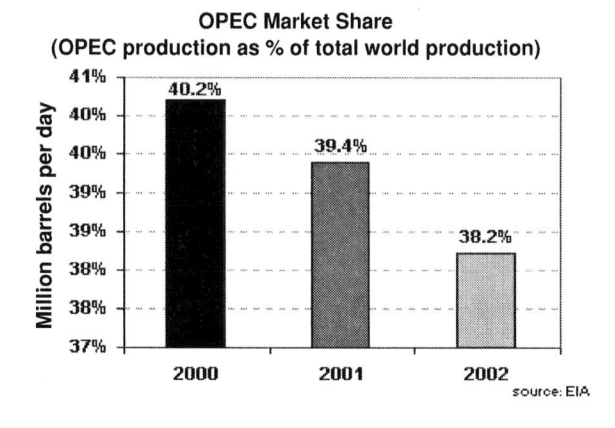

OPEC Market Share
(OPEC production as % of total world production)

- 2000: 40.2%
- 2001: 39.4%
- 2002: 38.2%

Million barrels per day
source: EIA

---

[3] www.eia.doe.gov

Graph 7.4.2: OECD stock levels and OPEC basket prices[4]

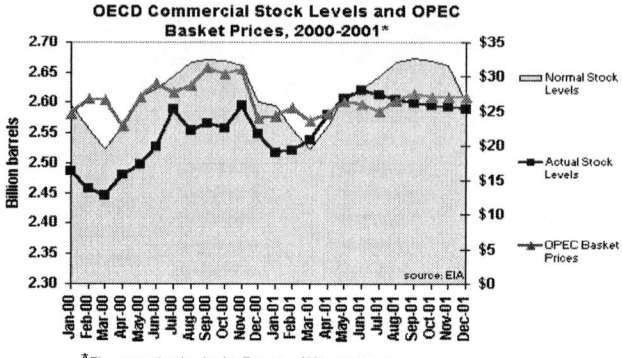

OECD Commercial Stock Levels and OPEC Basket Prices, 2000-2001*

*Please note that data for July-December 2001 are estimates.

Graph 7.4.3: OPEC basket price and price band[5]

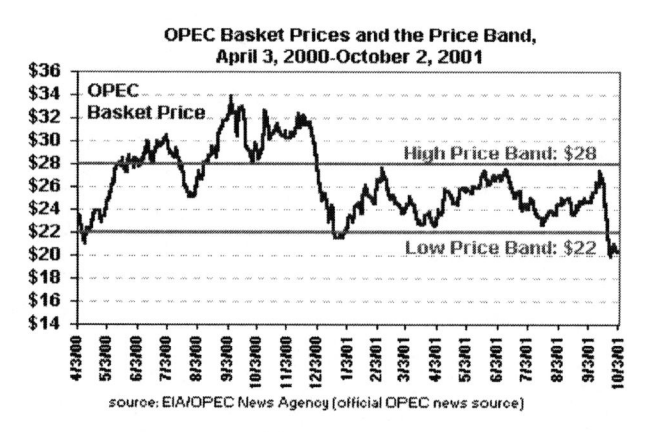

OPEC Basket Prices and the Price Band, April 3, 2000-October 2, 2001

source: EIA/OPEC News Agency (official OPEC news source)

During its March 2000 meetings, OPEC adopted an informal price band mechanism (formally ratified on January 17, 2001) whereby the OPEC basket price being higher than $28 per barrel or lower than $22 per barrel would trigger automatic production adjustments. Prices sustained above the price band's target for 20 trading days are to result in an automatic production increase of 500,000 BBL/D, while prices below the target range for 10 trading days are to result in cuts of 500,000 BBL/D. OPEC has specified that supply adjustments are not automatic but require approval by an OPEC conference.

---
[4] www.eia.doe.gov
[5] www.eia.doe.gov

Oil prices collapsed on September 24, in the largest single-day drop since January 1991. The September 11 terrorists' attacks inside the US, and the world economic downturn, appear to have precipitated new OPEC flexibility regarding its $25 price target for its basket of crude oils.

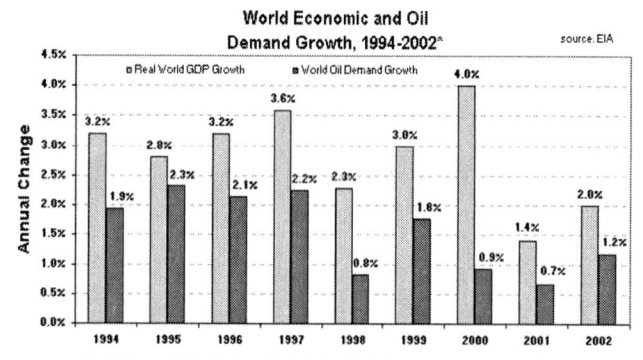

Graph 7.4.4: World economic and oil demand growth[6]

World Economic and Oil Demand Growth, 1994-2002*
source: EIA

Year	Real World GDP Growth	World Oil Demand Growth
1994	3.2%	1.9%
1995	2.8%	2.3%
1996	3.2%	2.1%
1997	3.6%	2.2%
1998	2.3%	0.8%
1999	3.0%	1.6%
2000	4.0%	0.9%
2001	1.4%	0.7%
2002	2.0%	1.2%

Graph demonstrates the imperfect relationship between economic and oil demand growth. In 1995, oil demand grew more than it had in 1994, even as economic growth was slower than in 1994. In 2000, economic growth was stronger than in 1999, but oil demand growth was weaker than in 1999.

*Please note that data for 2001 and 2002 are estimates.

The oil demand during the past decade grew by at least 1 million barrels per day except during periods of serious international crises. Since the events of September 11, 01, the world has entered serious political and economic crises, and moved closer to a global recession. In the near-term, the largest influence is expected to come from the large drop in global demand for jet fuel. Worldwide jet-fuel demand fell by about 10% outside the US and around 20% within the US. Energy Information Administration's (EIA) outlook for 2002 assumes that, following the initial stages of the crisis, commercial jet fuel use will recover somewhat, and that global jet fuel demand will be down by roughly 5%. Growth in world oil demand in 2002 is now estimated at 900,000 barrels per day, down from 1.4 million barrels per day in EIA's previous review.

---

[6] www.eia.doe.gov

Graph 7.4.5: Monthly crude oil prices[7]

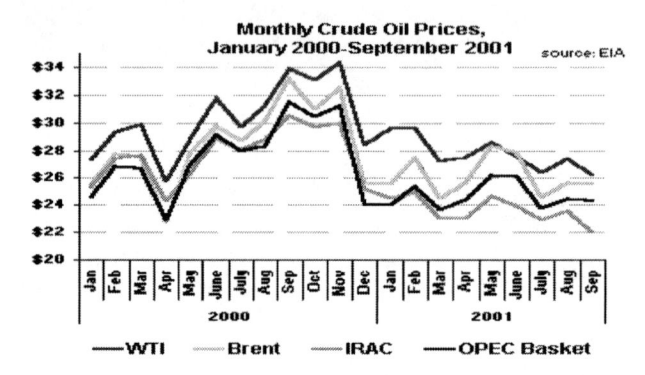

Monthly Crude Oil Prices, January 2000-September 2001 source: EIA

— WTI   — Brent   — IRAC   — OPEC Basket

OPEC collects pricing data on a "basket" of seven crude oils, including: Algeria's Saharan Blend, Indonesia's Minas, Nigeria's Bonny Light, Saudi Arabia's Arab Light, Dubai's Fateh, Venezuela's Tia Juanna Light and Mexico's Isthmus. It uses the price of this basket to monitor world market conditions, and the basket price triggers the price band mechanism.

Major crude oils important for oil pricing (benchmark crudes), include US West Texas Intermediate and North Sea Brent crude.

Traders

The physical oil traders and the futures traders are the ones who provide the market with two-way pricing. They take positions according to their view of the marketplace.

---

[7] www.eia.doe.gov

Gold

Producers

Table 7.4.3: Top 20 Producing Countries

Producing countries	Rank 2001	Rank 2000	Production 2001 (t)	Production 2000 (t)
South Africa	1	1	394	428
United States	2	2	335	355
Australia	3	3	285	296
Indonesia	4	7	183	140
China	5	4	173	164
Russia	6	6	165	154
Canada	7	5	157	155
Peru	8	8	134	133
Uzbekistan	9	9	85	88
Ghana	10	11	72	74
PNG	11	10	68	76
Brazil	12	12	51	53
Mali	13	15	45	30
Chile	14	13	40	50
Tanzania	15	21	34	17
Philippines	16	14	32	35
Argentina	17	17	31	26
Mexico	18	16	26	27
Kyrgyzstan	19	19	25	22
Zimbabwe	20	18	22	25
Rest of World			249	236

Source: Gold Fields Mineral Services (GFMS)

Table 7.4.4: Top 15 Gold Producing Companies

Producing companies	Rank 2001	Rank 2000	Output 2001	Output 2000
AngloGold (RSA)	1	1	217.2	225.3
Barrick Gold (CAN)	2	4	190.5	116.4
Newmont Mining (USA)	3	2	168.1	153.7
Gold Fields Limited (RSA)	4	3	117.1	121.2
Rio Tinto (UK)	5	6	111.3	84.9
Placer Dome Inc. (CAN)	6	5	85.7	92.8
Freeport-McMoRan (USA)	7	10	82.3	59.8
Normandy Mining (AUS)	8	9	75.9	64.5
Harmony Gold (RSA)	9	8	71.4	66.8
Ashanti Goldfields (Ghana)	10	11	51.5	54.0
Durban Roodepoort Deep (RSA)	11	12	32.4	35.7
Cia. de Minas Buenaventura (Peru)	12	14	32.3	28.5
Kinross Gold (USA)	13	13	29.2	29.0
WMC Ltd. (AUS)	14	16	25.8	23.1
Newcrest Mining (AUS)	15	15	21.9	27.9
Homestake Mining (USA)		7	–	68.6

Source: Gold Fields Mineral Services (GFMS)

IMF and Central banks

In the past, central banks were mainly seen on the demand side of the market. In 1975, the US started gold auctions. On 1st April 1978, the 2nd Amendment to IMF Articles of Agreement came into effect, and gold's formal role in the international monetary system disappeared.

IMF[8]

In 1999, the IMF planned gold sales to support heavily indebted poor countries but, due to pressure from the international community, the IMF decided, on the 22nd of September 1999, to search for alternative methods of financing its contribution to debt relief for the world's poorest countries

Bank of England[9]

On 7th May 1999, the UK Treasury announced its intention of selling 415 tonnes of gold reserves over the medium term and thereby reducing its holding to 300 tonnes from 715 tonnes. The announcement had an immediately damaging effect on the gold price, which fell by nearly $7.50 to $ 281.50 an ounce. By selling 415 tonnes of its gold reserves, the gold % in the total reserves would drop from 16.7% to about 7%, which was below international standards of 15%. According to the Bank of England, the gold auctions are no more than a prudent restructuring of the reserve holdings.

Swiss National Bank[10]

In April 1999, Swiss voters approved, by referendum, a new constitution, paving the way for legislation to remove the constitutional link between the Swiss franc and gold. Agreement on other legislative and constitutional factors must still be sought before Switzerland will be in a position to sell any gold as proposed (May 1999 demand report). The Swiss National Bank announced its intention to sell 1,300 tonnes of its gold reserves. Even after the gold sales, their gold reverses still would be high compared to other countries.

---

[8]Press release 22 September 1999, *World Gold Council Welcomes IMF's Search for Alternative Methods of Funding Debt Relief*, www.gold.org
[9]Press release 7 May 1999, *UK Treasury Gold Sales*, www.gold.org
[10]World Gold Council, *20 questions about Switzerland's gold*, www.gold.org

Table 7.4.5: Gold reserves per capita (May 2000)

		Troy ounces			Troy ounces
1	Switzerland	11.90	14 Belgium		0.83
2	Switzerland (after sales)	5.93	15 Sweden		0.66
3	Lebanon	2.31	16 Venezuela		0.43
4	Iceland	1.95	17 Spain		0.43
5	Portugal	1.95	18 Greece		0.39
6	Netherlands	1.83	19 United Kingdom		0.33
7	France	1.65	20 Finland		0.32
8	Austria	1.64	21 Denmark		0.31
9	Netherlands (after sales)	1.43	22 Norway		0.30
10	Germany	1.36	23 Bahrain		0.25
11	Kuwait	1.27	24 Italy		0.22
12	United States	0.97	25 Saudi Arabia		0.22
13	Libya	0.92			

Source: World Gold Council

Washington Agreement 26th September 1999[11]

The central banks of Austria, France, Italia, Portugal, Switzerland, Belgium, Germany, Luxembourg, Spain, Great Britain, Sweden, Ireland, Netherlands, Finland and the ECB agreed to limit sales of gold from official reserves to a maximum of 2,000 tonnes over the next five years, approximately 400 tonnes a year. These figures include the potential sales of 1,300 tonnes by the Swiss National Bank and the sales by the Bank of England. The central banks have also agreed not to increase their gold lending arrangements and derivative operations above the current levels for the next five years. The Washington pact meant a degree of beneficial market stability was achieved. As a result, the gold price spiked to a high of $325.

Statement on Gold[12]

In the interests of clarifying their intentions with respect to their gold holdings, the above institutions make the following statement.
1. Gold will remain an important element of global monetary reserves.
2. The above institutions will not enter the market as sellers, with the exception of already decided sales.
3. The gold sales already decided will be achieved through a concerted program of sales over the next five years. Annual sales will not exceed approximately 400 tonnes and the total sales over this period will not exceed 2,000 tonnes.
4. The signatories to this agreement have agreed not to expand their gold leasings and their use of gold futures and options over this period.
5. This agreement will be reviewed after five years.

---

[11] World Gold Council, *20 questions about Switzerland's gold*, www.gold.org
[12] Press communiqué by central banks on the *Washington Agreement 26 September 1999*, www.gold.org

Chapter 7

Traders

Gold traders and gold futures traders form the last group of strategic thinkers. They give the two-way pricing and decide which position they want to hold based on their view about the market.

7.5 DESIGN APPROACH I: BUSINESS PLAN

Product plan

The products represented within Division II (Commodity Market):
1. OIL
2. GOLD

Oil

The principals of oil refining and the oil products can be found in the following book: "Trading in Oil Futures and Options" by S. Clubley.

Gold

The purposes of gold are as stated below:
- Jewelry
- Gold reserves of central banks
- Safe-haven in times of uncertainty or distress.
- Industrial uses

The largest market for gold is India, based on the demand during marriages and the festival season. In 2000, an abnormally small number of auspicious days for weddings in the Hindu calendar, coupled with a patchy monsoon, restrained demand in India. In the first quarter of 2001 gold demand in India rose 23% higher than Q1 of 2000 due to a season of marriages and festivals during the quarter, especially in the south. The devastating Gujarat earthquake in January of 2002 is likely to have some negative influence. The gold demand in India comes overwhelmingly from the rural areas[13].

---

[13]World Gold Council, *Gold Demand Trends, Issue No. 35 May 2001*, www.gold.org

Table 7.5.1: World demand in key markets worldwide (tonnes) 1995-2001[14]

	1995	1996	1997	1998	1999	2000	2001 Q1
Gold price	*384.1*	*387.9*	*331.3*	*294.1*	*278.6*	*279.1*	*263.5*
India	477.2	507.8	736.7	815.0	838.8	855.2	243.3
Pakistan	43.2	53.7	81.8	98.2	121.8	119.1	29.8
Greater China	427.3	374.4	406.4	314.6	343.3	329.3	82.8
Japan	272.2	152.2	107.1	110.4	121.8	98.0	21.8
S Korea	121.0	125.5	114.4	-162.5	118.5	120.5	29.5
SE Asia	324.7	329.6	204.0	51.5	265.5	267.3	76.1
Saudi Arabia	193.1	184.9	199.0	208.4	199.4	221.0	63.5
Gulf States	104.6	118.0	142.1	144.2	144.7	157.8	48.5
Egypt	67.0	75.7	97.6	104.4	124.8	119.7	31.0
Turkey	139.4	153.0	202.0	171.0	139.0	207.0	31.0
Americas	399.7	431.7	469.0	547.4	586.3	536.7	116.7
Europe	295.2	273.0	293.0	308.6	278.3	258.8	51.9
WGC Mkt Total	**2864.5**	**2779.5**	**3053.6**	**2712.1**	**3282.3**	**3290.3**	**825.9**

Source: World Gold Council

Japan is also a major market for gold since Japan is the major fabricator of electronics products and the leading dental gold fabricator[15]

Determinants for the goldprice are:
- Hedging activity of the gold miners.
- Natural disasters in countries with high gold demand.
- International conflicts, tensions, or unrest.
- Uncertainty in other financial markets such as sell-off in equity markets.
- Gold sale by central banks.

---

[14] World Gold Council, *Gold Demand Trends, Issue No. 35 May 2001*, www.gold.org
[15] World Gold Council, *Industrial Uses of Gold*, www.gold.org

Production plan

The production plan describes everything that is needed to sell the products in the product plan.

Oil

1. Refining of oil
2. Upgrading residual fuel
3. Physical markets
4. Futures markets
5. Options market

I would recommend the following books to learn more about the oil market.
- "Trading in Oil Futures and Options" by S. Clubley, Woodhead Publishing Limited, 1998.
- "The Futures Game: Who Wins, Who Loses, & Why" by R.J. Teweles & F.J. Jones, McGraw-Hill, 1999, 3rd edition.

Gold[16]

1. Mining
2. Financing
3. Markets
4. Gold lease
5. Hedging

Financing[17]

The gold mining industry, in South Africa, Australia and elsewhere, has been undergoing massive structural change. With the market having expanded in the early 1980s in response to the upswing in gold prices, producers faced a different challenge when prices fell and the principal need was to reduce costs. To finance the re-organizational processes demanded in this volatile situation, the industry found it made sense to literally borrow gold to be repaid from future output. The cost of borrowing gold was more attractive than the cost of borrowing money. So the gold producers, with the help of banks, developed hedging techniques, which reflected financial developments taking

---

[16] A. Doran, *Trends in Gold Banking*, Research Study No. 19, World Gold Council, www.gold.org
[17] A. Doran, *Trends in Gold Banking*, Research Study No. 19, World Gold Council, www.gold.org

place in many other sectors. Gold producers are borrowing in gold rather than in currency to finance mining developments and to hedge against price drops.

Markets[18]

The volume of gold trading, measured at its broadest base to include physical and paper contracts, has reached over 100,000 tonnes per year, well in excess of 100 times the annual output of newly mined gold. Gold trading occurs around the clock, with the London market overlapping those of New York and Tokyo. The daily clearing volume in London is of the same order as major currency pair. The key trading houses are the international bullion banks including the two Swiss giants UBS and Credit Suisse; Republic National Bank of New York; and NM Rothshild. London is the dominant center for physical gold trading, both spot and forward, followed by Zurich. For gold futures and traded options, the New York Commodity Exchange (COMEX) dominates the market. Zurich is the premier physical market in wholesale terms. The two major Swiss banks, UBS and Credit Suisse, are both major dealers in gold. Together they form the Zurich Gold Pool, which provides an informal clearing and price setting mechanism. Zurich absorbs, initially, most of the newly mined South Africa output. The large Swiss banks have their own refineries, producing a wide range of bars to suit regional trading specifications around the world.

Gold lease[19]

The growth to such a large volume of trading has been possible through the liquidity supplied to the market from aboveground stocks. This liquidity has not been in the form of sales, but in the form of loans, that is, the lending of gold from aboveground stocks held by private or official bodies. It is the availability of this gold credit supply that permits the necessary gold borrowing. The presence of a liquid gold market is vital for:
- Hedging programs by mining companies (65% of demand for gold credit); or
- financing of refiners, fabricators and jewelry stock holders (20%); or
- speculative and investor activity (15%).

The duration of the gold leasing agreements (lending agreements) is less than one year. In such activity, commercial bullion banks are again key intermediaries. The most common transaction type is acceptance of time deposit, on which interest is paid in gold. Bullion banks also arrange currency swaps under which there is a repurchase agreement for the gold at a fixed price. In London, the Bank of England holds stocks of gold on behalf of many central banks like the Federal Reserve Bank in New York. So they are the center of unallocated account-clearing facilities for the bullion dealers and holders.

---

[18] A. Doran, *Trends in Gold Banking*, Research Study No. 19, World Gold Council, www.gold.org
[19] A. Doran, *Trends in Gold Banking*, Research Study No. 19, World Gold Council, www.gold.org

Physical demand and supply must match each period. Newly mined supply is inelastic in the short-term so the price is the only determinant left. The derivatives market does give a rise to accelerate supply and according to analysts the spot price of gold is 10-15% below the level which it would be without the hedging activities by producers and fabricators through the derivatives market. The derivatives market has also created for gold owners an opportunity to get extra income. However, the growth of the derivatives market wouldn't be possible without the existence of large stocks of gold, largely in the official sector, and the readiness of this sector to lend its gold[20]

Hedging[21]

Two-thirds of the demand for gold credit arises from hedging programs carried out by mining companies. Gold financing techniques can provide three benefits.
- A reduction in the exposure to gold price falls and hence more certainty of cash flows.
- a reduced financing cost unit
- keeping the amount of borrowing to a minimum

In hedging, the basic strategy is to sell gold forward. The forward price of gold has nearly always been higher than its spot price (contango). The contango in the gold market is a direct result of the low cost of borrowing. The amount of the contango is arrived at by adding to the spot price the deposit rate earnable on local currency raised from the sale of spot gold over the period concerned, less the costs of borrowing gold over the same period. If the local interest rates are high, and the gold lease rate is low, the contango will be steep and the advantage to the mine owner is large. Other possibilities to hedge are the use of options, futures and swaps.

---

[20] A. Neuberger, *Gold Derivatives: the Market Impact*, World Gold Council, www.gold.org
[21] A. Doran, *Trends in Gold Banking*, Research Study No. 19, World Gold Council, www.gold.org

Chapter 7

Marketing plan

Clients

Oil

- Refineries
- Traders
- Speculators

Gold

- India (26%)
- Japan (industrial business, 3%)
- Investors
- Traders
- Speculators
- Private clients

Competitors

For oil, the main competitors are the cleaner environmental ways of energy like wind energy, water and sun energy, and also natural gas. The main competitors for gold are currency blocks and a stable global environment. When the global environment is stable the demand for gold is lower. Gold is bought in times of uncertainty. However the main competitors for Division II are the other Divisions (FX Option Market, Equity Market, International Debt Market, and S-T-I-R Market).

Outcome Business Plan

Table 7.5.2 Business Plan

Business Plan	Questions	Answers
Product plan	Products?	Oil products
		Gold products
Production plan	What's needed?	Oil:
		Refinery, upgrading residual fuel, physical markets, futures markets, options market
		Gold:
		Mining, financing, markets, gold lease, hedging.
Marketing plan:	Clients?	Oil: refineries, traders, speculators
		Gold: India, Japan, investors, traders, speculators, private clients
	Competitors?	Division I (FX Option Market)
		Division III (Equity Market)
		Division IV (International Debt Market)
		Division V (S-T-I-R Market)

Strategy:
Both products (oil and gold) are important for the organization as a whole, especially oil. Gold played an important role in the past, but is losing its importance. However, in some parts of the world, gold still plays an important role, only this one is different from its store value. Furthermore, in situations of uncertainty, hoarding is inevitable.

7.6 DESIGN APPROACH II: SWOT ANALYSIS

Commodity Market as driver of EUR/USD Interbank Market

Strengths

Oil price movements as explanation for EUR/USD movements

Graph 7.6.1: Brent price versus EUR/USD, Source : Reuters

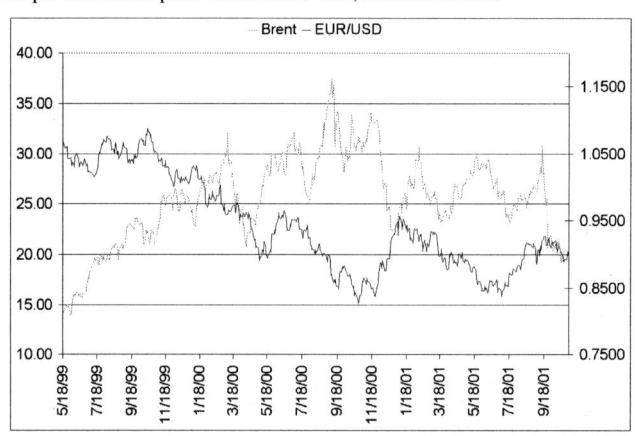

The first strength is that oil explains the weakness in EUR/USD since its start in 1999. The US is the main importer of oil and when the oil prices are moving higher more USD are needed to finance the constant demand for oil in the automobile dominated society where cars are also used mainly for longer distance. Further, oil is quoted in USD so an increase in oil price automatically means more demand for USD. Since the beginning of 1999, oil (Brent) started a move up which seemed to come to an end in September/October 2000 after making a double top. From that time on, oil prices (Brent) moved sideways. Brent moved up from $10 in January 1999 to a high of around $36 in September/October 2000, while in that period the EUR/USD moved down from around 1.1700 (start in 1999) to the low of 0.8228 (end of October 2000). Every time that oil makes a correction downwards, the EUR/USD corrects upwards, see graph (correlation = -0.60).

Table 7.6.1: Brent-EUR/USD correlation table based on Reuters daily data

	Correlation with EUR/USD
18/05/99-31/10/01	-0.60
1999	-0.28
2000	-0.56
1st half 2000	-0.18
2nd half 2000	-0.49
2001	-0.20
1st half 2001	-0.36
2nd half 2001	-0.13

September 11 impact on correlation between Brent and EUR/USD

The September 11 events changed the market and the strong negative correlation between Brent oil and EUR/USD. Up to September 11, the correlation was -0.67. After that the correlation moved from -0.67 to -0.35 including 3 April 2002.

Graph 7.6.2: Before September 11, 2001

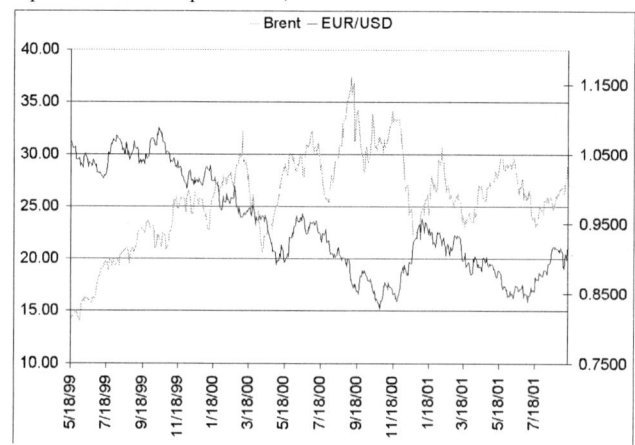

Source: Reuters daily data

Graph 7.6.3: After September 11, 2001

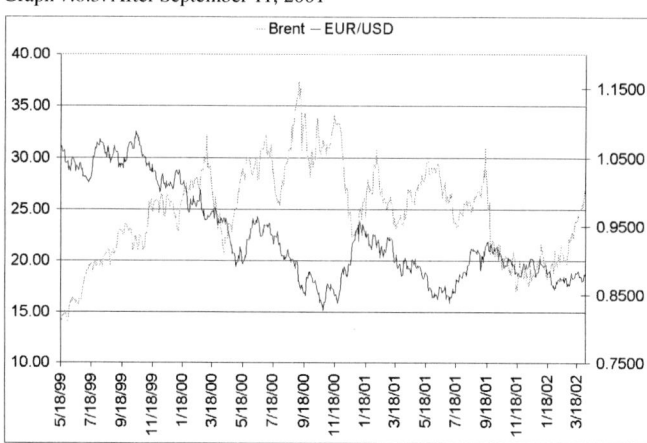

Source: Reuters daily data

What happened?
1. Market changed from a supply-driven "minded" market to a demand "minded" market.
    – Supply minded: market reacts on information about shortage of supply such as API data and fear of supply disruption due to threat of war.
    – Demand minded: markets reacts on information about the state of the airline industry (less passengers)and the state of US and world economy.

2. In 2002, market is slowly changing back towards supply minded market.
    – Markets pricing in US and global recovery.
    – Oil is sensitive for tensions in Middle East, Israel/Palestine conflict and the threat of Iraq and Iran to use oil as a weapon against the US.

So after a few months (Sep-Dec 2001) of low negative correlation between Brent oil and EUR/USD, this correlation is starting to pick up again because of a supply minded market. A wider spread Middle East conflict could move oil higher and prospects of peace could move oil lower. A lower oil price would give EUR/USD the opportunity to break higher while a higher oil price would diminish this upside potential.

Gold price movements as explanation for EUR/USD movements

Graph 7.6.4: Gold price versus EUR/USD, Source: Reuters

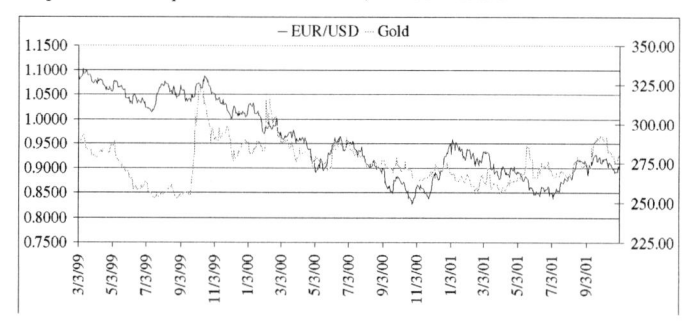

The movements in the gold price could give an explanation for the movements in the EUR/USD. From January 1999 until now, the correlation between the EUR/USD and the Gold price is 0.27. Unlike the oil price, the gold price has a much higher (positive) correlation with the EUR/USD on the shorter-time frame and is, in some cases, even leading.

Table 7.6.2: Gold-EUR/USD correlation table based on Reuters daily data

	Correlation with EUR/USD
03/03/99-31/10/01	0.27
1999	0.20
1st half 1999	0.86
2nd half 1999	0.07
2000	0.79
1st half 2000	0.53
2nd half 2000	0.83
2001	0.10
1st half 2001	-0.39
2nd half 2001	0.80

Week 08-12 October 2001:

Sunday — The US started the military counter attack overnight with missile strikes on targets inside Afghanistan.

Monday — In the currency markets the CHF strenghtened due to safe-haven flows.
In the Commodity Market, Gold strengthened against the USD (high around $293.75).

Tuesday — The USD/CHF and the EUR/USD were facing problems to take out important technical levels. Gold had problems with a $294.00 key resistance level.

Wednesday — Currency markets give the signal that the worst is over. Gold dropped almost $4 and the USD/CHF popped up above 1.6200.

Thursday — Gold **dropped to the $282.50** level and this is adding to the sentiment supporting USD. This drop in Gold was followed later that day by a sell-off in the EUR/USD and other currencies against USD.

Table 7.6.3: Gold price versus EUR/USD

	Gold open	Gold high	Gold low	Gold close	EUR/$ open	EUR/$ high	EUR/$ low	EUR/$ close
11 Sep 01	271.15	289.80	271.00	286.00	0.8982	0.9169	0.8947	0.9140
12 Sep 01	290.00	290.00	275.50	278.00	0.9112	0.9149	0.9005	0.9068
13 Sep 01	277.00	281.00	277.00	281.00	0.9067	0.9125	0.9044	0.9107
14 Sep 01	280.00	288.50	280.00	285.30	0.9106	0.9248	0.9077	0.9206
16 Sep 01					0.9210	0.9220	0.9209	0.9220
17 Sep 01	290.00	294.00	284.50	289.20	0.9233	0.9333	0.9169	0.9243
18 Sep 01	289.00	289.50	286.25	287.50	0.9247	0.9282	0.9184	0.9273
19 Sep 01	287.25	291.00	286.25	289.90	0.9268	0.9325	0.9223	0.9266
20 Sep 01	290.00	290.50	287.50	288.40	0.9260	0.9293	0.9226	0.9276
21 Sep 01	288.50	294.50	288.00	291.20	0.9274	0.9275	0.9082	0.9147
22 Sep 01	291.00	292.00	290.50	290.50	0.9146	0.9150	0.9135	0.9135
23 Sep 01	290.50	290.50	290.50	290.50	0.9132	0.9140	0.9132	0.9140
24 Sep 01	290.75	292.50	286.90	289.00	0.9133	0.9204	0.9100	0.9168
25 Sep 01	289.00	290.25	286.50	289.25	0.9165	0.9249	0.9143	0.9230
26 Sep 01	288.50	293.40	288.50	292.50	0.9229	0.9243	0.9188	0.9230
27 Sep 01	292.25	292.80	288.65	291.40	0.9227	0.9232	0.9154	0.9181
28 Sep 01	291.00	293.65	289.55	292.45	0.9178	0.9181	0.9079	0.9114
29 Sep 01	292.50	293.50	292.00	292.00	0.9114	0.9119	0.9114	0.9114
30 Sep 01	292.00	292.00	292.00	292.00	0.9114	0.9114	0.9095	0.9098
01 Oct 01	291.45	292.50	290.40	291.45	0.9100	0.9177	0.9057	0.9173
02 Oct 01	291.65	292.60	288.40	289.20	0.9169	0.9197	0.9129	0.9188
03 Oct 01	289.50	290.80	288.75	289.20	0.9181	0.9235	0.9124	0.9144
04 Oct 01	288.75	291.10	288.25	289.60	0.9141	0.9185	0.9107	0.9178
05 Oct 01	289.75	292.00	289.75	290.75	0.9177	0.9207	0.9153	0.9183
06 Oct 01	290.75	291.75	290.75	290.75	0.9183	0.9185	0.9183	0.9185
07 Oct 01	290.75	290.75	290.45	290.50	0.9185	0.9191	0.9178	0.9191
08 Oct 01	292.25	293.75	290.20	291.65	0.9180	0.9244	0.9161	0.9210
09 Oct 01	291.50	291.50	287.60	287.75	0.9206	0.9226	0.9123	0.9130
10 Oct 01	288.50	288.80	283.60	284.60	0.9128	0.9158	0.9098	0.9110
11 Oct 01	285.00	285.00	280.00	281.00	0.9106	0.9122	0.8984	0.9022
12 Oct 01	282.05	284.60	281.00	284.20	0.9025	0.9125	0.9010	0.9113

Source: Reuters daily data

Weakness

Correlation between Gold and EUR/USD is not stable

The main weakness is that the correlation between gold price and EUR/USD is not stable. This correlation is very important in times of high uncertainty, because safe-haven flows cause an extra demand for gold against the USD. In normal market circumstances, the gold price is reacting to the US interest rates, dollar strength relative to other currencies, the lease rate of gold, recession outlook, gold auctions and the hedge activities of producers.

At the start of this year, gold came under pressure despite a lower USD (rally in EUR/USD to 0.9600) and weaker stock markets. The unexpected 50bp inter-meeting interest rate cut by the Fed made a sudden short covering happen. However, the upmove was not for long. The Bank of England gold auction, and the renewed strength of the USD, put pressure on the gold price. News of the devastating earthquake in Gujarat, which the market feared could lead to a reduced demand for gold in India (main importer), pushed gold to the new low end of its trading range on January 29. At the beginning of February, gold lease rates showed early signs of tightness developing in the physical market, with the one month rate, which had held close to 0.50% throughout 200, firming up to 0.76%. But with the dollar recovering strongly, gold came under renewed pressure. On February 9, gold dipped below $260. The release of US producer price statistics, showing an unexpectedly large gain of 1.1%, then provided some support for gold prices. The gold lease rates for nearby maturity continued to rise strongly as the availability of short-term liquidity tightened once more. The one-month lease rate increased to 1.08%. By February 26 the one-month rate had surged to 2.26%. On February 27 the one-month lease rate soared towards 5%. Additional support was provided by reports of a 6% decrease in US durable goods orders in January, which raised the specter of recession and increased the likelihood of lower US interest rates. In March, gold was sold off as a result of the Bank of England gold auction, the dollar's strength relative to the EUR and the Australian dollar and the disappointed 50bp interest rate cut by the Fed[22].

---

[22]World Gold Council, *Gold Demand Trends, Issue No. 35 May 2001*, www.gold.org

Opportunities

The opportunity is that gold will be restored to dominance in the international financial markets and thereby play a more dominant role than it does currently. The situations when this occurs are during periods of financial stress or instability (terrorist attacks of the 11th of September). Investors can protect themselves against these periods by building diversified portfolios including gold[23]. Since there are always risks in global markets. gold will be able to be restored to power for just short periods.

Threats

The threats are that the other divisions will give a better explanation of the movements in the EUR/USD than the Commodity Market. So far, Division II has been leading due to a solid explanation from the oil side. Division II is followed by Division III (Equity Market), in which M&A together with oil, gave the EUR/USD a horrible time.

Outcome SWOT Analysis

Table 7.6.4: SWOT Analysis

Strengths	Weaknesses
Oil	Gold and EUR/USD correlation not stable
Gold	

Opportunities	Threats
In times of uncertainty in stress gold is back in favor	FX Option Market, Equity Market, International Debt Market, Short-Term-Interest-Rate Market

The strategy resulting from this SWOT Analysis is the following:
Since oil gives a solid explanation for the movements in the EUR/USD, it is the key market to watch. Gold has lost its dominant position but will play an important role in times of uncertainty. In such times, gold is appreciating against the dollar. However, upfront it's not always clear if the dollar also appreciates against the other major currencies.

---

[23]Gold Portfolio Letter no.11, December 2000, *Managing Portfolio Risk for Periods of Stress,* World Gold Council, www.gold.org

The following strategy is defined to overcome the major weakness. There is no stable correlation between gold and EUR/USD:

Graph 7.6.5: Gold/Oil versus EUR/USD

USE THE GOLD PRICE RELATIVE TO OIL PRICE AS MAIN DRIVER FOR MOVEMENTS IN EUR/$ (GOLD PRICE/OILPRICE). GRAPH 7.6.5 AND TABLE 7.6.5 WILL SHOW THIS.

Source: Reuters daily data

Table 7.6.5: Gold/Brent-EUR/USD correlation based on Reuters daily data

	Correlation with EUR/USD
18/05/99-31/10/01	0.65
1999	0.29
2000	0.68
1st half 2000	0.33
2nd half 2000	0.60
2001	0.19
1st half 2001	0.26
2nd half 2001	0.36

7.7 POSITIONING APPROACH I

Considering the position of this division compared to the other divisions in the EUR/USD Interbank Market Organization, the key question is:

Is this division able to explain the movements in the EUR/USD Interbank Market and how is this compared to competitors?

Potential entrants:
The potential entrants are low since almost all the financial markets are defined as a division in the EUR/USD Interbank Market Organization. The only market left is the real-estate market, including the funds operating in this market.

There is an intensity of rivalry among existing competitors:
The competitors of this division are:
- FX Option Market Division
- Equity Market Division
- International Debt Market Division
- Short-Term-Interest-Rate Market Division

This division and the Commodity Market Division have played a very prominent role in the EUR/USD Interbank Market Organization. The power shifts from one division to another creating rivalry.

Bargaining power of buyers:
The buyers are the refineries (oil), investors, speculators, traders and private clients. There are not alternative opportunities for the buyers, because the other financial markets don't deliver similar products. Further, the demand for oil and gold is sentiment driven. When the oil market is focused on the supply side, tension in the Middle East or in other oil producing countries will push the oil price up. The demand for gold (hoarding) will also be higher in an uncertain environment, such as tension in the Middle East, September 11 attacks and accountancy problems of major companies in the U.S.A.

Bargaining power of suppliers:
The suppliers in this market are: OPEC members and non-OPEC members in the oil market and mining companies and central banks in the gold market. The power of the suppliers is high because the industrialized world cannot live without oil. The gold supply is quite inelastic not only because the mining process is time consuming, but also the Washington Agreement limits the selling of gold by central banks.

Pressure from substitute products:
The substitute products are the products offered by the other divisions in the EUR/USD Interbank Market Organization.
- FX Options
- Equity products
- International Debt Market products
- Short-Term-Interest-Rate Market products.

Other products are no substitute for oil and gold, so pressure from substitute products is low.

7.8 THE POSITIONING APPROACH II: CONCEPTS OF INDUSTRY EVOLUTION

Division II is based on industry creation and not on the concepts of industry evolution. There are some variables that cannot be influenced including economic, technological, social and political factors. However, the rest of the variables can influenced by strategists. OPEC is a very good example of this. They control 40% of the oil market and are trying to increase their power by buying or building refineries or signing long-term supply contracts. The oil suppliers are the ones who control the industry and, if they help each other, they are able to create the environment they prefer, since people are dependent on oil. A similar kind of situation is going on in the gold market. The only difference is that the producers met some new suppliers in gold in the market (central banks). However, the supply is for the coming five years and is restricted by the Washington Agreement. Gold has lost its dominant power but will continue playing an important role in financial markets, especially in situations of distress and uncertainty. The reader can find out more about industry evolution versus industry creation in the following book: "Strategy Process, Content, Context" by Bob de Wit & Ron Meyer.

7.9 APPENDIX A

Table A, Source: www.eai.doe.gov

1999	Sources include Dow Jones (DJ), New York Times (NYT), Wall Street Journal (WSJ), the Washington Post (WP), World Markets Online (WMO), Oil Daily (OD), Los Angeles Times (LAT).
Jan 1	British Petroleum Company and Amoco Corporation complete their $53 billion merger. (DJ)
Feb 4	Italy's ENI SpA and Russia's RAO Gazprom, the world's largest natural gas producer, agree to build a natural gas pipeline from Russia to Turkey at a cost of nearly $3 billion. Each project partner will hold a 50 percent stake in the project (Asian WSJ).
Feb 10	U.S, Energy Secretary Bill Richardson visits Saudi Arabia to discuss potential U.S, investment in the Kingdom's oil and gas sectors. Following his visit, Richardson says the Saudis are primarily interested in foreign investment in the natural gas sector and in the oil refining and marketing sectors, rather than in the upstream crude oil sector. (DJ), (USA). (WSJ)
Mar 23	In an effort to raise oil prices, OPEC and non-OPEC countries agree to cut oil output by a combined 2.104 million barrels per day, effective April 1, 1999, for one year. OPEC members have pledged to cut 1.716 million barrels per day, while several non-OPEC countries have pledged total reductions of 388,000 barrels per day. (DJ, NYT)
Mar 31	Arco agrees to be acquired by BP Amoco PLC for $26.6 billion in stock. If approved, the merger will create the largest oil producer in the United States and one of the largest energy companies in the world. (DJ), (WSJ).
Apr 15	The U.S, Department of Energy (DOE) announces that it will begin taking oil deliveries within the next few days under its plan to add 28 million barrels of oil to the U.S, Government's Strategic Petroleum Reserve (SPR) from federal oil royalty payments. (DJ)
Apr 17	An oil pipeline that transports oil from Baku, Azerbaijan, to Suspa, Georgia, is officially opened.
Apr 28	The U.S, Department of Treasury's Office of Foreign Asset Control (OFAC), notifies Mobil that it has turned down Mobil's request for a license to swap crude oil it produces in Turkmenistan in exchange for Iranian oil. (DJ, WP)
May 10	The Board of Argentine oil company YPF unanimously approved a $13.4 billion offer from Repsol, a Spanish company. (WSJ)
May 12	The Caspian Pipeline Consortium (CPC) begins construction of a 981-mile pipeline that will carry crude oil from the Caspian Sea to the Russian port of Novorossisk for export to foreign markets.
May 17	The Environmental Protection Agency (EPA) states that it will not change its "Tier Two Plan" to cut gasoline sulfur content and tailpipe emissions, in response to a recent appellate court ruling that the EPA had overstepped its mandate in implementing some provisions of the Clean Air Act.
May 27	Exxon and Mobil shareholders approve an $81.2 billion merger, in which Exxon will issue 1.32 shares for each share of Mobil's approximately 780.2 million shares outstanding. (DJ)
June 1	Sudan starts pumping oil through its pipeline linking the Heglig oil field in Western Kordofan province to Port Sudan on the Red Sea. (DJ)
Sep 14	French oil companies Total Fina and Elf Aquitaine agree to merge, after a lengthy takeover battle, in a deal, which will form the world's fourth largest oil company. (WP, WSJ)
Sep 22	The Organization of Petroleum Exporting Countries (OPEC), at a meeting of its member states' oil ministers, decides to maintain current production cuts until March 2000, despite the fact the crude oil prices have doubled since early 1999. (DJ)
Sep 28	Iranian Oil Minister Bijan Zanganeh announces that the National Iranian Oil Company has discovered a new oilfield, Azadegan, with 26 billion barrels of crude oil in Khuzestan province.

Oct 4	The United Nations Security Council agrees to raise the monetary ceiling on Iraqi oil sales to $8.3 billion from $5.26 billion, guaranteeing the continuation of Iraqi production until the November 20 end date for the current six-month extension of the "oil-for-food" program. (DJ)
Nov 18	The heads of state of Turkey, Azerbaijan, and Georgia sign an agreement to build a pipeline for the export of crude oil from the Caspian Basin. (WP, NYT)
Nov 30	The Federal Trade Commission (FTC) grants approval for the proposed merger between oil giants Exxon and Mobil. (DJ)
Dec 21	(DJ) The Export-Import Bank drops a proposed $500 million loan to Russia's Tyumen Oil after Secretary of State Madeleine Albright exercises her statutory authority to block the transaction.
Dec 31	The Panama Canal Zone reverts to Panamanian sovereignty at noon, after nearly a century of American control. More than a half-million barrels of crude oil and petroleum products transit the Canal each day. (DJ) After nearly two years of construction, ExxonMobil completes the Sable Offshore Energy Project, a $2 billion project to bring natural gas from field's offshore Nova Scotia to the northeastern United States. The fields are estimated to contain 3.5 trillion cubic feet of natural gas. (DJ) Russian President Boris Yeltsin makes a surprise announcement that he is resigning immediately, Vladimir Putin becomes Acting President, and presidential elections will be held within 90 days, with a date to be set by the State Duma. Russia is the largest exporter of energy in the world. (DJ)

Table B, Source: www.eai.doe.gov

2000	Sources include Dow Jones (DJ), New York Times (NYT), Wall Street Journal (WSJ), the Washington Post (WP), World Markets Online (WMO), Oil Daily (OD), Los Angeles Times (LAT).
Jan 26	The United Nations Security Council reaches agreement on the appointment of Hans Blix of Sweden, the former head of the International Atomic Energy Agency (IAEA), to lead the new United Nations weapons inspection organization for Iraq. Iraq has indicated that it does not intend to accept the new Security Council resolution. (DJ)
Feb 2	The Federal Trade Commission (FTC) acts to block the proposed merger between BP Amoco and Atlantic Richfield, saying the merger would unduly restrict competition along the West coast of the United States. (WSJ, WP)
Mar 6	The United States Supreme Court overturns the State of Washington's law establishing state regulation of oil tankers, ruling unanimously that federal laws take precedence. (WP, NYT)
Mar 7	New York Mercantile Exchange front-month West Texas Intermediate crude oil futures contract closes at $34.13 per barrel, the highest level in nine years. (WSJ)
Mar 15	Phillips Petroleum announces that it has agreed to purchase Atlantic Richfield's assets in Alaska for $6.5 billion. (DJ, NYT, WSJ)
Mar 26	Vladimir Putin is elected president of Russia on the first ballot, winning 53 percent of the popular vote. Putin took office as acting president in December 1999 after the resignation of Boris Yeltsin. (DJ)
Mar 28	After two days of meetings, oil ministers of the OPEC agree on an increase in oil production of 1.452 million barrels per day by its members, excluding Iran and Iraq. (DJ)
Apr 12	Several Chief Executive Officers of major US oil companies meet with senior Saudi Arabian officials to discuss possible investments in natural gas and petrochemical projects. (WP)
Apr 14	BP Amoco receives approval from the Federal Trade Commission (FTC) for its $28 billion takeover of Atlantic Richfield Corporation (ARCO). (WP, WSJ)
May 16	Several sources, including the Washington Post, report major oil finding at the Kashagan field offshore from Kazakhstan, with reserves reportedly greater than 8 billion barrels. (WP, DJ)
May 17	The Environmental Protection Agency (EPA) formally proposes a rule, which, if finalized, would reduce allowable sulfur levels in diesel fuel by 97 percent over the next five years. (DJ)
	The Energy Information Administration releases a study of oil reserves in the Arctic National Wildlife Refuge (ANWR), which currently is off-limits to oil exploration. (WSJ)
June 6	The World Bank executive board votes to approve a loan of $193 million to support a project to build a crude oil pipeline from Chad to the coast of Cameroon. (DJ)
June 8	The Brazilian government conducts an auction of oil exploration and production concessions covering a total of 21 blocks, both onshore and offshore. (NYT)
June 9	The United States and Mexico sign a treaty resolving the issue of economic rights over the deepwater "doughnut hole" area in the Gulf of Mexico between the two countries. (DJ)
June 21	Oil ministers from the OPEC, meeting in Vienna, agree to raise crude oil production quotas by a total of 708,000 barrels per day. (DJ)
July 27	Italy's ENI signs a deal with Iran worth $3.8 billion for the development of the country's South Pars gas field in the Persian Gulf. (DJ)
Aug 10	Venezuelan President Hugo Chavez meets with Iraqi President Saddam Hussein in Baghdad as part of a tour of members of the Organization of Petroleum Exporting Countries. (NYT, WP)
Aug 23	The Energy Information Administration reports that crude oil stock levels in the United States have fallen to their lowest level since 1976. Crude oil for October delivery closes at $32.02 on the New York Mercantile Exchange (NYMEX), up 80 cents. (DJ)
Aug 30	The Department of Energy awards contracts to create a two-million-barrel reserve of heating oil.
Sept 8	Truck drivers in Britain begin a blockade of oil refineries to protest high fuel prices. The blockade follows a similar protest in France. (DJ)

Sept 10	The OPEC, at a meeting of OPEC oil ministers in Vienna, agrees to raise production quotas by 800,000 barrels per day (to 26.2 million barrels per day, not counting Iraq) in an attempt to push crude oil prices back under $28 per barrel. (DJ)
Sept 20	Oil prices close at $37.20 on the New York Mercantile Exchange (NYMEX), after trading as high as $37.80 during the day's trading session. The price spike comes amid an increase in tensions between Iraq and Kuwait. This level sets a new ten-year high for NYMEX crude oil. (DJ)
Sept 22	President Clinton authorizes the release of 30 million barrels of oil from the Strategic Petroleum Reserve (SPR) over 30 days to bolster oil supplies, particularly heating oil in the Northeast. Crude oil for November delivery falls four percent, to $32.68, on the New York Mercantile Exchange (NYMEX).
Sept 26	A summit of heads of government of the OPEC opens in Caracas, Venezuela. (DJ)
Sept 28	The United Nations Compensation Commission, which handles claims for reparations arising from Iraq's 1990 invasion of Kuwait, approves by consensus a $15.9 billion claim by Kuwait for compensation for lost oil production and damage to oil reserves and equipment. (DJ)
Oct 12	Oil prices rise sharply on news of a terrorist attack on an American warship, the USS Cole, in the Yemeni port of Aden, as well as escalating violence between Palestinians and Israeli security forces. (WSJ)
Oct 15	Chevron agrees to purchase Texaco for $35.1 billion in stock. (WSJ)
Oct 30	The president of the OPEC, Venezuelan oil minister Ali Rodriguez, announces that the cartel will raise production quotas by 500,000 barrels per day, beginning Nov 1st. (DJ, WP, WSJ)
Oct 31	The United Nations Sanctions Committee approves an Iraqi request to be paid in Euros, rather than United States dollars, for oil exported under the "oil for food" program, which is part of the sanctions regime stemming from Iraq's 1990 invasion of Kuwait. (DJ)
Nov 3	Russia's Lukoil announces that it will purchase Getty Petroleum Marketing of the United States for $71 million. (DJ)
Nov 12	Oil ministers of the OPEC, meeting in Vienna, announce a decision to put any further production increases on hold until their next meeting scheduled for Jan 17, 2001. (NYT, WSJ)
Nov 16	Iraq's State Oil Marketing Organization (SOMO) demands that companies lifting cargoes of Iraqi crude oil begin paying a fifty-cent per barrel surcharge starting on December 1, 2000. (DJ)
Dec 1	Vicente Fox is inaugurated as Mexico's president, Ernesto Martens takes office as the new Minister of Petroleum. (DJ)
Dec 4	California utilities are forced to cut off electricity supplies to some "interruptible" customers due to a supply shortage. (DJ)
Dec 5	The United Nations Security Council approves a six month extension to the Iraq "oil for food" program. (DJ)
Dec 21	The Environmental Protection Agency (EPA) announces new regulations, which will drastically reduce the allowable sulfur content in diesel fuel in the United States. (DJ)
Dec 27	Natural gas prices in the United States surge above $10 per million British Thermal Units (BTUs) first time ever in response to cold weather and stockdraws reported by the American Gas Association (AGA), Henry Hub natural gas closes at $9.978, after falling slightly from its intraday peak price. (DJ)
	Venezuelan President Hugo Chavez appoints Alvaro Silva Calderon to replace Ali Rodriguez as Minister of Petroleum. (DJ)
Dec 31	Saudi oil minister Ali Naimi says that the Organization of Petroleum Exporting Countries (OPEC) will cut production when ministers meet in Vienna on January 17, 2001. (DJ)

Table C, Source: www.eai.doe.gov

2001	Sources include Dow Jones (DJ), New York Times (NYT), Wall Street Journal (WSJ), the Washington Post (WP), World Markets Online (WMO), Oil Daily (OD), Los Angeles Times (LAT).
Jan 5	The State of Texas sues ExxonMobil, alleging that the company had produced oil from state-owned land in Texas without paying royalties (DJ, WP).
Jan 6	California power utility Southern California Edison announces that it will cut 1,450 jobs and reduce equipment maintenance in an effort to avoid bankruptcy (DJ).
Jan 11	Crude oil prices rise sharply on indications that the OPEC will cut output quotas at its next meeting scheduled for January 17th in Vienna, The NYMEX contract for February crude closes $29.48 per barrel, up $1.84 or about 7%. (DJ)
Jan 12	California narrowly avoids rolling blackouts as its crisis reaches a Stage 3 alert (WSJ).
Jan 17	OPEC agreed to cut production quotas by 1.5 million bbl/d February 1, 2001. (NYT, WP) California utilities impose rolling blackouts on large portions of the State, as demand for electricity exceeds available supplies (DJ, LAT, WSJ).
Jan 31	The California Senate passes a bill to authorize the state government to spend up to $10 billion for the purchase of electricity, to be financed by the issuence of state bonds (DJ),
Feb 12	A federal judge denies a request by Southern California Edison to remove a rate freeze which has kept the company from recouping the costs imposed on it by wholesale power prices from its customers (DJ).
Feb 14	Kuwait's Prime Minister appoints Adel-al Subeih as Minister of Petroleum (DJ).
Feb 16	US and British aircraft strike Iraqi air defence targets near Bagdad (DJ).
Feb 16	Ecuador's government signs an agreement with a multinational consortium to build a $1.1 billion oil pipeline linking the country's Amazon jungle to an export terminal on its Pacific coast (DJ).
Feb 21	The Federal Energy Regulatory Commission gives final approval for the construction of the Gulfstream Natural Gas System, aproposed $1.7 billion pipeline designed to deliver natural gas to growing markets in Florida (DJ).
Feb 22	For the first time in six weeks, California lifts all alerts on its electric power grid (DJ).
Mar 2	California's largest utility, Pasific Gas and Electric, secures a $1 billion loan to pay its creditors and avoid bankruptcy (LAT).
Mar 4	Tests in recent days confirm the world's largest oil find in three decades in the Kashagan field in the Caspian Sea (WSJ).
Mar 5	Governor Gray Davis of California announces that the state has reached forty separate agreements worth $40 billion to buy power over the next ten years.
Mar 7	Royal Dutch/Shell group announces an unsolicited $1.8 billion takeover bid for Denver-based natural gas producer Barrett Recources Corporation (NYT).
Mar 8	Barret rejects Royal Dutch/Sheel group's $1.8 billion takeover bid and invites other offers (WSJ).
Mar 13	ExxonMobil temporarily shuts down on-shore natural gas operations in the Indonesian region Aceh due to escalating violence and risk to employees and contractors (WSJ).
Mar 15	The world's largest oil rig, located 80 miles offshore Brazil and operated by the Brazilian state oil company Petrobas, suffers three explosions (WSJ).
Mar 17	OPEC agreed to cut production quotas by 1 million bbl/d, effective April 1, 2001
Mar 21	BP and ENI agree to build a $2.5 billion gas liquefaction plant in Egypt with the Egyptian Petroleum Corp (WSJ).
Mar 26	Kazakhstan's Prime Minister opens an oil pipeline from the giant Tengiz field to the Russian port of Novorossiisk (NYT).
Mar 27	California regulators approve 40-46% rise in electricity prices (LAT, NYT, WP).
Mar 28	Oil workers in Venezuela, the world's third largest oil exporter, begin a strike (Reuters).

Chapter 7

Mar 30	The Western Hemisphere climate conference ends with the US declining to go along with a Latin American plan for industrialized countries to reduce their emissions (NYT).
Apr 6	Pacific Gas and Electric formally files for Chapter 11 bankruptcy protection, The utility is attempting to get relief from $9 billion in debt (NYT).
Apr 10	E.ON AG of Germany announces plan to take over Powergen PLC of the UK in a $7.4 billion deal that would create the world's second largest electricity provider (WSJ).
Apr 10	The front month gasoline futures price rises 3.4% to its highest level since June 2000. following a fire that shut down El Paso Energy's Coastal Refinery in Aruba (WSJ).
Apr 12	ExxonMobil Corp, announces that it has made a major oil discovery in Indonesia (DJ).
	Data released by the International Energy Agency show that the OPEC continued to produce oil above its target level in March (DJ).
Apr 16	Conoco's Killingholme refinery in the UK suffers an explosion, shutting down the refinery and killing two workers (Reuters).
Apr 17	Chevron announces that oil reserves in the Tengiz field are about 368 million barrels according to its latest estimates. This is more than double previous estimates (WMO).
Apr 19	US President Bush states publicly that the US government has no intention of removing economic sanctions on Iran and Libya (WP).
Apr 22	The Summit of the Americas in Quebec ends, with all countries except Venezuela and Cuba agreeing to establish a Free Trade Area of the Americas by the end of 2005.
Apr 23	The Australian Government rejects Royal Dutch/Shell Group's planned takeover of Woodside Petroleum Ltd, Australia's largest energy company (WSJ).
Apr 24	Venezuela calls upon foreign companies operating in the country to cut their crude oil output in order for the country to meet its OPEC production quota (WMO).
Apr 26	The directors of the Dabhol Electricity Plant of India, owned by Enron, decide to halt electricity sales to the Maharashtra state electricity board (WMO). Apr 27 Saudi Arabian Energy Minister Ali al-Naimi meets a number of senior US officials (WMO. Reuters).
May 3	ExxonMobil announces that it has made a major oil discovery offshore Angola (WMO).
May 4	California Governor Gray Davis announces a $7 billion agreement by the State to buy electricity over 10 years from Sempra Energy (LAT).
May 7	The Williams Companies announces that it has acquired Barret Resources for $2.5 billion in cash and stock (NYT, WMO).
	Valero Energy announces that it has reached an agreement to acquire Ultramar Diamond Shamrock for $6 billion (NYT, WMO).
May 9	Four people are killed in the Aceh region of Indonesia when two bombs explode, damaging a natural gas pipeline and pumping station owned by ExxonMobil (WMO).
	BP Trinidad and Tobago announces the discovery of a one-trillion-cubic-foot natural gas field off the east coast of Trinidad, enough to power the entire country's electricity needs for about 50 years (WMO).
May 15	The California Public Utilities Commission approves a plan that calls for a $5.7 billion rate increase, much of it falling on residential customers (LAT).
May 16	Norwegian Oil Minister Olav Akselsen announces that Norway's oil production has plateaued and that there are no plans to raise or lower in concert with OPEC (Reuters).
May 17	President Bush issues the administration's new energy policy (LT, WP, WSJ).
	BP and Shell say that they will build a $150 million, 100-mile natural gas pipeline in the Gulf of Mexico WSJ).
May 18	Brazil orders consumers and citizens to cut electricity consumption by 20% to avoid blackouts (NYT).
	Saudi Arabia selects the eight companies to take part in its "Gas Initiative", three core venture gas projects that have an anticipated worth of $25 billion. They are: Core Venture1: ExxonMobil, Shell, BP and Philips; Venture 2: ExxonMobil, Occidental and Enron; Venture 3: Shell, TotalFinaElf and Conoco (WMO).

May 21	The price of Brent futures crude oil for delivery in early June peaks at $29.68 per barrel, the highest in a year. This comes as concern increases over US gasoline supplies, heightening Israeli-Palestinian tensions, a possible Iraqi halt in oil exports and OPEC statements to the effect that a production quota increase in June is unlikely (WMO).
	The Enron Corporation's power generating venture in India, the Dabhol Power Company, serves formal notice that it will terminate its power supply contract and pull out
May 23	Shell announces that it has discovered a huge reserve of oil in Oil Mining Lease 118 offshore Nigeria (WMO).
May 30	Iraqi Oil Minister Amir Mohammad Rasheed signs an oil and gas cooperation agreement with his Algerian counterpart (WMO).
May 31	The US and Britain win Security Council approval of a one-month extension of the UN oil-for-food program (WSJ).
June 3	Iraq announces that it will halt crude exports in response to a UN Security Council resolution that extends the oil-for-food program by only one month, instead of the normal six-month period (NYT).
June 5	OPEC held its 115th extraordinary meeting to review the state of world oil markets, leaving quotas unchanged.
	Eqypt and Jordan signa 30-year agreement to export Egyptian natural gas to Jordan through a pipeline (DJ).
June 7	BP announces that it will build a new $600-million platform offshore Trinidad that is expected to double the company's production of natural gas by 2004 (DJ).
June 11	Saudi Arabia announces that it has seized ownership, effective June 7, of the 1.6-million barrel-per-day IPSA pipeline that had carried Iraqi crude oil to the Saudi Red Sea port of Mu'jiz prior to Iraqi invasion of Kuwait (DJ).
June 14	The California Supreme Court reject allegations that nine of the largest oil companies in the US conspired to fix gasoline prices in California (DJ).
June 16	The Iraqi Trade Minister, Mohammed Mehdi Saleh, states that Iraqi crude oil exports will not resume as long as the US-British changes to the memoranum governing the oil-for-food program are being considered (AP).
June 18	Statoil, the Norwegian state-owned oil company, takes part in an initial public offering (NYT).
June 19	Hunt Oil Company of the US agrees to pay $600 million to acquire Chieftain international of Canada (WSJ).
	Administrative workers for Shell in Nigeria go on strike (Reuters).
June 22	Electricity prics in the western US fall to their lowest level in over a year in the wake of federal price controls and declining natural gas prices (WSJ).
June 24	Qatar signs a contract with Edison Gas of Italy to supply 3.5 million metric tons of liquefied natural gas per year for 25 years, starting in 2005 (Reuters).
June 27	Crude oil and gasoline futures on the NYMEX collapse to their lowest level in over a year. This comes in the wake of reports that inventories are steady or rising for gasoline and crude oil (DJ)
June 30	ENI of Italy signs a $550 million contract to develop Iran's Darquain field, with expected production of 160,000 barrels per day (LAT).
July 2	The UN Security Council, facing almost certain Russian veto, agrees to postpone indefinitely a vote on the US-led package for Iraq, despite support by the four council members. Instead it will extend the program that allows Iraq to export oil and import food and other commodities under UN supervision (WP).
July 3	OPEC agrees to maintain current production quotas (WP).
July 9	California State officials and power suppliers fail to reach agreement on disputed charges worth $8.9 billion (WP).
July 11	Iraq resumes oil exports. The oil-for-food program will be extended for five months (NYT).

July 12	A bomb attack shuts down pumping at Colombia's Cano Limon Pipelinem the country's second-largest crude oil export pipeline (OD, DJ).
July 16	BP agrees to buy a 51% stake in German energy conglomerate E.On's Veba Oel petroleum station and oil unit in a deal valuing the business about $5.56 billion (DJ).
July 18	Crude oil futures fall to their lowest level in 14 months after data from the Energy Information Administration and the American Petroleum Institute show larger-than expected build in crude oil stocks (DJ).
July 23	Endesa agrees to buy Electrogen of Italy for $3.2 billion. making Endesa the third largest electricity generator in italy (NYT).
July 24	An Iranian warship in the Caspian Sea threates a BP oil exploitation ship off the coast of d Azerbaijan. This prompts BP to suspend exploration in the area (NYT).
July 25	OPEC agree to cut crude oil production quotas by about 4% (DJ).
Aug 1	The US House of Representatives votes to allow oil drilling in the Arctic National Wildlife Refuge (WP).
Aug 2	Crude oil futures prices for September delivery on NYMEX rise $0.94 to $27.71 per barrel. their highest level in six weeks. This comes after a July 31 report by American Petroleum Institute showing a decline in US petroleum inventories for the first time in more than a month (WSJ).
Aug 8	The Energy Information Administration announces that petroleum demand in July is the second highest July figure ever recorded (DJ).
Aug 10	The US and Great Britain reject a proposal by UN Secretary General Kofi Annan to permit the Iraqi government to use $1 billion per year to fund Infrastructure improvements and to increase oil production capacity (WMO).
Aug 13	Iraqi Vice-President Ramadan announces that Syria will soon hire contractors to build a new oil pipeline stretching from the Iraqi boarder to Syria (DJ).
	BP signs an agreement with Algerian state oil and gas company Sonatrach for the development of the 7.1-trillion-cubic-foot in Salah natural gas field (WMO).
Aug 14	Devon Energy buys Mitchell Energy for $3.1 billion in cash and stock (WSJ, DJ).
Aug 24	The US decides to support a modified British proposal to tighten procedures for pricing Iraqi crude oil (WP).
	Iranian President Khatemi and Turkish President Niyazov call for a suspension of oilfield development in disputed sectors of the Caspian Sea (WMO).
Aug 28	The European Commission approves the $5.3 billion takeover of Italian power company Montedison by Italenergia, a holding company led by the Fiat Group (NYT).
Sep 3	Libya's Foreign Minister announces that US companies will be given one year to resume oil operations in the country before Libya decides whether their licenses should be revoked and given to other firms (Reuters).
Sep 4	Devon Energy agrees to buy natural gas-producer Anderson Exploration of Canada for $3.4 billion (DJ).
Sep 5	The NYMEX begins trading of 14-day Brent futures contracts, which had previously been traded on the International Petroleum Exchange in London. The price of Brent crude is an important international benchmark used in pricing formulas for up to two-thrids of the world's crude oil (DJ).
Sep 7	The US Fedral Trade Commission approves Chevron's bid to buy Texaco (DJ).
Sep 11	Terrorist attacks in the US.
Sep 13	Relative calm returns to world oil markets as US retail gasoline prices return to normal levels and Brent futures fall back to $28.02 per barrel for October delivery after spiking to above $31.00 in the aftermath of the September 11 attacks (WMO).
Sep 17	Philips completes its $7.36 billion stock acquisition of Tosco, after getting approval from the US Federal Trade Commission (WSJ, LAT).

Sep 20	Iraq accuse Kuwait of excessive extraction of the joint al-Ratqa border oilfield (Reuters). PG&E, California's largest utility, files its bankruptcy plans (NYT).
Sep 24	Crude oil and petroleum products futures fall to their lowest level in nearly two years amid fears that a recession will reduce energy demand. Over the past six trading sessions crude oil and gasoline futures have fallen more than 26% and heating oil futures have fallen nearly 29%.
Oct 4	The US EIA releases its Winter Fuels Outlook 2001/2002, which predicts lower gasoline, heating fuel, and electricity costs for this winter as compared with the previous one (NYT).
Oct 7	Air raids by the US and its coalition partner, Great Britain, begin against Taliban and al-Qaeda targets in Afganistan (Reuters).
Oct 8	Burlington Resources agrees to purchase Canadian Hunter Exploration for $2.08 billion (WSJ).
Oct 8	Enron agrees to sell its Portland General Electric to Northwest Natural Gas for $1.88 billion in cash and stock (DJ).
Oct 9	Royal Dutch/Shell announces that it will acquire Texaco's interests in two US refining ventures, Motiva Enterprises and Equilon Enterprises, for $2.1 billion in cash, $1.4 billion in debt, and $300 million in pension liabilities (DJ).
Oct 9	The US House of Representatives passes a measure urging the Bush administration to pump more oil into the Strategic Petroleum Reserve (AP).
Oct 18	Crude Oil for November delivery falls to its lowest level since August 1999 on the New York Mercantile Exchange (NYMEX). Poor economic prospects in the next few months, and OPEC's inability to respond so far are seen as factors contributing to the sliding prices of crude oil (Oil Daily).
Oct 22	OPEC announces that its 10 members with output restrictions implemented only 539,000 barrels per day of a promised one million cut in September (Reuters).
Oct 28	Mexican President Vicente Fox states that Mexico would not cut or freeze Pemex's crude output for now (Reuters).
Oct 31	OPEC President Chakib Khelil states that OPEC oil producers are prepared to cut supply to get weak oil prices back up to the group's $25-per-barrel target price.

SUMMARY 7

Outcome of the Business Plan Division II, Commodity Oil & Gold Market, table 7.5.2

Business Plan	Questions	Answers
Product plan	Products?	Oil products Gold products
Production plan	What's needed?	Oil: Refinery, upgrading residual fuel, physical markets, futures markets, options market Gold: Mining, financing, markets, gold lease, hedging.
Marketing plan	Clients?	Oil: refineries, traders, speculators Gold: India, Japan, investors, traders, speculators, private clients
	Competitors?	Division I (FX Option Market) Division III (Equity Market) Division IV (International Debt Market) Division V (S-T-I-R Market)

Outcome of the SWOT Analysis Division II, table 7.6.4

Strengths	Weaknesses
Oil	Gold and EUR/USD correlation not stable
Gold	

Opportunities	Threats
In times of uncertainty or stress gold is back in favor	FX Option Market, Equity Market, International Debt Market, S-T-I-R Market

Division II (Commodity Oil & Gold Market) as a Machine Configuration.

Chapter 8 on Division III (Equity Market), will cope with the the following subjects:
1. The Configuration approach and Division III.
2. The Entrepreneurial approach and Division III.
3. The Design approach and Division III.
4. The Positioning approach and Division III.

REFERENCES

Doran, A. (1998). "Trends in Gold Banking", Research Study No.19, World Gold Council.
Green, T (1999). "Central Banks Gold Reserves", World Gold Council
Mintzberg, H., *STRUCTURES IN FIVES: Designing Effective Organizations,* Copyright © 1993. Reprinted by permission of Pearson Education, Inc., Upper Saddle River, New Jersey.
Mintzberg, H., B. Ahlstrand, J. Lampel, *STRATEGY SAFARI: The Complete Guide Through the Wilds of Strategic Management,* Copyright © 1998. Reprinted by permission of Pearson Education Ltd, 128 LongAcre, London WC2E 9AN
Neuberger, A. (2001). "Gold derivatives: the market impact", World Gold Council.
World Gold Council (2000). "20 questions about Switzerland's gold"
World Gold Council (2000). "Managing Portfolio Risk for Periods of Stress", Gold Portfolio Letter, No.11.
World Gold Council (2001). "Demand trends", Issue No. 35.
World Gold Council. "Industrial Uses of Gold"

RECOMMENDED BOOKS

Clubley, S. (1998). "Trading in Oil Futures and Options", Woodhead Publishing Limited.
Jones, F.J. and R.J. Teweles (1999). "The Futures Game: Who wins, Who loses & Why", Mc-Graw-Hill.
Meyer, R. and B. de Wit (1998). "Strategy Process, Content, Context". International Thomson Business Press.

Chapter **8**

DIVISION III
EQUITY MARKET

8.1 INTRODUCTION

Division III (Equity Market) is the third division of the EUR/USD Interbank Market organization. Division I (the FX Option Market) and the Division II (the Commodity Market) have already offered explanations for the movements in the EUR/USD over the last 2½ years. Division III (the Equity Market) also played a very important role in the EUR/USD downtrend.

The following conclusions are made in the SWOT Analysis:
1. Higher return on US investments and higher US GDP growth.
2. M&A cash financing has a large influence on the EUR/USD.
3. M&A stock swap financing is also important for EUR/USD movements.
4. Merger arbitrage activity gives an explanation for pressure on the EUR/USD.
5. MSCI adjustments weigh down on the EUR/USD.
6. Higher USD turnover in the equity derivative market.
7. Capital flow data of US Treasury Bulletin (TIC) and ECB balance of payments data are preferable to use as background information.
8. Division III (the Equity market) lost its important role in explaining the EUR/USD movements during the equity sell-off in 2000.
9. Division IV (the International Debt Market) and Division V (the S-T-I-R Market) took over this role.

We start this division with the Configuration approach, followed by the Entrepreneurial approach, the Design approach (I + II) and the Positioning approach (I + II). These approaches are explained in detail in chapters 1 and 2.

8.2 CONFIGURATION APPROACH

The structure of an organization can be defined as the different ways in which work is divided into different tasks and how these tasks are coordinated. In the organization, Division III, the main product is the Equity Market. This is the general product, which can be divided into two sub-products: equity markets (stock indices, merger & acquisition, hedge fund strategies) and derivative markets. The different EUR/USD sub products are used for different clients based on different knowledge levels.

Organizational parts
Strategic Apex
The equity market makers are responsible for Division III (the Equity Market). They are the strategists of the organization.

Support Staff
This organizational group has the task of influencing the work of others in the organization. They do this by training the people in Division III and by making sure that the technology is updated so that the Strategic Apex receives live prices and news. Further, the **salespeople match the clients and products.**

Techno Structure
The Techno Structure for Division III (Equity Market) is the same as for the total EUR/USD Interbank Market organization and can be divided into:
1. Fundamental Analysis (Chapter 4)
2. Technical Analysis (Chapter 5)
Division III uses a combination of both specialties.

Middle Line
The middle line of Division III is the group of other traders in this division, such as the M&A desks, traders on hedge fund (client group) desk, equity sales-traders, futures traders, options traders and convertible traders.

Operating Core
The operating core has four main functions:
1. Supply the general Equity Market product for the production.
2. Transform the general Equity Market product into the differentiated sub-products: stocks and derivatives.
3. Distribute the differentiated Equity Market sub-products
4. Provide direct support to input, transformation and output.

Coordination mechanism
The coordination mechanism used in Division III is standardization of output. The general Equity product (input) is transformed into two sub-products (output), which will be tailor-made to meet the needs of the clients.

Decentralization
The Equity Market traders are responsible for the strategy and building of the sub-products. The power is decentralized over the middle-line managers. However, inside this division, power is centralized.

Configuration
Division III (Equity Market) uses standardization of output as the coordination mechanism. Further, the Middle Line is the dominant force (with help of the salespeople) in the organization because it influences which of the Equity sub products is used in the market. The power is decentralized over the Middle Line (partial vertical decentralization). So Division III division also has a **Diversified Configuration (see chapter 1 for a visualization)**.

Outcome

Table 8.2.1

Division III: Equity Market	Definition
Strategic Apex	Equity Market traders
Support Staff	Systems
	Sales force to match the clients with the products
Techno Structure	Fundamental Analysis (Chapter 4)
	Technical Analysis (Chapter 5)
Middle Line	Traders on hedge fund desk
	Equity sales-traders
	Futures traders
	Option traders
	Equity swap traders
	Merger & Acquisition desks
Operating Core	Stock indices
	Hedge fund market
	Merger & Acquisition market
	Convertible market
	Index futures market
	Equity options market
	Equity swap market
Coordination mechanism	Standardization of output
Decentralization	Partial vertical decentralization
Configuration	Diversified organization
Culture	Market Psychology (Chapter 3)

8.3 ENTREPRENEURIAL APPROACH

Within Division III (Equity Market), traders and strategists make the decisions where, when and how to take positions in the market. Their decisions are based on their vision of the market. However, quantitative funds take the decision about positioning in the market based on models (analytical, Positioning approach)

The Equity Market can be divided into two sub markets.
1. EQUITY MARKETS
2. DERIVATIVE MARKETS

In the product plan, all the products of the different sub-markets will be described. The thinking is done by the market makers in the different Equity Markets. They decide about their pricing and position. However, the clients also make decisions about strategy, which makes them a very powerful client group.

DIVISION III EQUITY MARKET

8.4 DESIGN APPROACH I: BUSINESS PLAN

Product plan

The products represented within Division III (Equity Market):

EQUITY MARKETS
1. Stock indices
2. Hedge fund strategies
3. M&A

DERIVATIVE MARKETS
1. Swaps
2. Futures
3. Options

Equity markets

Stock indices
All stock indices are build up out of individual stocks. The stock selection is dependent on region, market capitalization, stock turnover, industry, and performance. An overview of the most important stock indices will be given below.

US
Dow Jones Industrial Average:
The Dow Jones Industrial is a price-weighted index. Table 8.4.1 shows the Dow Jones Industrial Average member weightings.

Table 8.4.1

No	Stock	%	No	Stock	%
1.	Alcoa Inc	2.605%	16.	Honeywell Intern	2.303%
2.	American Express	2.505%	17.	Intel Corp	1.860%
3.	AT&T Corp	1.455%	18.	IBM	6.969%
4.	Boeing Co	3.553%	19.	International Pa 2	.331%
5.	Caterpillar Inc	3.246%	20.	Johnson & Johnson	3.299%
6.	Citigroup Inc	3.324%	21.	JP Morgan Chase	2.913%
7.	Coca-Cola Co	2.919%	22.	McDonald's Corp	1.737%
8.	Disney Co	1.813%	23.	Merck & Co Inc	4.152%
9.	Du Pont	3.023%	24.	Microsoft Corp	4.323%
10.	Eastman Kodak Co	2.949%	25.	Minnesota Mining	7.499%
11.	Exxon Mobil Corp	5.680%	26.	Philip Morris Co	2.991%
12.	General Electric	3.068%	27.	Procter & Gamble	4.254%
13.	General Motors Co	4.047%	28.	SBC Communication	2.618%
14.	Hewlett-Packard	1.730%	29.	United Technologies	4.767%
15.	Home Depot Inc	2.968%	30.	Wal-Mart Stores	3.098%

Source: Bloomberg, July 2001

NASDAQ:
NASDAQ is a capital weighted index. The NASDAQ Composite Index group weightings are as follows.

Table 8.4.2

No	Group	%
1.	NASDAQ Computer	41.562%
2.	NASDAQ Industrials	23.194%
3.	NASDAQ Telecomm	9.126%
4.	NASDAQ Bank Inde	6.666%
5.	NASDAQ Other Fin	1.223%
6.	NASDAQ Transport	1.218%
7.	NASDAQ Insurance	0.939%

Source: Bloomberg, July 2001

S&P 500:
The S&P 500 is also a capital weighted index. The S&P 500 Economic Sectors group weightings are as follow.

Table 8.4.3

No	Group	%
1.	S&P Technology	18.380%
2.	S&P Financials	18.099%
3.	S&P Consumer Sta	12.989%
4.	S&P Health Care	12.760%
5.	S&P Capital Good	9.361%
6.	S&P Consumer Cyc	8.684%
7.	S&P Energy	6.754%
8.	S&P Communication	5.661%
9.	S&P Utilities	3.922%
10.	S&P Basic Materials	2.659%
11.	S&P Transportation	0.739%

Source: Bloomberg, July 2001

Eurozone
In the Eurozone we have: DAX (Germany), FTSE (UK), CAC 40 (France), SMI (Switzerland), MIB30 (Italy), IBEX 35 (Spain), BEL 20 (Belgium), AEX (The Netherlands), Dow Jones STOXX 50 and Dow Jones Euro STOXX 50. The difference between the last two is that the Dow Jones STOXX 50 Index is representing the largest and most liquid 50 blue chip stocks in Europe and the UK and Dow Jones Euro STOXX 50 represent only the ones in Europe.

Dow Jones Euro STOXX 50 Index:

Table 8.4.4

No	Stock	%	No	Stock	%
1.	Royal Dutch Petroleum	9.020%	26.	Alcatel Alsthom	1.640%
2.	Allianz	5.520%	27.	Endesa 1.640%	
3.	Deutsche Telekom	4.060%	28.	Generale des Eaux	1.590%
4.	ENI	3.630%	29.	RWE ord	1.460%
5.	France Telecom	3.530%	30.	Nokia	1.420%
6.	ING Groep	3.160%	31.	LVMH	1.270%
7.	Unilever	3.080%	32.	Rhone-Poulenc A	1.250%
8.	Daimler-Benz	2.970%	33.	Paribas	1.230%
9.	Telecom Italia ord	2.860%	34.	Ahold	1.130%
10.	Deutsche Bank	2.860%	35.	Societe Generale	1.090%
11.	Siemens	2.770%	36.	Electrabel	1.070%
12.	Veba	2.690%	37.	Akzo Nobel	1.030%
13.	Bayer	2.500%	38.	Repso	1 1.020%
14.	Telefonica Espana	2.400%	39.	Fiat ord	0.950%
15.	ABN Amro	2.350%	40.	Elsevier	0.940%
16.	Elf Aquitaine	2.330%	41.	Saint-Gobain	0.920%
17.	Assicurazioni Generale	2.320%	42.	Air Liquide	0.890%
18.	Axa	2.300%	43.	Credito Italiano ord	0.840%
19.	Aegon	2.240%	44.	Fortis	0.810%
20.	L'Oreal	2.230%	45.	Portugal Telecom	0.780%
21.	Banco Bilbao Vizcaya	2.060%	46.	Allied Irish Bank	0.750%
22.	Philips Electronics	1.820%	47.	Schneider	0.690%
23.	Carrefour	1.730%	48.	Metro ord 0.670%	
24.	Koninklijke PTT NL	1.650%	49.	Petrofina	0.640%
25.	Mannesmann	1.650%	50.	Deutsche Lufthansa	0.540%

Source: www.infobourse.online.fr/htm/DJES50.htm July 2001

Morgan Stanley Capital International (MSCI) Indices[1]

The MSCI Indices are the benchmarks most widely used by global portfolio managers. According to a survey conducted by Pensions & Investments, over 90% of international equity assets in the USA are benchmarked to the MSCI Indices. MSCI estimates that it has a similar market share in Asia. In Europe, MSCI is the index provider of choice for two thirds of Continental European fund managers compared to other cross-border index providers, according to Merrill Lynch/Gallup surveys. The business of MSCI is to provide benchmark products and services to the investment management community, to distribute index and company-level data, and to license the MSCI Indices to third parties for the purpose of creating derivative and proprietary products. The Benchmark Research Group (BRG) is responsible for research and analysis in connection with the MSCI Indices. The members of the BRG provide expertise in country and company research and analytic research. The Index Committee is responsible for all editorial

---

[1] MSCI, WWW.MSCI.COM

decisions affecting the MSCI Indices, including additions and deletions of constituents within the MSCI Indices.

The members of the Committee are from MSCI and the BRG. The EAB serves MSCI in an advisory capacity, providing input on index construction methodology and new product developments. The EAB comprises approximately 18 members from leading pension funds, asset management firms, consultants and academicians around the world[2].

On December 9, 2000, MSCI announced that it would make two major changes to its rules. These are[3]:
1. Adjust all constituents for free float, rounding up to the nearest 5%
2. Increase market coverage from 60% (on a non-float-adjusted basis) to 85% on a float-adjusted basis. Coverage is calculated within each industry of each country.

The new rules will be implemented in two stages: the first half of the adjustment took place on November 30, 2001 and the second half took place on May 31, 2002. Deletions were made in one phase on November 30, 2001. MSCI also created a "preliminary index", which will reflect all the changes, on May 31, 2001. The preliminary index allowed managers to move immediately to the new methodology, and to implement it on a different schedule to the November 2001 - May 2002 timetable that the official index uses. On May 19, 2001, MSCI announced the additions, deletions, weight increases and weight decreases to the index as a result of the new rules.

All Country World Index (ACWI) Free:
The MSCI ACWI Free Index represents 49 of the world's developed and emerging equity markets. The overall free float-adjusted market capitalization of the MSCI Provisional ACWI Free Index will be lower than the total market capitalization of the MSCI Standard ACWI Free Index. The largest increases in weights are:

Country	Standard	Provisional
USA Index	49.1%	55.3%
UK Index	9.3%	10.4%

The largest decreases in country weights occur in the Japanese, French and German Indices (-1.3, -1.2 and –1.0%).

The MSCI EURO Index includes all the important European stocks. The MSCI PAN EURO Index also includes the important stocks of the UK and Switzerland.

---

[2] MSCI, WWW.MSCI.COM
[3] MSCI press release, Geneva May 19 2001, *MSCI Announces Provisional Index Constituents*, Goldman Sachs, Equity Index Research, *The New MSCI Indices,* May 19, 2001

MSCI EURO Index:

Table 8.4.5

No	Stock	%	No	Stock	%
1.	ABN AMRO holding	1.104%	51.	IntesaBci SpA	0.740%
2.	Accor SA	0.314%	52.	KBC Bancassurance	0.473%
3.	Aegon NV	1.668%	53.	Royal KPN NV	0.198%
4.	Koninklijke Ahold	1.021%	54.	L'OREAL	1.908%
5.	Air Liquide	0.523%	55.	Lafarge SA	0.501%
6.	Akzo Nobel NV	0.510%	56.	Lagardere S.C.A.	0.278%
7.	Alcatel SA	0.780%	57.	Linde AG	0.208%
8.	Allianz AG	2.797%	58.	LVMH Moet Hennes	1.015%
9.	Allied Irish Bank	0.406%	59.	Mediaset SpA	0.381%
10	ASML Holding NV	0.364%	60.	Mediabanca SpA	0.312%
11.	Autostrade Conce	0.353%	61.	Metro AG	0.553%
12.	Aventis SA	2.430%	62.	Muenchener Rueck	2.143%
13.	Axa	2.091%	63.	Nokia OYJ	3.351%
14.	Banca di Roma Sp	0.177%	64.	Peugeot SA	0.544%
15.	Banco Bilbao Viz	1.620%	65.	Koninklijke Philips	1.409%
16.	Banco Comercial	0.379%	66.	Pinault-Printemp	0.703%
17.	BASF AG	1.026%	67.	Pirelli SpA	0.168%
18.	Bayer AG	0.959%	68.	Portugal Telecom	0.349%
19.	Bayerische Hypo	0.883%	69.	Preussag AG	0.239%
20.	Bipop-Carire SpA	0.223%	70.	Qiagen N.V.	0.117%
21.	BNP Paribas	1.667%	71.	RAS SpA	0.388%
22.	Bouygues	0.474%	72.	Repsol YPF SA	0.833%
23.	BSCH	1.650%	73.	Royal Dutch Petr	4.905%
24.	Cap Gemini SA	0.359%	74.	RWE AG	0.956%
25.	Carrefour SA	1.614%	75.	Sanofi-Synthelab	2.005%
26.	Casino Guichard	0.313%	76.	Sanpaolo IMI SpA	0.707%
27.	CRH Plc	0.396%	77.	SAP AG	1.781%
28.	DaimlerChrysler	1.831%	78.	Schering AG	0.438%
29.	Groupe Danone	0.816%	79.	Schneider Electr	0.394%
30.	Deutsche Bank AG	1.747%	80.	Siemens AG	1.798%
31.	Deutsche Lufthansa	0.240%	81.	Societe Generale	1.031%
32.	Deutsche Telecom	1.858%	82.	Solvay SA	0.196%
33.	E.ON	1.765%	83.	Sonera Oyj	0.155%
34.	Electricidade de	0.341%	84.	Cie de Saint-Gob	0.550%
35.	Eircom Plc	0.111%	85.	STMicroelectroni	1.178%
36.	Elan Corp Plc	0.722%	86.	Suez SA	1.471%
37.	Electrabel	0.500%	87.	Telecom Italia	0.172%
38.	Elsevier	0.393%	88.	Telecom Italia	1.331%
39.	Endesa SA	0.713%	89.	Telefonica SA	2.131%
40.	Enel SpA	1.019%	90.	ThyssenKrupp AG	0.286%
41.	ENI-Ente Naziona	2.105%	91.	TIM SPA	1.931%
42.	Fiat SpA	0.351%	92.	TotalFinaElf	4.425%
43.	Fortis (B)	0.797%	93.	UCB S.A.	0.244%
44.	France Telecom	1.592%	94.	Unicredito Itali	0.896%
45.	Fresenius Medica	0.326%	95.	Unilever NV	1.424%

46.	Gas Natural SDG	0.356%	96.	Union Fenosa SA	0.222%
47.	Assicurazioni Generali	1.674%	97.	UPM-Kymmene Oyj	0.326%
48.	Groupe Bruxelles	0.302%	98.	Vivendi Universal	2.478%
49.	Iberdrola SA	0.516%	99.	Volkswagen AG	0.575%
50.	ING Group NV	2.657%	100.	Wolters Kluwer NV	00.253%

Source: Bloomberg, August 2001

MSCI USA:

Table 8.4.6: Sector weights

Sector	Percentage
Energy	5.63
Materials	2.53
Industries	11.11
Consumer Discretionary	11.78
Consumer Staples	8.66
Health Care	15.18
Financials	19.55
Information Technology	15.03
Telecommunication Services	6.90
Utilities	3.63

Sources: MSCI, WWW.MSCI.COM

Hedge Fund strategies by Tsatsaronis (BIS)[4]

"The selection of stocks from which the investors can choose depends on their time horizons, views on the country, sector, industry, small cap or blue chips. Since the possibilities are enormous, more investors decide to invest their money with hedge funds. Hedge funds are investment companies with legal and organizational structures conducive to an aggressive investment style. They typically operate as limited partnerships or choose to register offshore, in order to minimize reporting and regulatory requirements that apply to more widely marketed investment companies such as mutual funds. To minimize liquidity requirements, the funds place restrictions on withdrawals by investors. Management fees are highly sensitive to performance, which is in turn measured in absolute terms rather than relative to the peer group. Hedge funds market themselves as following specialized investment strategies, or investment styles. Two broad categories of investment style, based on fundamental investment philosophy, can be distinguished. Funds in the first category take directional positions in expectation of an appreciation or decline in a specific asset's price. These strategies represent bets that existing relationships between asset prices are not sustainable. The global macro fund style is representative of this category. The second category comprises styles that aim at exploiting pricing anomalies or temporary distortions of securities' prices using combi-

---

[4] K. Tsatsaronis, *Special feature: Hedge funds*, BIS Quarterly Review, November 2000

nations of both long and short positions on similar securities. These long-short positions are based on the expectation that historical relationships will eventually reassert themselves. Leverage is also used to magnify potential profits since the pricing discrepancies that the funds attempt to exploit are typically very narrow. The strategy often relies on financial derivative instruments (frequently contracted in the OTC market) to help insulate portfolio returns from other market risks unrelated to the specific pricing anomaly that is being exploited. Investment styles such as Market Neutral and Relative Value Arbitrage fall into this category".

Table 8.4.7

		1997	1998	1999	2000	Leverage
Global Macro	Number of funds	74	74	66	66	161%
	Assets under management	32.2bn	30.4bn	24.9bn	14.3bn	
Global established	Number of funds	218	154	142	148	139%
	Assets under management	20.4bn	8.7bn	10.2bn	10.2bn	
Long only	Number of funds	27	25	25	24	223%
	Assets under management	0.4bn	0.3bn	0.6bn	0.5bn	
Short sellers	Number of funds	20	22	20	21	113%
	Assets under management	0.6bn	0.8bn	11.8bn	1.1bn	
Sectoral	Number of funds	80	83	100	133	124%
	Assets under management	3.4bn	4.0bn	5.0bn	9.2bn	
Market neutral	Number of funds	276	288	277	292	256%
	Assets under management	23.8bn	26.3bn	27.6bn	32.0bn	
Event-driven	Number of funds	135	129	118	133	133%
	Assets under management	10.4bn	11.6bn	13.1bn	16.6bn	
Total (excl funds of funds)	Number of funds	1,114	1,089	949	1146	168%
	Assets under management	132.1bn	127.9bn	130.9bn	121.9bn	
Funds of funds	Number of funds	314	296	318	346	114%
	Assets under management	22.3bn	21.7bn	25.0bn	27.4bn	

Source: BIS Quarterly Review, November 2000, Special feature, Hedge funds

"On average, hedge funds have generated handsome returns for their investors, outpacing market benchmarks as well as other investment vehicles such as mutual funds. The fact that this investment performance typically exhibits a low correlation with broad market Indices is an additional attractive feature of hedge fund investments. The risk adjusted return is measured by the Sharp-ratio".

Table 8.4.8: Financial performance of hedge funds

Strategy	1998		1999		2000	
	Return	Sharp ratio	Return	Sharp ratio	Return	Sharp ratio
Convertible arbitrage	-4.41	-1.10	16.04	5.37	34.53	9.61
Dedicated short bias	-6.00	-0.35	-14.22	-1.29	-19.55	-1.21
Emerging markets	-37.66	-1.61	44.82	2.05	8.23	0.14
Equity market neutral	13.31	2.48	15.33	5.45	19.25	9.18
Event-driven	-4.87	-0.70	22.26	4.43	10.73	1.35
Fixed-Income arbitrage	-8.16	-1.49	12.11	3.47	6.26	0.27
Global Macro	-3.64	-0.45	5.81	0.07	3.32	-0.22
Long/short equity	17.18	0.74	47.23	2.82	9.18	0.15
Managed futures	20.64	1.20	-4.69	-1.13	-10.15	-3.48
All hedge fund styles	-0.36	-0.42	23.43	1.91	8.08	0.18
S&P 500	26.10	0.99	18.75	1.08	-2.50	-0.45
MSCI world equity	22.54	0.90	22.01	1.43	-10.96	-1.06
Merrill Lynch corporate master bond index	5.45	0.10	-12.02	-3.91	4.24	-0.34

Source: BIS Quarterly Review, November 2000, Special feature, Hedge funds

Merger & Acquisition

By Andrade, Mitchell and Stafford[5]
"M&A activity occurs in readily identifiable waves over time, however these waves are not alike. If mergers come in waves, but each wave is different in terms of industry composition, then a significant portion of merger activity might be due to industry-level shocks. Industries react to these shocks by restructuring, often via a merger. These shocks are unexpected, which explains why industry-level takeover activity is concentrated in time, and is different over time, which accounts for the variation in industry composition for each wave. Examples of shocks include:
1. Technological innovations, which can create excess capacity and the need for industry consolidation.
2. Supply shocks, such as oil prices.
3. Deregulation

Deregulation creates new investment opportunities for the industry and it removes potentially long-standing barriers to merging and consolidating. The following industries have undergone substantial deregulation since 1973: airlines (1978), broadcasting (1984 and 1996), entertainment (1984), natural gas (1978), trucking (1980), banks and thrifts (1994), utilities (1992) and telecommunications (1996)[6]".

---

[5] G. Andrade, M. Mitchell and E. Stafford, *New Evidence and Perspective on Mergers,* May 2001
[6] G. Andrade, M. Mitchell and E. Stafford, *New Evidence and Perspective on Mergers.* May 2001

By Gondhalekar and Bhagwat[7]
"According to Berkovitch and Narayanan (BN 1993) the three major motives for takeovers are synergy, agency and hubris. In synergy-motivated takeovers, the managers of acquirers act in the interest of their shareholders by creating value via economic gains. Empirically, studies have found total gains to be positive, suggesting the presence of synergy, in different sub-sets of takeovers. In agency-motivated takeovers, the managers of acquirers pursue self-interest by wasting the resources of their shareholders. In hubris-motivated takeovers, the managers of acquirers end up overpaying the targets because of overconfidence about their ability to access and or extract takeover gains (Roll, 1986). An important aspect is takeovers is the method-of-payment. Purely stock-financed takeovers increased from 12% in the before-crash period to 29% in the after-crash period" (1987).

Table 8.4.9: Characteristics and descriptive statistics of M&A by decade. 1973-1998

	1973-1979	1980-1989	1990-1998 1	973-1998
N	789	1,427	2,040	4,256
All cash	38.3%	45.3%	27.4%	35.4%
All stock	37.0%	32.9%	57.8%	45.6%
Any stock	45.1%	45.6%	70.9%	57.6%

Source: Andrade, Mitchell, Stafford, *New Evidence and Perspective on Mergers*

Cross-border mergers and acquisitions result in cross-border capital flows. When a foreign company acquires a US firm, the main forms of financing the deal are:
1. Cash mergers or tender offers
2. Stock swap
3. IPO
4. Issue of bonds
5. Issue of CP
6. Syndicated loan

In the first situation, the foreign company pays in cash for the acquisition of (for example) a US company. When the foreign company has the cash amount already in USDs there will be no effect in the foreign exchange market. However there will be a direct effect when the foreign company has the cash amount in another currency. The time of influence will depend on the expectations of the foreign company on the currency exchange rate and when it needs to deliver the cash. The second way of financing a merger is through stock swaps. The shareholders of the US firm are given stocks in the foreign firm (which may have negative tax repercussions on the American stockholder.)

---

[7] V. Gondhalekar and Y. Bhagwat, *Motives in the Acquisitions of Nasdaq Targets During the Aftermath of the 1987 Crash*, The Financial Review Vol 37, No 4, 2002

CHAPTER 8

The other ways mentioned of financing an M&A deal will also have an important influence on the foreign exchange market, however it will be an indirect influence, which is often not that visible. When the foreign company decides to do an IPO in a country other than the US (not likely) then it needs to convert the IPO result into USDs. The influence of a non-USD denominated bond issue or non-USD syndicated loan can be found in our next division, the International Debt Market. The influence of a non-USD CP program can be found in Division V (S-T-I-R Market). The effects of M&A deals are seen in all these three divisions.

Derivative markets

Swaps[8]
Equity swaps are transactions in which payments, referenced to the change in a certain index and an interest rate, are exchanged, and are annually based on a fixed notional amount.

Futures[9]
Stock index futures are futures on various stock indices and are traded on most of the major exchanges.

Options[10]
Stock index and Equity options
Stock index options are options on either the cash value of the indices or on the stock index futures. Equity options are options on the individual stocks and are also traded on most major exchanges. (Chicago Board Options Exchange, New York Stock Exchange, American Stock Exchange and Philadelphia Stock Exchange).

Warrants
Warrants are longer-term options on either individual stocks or on certain indices.

Equity-linked-notes
These are fixed-income securities issued by a corporation, bank or sovereign in which the principal repayment of the note at maturity is linked to the performance of an equity index.

---

[8]Federal Reserve Board, *Trading and Capital-Markets Activities Manual, Equity Derivatives,* February 1998
[9]Federal Reserve Board, *Trading and Capital-Markets Activities Manual, Equity Derivatives,* February 1998
[10]Federal Reserve Board, *Trading and Capital-Markets Activities Manual, Equity Derivatives,* February 1998

Production plan

The production plan describes everything that is needed to sell the products in the product plan.
1. Training in economic fundamentals and stock fundamentals
2. Building knowledge and constructing a diversified portfolio
3. Training in Econometrics and building quantitative models
4. Training in derivative markets
5. Live news, prices and other information.

Economic fundamentals
For economic fundamentals see the Chapter on Fundamental Analysis (Chapter 4).

Stock fundamentals[11]
Every stock has its own value, however it can be compared with the peer in the industry. There are several methods of valuing a company. One of them utilizes discounted cash flows. To understand value creation one must use a long-term point of view, manage all cash flows on both the income statement and the balance sheet and understand how to compare cash flows to the different time periods on a risk-adjusted basis. It is nearly impossible to make good decisions without complete information. Let's take the present value of the following:
- Consumer's surplus
- Labor's claim
- Supplier's claim
- Debt claim (interest expenses)
- Government claim (taxes)
- Equity claim (dividend)
- Uses of working capital
- Uses of physical capital
- Sources of working capital
- Sources of debt
- Sources of equity

Further:
- Review market performance
- Analyze comparative corporate performance
- Understand corporate cash flows
- Synthesize market views
- Look at management

---

[11] T. Copeland, T. Koller, J. Murrin, *Valuation*, Chapter 1 and 2 , McKinsey & Company, Inc, August 1995

Table 8.4.10: Sector approach by Morgan Stanley

Sector	Best correlation with these sectors	Macro factors The sector outperforms if...	Sub sector	Micro factors
Automobiles & Components	US Autos	Bond yields rise CPI rises GDP growth is strong	Automobiles Components	Pricing, Market share Global presence
Banks	Div. Fin Insurance US Div. Fin	European bond yield falls. US-Europe bond yield spread falls.		Internet strategy ROE
Capital Goods	Materials Consumer Durables US Cap Goods	Bond yields rise Inflation rises European short rate rises	Machinery Defense	VDMA Orders Capex budgets Airline profitability Budget deficits
Commercial Services & Supplies	Hotels	Bond yields rise CPI rises Earnings momentum one month ago is strong		Outsourcing trends Employment growth
Consumer Durables & Apparel	Cap Goods Materials US Cap Goods	European yield curve widens Inflation rises		Brand differentiation Size/global muscle Travel trends Wealth effect
Energy	US Energy Real Estate	Oil prices rise, US interest rates rise European yield curve widens	Oil & Gas (integrated) Oil & Gas (E&P) Energy Equip & Services	Refining & Petrochemical margin, Cost control, Business mix Sustainability of debt service. Major discoveries, Cash driven M&A, Outsourcing trends
Food & Drug Retailing	Retail Food Bev Utilities	US interest rates fall CPI falls Growth is weak		LFL sales growth
Food Beverage & Tobacco	US Food Beverages Food Retail US Utilities	US-Europe bold yield spread narrows European interest rates rise. Confidence falls	Food Products Beverages Tobacco	Business portfolio optimization, Emerging markets Employment growth Regulation/legal
Hotels Restaurants & Leisure	Comm Service Transport Cap Goods	CPI rises Bond yields rise Nom GDP growth is strong		REVPAR momentum,M&A, Earnings momentum/ visibility

DIVISION III EQUITY MARKET

Insurance	Banks	US yield curve is flat Consumer is strong Bond yields fall		Mutual-funds flow, Profitability and growth, Innovation
Materials	Cap Goods US Materials Consumer Durables	Bond yields rise Inflation rises Consumer is weak	Paper & Forest products	Capacity announcements Pulp price > cash cost of production,
			Chemicals	Operating rates, Output price expectations
			Metals & Mining	Capacity cycle, Innovation, Restructuring
			Construction Materials	Commodity inventories Scale economies Earnings momentum Productions growth Construction activity
Media	Retailing	European yield curve widens European interest rates fall CPI falls		Corporate advertising budgets
Pharma & Biotechnology	US Pharma US Health Care Food Bev	Inflation falls Bond yields fall European short rates fall		Long-term growth relative to expectations, Pipeline/patent expiry, Industry regulation
Real Estate	Utilities US Utilities Energy	CPI rises Bond yield rise European short rates rise		Stage of real estate cycle Gearing, Vacancy rates
Retailing	Food Bev US Utilities	Consumer is weak US yield curve widens Short rates fall Real GDP growth is weak		Brand and execution
Software & Services		Bond yields fall European short rates fall, Inflation falls Earnings momentum is strong		Earnings surprises, Product cycle, PC demand, US product sales into Europe

Technology Hardware & Equipment	US Tech Hardware	Consumer is strong US-Europe bond yield spread rises European bond yield falls	Communication Equipment Semiconductor Equipment	Earnings surprises, Penetration rate of wireless, Product cycle Capex/sales < 25% = outperformance Earnings surprises, Capacity utilization, PC demand
Telecommunication Services		Bond yields fall CPI falls Consumer is strong		Penetration rate of wireless, Subscriber acquisition costs, Average revenue per user
Transportation	Hotels Capital Goods Materials	Bond yields rise Inflation rises Growth is strong	Airlines Transportation Infrastructure	Regulation, Capacity cycle, Yields, Unit costs, Leasing costs, Construction costs Planning permission Consumer behavior, Restructuring potential/likelihood
Utilities	Food Retail Real Estate Food Beverage	US interest rates fall Prices fall		

Source: Morgan Stanley Equity Research Europe, Strategy, August-September 2001

Portfolio construction

By Berset, Condorelli, Hoebrechts and Rampa[12]

"In the financial literature ßim (systematic risk of asset i) is often called to be the true factor of risk. The Modern Portfolio Theory shows that investors can always diversify their portfolio in order to reduce the total risk to a minimum. The only risk an investor cannot avoid is the risk of the economy as a whole (the non-diversifiable risk). So, the market risk remains the same. The investor is willing to bear higher systematic risk only if the investment shows a commensurately high performance".

By Arnswal[13]

The Economic Research Centre of the Deutsche Bundesbank did a research project about the Investment Behavior of German Equity Fund Managers: here are the results. "For a long time, institutional investing played a merely subordinate role in Germany, in particular, when compared with the UK and the US. This appears to be changing. By the end of 1999, German banks, insurance companies and mutual funds already owned

---

[12] J. Berset (UBP) S.Condorelli (UBP), P.Hoebrechts(UBP) and A. Rampa (UBP), *Understanding Hedge Funds*, Working Paper II, UBP and Alternative Asset Management Group.
[13] T. Arnswald, *Investment Behaviour of German Equity Fund Managers*, March 2001, Economic Research Centre of the Deutsche Bundesbank

36% of all national assets held in equity. The ongoing intermediation of portfolio equity investments is mainly driven by two factors: First, private households progressively purchase certificates of share-based mutual funds instead of direct holdings in stock markets, and secondly, banks and insurance companies themselves increasingly favor portfolio investments in specialized funds reserved for institutional investors. In principle, the concentration of assets in the hands of investment professionals bodes well for improved and consistent decision-making. Institutionalization may enhance trading liquidity on stock markets as much as it enhances the efficiency of equity pricing. However, trading liquidity appears on the risk side of institutionalization as well. An excessive clustering of assets could, at least in some market segments, reduce the number of trading partners, effectively jeopardizing market depth (more blue chip and less small-cap investments).

Some key findings with implications for market efficiency and stability are briefly summarized as follows:
1. Fund managers generally identify longer-term price inefficiencies on stock markets and pursue predominantly active strategies with the principle aim of achieving above-average returns for their clients.
2. In analyzing investment patterns, there are three types of managers: fundamentalists, tacticians and methodologists. Fundamentalists use mainly fundamental analysis; tacticians use technical and fundamental analysis together, and the methodologists use fundamental analysis, an econometric model, and portfolio optimization. Informational-based herding, intentional copying of other market players, or the practice of following non-fundamental market signals is more common among tacticians and methodologists.
3. Fundamentalists seem to be best suited for the role of arbitrageurs, returning equity prices to, and stabilizing them at, fair and sound levels.
4. Institutional investors can generally contribute to more efficient stock market pricing. Managers from all groups demonstrate a clear preference for stock analysis based on underlying economic factors.
5. Fund managers generally assign to fundamental buy signals.
6. Fund managers rely to a great extent on information from external analysts, the media and professional colleagues.
7. There is evidence that fund managers tend to favor stocks which receive a lot of attention from analysts or in reports; they also prefer stocks with a proven record of outstanding corporate and stock price performances".

Chapter 8

Econometrics[14]

Econometrics is by no means the same as economic statistics. Nor is it identical with what we call general economic theory, although a considerable portion of this theory has a definitely quantitative character. Nor should econometrics be taken as synonomous with the application of mathematics to economics. Experience has shown that each of these three viewpoints, that of statistics, economic theory, and mathematics, is a necessary, but not by itself a sufficient, condition for a real understanding of the quantitative relations in modern economic life. It is the *unification* of all three that is powerful and it is this unification that constitutes econometrics (Frisch, 1933). Econometrics is the field of economics that concerns itself with the application of mathematical statistics and the tools of statistical inference to the empirical measurement of relationship postulated by economic theory. In order to understand the economic/financial models and all the different hedge fund strategies and their market influence in depth, knowledge of Econometrics is absolutely essential.

Derivative market training

The trading of derivative securities, especially over-the-counter derivatives, is designed to implement a specific view and maximize the returns in some particular environment that can not be achieved by standard securities. That is why derivative securities are more sensitive than standard securities such as stocks and bonds when the environment changes. The changes in the derivatives prices often offer early warning signals of uncertainty, changing environment or volatility in financial markets.

Equity swap by Chen[15]
"Essentially this is a loan with equity as collateral. In some situations the controlling shareholders of a company don't have enough cash to make additional investments and they are reluctant to sell their share holdings because that would reduce their control over their company. They usually prefer to borrow money against their share holdings. If they go to a commercial bank, the bank may lend at most 30% of the face value of the shares for non-blue chip stocks. However an investment bank, which is trading oriented, thinks it can monitor and manage risk better and is often willing to lend cash at 70% of the face value of the shares. So the controlling shareholders usually turn to investment banks for an equity swap, or a loan using equity as collateral. The borrowers very often buy more of their companies to push up the share prices. When the share price becomes higher, they can use more shares for another equity swap, this time at a higher price. As the share prices move higher and higher, they can borrow more and more money to buy the shares. The high share price puts a company in a strong position to negotiate new mergers and acquisitions or to spin off an entity from the company at a good price. When well planned in a bull market, the financial leverage can often be transformed into a permanent increase in equity value. The over-the-counter derivative contracts, such as equity swaps, are off-balance-sheet and the information is not available to the public. When the price falls, the investment banks need to sell shares to reduce their exposure, so the domino effect is started.

---

[14]Greene, W.H., *ECONOMETRIC ANALYSIS, 4/E,* Copyright © 2000, Reprinted by permission on Pearson Education, Inc., Upper Saddle Rive, New Jersey .
[15]J. Chen, *Derivative securities: What they tell us?*, March 1999

When a client approaches an investment bank for an equity swap deal, the bank knows he probably has many deals with other banks and the share prices are likely to be inflated. However the bank is also confident the client is going to sign more deals after that. So as long it is not the last one in the chain, the bank should have enough time to ask for more collateral or to unload the positions when the price trend reverses. The risk (definition by banks) of equity swap is defined as credit risk. However the market movement triggers the credit risk, so in fact it is a market risk. Further, all the parties involved have a keen interest in moving the share price higher, so as a result most of the report will be bullish. A good trading strategy for the banks involved is if the stocks start to drop, they will sell their holdings immediately, because they know it will drop sharply. So a domino effect is started. (Chen, 1999)".

Products and markets are getting more complex and the influence of derivatives is becoming more important. The OTC off-balance-sheet derivatives are playing an important role because the information is not public but the market influence is enormous. Be aware—it's better to start training yourself in off balance sheet derivatives as early as possible.

Live news and prices
Without live news and prices there are no financial markets as we know them today.

Marketing plan

Market	Sub-market	Clients
Equity market	Stock indices	Market makers
		Fund managers
	Hedge fund strategies	Hedge funds
	M&A	Corporates
		Speculative accounts
		Hedge funds
Derivatives	Futures	Funds
	Options	Funds
	Convertibles	Hedge funds

Equity markets

Stock indices
Market makers:
Market makers of individual stocks and sectors use the stock indices as a hedge against their open positions. They buy or sell index futures and options because the liquidity in these derivatives is much higher than in an individual stock. If a specific stock has a high weighting in an index, hedging via the derivative market is the best option because when the stock is under pressure it will drag down the index as well. Microsoft and Intel are good examples of stock with a high weighting in the index.

Fund managers:
Fund managers build their portfolios to be similar to the benchmark. The most important and followed indices are the Morgan Stanley Capital International (MSCI) Indices. Changes and adjustments in country weighting should have an influence on the currency pairs involved as well. The active managers will be unlikely to make significant portfolio changes as a result of the benchmark changes. Passive managers have a quite different problem from active managers. These managers have carefully focused on the MSCI Index changes. Most managers are likely to develop a schedule for rebalancing their portfolios over the coming months.

Funds:
The third group is the group of fund managers who do their own research (buy-side). They take positions in a stock based on their portfolio composition, diversification and view about the stock and the sector.

Hedge funds strategies by Berset, Condorelli, Hoebrechts and Rampa[16]
The hedge funds managers are a very important group of decision-makers. Their decisions in the Equity Market are based on their strategies such as Long-Short Equities, Arbitrage, Market Neutral, Distressed Securities and Event Driven.

Long-Short Equities:
" 'Classic' hedge fund strategies are those strategies that apply the original Hedge Fund model: using leverage to combine fundamentally researched long and short equity positions in a portfolio with reduced net exposure to the market. By reducing the exposure to market risk, the overall risk of the portfolio is lowered and the return is derived from stock selection becomes larger relative to the total portfolio risk".

Equity Index Arbitrage
"These managers engage primarily in the practice of Index Arbitrage: purchasing and/or selling securities against related securities such index options or stock options to take advantage of pricing disparities."

Market Neutral
"Market Neutral strategies invest long and short in equity securities, usually in the same industry sector, with an approximate match between the total value of the long and the short holdings in the portfolio. Going long those stocks that are expected to outperform over an investment horizon of three to nine months and shorting those stocks expected to underperform".

Distressed Securities
"Distressed Securities strategies are based on the observation that securities of companies involved in bankruptcy proceedings are frequently undervalued, providing the prospect of greater appreciation in value than the securities of more financially stable issuers".

Event-Driven
"Event-Driven strategies focus on the securities of corporations involved in significant transactions, including mergers, acquisitions, divestitures, tender offers, liquidations, restructurings and other similar corporate events. These strategies profit from the successful completion of the transaction by purchasing the securities at a discount to the value that will be realized upon completion of the transaction".

---

[16]J. Berset (UBP) S. Condorelli (UBP), P Hoebrechts(UBP) and A. Rampa (UBP), *Understanding Hedge Funds*,Working Paper II,, UBP and Alternative Asset Management Group.

Merger & Acquisition
Speculative accounts:
The CEOs of both companies first make the decision about the intentions to merge, or one company declares its interest in the other company. From the time the rumor or the news enters the market, the speculative account managers take positions in both companies' stocks. They buy the company, which is taken over, and they sell the acquiring company. By doing this they are pushing the price of the first company up and the second company down. Especially in the foreign exchange market, these accounts have a very large influence when we talk about cross-border mergers & acquisitions. In the year 2000, European companies bought a not unimportant number of US companies for very large amounts, to meet their expansion aspirations. These deals were creating large flows out of EURs into USDs and putting the EUR/USD under heavy pressure as a consequence. Even rumors about M&A activity could result in a sell-off of EUR/USD. At that moment, the information about how the deal would be financed, whether by cash, debt, share swap or a combination of these, was not released because the companies involved were still in the talking phase. But the traders' suspicion that, for example, another 2 yard sell order was hanging over the market, was already enough information to sell the currency pair spot. In the meantime the deal was completed and about half a year later the cash part of the deal was executed. At that time players were wondering what the reason for the weakness was, and when they found out, the deal was already done. **The memory of market participants is very short.**

Hedge funds
Merger Arbitrage[17]
"A merger arbitrage strategy is a strategy where the manager capitalizes on pricing discrepancies between two companies involved in a merger".

Derivative markets

Futures market
Market participants use futures to hedge market risk, arbitrage price discrepancies within and between markets, take positions on future market movements and profit by acting as market makers or brokers. Financial institutions, money managers, corporations and traders use these instruments for managing, for example, equity risks[18]. There are, for example, index futures available on the Dow Jones Industrial Average, NASDAQ, S&P, DAX, FTSE etc.

---

[17]J. Berset (UBP) S. Condorelli (UBP), P. Hoebrechts (UBP) and A. Rampa (UBP), *Understanding Hedge Funds*,Working Paper II, UBP and Alternative Asset Management Group.
[18]Federal Reserve Board, *Trading and Capital-Markets Activities Manual, Financial Futures,* February 1998

Options market
The market makers provide prices to the market and take positions based on their view, as do speculators. Fund managers use the index options as a hedge against their portfolios. There are also options on individual stocks (no futures), which is an advantage in hedging and speculating.

Convertible market
Market makers provide prices and liquidity to the market and take positions based on their view. The other main players are the hedge funds.

Outcome/Business Plan

Table 8.4.11 Business Plan

Business Plan	Questions	Answers
Product plan	Products?	Stock indices
		Hedge fund strategies
		Merger & Acquisition
		Swaps
		Futures
		Options
Production plan	What's needed?	Economic fundamental knowledge
		Stock fundamental knowledge
		Constructing portfolio training
		Econometric knowledge
		Derivative market knowledge
		Live prices and news
Marketing plan	Clients?	Private clients, fund managers and hedge funds, market makers, corporates, speculative accounts
	Competitors?	Division I (FX Option Market)
		Division II (Commodity Market)
		Division IV (International Debt Market)
		Division V (S-T-I-R Market)

Strategy:
Division III (Equity Market) offers its clients specialized products for every knowledge level. Further, adjustments in some of the indices, M&A and hedge fund activities can have an important influence in the foreign exchange currency market. The SWOT Analysis can tell you whether the strengths are able to explain the movements in the EUR/USD.

8.5 DESIGN APPROACH II: SWOT ANALYSIS

Equity Market as driver of EUR/USD Interbank Market

Strengths

Higher return on your US investment and higher US growth

By Nowak[19]
"Empirical research shows that in the US and Germany, corporate investment creates value in excess of cost, but the US industrial sector seems to be more efficient in making value-enhancing investments. In 1991, a dollar of assets invested in a public stock company in the US generated $1.21 in value whereas a Deutsche Mark invested in German stock companies generated only DM 1.14 on average. This discrepancy widens if the banks and insurance companies are taken into account. There are two interpretations that might throw some light on this issue. First, the market value of shares of domestic companies as a percentage of GDP is only 20.3 % in Germany compared to 77.3% in the US. Therefore most of the investment activity that is going on in Germany is not reflected in the stock market. Second, maximizing shareholder value has not always been the main objective for corporations in Germany. Traditionally, social consensus between stakeholders has been a guideline of corporate governance in Germany. At margin, investment decisions in Germany seem to generate less value."

Maximizing shareholders' value is nowadays the main goal of every large firm. However, it is an undeniable fact that the US firms are still ahead in this game. Since maximum share value is the first interest of equity investors, they will invest more of their capital in US firms than in Eurozone firms. This will create capital flows from the Eurozone to the US. Table 8.5.1 shows the capital flows between the Eurozone and the US. Negative figures indicate a net flow from the US to the Eurozone. To see the effect on the EUR/USD, the open, high, low and close are also put into this table.

---

[19] E. Nowak, *Finance, Investment, and Firm Value in Germany and the US*, A Comparative Analysis, Discussion Paper 49, DFG Sonderforschungsbereich 373, Humboldt-University Berlin, May 1998.

Table 8.5.1:
Net Eurozone transactions in US stocks; in Millions of dollars: positive sign means net inflow into the US

Period	Corporate stocks	EUR/$ Open	EUR/$ High	EUR/$ Low	EUR/$ Close
1999	46,044	3 Jan 99 1.1670	1.1906	0.9986	1.0070
Q1	9,859	1.1670	1.1906	1.0678	1.0765
Q2	12,284	1.0771	1.0883	1.0254	1.0352
Q3	5,686	1.0359	1.0826	1.0104	1.0682
Q4	18,327	1.0676	1.0911	0.9986	1.0070
2000	84,851	1.0050	1.0414	0.8225	0.9422
Q1	33,440	1.0050	1.0414	0.9390	0.9560
Q2	22,238	0.9560	0.9750	0.8844	0.9523
Q3	14,800	0.9522	0.9597	0.8437	0.8837
Q4	14,281	0.8840	0.9425	0.8225	0.9422
2001	30,981	0.9423	0.9595	0.8344	0.9098
Q1	17,492	0.9423	0.9595	0.8748	0.8774
Q2	10,902	0.8742	0.9091	0.8408	0.8495
Q3	2,507	0.8495	0.9333	0.8344	0.9098

Sources: United States, Department of Treasury, Treasury Bulletin (various issues), Reuters daily & weekly data

The net high capital outflow from the Eurozone to the US had a negative influence on the EUR/USD exchange rate. The decrease of outflow after the first quarter of 2000 indicates the sell-off in the US equity markets. However, the capital outflow is large enough to keep the EUR/USD under pressure.

By Bartram and Dufey[20]
"Since investment opportunities are no longer restricted to domestic markets, financial capital can seek opportunities abroad with relative ease. The international competition for funds has caused an explosive growth in international flows of equities as well as fixed-income and monetary instruments. The US securities markets are the largest in the world and they also have the best reputation from a technical point of view: they are well regulated, and are characterized by breadth, depth and resilience. US investors still hold only a small amount of foreign securities in contract to foreign holdings of US securities, which are about twice as large. Foreign portfolio investors, at the end of 1999, held $3,170.0 billion in US securities. This is up 15.6% from the 1998 level of $2,742.1 billion. Foreign investors found that the attractiveness of the US as an investment opportunity had increased. Of the $3,170.0 billion, 45.6% or $1,445.6 billion, consisted of stocks. High economic growth usually goes hand in hand with high growth in the country's capital market and thus attracts investors from abroad".

---

[20]S.M. Bartram and G. Dufey, *International Portfolio Investment: Theory, Evidence, and Institutional Framework*, Financial Markets, Institutions & Instruments, Vol10 (3), August 2001, pp.85-155

The US GDP growth averaged 3.5% per annum, more that double the 1.6% average pace of German GDP growth. The persistent underperformance of the German and Euroland economies, according to the BIS annual report, has given rise to an asymmetry in the response of global investors to favorable and unfavorable data releases out of Euroland. Investors have become accustomed to longer-term disappointing data from Euroland and therefore treat favorable data releases as transitory events and unfavorable data releases as more permanent events. Given the market's asymmetric behavior, the Euro has traded with a sustained downward bias.

Table 8.5.2: GDP

Period	US GDP (chain yoy %)	Eurozone GDP constant	Difference	EUR/$ open	EUR/$ close
1999 Q1	4.0	2.0	2.0	1.1670	1.0765
1999 Q2	3.9	2.2	1.7	1.0771	1.0352
1999 Q3	4.0	2.8	1.2	1.0359	1.0682
1999 Q4	4.4	3.6	0.8	1.0676	1.0070
2000 Q1	4.2	3.6	0.6	1.0050	0.9560
2000 Q2	5.2	3.9	1.3	0.9560	0.9523
2000 Q3	4.4	3.2	1.2	0.9522	0.8837
2000 Q4	2.8	2.8	0.0	0.8840	0.9422
2001 Q1	2.5	2.5	0.1	0.9423	0.8774
2001 Q2	1.2	1.6	-0.4	0.8742	0.8495
2001 Q3	0.5	1.3	-0.8	0.8495	0.9098

Sources: Bloomberg, Reuters daily data

Mergers & Acquisitions

Cash effect
A continuing trend in the M&A sector has been the increase in foreign acquirers bidding for US firms. More than $356 billion, or nearly 20% of the announced deals, proceeded in the US and had a foreign acquirer in 2000. European firms made up the lion's share of foreign buyers in the US. *Thomson Financial Securities Data*

Table 8.5.3: Transatlantic M&A activity end 1998-2001

Announcement	Target company	Acquiring company	Amount	Method of finance
30 Nov 1998	Bankers Trust (US)	Deutsche Bank (Germany)	$10.1bn	Capital increase Cash Issue bonds and convertible bonds or bonds with warrants[21].
18 Jan 1999	AirTouch (US)	Vodafone (UK)	$56.0bn	Cash Stock[22]
17 Jan 2000	Glaxo Welcome (US)	SmithKline Beecham (UK)[23]	$76.0bn	
12 Apr 2000	SlimFast Foods Company (US)	Unilever (UK/Netherlands)	$2.3bn	Cash[24]
06 Jun 2000	Bestfoods (US)	Unilever (UK/Netherlands)	$24.3bn	Cash Bond issue[25]
12 Jul 2000	PaineWebber (US)	UBS (Switzerland)	$11.8bn	Cash Stocks[26]
24 Jul 2000	VoiceStream Wireless Corporation (US) Powertel Inc (US)	Deutsche Telekom (Germany)	$50.7bn	Cash Stocks[27]
30 Aug 2000	DLJ (US)	Credit Suisse Group (Switzerland)	$11.5bn	Cash Stocks[28]
15 Jan 2001	Ralston Purina (US)	Nestle (Switzerland)	$10.1bn	[29]
12 Mar 2001	American General Corporation (US)	Prudential plc (UK)	$24.6bn	[30]
09 Oct 2001	Royal Dutch/Shell (Eurozone)	Motiva Enterprises (US) and Equilon Enterprises (US)	$3.8bn	$2.1bn in cash, $1.4bn in debt and $300mn in pension liabilities[31].

---

[21] Deutsche Bank, Press release, November 30, 1998
[22] Vodafone has the AirTouch, 18 January 1999, www.wired.com/news/topstories
[23] GlaxoSmithKline, Merger information, Press release 17 January 2000, Thomson Financial Services
[24] Unilever press release, 12 April 2000
[25] Unilever press release 6 June 2000 and 6 December 2000
[26] UBS and PaineWebber press release 12 July 2000 and 6 November 2000
[27] VoiceStream Press Room, 24 July 2000 and 31 May 2001
[28] CS nabs DLJ for $11.5b, 30 August 2000, www.cnnfn.cnn.com
[29] Ralston press release, 21 May 2001, Report: Ralston Purina accepts offer from Nestle, 15 January 2001, www.suntimes.com
[30] Prudential plc and American General Corporation press release, 12 March 2001 Thomson Financial Services
[31] Dow Jones

Table 8.5.4

Announcement	M&A activity	Amount	EUR/$ Open	EUR/$ High	EUR/$ Low	EUR/$ Close
30 Nov 1998	Bankers Trust & Deutsche Bank	$10.1bn	1.1607	1.1618	1.1455	1.1484 [32]
18 Jan 1999	Airtouch & Vodafone	$56.0bn	1.1713	1.1753	1.1583	1.1670
17 Jan 2000	Glaxo Wellcome & SmithKline Beecham	$76.0bn	1.0125	1.0146	1.0066	1.0115
12 Apr 2000	SlimFast Foods Company & Unilever	$2.3bn	0.9585	0.9600	0.9518	0.9586
06 Jun 2000	Bestfoods & Unilever	$24.3bn	0.9464	0.9601	0.9447	0.9543
12 Jul 2000	PaineWebber & UBS	$11.8bn	0.9517	0.9526	0.9389	0.9421
24 Jul 2000	VoiceStream Wireless & Deutsche Telekom	$50.7bn	0.9360	0.9374	0.9307	0.9335
30 Aug 2000	DLJ & Credit Suisse	$11.5bn	0.8921	0.8947	0.8865	0.8943
15 Jan 2001	Ralston Purina & Nestle	$10.1bn	0.9517	0.9530	0.9407	0.9422
12 Mar 2001	American General Coporation & Prudential plc	$24.6bn	0.9324	0.9342	0.9255	0.9285

Sources: Reuters daily data, Thomson Financial Securities Data and various press releases.

The method of financing will determine the influence on the EUR/USD. Cash financing will have an immediate influence on the exchange rate, even when the acquirer already has the cash amount in the needed currency. The reason for this is that interbank traders react right away on M&A news or rumors. If a Eurozone company takes over a US company, EUR/USD is sold-off right away, without disclosure of any details. At the time that the cash amount is going through the foreign exchange market, traders wonder why EUR/USD is under pressure. Market participants find out the reason after the deal is done in the market (sometimes before the announcement). So we are dealing with two impacts: announcement or rumor impact and real transaction impact. The continuous trend in 1999 and 2000 of European firms buying US firms has put EUR/USD under severe pressure. EUR/USD went down from 1.1607 (end of November 1998) to 0.8611 (beginning of November 2000). The short time interval between the announcements gave EUR/USD little time to recover. The recovery time came in November/December 2000 when most of the deals were completed or the market impact of the financing had already happened.

Table 8.5.5

M&A activity	Completion
Bankers Trust & Deutsche Bank	04 June 1999
PaineWebber & UBS	06 November 2000
Bestfoods & Unilever	06 December 2000
Glaxo Wellcome & SmithKline Beecham	27 December 2000
VoiceStream Wireless & Deutsche Telekom	31 May 2001

---

[32] Reuters weekly data

In the product plan of EUR/USD interbank organization, I explained that EUR/USD can be divided into two products: direct EUR/USD and indirect EUR/USD. The M&A deals Bankers Trust/Deutsche Bank and VoiceStream Wireless/Deutsche Telekom have had a direct influence on EUR/USD because a Eurozone firm took over a US firm. The other deals have had an indirect EUR/USD influence. UBS/PaineWebber, Credit Suisse/DLJ and Ralston Purina/Nestle are deals which have had a direct influence on the USD/CHF rate. Since the USD/CHF market is an illiquid market, traders create USD/CHF through EUR/USD and EUR/CHF. They sell EUR/USD and buy EUR/CHF to buy, in the end, USD/CHF. So these M&A deals between Suisse firms and US firms had a large negative influence on the EUR/USD. The deals Glaxo Wellcome/ SmithKline Beecham, Vodafone/AirTouch and Prudential/American General Corporation have selling activity in GBP/USD as result of selling EUR/USD and buying EUR/GBP. The Unilever deals can pop up in direct EUR/USD market or via the GBP market. The EUR/USD is the most liquid currency pair so every large deal in one of the markets goes through the EUR/USD market.

Table 8.5.6[33], 1999

Buying companies	US	US	Non-US	Non-US	Total
Targets companies	US	Non-US	US	Non-US	
Actual amount of deals	6,801	1,380	970	259	1,923
Deals with data on the value of transaction	2,961	528	531	4,540	8,560
Recorded value of deals: million	$ 921,629	103,387	224,841	714,193	1,964,050
Estimated value of all deals: million	$ 1,098,688	130,560	251,350	876,548	2,348,147

Source: F.L.Pryor, *Dimensions of the Worldwide Merger Boom,* Journal of Economic Issues, February 2001

Stock swap effect by Warnock and Mason[34]
"US investors have acquired a substantial number of foreign stocks, mostly European, through mergers that involved stock swaps (see table 8.4.6). Net acquisitions through stock swaps amounted to $96 billion in 1998, $123 billion in 1999, $84 billion in 2000 and a characteristically low $40 billion in the first three quarters of 2001. These stock swaps are not reported under the Treasury International Capital reporting system (source of table 8.4.4[35]). The use of stock swaps to finance cross-border M&A is a relatively recent phenomenon that became more important in 1998 and 1999. US residents acquired over $100 billion annually in foreign stocks through swaps, due largely to the mega mergers of DaimlerChrysler (1998), BP Amoco (1998) and Airtouch Vodafone (1999). If the acquisition of foreign stocks through swaps results in a greater than desired weighting on foreign stocks in US equity portfolios, US residents will subsequently sell foreign stocks to rebalance their portfolios".

---

[33] F.L.Pryor, *Dimensions of the Worldwide Merger Boom*, Journal of Economic Issues, February 2001
[34] F.E. Warnock and Molly Mason, *The Geography of Capital Flows,* Emerging Markets Quarterly, 5 (1) pp.15-29 Spring 2001
[35] United States Department of Treasury, *Treasury Bulletin*, various issues

In the case of the Deutsche Telekom/VoiceStream Wireless deal, the portfolio rebalance has started. The lockup period of Deutsche Telecom shares expired on 4th September 2001. Deutsche Telecom had issued 1.2 billion shares to fund its purchase of VoiceStream Wireless. The lockup period for every stock swap out of M&A transactions is different, and will usually not be made public. US residents will only sell the shares if the company is not part of the MSCI Index or if they are overweighted in one of the industries.

In the April 2001 Exchange Rate Perspectives of Deutsche Bank, it is mentioned that the Euro remains vulnerable to equity related outflows. This reflects:

1. Structural outflows by Euroland investors looking to raise their overseas weightings (see higher returns of US investments or the MSCI effect).
2. Continued selling of Euroland equity by those US investors who involuntarily acquired Euroland as a result of M&A outflows from Euroland to the US in recent years (share swaps).

The Eurozone-stocks selling activity of US residents can be seen as a post-M&A effect. Another effect is that the European company needs to make investments in its newly acquired US subsidiary (direct investments). Direct investments can be divided into equity capital and reinvested earnings and other capital, mostly inter-company loans.

The M&A activity calmed down in 2001 as a result of the sell-off in the equity markets. There is simply no money to make cross-border mergers and acquisitions because firms need it to restructure the companies and write-off inventories. The sell-off in the equity markets had a shift towards the international debt division as a result. Emission of shares or share swaps were not the appropriate finance methods anymore due to low share prices, volatility, uncertainty and negative sentiment in the market. Cash was the favorable finance method, however a shortage of cash made firms turn to the International Debt Market. They turned first to the international money market (S-T-I-R Market) and later to the International Debt Market.

Table 8.5.7 will show the capital flows from and to the Eurozone. A negative sign indicates an outflow of capital. In most cases, the outflow of direct investment and equity from the Eurozone had a negative influence on EUR/USD.

Table 8.5.7 in billions, inflows Eurozone (+); outflows (-)[36]

		Direct investment	Equity	EUR/USD	
	Total			Open	Close
1999	Jan	-2.9	3.1	1.1670	1.1355
	Feb	-8.3	-2.4	1.1355	1.0921
	Mar	-3.1	-27.9	1.0921	1.0765
	Apr	-16.8	-3.5	1.0771	1.0565
	May	-18.2	-4.9	1.0586	1.0420
	Jun	-14.6	2.5	1.0426	1.0352
	Jul	-10.7	3.7	1.0359	1.0705
	Aug	-7.3	-9.0	1.0680	1.0562
	Sep	1.0	0.1	1.0564	1.0682
	Oct	-6.7	-3.6	1.0676	1.0548
	Nov	-12.9	-2.8	1.0548	1.0089
	Dec	-17.8	-4.8	1.0091	1.0070
2000	Jan	-1.3	-14.6	1.0050	0.9693
	Feb	142.4	-161.2	0.9701	0.9646
	Mar	-1.8	-46.9	0.9643	0.9560
	Apr	1.0	-20.4	0.9560	0.9120
	May	-13.4	-10.2	0.9118	0.9377
	Jun	-8.6	36.6	0.9369	0.9523
	Jul	-19.1	-18.2	0.9522	0.9259
	Aug	-35.4	1.7	0.9263	0.8886
	Sep	-32.5	-3.2	0.8885	0.8837
	Oct	-18.4	-6.4	0.8840	0.8490
	Nov	1.4	-8.8	0.8484	0.8722
	Dec	3.4	-6.2	0.8722	0.9422
2001	Jan	-9.9	-21.1	0.9423	0.9362
	Feb	2.4	-0.1	0.9370	0.9230
	Mar	-33.2	10.8	0.9235	0.8774
	Apr	0.7	-4.1	0.8742	0.8880
	May	-40.9	46.1	0.8888	0.8456
	June	-10.4	30.1	0.8446	0.8495
	July	7.2	4.4	0.8495	0.8761
	Aug	-6.0	12.7	0.8761	0.9122
	Sep	-13.1	28.3	0.9123	0.9098

Source: ECB Monthly Bulletin various issues, Bloomberg, Reuters daily data

According to Deutsche Bank Foreign Exchange Research (3 September 2001), the bi-lateral US/Euroland flows turned around. This improvement is due to a sharp reduction in investment into the US by Euroland companies. In 2001, the FX flow related to M&A deals was a key determinant of exchange rate movements. This year however, the global volume of M&A deals dropped by 48% and as a result the significance of M&A flow for exchange rates has diminished markedly (Paul Meggyesi, Deutsche Bank).

---

[36]The idea to look at the balance of payments data is coming from ABN AMRO Global Head of FX Strategy: Tony Norfield

Merger arbitrage
The third effect of M&A activity on the EUR/USD is through merger arbitrage. Hedge fund managers will take positions mainly in the large M&A deals. Merger arbitrageurs first study all the released documents and develop a view about risks and returns. Based on this view they take the decision to enter arbitrage positions in only the M&A deals with the liquid stocks. Speculators and merger arbitrage specialists will buy the stock of the company to be acquired and sell the acquiring company. They take indirect currency positions when the M&A deals are cross-border. In the event that a European company is acquiring a US company, the stock of the European company is sold and the stock of the US company is bought. When both stocks are listed in New York, then part of these transactions don't involve the currency market.

Another indirect influence of the individual stocks on the EUR/USD is the use of the different cross-border strategies by hedge funds. Hedge fund managers take a long position in one stock and go short in a similar stock or sell index futures. When they go long in General Electric and go short in Siemens (shares trading in Europe), for example, they will have an indirect currency position. The same story applies with Relative Value Arbitrage. Relative Value Arbitrage managers are making spread trades so, for example, they go long Boeing and short Airbus. If the positions are large this will have an influence on the EUR/USD.

Stock indices

The adjustments in the Morgan Stanley Capital International Indices can explain the weakening of the EUR against the USD. The US was one of the main beneficiaries of the adjustments while the Eurozone weighting was decreased. The release of this information had a negative influence on the EUR/USD. The negative effect is twofold: less confidence in the Eurozone than in the US in terms of equities and the actual flow required to sell the Eurozone canceled stocks and to buy the US stocks. The passive managers will take time to adjust their portfolios.

On the 14th of November, the EUR/USD is reported to be under pressure and one of the reasons is the first stage of the MSCI adjustments. The first part of MSCI's two-stage index adjustments (second phase 31 May 2002) took place on November 30. ABN AMRO Equity analysts expected to see European trades totaling USD 14 billion taking place on or close to November 30 as tracker funds (passive fund managers) rebalanced their portfolios. Analysis expected additional trading totaling USD 25 billion taking place over the month of November from funds benchmarked to the indices. The adjustments in the MSCI Indices are positive for the USD and the GBP against the EUR; France and Germany saw the largest outflows[37].

---

[37] Guy Fisher & Nick Aldred, *MSCI index rebalancing (2)*, ABN AMRO, 8 November 2001

Derivative markets

The effect of the equity derivative markets is essentially the leverage effect embodied in derivatives. "The US equity market is followed by the other equity markets around the globe. When the volatility in New York goes up, the correlation across the equity market goes up" (Frankel 1993)[38]. "Volatility of stocks tends to increase when the price drops. This effect is particularly important for the option market: not only does it imply that at-the-money volatilities tend to increase after price drops, but also that a significant skew in the volatility smile should appear. This skew reflects the fact that a negative volatility-return correlation induces a negative skew in the distribution of price returns. The leverage effect corresponds to a negative correlation between future volatility and past return. The leverage for stocks can be interpreted as meaning that the absolute price changes are related to an average level of the past prices. This interpretation is supported by the data on US, European and Japanese stocks. For stock indices however, this interpretation breaks down and a specific panic phenomenon seems to be responsible for the observed enhancement of the negative correlation between volatility and returns" (Bouchard, Matacz, Potters 2001)[39].

By Jeanneau (BIS)[40]
"In the fourth quarter of 2000, the dollar value of exchange-traded activity increased moderately, with equity contracts leading the expansion. Renewed downward pressures in global equity markets lifted actual and implied volatilities, apparently prompting investors to hedge their positions. Within the equity-related market, trading in technology stock indices was particularly buoyant. The value of turnover on the CBOE's NASDAQ 100 contract expanded by 77%[41]. The shifting sentiment in the first quarter of 2001, about the depth and length of the US economic slowdown, accentuated volatility in most major equity markets, leading to a further recovery of activity in equity index contracts. The options contract grew more rapidly than futures (by 21% versus 12%). European markets also witnessed a fairly rapid expansion of activity. Overall, the increased volatility in equity markets has resulted in the turnover of US exchange traded option contracts increasing more than the Eurozone exchange traded contracts"[42].

The following reasons can be found. US equity markets are widely followed by the other equity markets around the globe. An increase in volatility in New York also increases the correlation between the equity indices. **Investors hedge the risk at the origin (US). The higher demand for US exchange traded option contracts will indirectly have a higher demand for USDs as result.**

---

[38] J.A. Frankel, *The Internationalization of Equity Markets*, December 1993, National Bureau of Economic Research, Introduction of his book published by University of Chicago Press
[39] Jean-Philippe Bouchaud, Andrew Matacz and Marc Potters, *The Leverage Effect in Financial Markets:Retarded Volatility and Market Panic*, January 16, 2001
[40] S. Jeanneau, *Derivative Markets*, BIS Quarterly Review, March-June 2001.
[41] S. Jeanneau, *Derivative Markets*, BIS Quarterly Review, March 2001, pp.33-34
[42] S. Jeanneau, *Derivative Markets*, BIS Quarterly Review, June 2001.pp..30

Weaknesses

Lagging data

The ECB balance of payments data have a time lag of around two months. These data give good information as to what happened at that time. However, they are historical data, which don't give any explanations about what's driving EUR/USD at the moment. The same can be said about the capital flow data from the US Department of Treasury, Treasury Bulletin (TIC). To overcome this problem I try to focus more on the difference in the return on investment between the US and Eurozone, and announcements of the M&A activity. These announcements will enter the market as soon as they become public.

Stock indices

The movements in the currency markets are relative movements meaning the strengthening or weakening of one currency against another currency. When we try to explain these movements we should also come up with relative explanations. We should take into account the movements in the US equities markets compared to the movements in the European markets. If the movement in one of the markets is larger or smaller this can be seen as a reason for the preference of the currency with the stronger equity market performance. An analysis I did on June 17, 2002 had the following results. The correlation between Euro STOXX 50 future (excluding UK) divided by S&P 500 future + NASDAQ future with EUR/USD is -0.14 over the period May 17, 2000 – June 14, 2002. Over the same period the correlation between the S&P 500 future and EUR/USD was 0.09 and Euro STOXX 50 future divided by S&P future with EUR/USD -/-0.03.

It's a habit of currency traders to look mainly at US equities and index futures (the European equities and index futures are often ignored) to determine the USD sentiment. Often they find that the EUR/USD didn't move up even if there was a sell-off in the US stock markets. The EUR/USD didn't profit at all from the sell-off in the stock indices we have seen since March 2000. However, the opposite is valid in a positive USD environment: rallies in the US stock indices are used to sell-off EUR/USD. So it's used to sell-off EUR/USD in a negative EUR environment (positive USD).

Opportunity

For the moment, M&A activity is reasonably quiet after a period of USD favored M&A transactions. Firms first need to solve their internal and cash problems before this M&A activity can start again. The opposite activity should support the EUR/USD. For the time being the major roles are played by the FX Options Market, Commodity Market and International Debt Market (Divisions I, II and IV).

Threats

The main threats are the other divisions: the FX Option Market, Commodity Market, International Debt Market and S-T-I-R Market. This change in power had already happened in the period March-September 2000 when the Equity Markets faced big losses. From that time on, Division IV (International Debt Market) took over the role from the Equity Market. This handing over of the power from one to another division is like a flow in time. Division II (Commodity Market), Division III (Equity Market) and Division IV (International Debt Market) are longer-time-frame divisions. Division V (S-T-I-R Market) is more short-term oriented, while Division I (FX Option Market) is already very important and will become even more important over time.

Outcome SWOT Analysis

Table 8.5.8: SWOT Analysis

Strengths	Weaknesses
Higher return on US investments and higher US GDP growth.	Lagging data
Cash-effect of M&A activity	US stock indices
Stock swap effect of M&A activity	
Merger arbitrage	
MSCI Index adjustments	
Derivative markets	

Opportunities	Threats
Rebuild dominant role	FX Option Market, Commodity Market, International Debt Market, Short-Term Interest Rate Market

The strategy resulting from this SWOT Analysis is the following:
Following the announcements of M&A activity, GDP release, studies about the return on investments between the US and the Eurozone, and MSCI Index adjustments. Use the TIC data and ECB balance of payments data as background information. Further, be aware that traders buy $ if US Stock Index Futures are up in $ positive environment, and sell $ if US Stock Index Futures are down in $ negative environment (European stock exchanges are ignored).

8.6 POSITIONING APPROACH I

With the position of this division compared to the other divisions in the EUR/USD Interbank Market Organization, the key question is:

Is this division able to explain the movements in the EUR/USD Interbank Market and how is this compared to the competitors?

Potential entrants:
The potential entrants are low since almost all the financial markets are defined as a division in the EUR/USD Interbank Market Organization. The only market left is the real-estate market including the funds operating in this market.

Intensity of rivalry among existing competitors:
The competitors of this division are:
- FX Option Market Division
- Commodity Market Division
- International Debt Market Division
- Short-Term-Interest-Rate Market Division

Division III (Equity Market) is the third division of the EUR/USD Interbank Market organization. Division I (FX Option Market) and the Division II (Commodity Market) have already given good explanations for the movements in the EUR/USD over the last 2½ years. Division III (Equity Market) also played a very important role in the EUR/USD downtrend.

Bargaining power of buyers:
The buyers are the funds, investors, corporates and private clients. The buying power is high because they have the power to switch easily into other products such as International Debt and S-T-I-R Market products depending on the sentiment in the market.

Bargaining power of suppliers:
The suppliers in this market are the brokers, the providers of the trading system/pricing systemg/booking systems and information systems and the providers of specialized courses and seminars. Economic and stock fundamentals also belonging to the supply side. The suppliers are important in financial markets, but the buyers have more power.

Pressure from substitute products:
The substitute products are the products offered by the other divisions in the EUR/USD Interbank Market Organization.
- FX Options
- Commodities Oil and Gold
- International Debt Market products
- Short-Term-Interest-Rate Market products.

Especially the International Debt Market and S-T-I-R Market products are good substitutes for the Equity Market products depending on the market sentiment.

8.7 THE POSITIONING APPROACH II: CONCEPTS OF INDUSTRY EVOLUTION

The industry of Division II (Equity Market) is complex, with a number of forces interacting simultaneously. In this industry the products are specialized and there are different levels of knowledge interacting with each other. It's necessary to have knowledge at all levels before it's clear what's driving this industry. This industry is in a maturity phase, and the table below explains why. For more details about the concepts of industry evolution see "Competitive Strategy" of Michael Porter (1980).

Buyer and Buyer Behavior
A high percentage of people invest in stocks and they are looking in the alternatives to invest their money especially when stock markets are sold off, large companies ask protection under chapter 11, and accountancy is guilty of malpractice. They are choosing to invest in funds and stocks.

Products and products change
High quality because of research and advice (independent?). Standardization is seen in information, fees and sectors.

Marketing
There is a market segmentation to small investors, fund managers and hedge funds. Fund managers and hedge funds have high knowledge and use it to get the highest quality available. Efforts are made to extend life cycle by offering alternative investments to diversify to client's portfolio. The packaging is important, there is a more tailor-made approach towards clients.

Manufacturing and Distribution
There is some overcapacity of analysts. Banks are centralizing their analysts desks to reduce the costs.

Overall Strategy
The strategy to increase market share is buying another company or merging with another company.

Competition:
The competition among banks is fierce and the sales force tries to differentiate by selling stocks combined with information.

Margin and profits
The fees (prices) are falling. It is very difficult to cover all the costs made by the commissions earned.

SUMMARY 8

Outcome of the Business Plan Division III, Equity Market, table 8.4.11

Business Plan	Questions	Answers
Product plan	Products?	Stock indices
		Hedge fund strategies
		Merger & Acquisition
		Swaps
		Futures
		Options
Production plan	What's needed?	Economic fundamental knowledge
		Stock fundamental knowledge
		Constructing portfolio training
		Econometric knowledge
		Derivative market knowledge
		Live prices and news
Marketing plan	Clients?	Private clients, fund managers and hedge funds, market makers, corporates, speculative accounts
	Competitors?	Division I (FX Option Market)
		Division II (Commodity Market)
		Division IV (International Debt Market)
		Division V (S-T-I-R Market)

Outcome of the SWOT Analysis Division III, table 8.5.8

Strengths	Weaknesses
Higher return on US investments and higher US GDP growth.	Lagging data
Cash-effect of M&A activity	US stock indices
Stock swap effect of M&A activity	
Merger arbitrage	
MSCI Index adjustments	
Derivative markets	

Opportunities	Threats
Rebuild dominant role	FX Option Market, Commodity Market, International Debt Market, Short-Term Interest Rate Market

Division III (Equity Market) has a Diversified Configuration.

Chapter 9 on Division IV (International Debt Market), will cope with the the following subjects:
1. The Configuration approach and Division IV.
2. The Entrepreneurial approach and Division IV.
3. The Design approach and Division IV.
4. The Positioning approach and Division IV.

REFERENCES

Aldred, N. and G. Fisher (2001). "MSCI Index Rebalancing (2)", ABN AMRO, 8 November 2001.

Andrade, G., M. Mitchell and E. Stafford (2001). "New Evidence and Perspective on Mergers".

Arnswald, T. (2001). "Investment Behaviour of German Equity Fund Managers", Economic Research Centre of the Deutsche Bundesbank.

Bartram, S.M. and G. Dufey (2001). International Portfolio Investment: Theory, Evidence, and Institutional Framework

Berset, J.(UBP), S. Condorelli (UBP), P. Hoebrechts (UBP) and A. Rampa (UBP). "Understanding Hedge Fund", Working Paper II, UBP and Alternative Asset Management Group, April 2000.

Bhagwat, Y. and V. Gondhalekar (2000). "Motives in the Acquisitions of Nasdaq Targets During the Aftermath of the 1987 Crash", The Financial Review, Vol 37, No.4, November 2002.

Bouchaud, J-P, A. Matacz and M. Potters (2001), "The leverage effect in financial markets: retarded volatility and market panic".

Chen, J. (1999). Derivative securities: What they tell us?", preliminary draft.

Copeland, T., T. Koller and J. Murrin (1995). "Valuation", McKinsey & Company, Inc., Wiley Frontiers in Finance.

Federal Reserve Board (1998). "Trading and Capital-Markets Activities Manual: Equity Derivatives"

Federal Reserve Board (1998). "Trading and Capital-Markets Activities Manual: Financial Futures"

Frankel, J.A. (1993). The Internationalization of Equity Markets", National Bureau of Economic Research, Introduction of his book published by the University of Chicago Press.

Goldman Sachs. "Equity Index Research: The new MSCI indices", 19 May 2001.

Greene, W.H., *ECONOMETRIC ANALYSIS, 4/E,* ©2000, Reprinted by permission on Pearson Education, Inc., Upper Saddle Rive, New Jersey.

Mintzberg, H., *STRUCTURES IN FIVES: Designing Effective Organizations*, Copyright © 1993. Reprinted by permission of Pearson Education, Inc., Upper Saddle River, New Jersey.

Mintzberg, H., B. Ahlstrand, J. Lampel, *STRATEGY SAFARI: The Complete Guide Through the Wilds of Strategic Management,* Copyright © 1998. Reprinted by permission of Pearson Education Ltd, 128 LongAcre, London WC2E 9AN

MSCI. "MSCI Announces Provisional Index Constituents", WWW.MSCI.COM, 19 May 2001

Nowak, E. (1998). "Finance, Investment, and Firm Value in Germany and the US, A Comparative Analysis", Discussion Paper 49, DFG Sonderforschungsbereich 373, Humboldt-University Berlin, May 1998.

COMPETITIVE STRATEGY: Techniques for Analyzing Industries and Competitors by Michael E. Porter. Copyright © 1980, 1998 by The Free Press, an imprint of Simon & Schuster Adult Publishing Group. Reprinted with permission of the publisher.

Pryor, F.L. (2001). Dimensions of the Worldwide Merger Boom, Journal of Economic Issues.

Tsatsaronis, K."Special feature: Hedge funds, BIS Quarterly Review, November 2000

Warnock, F.E. and M. Mason (2001). "The geographyof capital flows", Emerging Markets Quarterly, 5 (1), pp.15-29, Spring 2001.

RECOMMENDED BOOKS

Jones, F.J. and R.J. Teweles (1999). "The Futures Game: Who wins, Who loses & Why", Mc-Graw-Hill.

Nicholas, J.G. (2000). "Market Neutral Investing: Long/short hedge fund strategies", Bloomberg Press Princeton.

Chapter **9**

DIVISION IV
INTERNATIONAL
DEBT MARKET

9.1 INTRODUCTION

Division IV (International Debt Market) is the fourth division in this EUR/USD Interbank Market organization. So far, the products from the FX Options Market (Division I), Commodity Market (Division II) and the Equity Market (Division III) have demonstrated rationale for the movements in EUR/USD. Division I and II were still dominant at the end of 2001, while Division III has lost most of its power, during the sell-off in the equity markets, since March of 2000. Early in calendar year 2000, investors began migrating from equities into bonds. Investors had begun to worry about the worldwide economic outlook, and economic deterioration usually follows an interest easing cycle, which generally portends a good future for bonds. The sell-off in the equity markets created an uncertain environment for investors, so the rally in the bond markets was the result. The bond markets' rally started around February/March 2000 and ended in November/December 2001, primarily due to the widely expected recovery of the US economy in 2002 (and inflation fears). The following conclusions are made in the SWOT Analysis:
1. US debt market offers better return.
2. US debt market is higher developed and has evolved into greater depth and breadth.
3. USD preferred as currency denomination in issues.
4. Market borrower driven.
5. Increase USD turnover in derivative market.
6. The drop in USD denominated issues and drop in oil prices explain the rally in EUR/USD in fourth quarter of 2000.

We start this division with the Configuration approach, followed by the Entrepreneurial approach, the Design approach (I + II) and the Positioning approach (I + II). These approaches are explained in chapter 1 and 2.

9.2 CONFIGURATION APPROACH

The structure of an organization can be defined as the different ways in which work is divided into different tasks and how these tasks are coordinated. In the organization of Division IV (International Debt Market), the main products are the international loan market, the international bond market and the derivatives market. These are the general products, which can be divided into the sub-products mentioned earlier.
The different sub products are used for different clients based on different knowledge levels and different strategy.

Organizational parts
Strategic Apex
The International Debt Market makers are responsible for this division. They are the strategists of the organization.

Support Staff
Organizationally, this group has the task of influencing the work of others in the organization. They do this by training the people in Division IV and making sure that technology is updated so that the Strategic Apex receives live prices and news. Further, the **salespeople match the clients and products.**

Techno Structure
The Techno Structure of Division IV (International Debt Market) is the same as for the total EUR/USD Interbank Market organization and can be divided into:
1. Fundamental Analysis (Chapter 4)
2. Technical Analysis (Chapter 5)
This division uses a combination of both specialties.

Middle Line
The middle lines are the other traders in this division, for example the government bond, Pfandbrief, futures, options and swap traders.

Operating Core
The operating core has four main functions:
1. Supply the general International Debt Market products for the production (see production plan, products like government bonds and agency bonds).
2. Transform these general products into the differentiated sub-products.
3. Distribute the differentiated sub-products
4. Provide direct support to input, transformation and output.

Coordination mechanism
The coordination mechanism used in Division IV is standardization of output. The general products (input) are transformed into the different sub-products (output) to meet the needs of the clients.

Decentralization
The International Debt Market traders are responsible for the strategy and building of the sub-products. The power is decentralized over the middle-line managers. However, inside this division, power is centralized.

Configuration
Division IV (International Debt Market) uses standardization of output as a coordination mechanism. Further, the Middle Line is the dominant force in the organization because it influences which of the sub products are used in the market. The power is decentralized over the Middle Line (partial vertical decentralization). Consequently this division also has a **Diversified Configuration.**

Outcome

Table 9.2.1

Division IV: International Debt Market	Definition
Strategic Apex	International Debt Market traders
Support Staff	Systems
	Sales force to match the clients with the products
Techno Structure	Fundamental Analysis (Chapter 4)
	Technical Analysis (Chapter 5)
Middle Line	Government bond traders
	Agency bond traders, MBS traders
	Corporate bond traders
	MTN traders
	Floaters traders
	Swap traders
	Futures traders
	Option traders
Operating Core	Government bond market
	Agency market
	MBS market
	Corporate bond market
	MTN market
	Floaters market
	Swap market
	Futures market
	Options market
	Hedge fund market
Coordination mechanism	Standardization of output
Decentralization	Partial vertical decentralization
Configuration	Diversified organization
Culture	Market Psychology (Chapter 3)

9.3 ENTREPRENEURIAL APPROACH

Within Division IV (International Debt Market), traders make the decisions where, when and how to take positions in the market. They follow the Enterpreneurial approach because their decision is based on their market view or vision. The International Debt Market can be divided into three sub-markets:
- INTERNATIONAL LOAN MARKET
- INTERNATIONAL BOND MARKET
- DERIVATIVE MARKET

In the product plan, all the products of the different sub market can be described. The thinking about strategy is done by the market makers in the debt markets. They decide pricing and position. Some clients also do strategic thinking, which makes them a very powerful client group.

9.4 DESIGN APPROACH I: BUSINESS PLAN

Product plan

These products are represented within Division IV (International Debt Market):
INTERNATIONAL LOAN MARKET
     – Loans
     – Syndicated loans
INTERNATIONAL BOND MARKET
     – Government bonds
     – Agency bonds and mortgage backed securities
     – Corporate bonds
     – Medium Term Notes
     – Floating-Rate Securities
DERIVATIVE MARKETS
     – Swaps
     – Futures
     – Options

International loan market

Loans
International banks are recycling large deposit flows from the depositors to the borrowers and creating interbank loans. Interbank loans are also created by transactions of banks with their offices abroad to channel substantial amounts into their subsidiaries. These subsidiaries will on-lend these funds to corporates and other borrowers in that country.

Syndicated loans
In the syndicated loan market, a few large banks together create a syndicate (with one loan contract) to offer large loans to their main borrowers. Borrowers are mainly using the syndicated loan market for the temporary finance of their M&A deals or management buyouts. The main form of syndicated loans is the bridge loan, a temporary or supplementary means of funding before or while the borrower is tapping the securities markets.

International bond market

Government bonds

US[1]

The US bills, notes and bonds are issued by the Treasury Department and represent direct obligations of the US government. They have little credit risk and are backed by the full faith and credit of the US Government.

Table 9.4.1

Issue Type	Security Type	Issues	Amount Outstanding November 30, 2001
Treasury bills	Discount	Cash-management 13-week, 26-week 52-week	$ 813 billion
Treasury notes	Coupon	2-year, 5-year, 10-year	$ 1,415 billion
Treasury bonds*	Coupon	30-year	$ 607 billion
Treasury inflation-indexed securities	Coupon	10-year, 30-year	$ 45 billion

Source: www.publicdebt.ustreas.gov/opd/opds112001.htm.

On October 31, 2001, the US Treasury said it was ending sales of its 30-year bond after 24 years of regular auctions. The government's slimmer borrowing requirements and the long bond's high interest rates made the one-time benchmark costly and unnecessary, Treasury officials argued[2] (*).

Eurozone

German Federal Government Bonds:

The federal government of Germany issues several types of securities: bonds (Bunds), notes (Bobls and Schatze) and Treasury discount paper (U-Schatze). U-Schatze are zero-coupon Treasury notes, with maturities of one to two years, which may not be purchased by foreigners. Short-term Treasury bills, with one-half to one-year maturities, can be purchased by foreigners. Bunds are issued regularly, usually in DM20 billion to DM30 billion blocks with maturities ranging from 8 to 30 years. Bunds are issued in minimum denominations of DM 1,000 and a typical issue carries a maturity of 10 years. Bunds are redeemable in a lump sum at maturity, at face value, with interest paid annually. Until 1990, all bonds issued by federal government and other public authorities were noncallable and bore a fixed coupon value. However, since February 1990, some callable floating-rate bonds have been issued[3]. The Federal government has issued special five-year federal notes (Bobls) since 1979, but foreign investment in these securities has been permitted only since 1988. In the past, medium-term notes with four-to six-year

---

[1]Federal Reserve Board, *Trading and Capital-Markets Activities Manual,US Treasury Bills, Notes , and Bonds Notes*, April 2002
[2]Financial Times, *US Treasury calls a halt to long bond sales*, Thursday November 1, 2001
[3]Federal Reserve Board, *Trading and Capital-Markets Activities Manual,German Government Bonds and Notes*, February 1998

maturities (Schatze) were issued irregularly by federal government, the Unity fund and the Federal Post Office and Railway. However, in 1995, the Ministry of Finance decided to discontinue the issuance of these securities to create more transparency in the market. All the Bobls and existing Schatze issues are fixed-coupon securities with bullet maturities[4].

Agencies and Mortgage Backed Securities
US[5]
Agency securities are debt obligations issued by the federal agencies or federally sponsored agencies. Federal agencies are direct arms of the US government; federally sponsored agencies are privately owned and publicly chartered organizations which were created by acts of Congress to support a specific purpose (GSE = government sponsored entities).

Federal agencies are arms of the federal government and generally do not issue securities directly in the market place. Examples of these agencies: Government National Mortgage Association (GNMA or Ginnie Mae), Export-Import Bank, Farmers Home Administration, General Services Administration (GSA) and Tennessee Valley Authority.

Government- sponsored entities include agencies in the following areas: housing, farm credit, student loans, small business and export funding.

GSEs issue both discount and coupon notes and bonds. These securities are not backed by the full faith and credit of the US government. GSEs issue direct debt obligations and guarantee various types of asset-backed securities. These are debt instruments that represent an interest in a pool of assets. Credit risk is an important issue in asset-backed securities because of the significant credit risks inherent in the underlying collateral and because issuers are primarily private entities.

Eurozone
Government agencies[6]:
German government agencies such as the Federal Post Office and the Federal Railway have also issued bonds (Posts and Bahns) and notes (Schatze). In addition, with the unification of West and East Germany in October 1990, the German Unity fund began to issue Unity Fund bonds (Unities) and notes (Schatze). The outstanding debt issues of the Post Office, Railway and Unity Fund have since been folded into the so-called Debt Inheritance Fund, which has led to an explicit debt service of these issues through the federal government, hence the full faith and credit of the federal government guarantees these issues.

---

[4] Federal Reserve Board, *Trading and Capital-Markets Activities Manual, German Governement Bonds and Notes*, February 1998
[5] Federal Reserve Board, *Trading and Capital-Markets Activities Manual, Government Agency Securities*, April 2001
Federal Reserve Board, *Trading and Capital-Markets Activities Manual, Asset-Backed Securities and Asset-Backed Commercial Paper*, Februari 2001
[6] Federal Reserve Board, *Trading and Capital-Markets Activities Manual, German Government Bonds and Notes*, February 1998

German Pfandbrief[7]:
The Pfandbrief is essentially a funding tool, which offers minimal, if any, risk transfer for the asset originator. The underlying cover asset remains on the balance sheet and the entire credit risk of the cover pool remains the obligation of the issuer. In this regard it differs from the traditional asset-backed-security, which usually transfers the asset off-balance-sheet, transfers the credit risk to the investor and clearly identifies any residual risk arising from third parties. Pfandbrief are standardized German law debt instruments that are strictly regulated by the Mortgage Bank Act and reviewed by the Federal Banking Supervisory Authority. Pfandbrief are medium to long-term bonds (traditionally up to 10 years) which are secured by a pool of specified assets that have to qualify under specified rules. There are two types of Pfandbrief:
- Public sector Pfandbrief that are secured by a pool of loans to public law entities.
- Mortgage Pfandbrief, which are secured on residential and commercial mortgages.

A Pfandbrief bond is a principal obligation of a particular issuer, but which benefits from a first ranking security interest over a pool of either public sector or mortgage obligations. The risk of the Pfandbrief could therefore be said to lie in the performance of the cover pool of assets, and the practical and economic ability of the issuer to fend off difficulties that might occur in the management of the pool. This cover pool is usually maintained at a level surplus to the specific requirement of the Pfandbrief in issuance; however no mandatory over-collateralization is required. Pfandbrief benefit from a theoretical sheltering from default risk under paragraph 35 of the German Mortgage Bank Act, as long as the underlying pool is sufficient to cover Pfandbrief obligations.

The public sector Pfandbrief are collateralized by an asset pool of loans to, or guaranteed by, European public sectors. The asset pool is based on the high credit of the Federal Republic of Germany, and the Federal States, as well as central governments in other EU member countries. The asset pool is strictly separated and under the supervision of an independent trustee appointed by the German Banking Supervisory Authority. Due to the character of the collateral, Public Sector Pfandbrief are regarded as European Agency products. The Pfandbrief market has grown rapidly since the mid 1990s. Before, that, domestic investors like banks and insurance companies were the main buyers of traditional Pfandbrief, which were small tailor-made bonds issues in a domestic market that was illiquid as well as fragmented. The introduction of the Jumbo Pfandbrief concept in 1995 marked the beginning of the standardization and internationalization of the German Pfandbrief market (issue size > 1 billion and 5 pip spread). This Jumbo Pfandbrief -was extended to the Global Pfandbrief in 1998.

---

[7]Commerzbank Securities, *All that glitters*, Appendix 4, 24 July 2001
Euromoney, *Pfandbrief issuers' business overhaul*, April 2001
www.depfa.com/treasury

Table 9.4.2[8]

	Traditional Pfandbrief	Jumbo Pfandbrief	Global Pfandbrief
Market	Fragmented	Start of standardization	Standardized
	Illiquid	Forced liquidity	High liquidity
	Domestic	Internationalization	Global distribution
Investor target group	Domestic Insurance Companies	International Insurance Companies	Relative Value Investors
	Domestic Banks	Domestic Funds	Central Banks
			International Funds
Investment criteria	Absolute Yield	Risk Weighting	Liquidity
	Tailor-made	Liquidity	Repo
			OTC options
			Benchmark

Table 9.4.3[9]

Global Pfandbrief #3	Global Pfandbrief #4	Global Pfandbrief #5
Launched January 1998, Maturity January 2005	Launched July 1998, Maturity July 2008	Launched January 1999, Maturity 15 January 2009
Initial issue size of DM 4 billion	Initial issue size of DM 5 billion	Initial issue size of Euro 3 billion
Spread performance tighter than comparable bonds.	Relative performance: 2-5bp after launch: tightening to +10bp	Largest single Euro-denominated non-government.
Significant step towards Pfandbrief benchmark. The Euro "agency" product.	Global Pfandbrief facility: Extension of Domestic Frequent Issuer Status US Market	Spread performance from +35bp to +29/+30bp over the Bund 01/09.
		Increased liquidity through OTC-bond options and repo back-stop facility at Euribor-70bp
Joint leads: Deutsche bank, Goldman Sachs	Joint leads: Commerzbank, Goldman Sachs	Joint leads: Commerzbank, Morgan Stanley Dean Witter

Introduction of OTC bond options:
- Tradable option prices quoted by the joint leads.
- Same conventions as Bund options enable transparent spread trading.
- Efficient tool to hedge against the increased volatility of credit spreads.
- Facilitates growing investor interest in option based trading strategies.

---

[8] www.depfa.com/treasury
[9] www.depfa.com/treasury

Repo back-stop facility at Euribor-70bp:
- The issuer will offer a certain repo facility for a specified minimum size of total issue size at a rate of Euribor –70bp to all market parties.
- Guaranteed liquidity in the repo market should lead to lighter bid-offer spreads quoted by the market makers.

Figure 9.4.1: The distribution of Global Pfandbrief #5 on the first day[10]

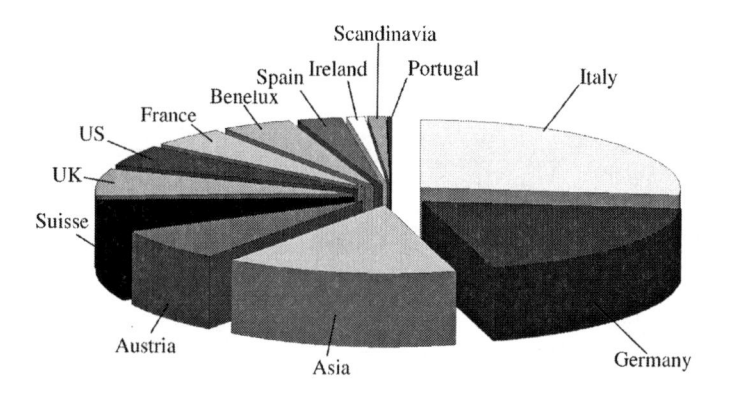

Figure 9.4.2: First day distribution by investor[11]

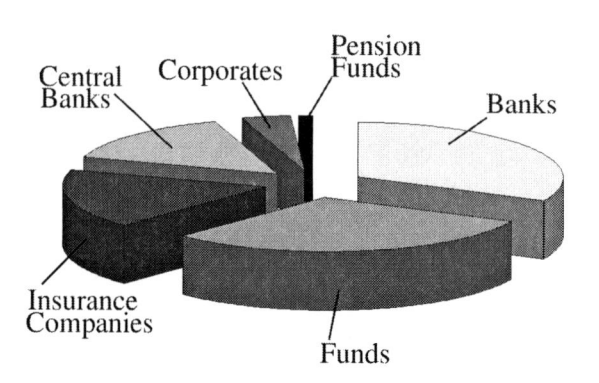

Since 1999, issuers under the Global program will have an initial volume of Euro 2-4 billion with potential increases up to Euro 5 billion.

---

[10] www.depfa.com/treasury
[11] www.depfa.com/treasury

Corporate bonds[12]
Corporate bonds are debt obligations issued by corporations. Corporate bonds may be secured or unsecured. If debt is unsecured, the bonds are known as debentures. Corporate bonds contain elements of both interest rate risk and credit risk. For investors, bond ratings are very important so they follow closely the ratings done by the two important rating agencies Moody's and S&P.

Floating-Rate Securities
These are securities with floating rates.

Derivative market

Swaps by McDougall[13]
A swap is a tool for changing risk. When hedging with a swap, first establish the existing position. The first leg of a swap matches the existing position. The second leg of a swap creates the required position. An interest rate swap (IRS) is a tool for changing interest rate risks:
> – An IRS is an agreement to exchange cash flows based on a given principal amount for a given time between two contractually bound counterparties.
> – An IRS is an arrangement, which alters the interest rate basis of the cash flows.
> – An IRS is a method for managing debts or investments.
> – An IRS is a tool for asset and liability management.
> – An IRS changes risk.

Swaps are an alternative financing technique, used when the cost of funds is lower than the cash market equivalent. In the same way that it is possible to use an interest rate swap as a means of changing proportions of fixed- and floating rate debt in a borrower's portfolio, it is possible to use a currency swap as a means of changing the proportion of currency debt in a multi currency debt portfolio.

---

[12]Federal Reserve Board, *Trading and Capital-Markets Activities Manual,Corporate Notes and Bonds*, February 1998
[13]McDougall, A., *MASTERING SWAP MARKETS*, Copyright © 2000. Reprinted by permission of Pearson Education, Inc., Upper Saddle River, New Jersey

Futures[14]

Futures contracts are exchange-traded agreements for delivery of special amount and quality of a particular product at a specified price on a specified date. These are essentially exchange traded contracts with standardized terms.

Options

On the future exchanges it is also possible to trade options on fixed-income securities and fixed-income futures.

---

[14]Federal Reserve Board, *Trading and Capital-Markets Activities Manual, Financial Futures,* February 1998

Production plan

The production plan describes everything that is needed to sell the products in the product plan.
1. Markets
2. Knowledge
3. Information systems

International loan market

Loan market by Wooldridge (BIS)[15]
"Members of the OPEC accounted for one third of the deposit flow from developing countries. Among developing countries outside OPEC, the largest deposits were from Taiwan and mainland China. The process of recycling the large deposit flows from developing countries contributed to an expansion of interbank loans. In the third quarter of 2000, banks in the UK received approximately one third of the deposit flows, and banks in the Euro area another quarter. The remainder was split between the US and offshore centers. These funds were rechannelled to borrowers in the developed countries as well as branches in offshore centers. Most of the deposits by developing countries were denominated in USD, with the EUR second, accounting for less than 15% of the deposits. Total amount of stock at the end of September 2000: USD 4,177.4 billion and EUR 1,199.9 billion. Swiss and US banks' transactions with their offices abroad also boosted interbank activity. Since the US investment banks and Swiss banks are dominant players in trust funds, these transactions were probably related to the fact that Swiss banks channeled substantial amounts into their subsidiaries in the US, which then onlent the funds to US corporations.

In the fourth quarter of 2000, an interbank activities surge capped a near-record year in the international banking market. According to the local banking statistics, cross border claims increased by $400 billion, $302 billion of which comprised interbank lending. Much of such activity was driven by efforts to recycle large inflows from emerging economies to borrowers in the industrial countries. Oil-exporting countries and emerging economies in East Asia were the main source of funds while borrowers in the US were among the principal recipients (like in Q2 and Q3). So funds made available through the interbank market supported an increase in lending to non-bank borrowers, especially in the US.

In the first quarter of 2001, the US dollar segment of the international market remained very active, but even larger flows were seen in the euro segment. The euro accounted for 51% of the total increase in the foreign currency claims of banks in the reporting area.

---

[15] P.D. Wooldridge, *The International Banking Market*, BIS Quarterly Review, March-September 2001

Banks located in the US were the most important source of cross border dollar funding. Foreign demand for dollars to support the purchases of US securities contributed to an unusually large $70.3 billion increase in dollar lending by banks in the US to banks abroad. Two thirds of this credit went to banks in Europe".

Table 9.4.4: International claims of BIS reporting banks

	1999 Year	2000 Year	Q1	Q2	Q3	Q4	2001 Q1	Stocks at end-March 2001
Total claims	333.4	1,372.1	573.5	148.0	230.6	420.0	838.8	12,698.8
USD	32.6	522.1	151.7	74.3	105.7	190.4	298.1	5,360.8
Euro	464.6	516.7	301.4	55.1	74.6	85.6	427.0	3,482.6
Intra-Euro	*295.4*	*140.5*	*106.6*	*-8.4*	*20.4*	*21.8*	*112.3*	*1,357.3*

Source: BIS Quarterly Review, September 2001

Syndicated loan market by Gadanecz (BIS)[16]

"In the first quarter of 2000, syndicated loans for M&A by telecommunications firms appeared to account for a significant part of the non-bank borrowers' lending flows. The two largest international lending deals signed in the first quarter were a EUR30 billion facility to support the takeover of Germany's Mannesmann AG by the UK's Vodafone Airtouch and a EUR13 billion facility to finance the acquisition of Germany's E-Plus by KPN.

The second quarter of 2000 was the most active for international syndicated credits since 1997. The telecommunications sector, where many of the mergers took place, continued to account for some of the biggest transactions. Developed countries made up nearly 90% of total new facilities, with US and British borrowers getting the lion's share. The largest deal was a GBP16 billion commercial paper backup facility for British Telecom. Seven large US banks and securities firms also borrowed at least $2 billion each. Outside the developed countries, there was a lot of activity in Hong Kong where borrowers obtained a total of $14 billion including $9 billion to finance the acquisition, by Pacific Century CyberWorks, of a majority stake in Hong Kong Telecom from parent company Cable & Wireless of the UK.

In the third quarter of 2000, activity related to M&As and bridge loans for telecommunications firms contributed to the strength. Deals to finance M&As and management buyouts rebounded to $55 billion from $43 billion in Q2. Borrowing by telecommunication firms picked up again, particularly in the form of bridge loans, a temporary or supplementary means of funding before or while tapping securities markets. The largest borrowers in the syndicated loan market were all Telecom firms: France Telecom (EUR 30 billion), Vodafone Airtouch ($15 billion), KPN (EUR 13 billion), and Telefonica de

---

[16] B. Gadanecz, The International Banking Market, BIS Quarterly Review, May 2000-March 2001, September 2001

Espana (EUR 8 billion). Facilities intended to support purchases of third-generation mobile phone licenses accounted for at least 20% of Telecom financing. US banks were the largest participants, providing approximately ¼ of Telecom financing during the first three quarters of 2000, followed by German and UK banks, which each provided around 10% of funds.

In the fourth quarter of 2000, the international syndicated credit market remained strong. North American companies were the most active telecoms in the market. The largest syndicated loan announced was a $25 billion facility arranged for AT&T, as backing for its commercial paper program. Syndicated credits arranged for telecoms firms totaled $256 billion in 2000, more than a threefold increase over 1999. The announcements related to M&As and buyouts increased by 22% in 2000 over the previous year to $214 billion. The poor performance of equities during 2000 may have prompted firms to turn from the stock markets to the syndicated loan market to finance M&As.

Syndicated lending activity rebounded in the second quarter of 2001 to a record high of $431 billion. The rebound was led by borrowers from the US, for whom banks arranged credits totaling $294 billion. EU nationals were also more active, raising $85 billion.

Some of the largest loans were arranged for borrowers who typically meet a large part of their short-term financing needs in the money market rather than the loan market. Telecommunications firms appear to have found bank financing more attractive than bond financing. Syndicated lending to telecoms almost doubled in the second quarter. Most of the telecom activity involved the rolling-over of facilities contracted in 1999 and 2000".

DIVISION IV INTERNATIONAL DEBT MARKET

International bond market by Sutton, Remolona and Cohen (BIS)[17]

Table 9.4.5: Gross issuance in the international bond and note market in billions of USD

	1999	2000					2001	
	Year	Year	Q1	Q2	Q3	Q4	Q1	Q2
Total announced issues	1,766.8	1,933.5	508.3	484.6	502.4	438.3	570.2	543.3
Floating rate issues	483.8	624.3	138.0	157.0	168.3	161.0	139.9	138.9
Straight fixed rate issues	1,230.9	1,252.7	356.0	315.7	317.6	263.5	418.3	387.9
Equity-related issues*	52.1	56.5	14.3	11.9	16.5	13.8	12.1	16.6
US dollar	775.4	859.3	216.9	206.6	240.8	194.9	263.1	249.2
Euro	677.9	647.8	186.8	153.1	150.7	157.2	214.6	193.9
Yen	118.9	204.6	49.2	76.1	51.2	28.1	36.4	51.3
Other currencies	194.6	221.8	55.3	48.7	59.8	58.1	56.1	48.9
Private sector	1,374.3	1,499.9	374.4	397.5	380.3	347.8	427.7	408.5
Financial institutions**	897.7	1,021.4	276.0	251.5	249.8	244.1	274.1	253.0
Corporate issuers	476.6	478.5	98.3	146.0	130.5	103.7	153.5	155.5
Of which telecoms	84.3	115.7	24.7	46.7	25.0	19.3	49.2	32.4
Public sector	314.7	363.0	113.4	66.7	107.7	75.2	125.7	111.6
Central government	94.2	93.0	46.0	18.7	23.7	4.7	28.5	20.8
State agencies and other	220.5	269.9	67.5	48.0	84.0	70.5	97.2	90.8
International institutions	77.8	70.7	20.5	20.4	14.5	15.3	16.9	23.2
Completed issues	1,771.2	1,935.3	474.9	485.2	501.0	474.2	559.1	520.2
Repayments	607.3	787.2	189.5	189.8	211.1	196.7	269.6	270.8

* Convertible bonds and bonds with equity warrants. ** Commercial banks and other financial institutions
Sources: BIS, Bank of England, Capital DATA, Euroclear, ISMA, and Thomson Financial Securities Data

---

[17] G.D. Sutton, E.M. Remolona and B.H. Cohen, The International Debt Secuirities Market, BIS Quarterly Review, August 2000-March 2001

Government bond market
US
Primary market[18]:
Treasury notes and bonds are issued through yield auctions of new issues for cash. Bids are separated into competitive bids and noncompetitive bids. Competitive bids are made by primary government dealers, while noncompetitive bids are made by individual investors and small institutions. Two types of auctions are currently used to sell securities: multiple –price auction and single price auction.

By A. Krishnamurthy[19]
"The Treasury currently auctions 30-year bonds on roughly a six-month cycle. Upon issuance, a bond is called the new bond and acquires benchmark status, replacing the bond that was issued six months prior (now old bond). One of the characteristics of new bonds is the high premium attached".

On October 31, 2001, the US Treasury said it was ending sales of its 30-year bond after 24 years of regular auctions. The government's slimmer borrowing requirements and the long bond's high interest rates made the one-time benchmark costly and unnecessary, Treasury officials argued[20].

Secondary market[21]:
Secondary trading in Treasuries occurs in the OTC market. In the secondary market, the most recently auctioned Treasury issue is considered "current", or "on-the-run". Issues auctioned before current issues are typically refered to as "off-the-run" securities. In general current issues are much more actively traded and have much more liquidity than off-the-run securities.

Eurozone
Primary market[22]:
Bunds are issued using a combination of syndication and bidding procedures. Part of the issue is offered at fixed terms to the members of the Federal Bond Consortium, which consists of German banks, foreign banks in Germany and Deutsche Bundesbank. The Bundesbank is the lead bank in the syndicate and determines the allocation of the offering among the syndicate members. These allocations are changed infrequently. During the syndicate meeting, the coupon rate, maturity and issue price are determined by the government and syndicate, although the total size of the issue is unknown.

---

[18]Federal Reserve Board, *Trading and Capital-Markets Activities Manual,US Treasury Bills, Notes , and Bonds Notes*, April 2002
[19]A. Krishnamurthy, *The Bond/Old-Bond Spread, February 11*, 2001
[20]Financial Times, *US Treasury calls a halt to long bond sales*, Thursday November 1, 2001
[21]Federal Reserve Board, *Trading and Capital-Markets Activities Manual,US Treasury Bills, Notes , and Bonds Notes*, April 2002
[22]Federal Reserve Board, *Trading and Capital-Markets Activities Manual,German Government Bonds and Notes*, February 1998

Syndicate members receive a fee from the government for selling bonds received through syndicate negotiations.

Bobls are issued on a standing-issue basis (similar to a tap form, in which a fixed amount of securities at a fixed price are issued when market conditions are considered favorable) with stated coupon and price. During the initial selling period the price is periodically adjusted by the Ministry of Finance to reflect changes in market conditions

Secondary market[23]:
German bonds are listed and traded on all eight German stock exchanges seven days after they are issued. Bobl issues are officially listed on the stock exchanges after the initial selling period of one to three months. In addition to the stock exchange transactions, substantial OTC trading occurs. In Germany, the secondary market for both stocks and bonds is primarily an interbank market.
The market for German government bonds and notes is active and liquid and price transparency is considered to be relatively high for these securities. Bonds are quoted as a percentage of par to two decimal places. Bonds are traded on a price basis, net of accrued interest. The bid-offer spread is usually eight pfennigs for liquid issues and 15 pfennigs for less liquid issues. For notes, bid-offer spreads are 5 to 10 pfennigs for liquid issues.

Agency securities market
US
Primary market[24]:
In the primary market, government agencies and GSEs sell their securities to a select group of commercial banks and investment banks. These banks advise the agencies on issuing debt, placing the debt with the end-users and making markets in these securities.

Eurozone[25]
Pfandbrief market:
Mortgage banks date back to the 19th century and are heavily constrained in their business scope, essentially being limited to residential and commercial lending and to public sector lending. Public sector lending is very important but margins have been eroded and demand for loans is falling. Margins have been eroded as a result both of changing fundamentals in the public sector business as well as greater investor and supervisory

---

[23]Federal Reserve Board, *Trading and Capital-Markets Activities Manual, German Government Bonds and Notes*, February 1998
[24]Federal Reserve Board, *Trading and Capital-Markets Activities Manual, US Government Agency Securities*, April 2001
[25]Commerzbank Securities, *All that glitters*, Appendix 4, 24 July 2001
Euromoney, *Pfandbrief issuers' business overhaul*, April 2001

focus on residual interest rate risk, thus promoting a less aggressive approach towards interest rate arbitrage. New loans to the public sector declined by 24% in 2000, reflecting a low demand as a result of shrinking state budget deficits as well borrowers' aspirations to go straight to the capital markets to raise funds. Mortgage lending has also declined, by 15% in 2000, as a result of higher interest rates and the economic downturn. The issue volume in 2000 was 19% lower than in 1999. The trend of decreasing issuance could become more visible after March 2002, when the newly implemented withholding tax- regime prevents issuers from increasing their existing issues. The Pfandbrief is no longer seen as a commoditised product. Investors are focusing on the true risk profile of the product as a function of the issuing bank. This causes differentiation amongst issuers based more upon perceived risk profiles of the issuers. Fundamentally, certain issues are more than adequately supported by their relevant cover pool assets; this reduces the importance of issuer risk.

The quantum of issuer risk is a function of:
- Credit quality of the cover pool.
- The degree of maturity and actual cash flow mismatch between the cover pool and the supporting liabilities.
- The degree of servicing risk associated with the day to day operational management of the cover pool.

Further, the rising cost of Pfandbrief funding relative to swap spreads is rapidly changing the economic basis for managing mortgage risk on the balance sheet.

In the second quarter of 2000 the German banks issued less paper. These institutions cut their net issuance from $45 billion in Q1 to $34 billion in Q2, reflecting the slowdown in the Pfandbrief market[26].

Mortgage Backed Securities market
For a detailed description of this market are recommended the following books:
- "The Handbook of Fixed Income Securities", by F.J. Fabozzi
- "Market Neutral Investing: Long/Short Hedge Fund Strategies", by J.G. Nicholas, including a chapter on Mortgage Backed Securities Arbitrage.

Corporate bond market by Remolona, Cohen and Wooldridge (BIS)[27].
"In the second quarter of 2000, non-financial corporations more than doubled their net debt issuance to $78 billion. Telecommunications companies and firm involved in mergers and takeovers were especially active. One of the largest borrowers was Deutsche Telekom, which announced a $14.6 billion package comprising eight separate bond issues (denominated in four currencies) on 27 June and $16.7 billion of bond and note issues during the quarter as a whole. Other large issuers included France Telecom ($5.9 billion), Worldcom ($5 billion), Unilever ($3.2 billion) and Vivendi ($1.9 billion). In the second quarter of 2001, the global economic slowdown seems to have dampened demand for new bond issues".

---

[26]E.M. Remolona and B.H. Cohen, *The International Debt Securities Market*, BIS Quarterly review, August 2000,
[27]E.M. Remolona and B.H. Cohen, *The International Debt Securities Market*, BIS Quarterly review, August 2000,
 P.D. Wooldridge, *The International Banking Market*, BIS Quarterly Review, September 2001.

Floating-Rate Securities Market[28]
The coupon rates for floating-rate notes are based on various benchmarks ranging from short-term rates to one-year and longer constant maturity Treasury rates. Coupons are usually quoted as spread above or below the base rate.

Derivative market

Swap market
Interest Rate Swap by McDougall[29]
Borrowers have created attractively priced funds through the swap markets for over 20 years. They issue bonds and swap the proceeds to reflect the required funding preference. The swap market is a way of arbitrage. Instead of asking for a loan at his bank, the borrower issues bonds and swaps the payments. The arbitrage (credit arbitrage) works because of the different perspectives of the providers of funds in the bond and in the loan markets. It is the difference between these perspectives, which creates the credit arbitrage, which drives the swap driven new issue process. The arbitrage between bond and loan pricing has been exploited in over 40 currencies. Credit arbitrage is created by different prices of credit in different markets. Further, it is easier to go short a credit in the bond markets than in the loan markets and it is easier to trade credit in the bond markets than in the loan markets. As a result, credit arbitrage creates a link between prices of loans and bonds.

Cross currency swaps[30]
The cross currency swap is an interest rate swap that involves two currencies. The cross currency swap is constructed from the two interest rates in the currencies and a currency spot rate. Further, there are three possibilities which must be considered concerning the amount to exchange.
1. Exchange of principal amounts at the beginning and the end of the swap.
2. Exchange of the principal amounts only at the beginning of the swap.
3. Exchange of the principal amounts only at the end of the swap.
4. No exchange of principal amounts at all.

In the first situation, the currency rate used is equal at the beginning and at the end of the swap. The overall position is squared but at the time the first exchange of principal amounts has taken place a spot position appears in the books. This position is re-valued against the currency moves and reflects the credit risk of the transaction. When the swap is terminated because of the default of the counterparty, this position becomes an actual one. Cross currency swaps are only done with good rated counterparties because of this credit risk.

---

[28] Federal Reserve Board, *Trading and Capital-Markets Activities Manual, Corporate Notes and Bonds*, February 1998
[29] McDougall,, A., *MASTERING SWAP MARKETS*, Copyright © 2000. Reprinted by permission of Pearson Education, Inc., Upper Saddle River, New Jersey
[30] Information from Lody Prijs, ABN AMRO Cross currency swap sales manager

In situations 2 and 3, the swap dealer is getting a currency position as a result of this deal. Since swap traders take positions in interest rates and not in currencies this forward currencies position is being hedged with the currency traders. In situation 4 the two parties pay the agreed interest rates in the chosen currency.

Futures market[31]
US
All futures have the following standardized terms: specific contract, quality, contract size, pricing convention and delivery data. The combination of contract standardization, centralized clearing and limited credit risk promotes trading of futures on excvhanges. Contracts on longer-terms instruments, such as Treasury notes (2-, 5-, and 10 year) and Treasury bonds (30-year) are listed on the Chicago Board of Trade (CBOT). Example of the terms on a futures contract for US Treasury notes traded on an exchange such as the Chicago Board of Trade.

Product	10-year Treasury notes
Contract size	$100,000
Price quoted	32nd of 100 percent
Delivery date	Any business day of delivery month (March, June, September, December, depending on the particular contract.
Delivery grade	Any US Treasury notes with maturity of 6½ to 10 years.

Eurozone
Table 9.4.6[32]

Market	Exchange	Contract size	Maturity
Euro-Bund	Eurex	EUR 100,000	8½ - 10½ years
	LIFFE	EUR 100,000	8½ - 10½years
Euro-Bobl	Eurex	EUR 100,000	4½ - 5½ years
Euro-Schatz	Eurex	EUR 100,000	1¾ - 2¼ years
Euro-Buxl	Eurex	EUR 100,000	20 – 30½ years
2-year Euro Swapnote	LIFFE	EUR 100,000	2 years
5-year Euro Swapnote	LIFFE	EUR 100,000	5 years
10-year Euro Swapnote	LIFFE	EUR 100,000	10 years

---

[31]Federal Reserve Board, *Trading and Capital-Markets Activities Manual,Financial Futures,* February 1998
[32]www.liffe.com/products/bonds/specs/
www.eurexchange.com/marketplace/products_specifications

Since the start of the EUR, the Eurex in Frankfurt (as part of Deutsche Termin Borse) became the main future market for the Bund future since the Bobl and Schatz futures are also traded there. The contract specifications on LIFFE and Eurex are the same.

Euro-Bund Futures[33]:

Unit of trading	EUR 100,000 nominal value of German government bond with 6% coupon.
Delivery months	March, June, September, December, such as the nearest three delivery months are available for trading.
Delivery day	Tenth calendar day of delivery month. If such is not a business day in Frankfurt then the Delivery Day will be the following Frankfurt business day.
Last trading day	12.30 Frankfurt time Two Frankfurt business days prior to the Delivery day.
Quotation	Per EUR 100 nominal value (LIFFE) In a percentage of the par value, carried out to two decimal places (Eurex).
Settlement	A delivery obligation arising out of a short position in a Euro-Bund futures contract may only be satisfied by the delivery of specific debt securities, namely German Federal Bonds (Bundesanleihen) with a remaining term upon delivery of 8½ to 10½ years. The debt securities must have a minimum issue amount of 2 billion EUR.

On 20 March 2001, LIFFE launched Swapnote, a suite of futures contracts that provide cost-effective and easy access to the EUR interest rate swap market. Since the launch, the Swapnote futures contracts have performed strongly with traded volume, open interest and market participation growing steadily.

Two-year Euro Swapnote, contract specification[34]:

Unit of trading	EUR 100,000 notional principal amount.
Notional Fixed Rate	6.0%
Maturities	Notional principal amount due two years from delivery day.
Delivery months	March, June, September, December, such as the nearest two delivery months that are available for trading.
Delivery day	Third Wednesday of the delivery month.
Last trading day	10.00 London time Two business days prior to the delivery day.
Quotation	Per EUR 100 nominal value.

---

[33] www.liffe.com/products/bonds/specs/bund
www.eurexchange.com/marketplace/products_specifications_fgbl
[34] www.liffe.com/swapnote/specs/2yr

Options market
US
For details about the option market see chapter 6.

Eurozone
Table 9.4.7[35]

Market	Exchange	Contract size
Euro-Bund future	Eurex	1 futures contract
	LIFFE	
Euro-Bobl future	Eurex	1 futures contract
Euro-Schatz future	Eurex	1 futures contract
2-year Euro Swapnote future	LIFFE	1 futures contract
5-year Euro Swapnote future	LIFFE	1 futures contract
10-year Euro Swapnote future	LIFFE	1 futures contract

In response to customer demand, and the positive start to the trading of the Swapnote futures contracts, LIFFE have introduced options contracts on the Swapnote futures product (24 July 2001).

---

[35] www.liffe.com/products/bonds/specs/
www.eurexchange.com/marketplace/products_specifications

Marketing plan

Clients
1. Interbank traders
2. Investors and portfolio managers
3. Hedge funds
4. Corporates
5. Private clients

Interbank traders
In the secondary US Treasury bond markets, the main players are interbank dealers, trading for clients or their own positions.

Investors and portfolio managers
They are trying to build optimal portfolios by combining equities; bonds and derivatives or they just build a Fixed-Income portfolio consisting of the different Fixed-Income securities.

Foreign investors, including banks, often purchase German government securities as a means of diversifying their securities portfolios. In particular, the low credit risk and deep liquidity of German government bonds and notes encourages the use of these instruments as non-US investment vehicles[36].

Hedge funds

Fixed-Income Arbitrage[37]
Fixed–income arbitrage strategies seek to profit from prices' inefficiencies between 2 or more related securities.

Convertible Bond Arbitrage[38]
Convertible Bond Arbitrage managers strive to take advantage of the relationship between convertible securities and the underlying common stock into which the bonds or preferred stocks are convertible. They aim to generate a predictable income stream from the coupon on the convertible security portion on their investments, and then to supplement their Fund's total return with the interest generated from the cash proceeds of the short sale.

---

[36] Federal Reserve Board, *Trading and Capital-Markets Activities Manual, German Government Bonds and Notes*, February 1998

[37] J. Berset (UBP) S.Condorelli (UBP), P.Hoebrechts(UBP) and A. Rampa (UBP), *Understanding Hedge Funds*, Working Paper II, (UBP and Alternative Asset Management Group.

[38] J. Berset (UBP) S.Condorelli (UBP), P.Hoebrechts(UBP) and A. Rampa (UBP), *Understanding Hedge Funds*, Working Paper II, (UBP) and Alternative Asset Management Group.

By Krishnamurthy[39]

"Arbitrageurs make convergence trades profit from the spread between the old bond and the new bond. The spread between the new and old bond is 12 basis points, while the spread between the previous new and old bond is only 3 basis points. Since the spread between the new and the old bond will converge towards zero as time passes, shorting the expensive new bond and purchasing the cheaper old bond has the potential to generate trading profits. In order to establish a short position, an arbitrageur must borrow the new bond in the repurchase market. Moreover, at times when the trade looks most profitable, the bond spread is high, and the repo costs are also high. Hedge funds, putting on the convergence trade, lost money during the period summer 1998 through the end of 2001. There are two reasons for this. First, the liquidity was more valued since the summer of 1998. Second, Treasury initiated a long bond buyback plan in the summer of 1999".

Corporates

The telecommunication companies were the main large borrowers in the international loan market, and large issuers in the international bond market, to finance their M&A deals and management buyouts. The conditions of the Division III (Equity Market) and Division IV (S-T-I-R Market) decide if they enter these markets or the International Debt Market.

Private clients

These clients are looking for a higher yield on their investments. Fixed-income securities are quite popular from the risk point of view.

---

[39] A. Krishnamurthy, *The Bond/Old-Bond Spread, February 11,* 2001

Outcome Business Plan

Table 9.4.8 Business Plan

Business Plan	Questions	Answers
Product plan	Products?	Loans
		Syndicated loans
		Government bonds
		Agency and mortgage-backed securities
		Corporate bonds
		Medium-Term-Notes
		Floating-Rate Securities
		Fixed-Income derivatives
		Swaps
		Futures
		Options
Production plan	What's needed?	Market
		Knowledge
		Information systems
Marketing plan	Clients?	Interbank dealers
		Investors and fundmanagers
		Hedge funds
		Corporates
	Competitors?	Private clients
		Division I (FX Option Market)
		Division II (Commodity Market)
		Division III (Equity Market)
		Division V (S-T-I-R Market)

Strategy:
Division IV (International Debt Market) offers its clients specialist products for every knowledge level. Further, the diversity of the US Debt Market gives itself a competitive advantage over the Eurozone Debt Market.

9.5 DESIGN APPROACH II: SWOT ANALYSIS

International Debt Market as driver of EUR/USD Interbank Market

Strengths

US debt market offers better return

Since 2000, the Fixed-Income balance has swung from a EUR 118.9 billion (total 2000) inflow to a EUR 42.8 billion outflow at end of third quarter of 2001 (ECB Monthly Bulletin). The increase in bond outflows from Euroland can be explained as follows. Foreign investors have been buying less Euroland debt or Euroland investors are buying more overseas debt. The following tables will give you a risk return overview. This information is based on Salomon Smith Barney Bond Index (Deutsche Bank)[40]

Table 9.5.1: Risk/Return Statistics based on five-year Monthly Returns in Local Currency

	Annualized Return (%)									August 2001		
	1992	1993	1994	1995	1996	1997	1998	1999	2000	Av	Ann Ret.	Ann Vol
US	10.5	11.2	7.5	9.4	6.9	7.3	7.2	7.4	6.5	8.2	7.6	3.7
DE	6.6	8.5	7.8	10.5	9.6	8.2	7.6	7.5	5.8	8.0	6.0	2.9

Table 9.5.2: Risk/Return Statistics based on five-year Monthly Returns in USD

	Annualized Return (%)									August 2001		
	1992	1993	1994	1995	1996	1997	1998	1999	2000	Av	Ann Ret.	Ann Vol
US	10.5	11.2	7.5	9.4	6.9	7.3	7.2	7.4	6.5	8.2	7.6	3.7
DE	6.0	9.0	9.7	11.4	9.3	6.0	8.5	2.7	-1.8	6.7	-1.5	10.2

According to these data the returns in the local currency in either the US or Germany are more or less equal. However taking the currency exposure into account, the US has performed better since the start of the EUR. This comes as no surprise, as a result of the move in EUR/USD from 1.0091 (January 2000) to 0.9123 (August 2001). Investors, consequently, would receive more return on their US investments against a lower volatility. The underperformance in terms of return is also the main reason for the preference for the US Fixed-Income market. Part of the European investment community also moved into US bonds, especially in the period of June 2000-September 2000 when the Treasury Bond had rallied and the German Bund moved side ways. However, the

---

[40]Deutsche Bank, *Exchange Rate Perspectives*, Monthly, July & September 2001.

rally in the Treasury Bond can also be partly explained by the buy backs of the 30-year bonds of the US Treasury.

Table 9.5.3: Spread difference on 10 year bonds

Year	Month	Euro area 10 year bond	US 10 year bond	Spread	EUR/USD Open	EUR/USD Close
1999	Jan	3.82	4.78	-0.96 3 Jan 99	1.1670	1.1355
	Feb	3.98	4.99	-1.01	1.1355	1.0921
	Mar	4.18	5.23	-1.05	1.0921	1.0765
	Apr	4.04	5.18	-1.14	1.0771	1.0565
	May	4.21	5.54	-1.33	1.0586	1.0420
	Jun	4.53	5.90	-1.37	1.0426	1.0352
	Jul	4.86	5.80	-0.94	1.0359	1.0705
	Aug	5.06	5.94	-0.88	1.0680	1.0562
	Sept	5.24	5.91	-0.67	1.0564	1.0682
	Oct	5.47	6.10	-0.63	1.0676	1.0548
	Nov	5.18	6.03	-0.85	1.0548	1.0089
	Dec	5.30	6.26	-0.96	1.0091	1.0070
2000	Jan	5.70	6.66	-0.96	1.0050	0.9693
	Feb	5.66	6.52	-0.86	0.9701	0.9646
	Mar	5.49	6.26	-0.77	0.9643	0.9560
	Apr	5.41	6.00	-0.59	0.9560	0.9120
	May	5.52	6.42	-0.90	0.9118	0.9377
	Jun	5.35	6.10	-0.75	0.9369	0.9523
	Jul	5.45	6.04	-0.59	0.9522	0.9259
	Aug	5.40	5.83	-0.43	0.9263	0.8886
	Sept	5.47	5.80	-0.33	0.8885	0.88375
	Oct	5.42	5.74	-0.32	0.8840	0.8490
	Nov	5.34	5.72	-0.38	0.8484	0.8722
	Dec	5.07	5.23	-0.16	0.8722	0.9422
2001	Jan	5.01	5.14	-0.13	0.9423	0.9362
	Feb	5.02	5.10	-0.08	0.9370	0.9230
	Mar	4.94	4.89	0.05	0.9235	0.8774
	Apr	5.10	5.13	-0.03	0.8742	0.8888
	May	5.26	5.37	-0.11	0.8888	0.8456
	Jun	5.21	5.26	-0.05	0.8446	0.8495
	Jul	5.25	5.23	0.02	0.8495	0.8761
	Aug	5.06	4.97	0.09	0.8761	0.9122
	Sept	5.04	4.76	0.28	0.9123	0.9098
	Oct	4.82	4.55	0.27	0.9100	0.8995

Source: ECB Monthly bulletin, various issues, Reuters daily & weekly data

In the period when the 10 year spread was in favor of the US, the USD was also stronger. The correlation between the 10 year Eurozone-US spread and changes in the EUR/USD is 0.20 (based on the data of table 9.5.3). Since July of 2001, the spread turned in favor of the Eurozone (more than 1 month). In this period the EUR/USD was able to recover from 0.8344 (6th of July) to 0.9325 (19th of September). The 10-year spread is not solely responsible for this move, however the difference in long-term interest rates has always been important for movements in a currency pair.

By Driessen, Melenberg and Nijman[41]
A study shows that, from 510 weekly observations from January 1990 until October 1999, the hedged bond returns in the US were higher than in Germany.

Table 9.5.4

Average hedged return in USD	
US 1-3 years	6.43%
US 3-5 years	7.26%
US 5-7 years	7.65%
US 7-10 years	7.82%
US > 10 years	8.49%
Germany 1-3 years	6.12%
Germany 3-5 years	6.95%
Germany 5-7 years	7.45%
Germany 7-10 years	7.34%
Germany > 10 years	8.26%

US Debt market is more sophisticated in its development, and has evolved into greater depth and breadth.

The US Fixed-Income market, compared to the Eurozone Fixed-Income market, has a better variety of products, higher returns and more liquidity, meaning narrow spreads in the corporate bond market. The US Fixed-Income market is more efficient than its European competitor. In the US, the policy of the Fed is to focus on economic growth. The Fed cuts interest rates if economic growth is in danger and increases the interest rate when the economy is overshooting. The Fed is the most active of the central banks world wide, followed by the Bank of England. The Bank of Japan is the least active and the ECB is in the middle. The ECB's main target is a stable price level. The Fed is likely to make interest rate cuts earlier in a high oil price environment, when economic growth is at stake, than the ECB. This fact will give the US Fixed Income market a higher potential under the described circumstances. Since January 1999, oil prices have started to rise (see Commodity Market, Chapter 7). At the beginning of 2000, the oil price exceeded the levels of 1997. The Fed started its easing cycle with an inter-meeting cut on the 3rd of January 2001. The Fed gained market respect with this change, as active central bank and market players gave the Fed the benefit of the doubt based on historical performance. The ECB hadn't yet built up the trust of the market, having not clearly presented one vision. Inflation is much more of a problem in the Eurozone than in the US due to the EUR/USD being under pressure, high local CPI rates, high M3 rate and the high oil price. The US is not bothered with imported inflation as a result of a weak currency because the dollar has been enormously strong over the last two years.

---

[41] J. Driessen, B. Melenberg and T. Nijman, *Common Factors in International Bond Returns*, February 7, 2000

US names are only willing to enter the market if the liquidity for larger amounts is more or less guaranteed. This is the case for most of the product traded in the US debt market.

By Jeanneau (BIS)[42]
"In the Eurozone, squeezes (on Eurex futures market) in the German government bond contract happen too often to guarantee this liquidity. The recent squeeze experienced by Eurex on its medium German government bond contract encouraged LIFFE to reintroduce futures on Euro-denominated swap rates in March. The Swapnotes contracts are expected to be less prone to squeezes because the Euro-denominated swap market is considerably larger than the stock of government securities underlying the futures contract. The swap curve's growing role, as a homogeneous Eurozone benchmark, should help to ensure market acceptance of these new contracts".

The acceptance of these contracts, and a higher liquidity as a result, will support the EUR against the USD since US entities are only prepared to enter liquid markets.

"Meanwhile, some US exchanges moved to capitalize on the upward trend in state agency and asset-backed financing by launching contracts on the US agency benchmarks and mortgage backed securities"[43]. "In the first quarter of 2001, US entities, including US agencies, increased their issuance of Euro-denominated bonds in 2000"[44].

When the Euro market is more developed, and offers a higher liquidity and more product development, the demand for EUR against USD will increase.

The reasons to invest in the US debt market currently, instead of the Eurozone debt market are:
 – Higher liquidity
 – Large product assortment in index traded and tailor-made products
 – More product development and innovation
 – Difference in return in favor for the US Fixed-Income market
 – More active stance of the Fed to cut rates.
 – Less confusing economic environment in the US.

These reasons explain the outflow of the Eurozone Fixed-Income market into the US Fixed-Income market; thereby, having a negative effect on the EUR/USD.

---

[42]S. Jeanneau, *Derivative markets*, BIS Quarterly Review, June 2001, pp.31
[43]S. Jeanneau, *Derivative markets*, BIS Quarterly Review, June 2001, pp.31
[44]G.D. Sutton, *The International Debt Securities Market,* BIS Quarterly Review, June 2001.

Table 9.5.5: in billions, inflows Eurozone (+); outflows (-)

		Portfolio investments: bonds and notes	EUR/USD open	EUR/USD close
1999	Jan	6.40	3 Jan 99 1.1670	1.1355
	Feb	-31.20	1.1355	1.0921
	Mar	-16.00	1.0921	1.0765
	Apr	12.90	1.0771	1.0565
	May	-32.50	1.0586	1.0420
	Jun	9.40	1.0426	1.0352
	Jul	-3.10	1.0359	1.0705
	Aug	5.20	1.0680	1.0562
	Sep	14.20	1.0564	1.0682
	Oct	-0.30	1.0676	1.0548
	Nov	9.90	1.0548	1.0089
	Dec	-7.60	1.0091	1.0070
2000	Jan	3.00	1.0050	0.9693
	Feb	-2.90	0.9701	0.9646
	Mar	8.10	0.9643	0.9560
	Apr	3.90	0.9560	0.9120
	May	12.40	0.9118	0.9377
	Jun	13.80	0.9369	0.9523
	Jul	18.30	0.9522	0.9259
	Aug	14.50	0.9263	0.8886
	Sep	4.10	0.8885	0.8837
	Oct	14.60	0.8840	0.8490
	Nov	16.30	0.8484	0.8722
	Dec	12.90	0.8722	0.9422
2001	Jan	-16.00	0.9423	0.9362
	Feb	-0.20	0.9370	0.9230
	Mar	3.10	0.9235	0.8774
	Apr	-15.00	0.8742	0.8888
	May	-28.30	0.8888	0.8456
	June	-1.60	0.8446	0.8495
	July	-4.90	0.8495	0.8761
	Aug	3.10	0.8761	0.9122
	Sep	16.60	0.9123	0.9098
	Oct		0.9100	0.8995

Source: ECB Monthly Bulletin various issues. Reuters daily & weekly data

Table 9.5.6 Net Eurozone transactions in US bonds; in millions of dollars: positive sign is inflow in US

Period	US Treasury bonds and notes	US Agencies	US Corporate bonds	EUR/$ Open	EUR/$ High	EUR/$ Low	EUR/$ Close
1999	-15,687	11,030	15,045	1.1670	1.1906	0.9986	1.0070
Q1	2,121	3,744	4,013	1.1670	1.1906	1.0674	1.0765
Q2	-8,290	2,408	2,351	1.0771	1.0883	1.0254	1.0352
Q3	-8,763	1,709	5,425	1.0359	1.0826	1.0104	1.0682
Q4	-913	3,169	2,622	1.0676	1.0911	0.9986	1.0070
2000	-5,971	16,052	16,405	1.0050	1.0414	0.8225	0.9422
Q1	439	3,688	2,755	1.0050	1.0414	0.9390	0.9560
Q2	-745	4,674	5,536	0.9560	0.9750	0.8843	0.9523
Q3	428	5,011	2,014	0.9522	0.9597	0.8437	0.8837
Q4	-6,093	2,679	6,179	0.8840	0.9425	0.8225	0.9422
2001	-10,731	5,040	1,759	0.9423	0.9595	0.8344	0.9098
Q1	-8,203	4,725	6,385	0.9423	0.9595	0.8748	0.8774
Q2	265	446	7,476	0.8742	0.9091	0.8408	0.8495
Q3	-2,793	-131	1,759	0.8495	0.9333	0.8344	0.9098

Sources: United States, Department of Treasury, Treasury Bulletin (various issues), Reuters daily & weekly data

---

[32] Reuters weekly data

USD preferred as currency denomination in issues

By Remolona, Cohen and Sutton (BIS)[45]

"The rebound of the net issuance in the first quarter of 2000 relative to Q4 1999 was largely confined to US dollar securities, which narrowly surpassed issuance in the Euro-denominated instruments. The pickup in USD issuance seemed largely to reflect a move towards more diversified funding sources by European issuers. Another factor promoting issuance in dollars was the growth in activity by emerging market borrowers, who continue to prefer the USD. Issuers tended to favor USD over EUR as the currency denomination. The pickup in Euro denominated issuance during the first quarter of 2001 was a continuation of the recovery, which had begun, in the fourth quarter of 2000. This in turn had reversed a slowdown during the first three quarters of 2000, after an exceptionally strong 1999. As in 1999, and in contrast to the previous quarter, the pickup occurred at a time when the EUR was depreciating against the dollar. This contrasts with a long-standing empirical pattern of issues favoring the stronger currency".

Table 9.5.7: Gross issuance in the international bond and note markets in billions of USD

Period	USD	EUR	Difference	Growth % diff.	EUR/$ Open	EUR/$ High	EUR/$ Low	EUR/$ Close
1998	603.10	335.40	267.70					
Q4	124.80	65.90	58.90					
1999	775.40	677.90	97.50	-63.59	1.1670	1.1906	0.9986	1.0070
Q1	197.40	147.60	49.80	-15.45	1.1670	1.1906	1.0674	1.0765
Q2	222.60	186.60	36.00	-27.71	1.0771	1.0883	1.0254	1.0352
Q3	200.00	179.10	20.90	-41.94	1.0359	1.0826	1.0104	1.0682
Q4	132.00	142.20	-10.20	-148.80	1.0676	1.0911	0.9986	1.0070
2000	859.30	647.80	211.50	116.92	1.0050	1.0414	0.8225	0.9422
Q1	216.90	186.80	30.10	395.10	1.0050	1.0414	0.9390	0.9560
Q2	206.60	153.10	53.50	77.74	0.9560	0.9750	0.8843	0.9523
Q3	240.80	150.70	90.10	68.41	0.9522	0.9597	0.8437	0.8837
Q4	194.70	157.20	37.50	-58.38	0.8840	0.9425	0.8225	0.9422
2001								
Q1	263.10	214.60	48.50	29.33	0.9423	0.9595	0.8748	0.8774
Q2	249.20	193.90	55.30	12.30	0.8742	0.9091	0.8408	0.8495

Sources BIS Quarterly Review various issues, and Reuters daily data

---

[45]E.R. Remolona, B.H. Cohen, G.D.Sutton, *The International Debt Securities Market*, BIS Quarterly Review, June 2000, March-June 2001

Table 9.5.8: Net issuance of international debt securities in billions of USD

Period	USD	EUR	Difference	Growth % diff.	EUR/$ Open	EUR/$ High	EUR/$ Low	EUR/$ Close
1998	410.70	223.80	186.90					
Q4	55.30	29.60	25.70					
1999	546.00	587.40	-41.40	-122.15	1.1670	1.1906	0.9986	1.0070
Q1	157.20	138.50	18.70	-27.23	1.1670	1.1906	1.0674	1.0765
Q2	171.60	152.50	19.10	2.14	1.0771	1.0883	1.0254	1.0352
Q3	141.80	164.80	-23.00	-220.42	1.0359	1.0826	1.0104	1.0682
Q4	75.40	118.90	-43.50	-89.13	1.0676	1.0911	0.9986	1.0070
2000	618.90	466.10	152.80	469.08	1.0050	1.0414	0.8225	0.9422
Q1	134.70	126.60	8.10	118.62	1.0050	1.0414	0.9390	0.9560
Q2	147.90	120.10	27.80	243.21	0.9560	0.9750	0.8843	0.9523
Q3	173.50	91.80	81.70	193.88	0.9522	0.9597	0.8437	0.8837
Q4	162.70	127.50	35.20	-56.92	0.8840	0.9425	0.8225	0.9422
2001								
Q1	150.30	141.40	8.90	-74.72	0.9423	0.9595	0.8748	0.8774
Q2	120.80	114.10	6.70	-24.72	0.8742	0.9091	0.8408	0.8495

Sources BIS Quarterly Review various issues, and Reuters daily & weekly data

These data show that the increased demand for USD issuance had a negative influence on EUR/USD in 2000. Further, they also show that pickup in EUR issuance in Q3 of 1999 and Q4 of 2000 supported EUR/USD.

Market borrower driven

In the international loan market the European and American telecommunication companies were the main borrowers. They needed to finance their third generation (3G) licenses and M&A activities. They first tried to finance licensing and development through IPO's. However, primarily due to the sell-off in the equity markets beginning early in March 2000, equity financing was not an option anymore. They went to the International Debt Market. First, they financed their short-term needs by syndicated bridge loans. It gave them space to prepare an issue in the money market (CP) and/or an issue in the international bond market. Telecom companies initially financed their needs mainly in the CP market. But a number of credit downgrades and the reduced willingness of banks to underwrite new issues made refinancing with CPs almost impossible.

By Sutton (BIS)[46]
"In the first quarter of 2001, the narrowing credit spreads in long-term debt markets was accompanied by a decline in the general level of interest rates, which brought issuers back to the market. The net issuance of straight fixed rate bonds and notes surged during the first quarter of 2001". Further there was a more than normal shift from

---

[46] G.D. Sutton, *The International Debt Securities Market,* BIS Quarterly Review, June 2001

short-term (S-T-I-R Market) to long-term funds. "In some instances, lower-rated corporate borrowers looked to the international bond market as a substitute for commercial paper issuance, which was not feasible as a result of credit downgrades and a reduced willingness of banks to provide backup credit facilities. The net issuance of money market instruments declined from the previous quarter's unusually high amounts as borrowers took advantage of favorable market conditions to lengthen the maturity of their debt. The increase in long-term issuance was due solely to the activities of low and medium-rated borrowers. Among the rated issues, gross issuance in the non-triple-A investment grade class rose markedly from $64 billion during the final quarter of 2000 to $126 billion in the first quarter of 2001. A large portion of the total increase in non-triple-A issuance was due to the activities of telecoms, whose gross issuance surged from $19 billion to $49 billion over the same period".

In a borrower driven market, players are focusing on the lowest interest rate. Since the Fed started an aggressive easing cycle at the beginning of 2001, the USD became, or rather, stayed, the favored currency for bonds and notes issues. It's simply a cost calculation. The issues were done in a strong dollar environment. A future weaker USD will diminish the borrowing costs for European corporates.

Increase USD turnover in derivative markets

By Jeanneau (BIS)[47]
"The 50bps inter-meeting rate cut by the Fed in early January also supported overall activity in longer-term instruments, with business rising by 29% to $17.5 trillion. However the turnover of instruments on European government bonds was rising by more than on US government bonds. In Europe there was a sharp increase of activity in government bond contracts traded on Eurex. The long-term contract, Bund future, expanded rapidly and remained by far the most active bond contract in the world. The turnover in the intermediate maturity contracts, Schatz future and Bobl future, grew even faster. While the overall increase in turnover of German contracts probably reflected expectations of an easing of monetary policy, the more rapid expansion of business in the Schatz and Bobl contracts may have been related to the growing acceptance of the intermediate German government securities as European benchmarks. The Fed's easing of policy rates in early January, together with mixed evidence concerning the duration of the US economic slowdown, underpinned a broad-based recovery of turnover in the US government bond contracts. The net repayments of US government debt, combined with a shift of issuance to intermediate maturities, have affected the liquidity of the US Treasury bond contract in recent periods".

---

[47] S. Jeanneau, *Derivative Markets*, BIS Quarterly Review, June 2001, pp.29-30

"In the second half of 2000, Euro-denominated contract interest rate instruments fell by 7%, while those denominated in USD maintained their rapid growth. The decline in the Euro-denominated swap business was spread across the three types of counterparties (reporting dealers, other financial, non-financial), but the most significant drop occurred in the inter-dealer group. Various factors may have accounted for this development. These included financial sector consolidation, reduced issuance of, for example, Pfandbrief (often hedged with swaps) and the efforts by banks to clean up their pre-Euro legacy currency portfolios. In the meantime, the stock of dollar-denominated swaps continued to grow at a sustained rate (10%). Net repayments of US government debt have affected the liquidity of the US government bond market and the effectiveness of traditional hedging instruments" [48].

Cross currency swaps

The activity in the swap market can have an important influence on the EUR/USD Interbank Market. When a company decides to do a cross currency swap with only one exchange of principals (and, it can be at the beginning or at the end) the swap trader is getting a currency position. For example, the daughter of a European corporate needs to borrow USD to make some investments. The mother company can decide to take a loan in EUR or launch an EUR bond issue because it's the cheapest way, and swap this position with a cross currency swap to USD. Further, the mother company decides only to do an exchange of principals at the beginning because at the end of the period the investment will pay off the principal. Swap traders play the interest rate market so therefore this currency position is hedged with the currency traders. If the cross currency swap is combined with a bond issue, the deal can have an amount of 1-2 billion and will have an influence in the currency market. These types of deals are as frequent as bond issues. Separate cross currency swaps are much smaller.

When a company decides to reduce its exposure (in loans), to the dollar, for example, and increase its exposure to EUR, it can do one of two things.
1. Borrow EUR, sell the proceeds of the borrowing spot, and buy USD.
2. A cheaper alternative is to swap the fixed rate interest payments into fixed EUR payments by entering a currency swap.

This currency swap is based on the view that paying interest rates in USD will become cheaper due to a decrease in interest rates or a depreciation of the USD against the EUR, or the view may be based on the EUR. The swap trader needs to hedge currency exposure. The easiest way to do this is to cover the currency risk by selling the present value of the EUR fixed interest receipts in the spot market; so, in fact, selling EUR/USD. In the light of the expectations of market participants that the Fed would cut rates, this strategy would work and put extra pressure on the EUR/USD rate.

---

[48] S. Jeanneau, *Derivative Markets*, BIS Quarterly Review, June 2001, pp.35-36

CHAPTER 9

Weaknesses

Also other reasons for the movements in EUR/USD

The rally in the EUR/USD in the period November 2000-January 2001 can not be explained only from the International Debt Market point of view, because in the same period oil price dropped from $34 to $22.50 (Brent crude). An increase in EUR denominated issues and the drop in oil price had a large influence on the EUR/USD as a result.

Lagging data

Further, the main weakness of using the ECB balance of payments data is that when received, data are lagging by two months. At the end of August, the June data will be released. Since these data are not available in real time, they are more valuable as background information. In fact it's old data and not useful for a market that is reacting to current news and events, because these data will not tell the market participant what's going on a real-time basis. Since the issues data can be found every day on the Reuters and Bloomberg markets (also future new issues) market participants elect to utilize this information as market signals.

Opportunity

Within the last year, the interest rate markets (long- and short-term) took over the important role from the equity markets. The International Debt Market will continue to play an important role in a low growth environment with moderate or low oil prices (prices within a range of $22-$27 per barrel). The drop in the oil price (Brent) since September 14, 2001, has eased the pressure on the Eurozone inflation and EUR/USD. Recently, the bond rally came under pressure due to expectations of an economic recovery in the US in 2002. Any disruption in these expectations will lift the bond markets again.

The Eurozone debt market is developing itself more and more into a liquid market with a good product variety and product innovation. This process will take some time, but when the Eurozone debt market is able to compete with the US debt market in terms of liquidity, product variety and product innovation, the US names will step into the market and create a higher demand for the EUR against the USD.

Threats

The main threats are Division I (FX Option Market), Division II (Commodity Market). Division III (Equity Market) and Division V (S-T-I-R Market). The first two market entities have already proved their influence on the EUR/USD. Division III (Equity Market) was surpassed in 2000 by Division IV (International Debt Market) because of the poor market performance of the Equity Markets. Up to November/December, in a low growth and low inflation environment, the bond markets have rallied. However, the recovery scenario of the US economy in 2002 made a partial shift of power back to the Equity Markets possible. The International Debt Market regained market share from the S-T-I-R Market as result of: 1) credit downgrades; and, 2) being close to the easing cycle of the Fed.

Outcome SWOT Analysis

Table 9.5.9: SWOT Analysis

Strengths	Weaknesses
US debt market offers higher return.	Also oil as explanation for Dec 2000- Jan 2001 EUR/USD rally.
Higher development performance US debt market.	Lagging ECB balance of payments data.
USD preferred as currency denomination with issues.	
Market borrower and low interest rate driven.	
Increase USD turnover in derivatives market	

Opportunities	Threats
Low growth and low inflation environment.	FX Options Market, Commodity Market, Equity Market, S-T-I-R Market
Better development Eurozone debt market.	

The strategy resulting from this SWOT Analysis is the following:
Division IV (International Debt Market) offers good explanations for the moves in the EUR/USD. However there is a need to keep a close eye on the competitors, the easing cycles of Fed and ECB, and the Eurozone debt market development.

9.6 POSITIONING APPROACH I

Let's examine the position of this division compared to the other divisions in the EUR/USD Interbank Market Organization. The key question is:

Is this division able to explain the movements in the EUR/USD Interbank Market and how is this compared to the competitors?

Potential entrants:
The potential entrants are low since almost all the financial markets are defined as a division in the EUR/USD Interbank Market Organization. The only market left is the real-estate market including the funds operating in this market.

Intensity of rivalry among existing competitors:
The competitors to this division are:
- FX Option Market Division
- Commodity Market Division
- Equity Market Division
- Short-Term-Interest-Rate Market Division

Division IV (International Debt Market) is the fourth division in this EUR/USD Interbank Market organization. So far, the products from the FX Options Market (Division I), Commodity Market (Division II) and the Equity Market (Division III) have demonstrated rationale for the movement in EUR/USD. Division I and II are still dominant at the end of 2001, while Division III has lost most of it power, during the sell-off in the equity markets, since March of 2000. Early in calendar year 2000, investors began migrating from equities into bonds. Investors had begun to worry about the worldwide economic outlook, and economic deterioration usually follows an interest easing cycle, which generally portends a good future for bonds. The sell-off in the equity markets created an uncertain environment for investors, so the rally in the bond markets was the result. The bond markets' rally started around February/March 2000 and ended in November/December 2001, primarily due to the widely expected recovery of the US economy in 2002 (and inflation fears).

Bargaining power of buyers:
The buyers are the funds, investors, corporates and private clients. The buying power is high because they have the power to switch easily into other products such as Equity Market and S-T-I-R Market products depending on the sentiment in the market.

Bargaining power of suppliers:
The suppliers in this market are Treasury, Agency, banks, coprorates the brokers, the providers of the trading system/pricing systemg/booking systems and information systems and the providers of specialized courses and seminars. Economic fundamentals also belong to the supply side. The suppliers are important in financial markets, however the buyers have more power.

Pressure from substitute products:
The substitute products are the products offered by the other divisions in the EUR/USD Interbank Market Organization.
- FX Options
- Commodities Oil and Gold
- Equity Market products
- Short-Term-Interest-Rate Market products.

The Equity Market and S-T-I-R Market products are good substitutes for the International Debt Market products depending on the market sentiment.

9.7 THE POSITIONING APPROACH II:

The industry of Division IV (International Debt Market) is complex, with a number of forces interacting simultaneously. In this industry the products are specialized and there are different levels of knowledge interacting with each other. It's necessary to have knowledge at all levels before it's clear what's driving this industry. This industry is in a maturity phase.

Buyer and Buyer Behavior
High percentage of people invest in bonds and they are looking to alternatives to invest their money especially when the easing cycle is over.

Products and products change
There is high quality research and advice and there are independent rating agencies. The standardization is seen in information, fees and sectors.

Marketing
There is market segmentation towards small investors, fund managers and hedge funds. Fund managers and hedge funds have high knowledge and use it to get the highest quality available. Efforts to extend life cycle by offering alternative investments to diversify to client's portfolio. The packaging is important, more tailor-made approach towards clients.

Manufacturing and Distribution
Fixed-income research departments are centralized.

Overall Strategy
The strategy to increase market share is buying another company or merging with another company.

Competition
The competition among banks is fierce, and development of structured products is key as a method to differentiate.

Margins and profits
The fees (prices) are falling. It is difficult to cover all the costs made by the commissions earned.

For more details about the concepts of industry evolution see "Competitive Strategy" of Michael Porter (1980).

SUMMARY 9

Outcome of the Business Plan Division IV, International Debt Market, table 9.4.8

Business Plan	Questions	Answers
Product plan	Products?	Loans
		Syndicated loans
		Government bonds
		Agency and mortgage-backed securities
		Corporate bonds
		Medium-Term-Notes
		Floating-Rate Securities
		Fixed-Income derivatives
		Swaps
		Futures
		Options
Production plan	What's needed?	Market
		Knowledge
		Information systems
Marketing plan	Clients?	Interbank dealers
		Investors and fundmanagers
		Hedge funds
		Corporates
		Private clients
	Competitors?	Division I (FX Option Market)
		Division II (Commodity Market)
		Division III (Equity Market)
		Division V (S-T-I-R Market)

Outcome of the SWOT Analysis Division IV, table 9.5.9

Strengths	Weaknesses
US debt market offers higher return.	Also oil as explanation for Dec 2000- Jan 2001 EUR/USD rally.
Higher development performance US debt market.	Lagging ECB balance of payments data.
USD preferred as currency denomination with issues.	
Market borrower and low interest rate driven.	
Increase USD turnover in derivatives market	

Opportunities	Threats
Low growth and low inflation environment.	FX Options Market, Commodity Market, Equity Market, S-T-I-R Market
Better development Eurozone debt market.	

Chapter 10 on Division V (S-T-I-R Market), will cope with the the following subjects:
1. The Configuration approach and Division V.
2. The Entrepreneurial approach and Division V.
3. The Design approach and Division V.
4. The Positioning approach and Division V.

REFERENCES

Berset, J.(UBP), S. Condorelli (UBP), P. Hoebrechts (UBP) and A. Rampa (UBP). "Understanding Hedge Fund", Working Paper II, UBP and Alternative Asset Management Group, April 2000.

Cohen, B.H., E.R. Remolona, G.D.Sutton, "The International Debt Securities Market", BIS Quarterly Review, June 2000, March -June 2001.

Commerzbank Securities. "All That Glitters", 24 July 2001.

Deutsche Bank. "Exchange Rate Perspectives", Monthly, July and September 2001.

Driessen, J., B. Melenberg and T. Nijman (2000). "Common Factors in International Bond Returns".

Euromoney. "Pfandbrief Issuers' Business Overhaul", April 2001

Federal Reserve Board (1998). "Trading and Capital-Markets Activities Manual: German Government Bonds and Notes".

Federal Reserve Board (2002). "Trading and Capital-Markets Activities Manual: US Treasury Bills, Notes and Bonds".

Federal Reserve Board (2001). "Trading and Capital-Markets Activities Manual: US Government Agency Securities".

Federal Reserve Board (1998). "Trading and Capital-Markets Activities Manual: Corporate Notes and Bonds".

Federal Reserve Board (1998). "Trading and Capital-Markets Activities Manual: Asset-Backed Securities and Asset-Backed Commercial Paper".

Federal Reserve Board (1998). "Trading and Capital-Markets Activities Manual: Financial Futures".

Jeanneau, S. "Derivative Markets", BIS Quarterly Review, June-September 2001

Gadanecz, B. "The International Banking Market", BIS Quarterly Review, August 2000-March 2001, September 2001

Krishnamurthy, A. (2001). "The Bond/Old Bond Spread".

McDougall, A. (1999). "Mastering Swap Markets", Financial Times Prentince Hall.

Mintzberg, H., *STRUCTURES IN FIVES: Designing Effective Organizations*, Copyright © 1993. Reprinted by permission of Pearson Education, Inc., Upper Saddle River, New Jersey.

Mintzberg, H., B. Ahlstrand, J. Lampel, STRATEGY SAFARI: The complete guide through the wilds of strategic management, Copyright © 1998. Reprinted by permission of Pearson Education Ltd, 128 LongAcre, London WC2E 9AN

COMPETITIVE STRATEGY: Techniques for Analyzing Industries and Competitors by Michael E. Porter. Copyright © 1980, 1998 by The Free Press, an imprint of Simon & Schuster Adult Publishing Group. Reprinted with permission of the publisher

Wooldridge, P.D. "The International Banking Market", BIS Quarterly Review, March-September 2001

RECOMMENDED BOOKS

Fabozzi, F.J. (2001). "The Handbook of Fixed Income Securities", McGraw-Hill, 6th edition.
Jones, F.J. and R.J. Teweles (1999). "The Futures Game: Who Wins, Who Loses & Why", McGraw-Hill.
Nicholas, J.G. (2000). "Market Neutral Investing: Long/Short Hedge Fund Strategies", Bloomberg Press Princeton.

Chapter **10**

DIVISION V
SHORT-TERM-INTEREST-RATE MARKET

10.1 INTRODUCTION

Division V (Short-Term Interest Rate, S-T-I-R, Market) is the fifth and last division in the EUR/USD Interbank Market organization. Division III (Equity Market) and Division IV (International Debt Market) are focused on a longer time horizon than this division. Both divisions have already proved that they provide explanations for the movements in EUR/USD. Flows continuously switch from the International Debt Market to S-T-I-R Market and vice versa. The role of Division V in the EUR/USD Interbank Market organization will be explained in this part. The following conclusions are made in the SWOT Analysis:
1. The US Debt growth will give an explanation for movements in the EUR/USD.
2. Changes in outstanding US CP have a correlation of –0.33 with changes in the EUR/USD.
3. The 3-month interest rate spread Eurozone versus US has a correlation of 0.16 with the changes in EUR/USD.
4. The relative monetary base growth will offer either a limited, or no, explanation for the movements in EUR/USD.
5. Higher demand for US money market derivative instruments.

We start this division with the Configuration approach, followed by the Entrepreneurial approach, the Design approach (I + II) and the Positioning approach (I + II). These approaches are explained in chapter 1 and 2.

10.2 CONFIGURATION APPROACH

The structure of an organization can be defined as the different ways in which work is divided into different tasks and how these tasks are coordinated. In the organization Division V (S-T-I-R Market), the main product is short-term interest rates. This is the general product, which can be divided into six sub-products: monetary base, Treasury bills, CP, repo, Eurocurrency and derivatives. The different sub products are used for different clients based on different knowledge and motivation.

Organizational parts
Strategic Apex
The S-T-I-R Market makers are responsible for this division. They are the strategists of the organization.

Support Staff
This organizational staff has the task of influencing the work of others in the organization. They do this by training the people in Division V (S-T-I-R Market) and by making sure that the technology is updated so that the strategic apex receives live prices and news. Further, the **salespeople match the clients and products.**

Techno Structure
The Techno Structure of Division V is the same as for the total EUR/USD Interbank Market organization and can be divided into:
1. Fundamental Analysis (Chapter 4)
2. Technical Analysis (Chapter 5)

This division uses a combination of both specialties.

Middle Line
The middle lines are the other traders in this division; for example, futures and options traders.

Operating Core
The operating core has four main functions:
1. Supply the general S-T-I-R Market product for the production (see production plan)
2. Transform the general S-T-I-R Market product into the differentiated sub-products.
    – US Debt growth EUR/USD (moves explained by US Debt growth)
    – M3 growth differential EUR/USD
    – Outstanding CP EUR/USD
    – 3 months interest rate spread EUR/USD
    – Turnover of US money market instruments
3. Distribute the differentiated S-T-I-R Market sub-products
4. Provide direct support to input, transformation and output.

Coordination mechanism

The coordination mechanism used in Division V (S-T-I-R Market) is standardization of output. The general S-T-I-R Market product (input) is transformed into seven sub-products (output) to meet the needs of the clients.

Decentralization

The S-T-I-R Market traders are responsible for the strategy and building of the sub-products. The power is decentralized over the middle-line managers. However, inside this division, power is centralized.

Configuration

Division V (S-T-I-R Market) uses standardization of output as a coordination mechanism. Further, the Middle Line is the dominant force in the organization because it influences which of the sub products are used in the market. The power is decentralized over the Middle Line (partial vertical decentralization). Consequently this division also has a **Diversified Configuration** (see chapter 1 for visualization).

Outcome

Table 10.2.1

Division V: S-T-I-R Market	Definition
Strategic Apex	S-T-I-R Market traders
Support Staff	Systems
	Sales force
Techno Structure	Fundamental Analysis (Chapter 4)
	Technical Analysis (Chapter 5)
Middle Line	Central Banks (money supply)
	Eurodollar and Euribor traders
	Repo traders
	CP traders
	Futures traders
	Option traders
Operating Core	Money supplies
	Eurodollar market
	Repo markets
	CP market
	Futures market
	Options market
Coordination mechanism	Standardization of output
Decentralization	Partial vertical decentralization
Configuration	Diversified organization
Culture	Market Psychology (Chapter 3)

10.3 ENTREPRENEURIAL APPROACH

Within Division V (S-T-I-R Market), traders make the decisions where, when and how to take positions in the market. They follow the Entrepreneurial approach because their decisions are based on their view about the market. The S-T-I-R Market can be divided into three sub markets.
- MONEY SUPPLY (MS)
- MONEY MARKET
- DERIVATIVE MARKET

Within the product plan, all the products of these different sub markets will be described. The strategic thinking is done by the market makers in the S-T-I-R markets. They decide about their pricing and position. The market makers of the Money Supply market are the central banks of the different countries.

10.4 DESIGN APPROACH I: BUSINESS PLAN

Product plan

The products represented within Division V (S-T-I-R Market):
MONEY SUPPLY:
- Money Supply of US
- Money Supply of Eurozone

MONEY MARKET
- Treasury Bills
- Commercial Paper
- Repurchase agreement
- Eurocurrency: (Eurodollar & Euribor)

DERIVATIVE MARKETS
- Futures
- Interest Rate Swaps
- Options

Money Supply

Money Supply US[1]
The Federal Reserve Board measures the money supply. There are three money supplies:

Table 10.4.1

Money Supply	Description
M1	Includes currency, non-bank travelers' checks and demand and other checking deposits.
M2	Includes M1 plus overnight repos, overnight Eurodollar deposits, general purpose and broker/dealer money market fund balances, money market deposit accounts and savings and small time deposits.
M3	Includes M2 plus large time deposits, term repos, term Eurodollar deposits and institutional money market mutual funds.

The data are reported weekly, with a ten-day lag, and are seasonally adjusted. The weekly changes, especially in M2, can be large. The monetary aggregates have faded in importance in recent years as their link with nominal GDP has broken down. Annual target ranges are set for M2 and M3 growth in order to meet the requirements of the Full Employment and Balanced Growth Act of 1978 (Humphrey-Hawkins)., but the Fed treats these as intermediate indicators for policy – and not highly critical ones for that – rather than as targets.

---

[1] JP Morgan, *Global Data Watch Handbook*, New York, January 1996

Money Supply Eurozone[2]
The European Central Bank mainly watches M3. The components of M3 are:
1. Currency in circulation
2. Overnight deposits
3. Deposits with agreed maturity of up to 2 years
4. Deposits redeemable at notice up to three months
5. Repurchase agreements
6. Money market fund shares/units and money market paper
7. Debt securities issued with maturity up to 2 years

Money Market

Treasury bill[3]
Treasury bills are issued by the Treasury Department and represent direct obligationsof the US government. They are backed by the full faith and credit of the US government. Treasury bills or T-Bills are negotiable, non-interest-bearing securities with original maturities of three months, six months, and one year. T-bills are offered by the Treasury in minimum denominations of $10,000, with multiples of $5,000 thereafter and are offered only in book-entry form. T-bills are issued at a discount from face value and are redeemed at par value.

Commercial paper[4]
Commercial paper (CP) is a short-term, fixed maturity, unsecured promissory note issued in the open markets as an obligation of the issuing entity. CP is usually issued with maturities of less than 270 days, with the most common having maturities of 30-50 days or less. CP is sold either directly by the issuer or through a securities broker. For entities with a sufficient credit rating, CP is generally banked by bank lines or letters of credit.

Repurchase agreement[5]
A repurchase agreement (repo) involves the sale of a security to a counterparty with an agreement to purchase it at a fixed price on an established future date. At initiation of the transaction, the buyer pays the principal amount to the seller and the security is transferred to the possession of the buyer. At expiration of the repo, the principal amount is returned to the initial buyer, and possession of the security reverts to the

---

[2]ECB, *Montly Monetary Developments in Euro area*
[3]Federal Reserve Board, *Trading and Capital-Markets Activities Manual,US Treasury Bills, Notes , and Bonds Notes,* April 2002
[4]Federal Reserve Board, *Trading and Capital-Markets Activities Manual,Commercial Paper,* April 2001
[5]Steiner, R., *MASTERING REPO MARKETS,* Copyright © 1997. Reprinted by permission of Pearson Education, Inc., Upper Saddle River, New Jersey.
ACI Diploma, *Chapter The Money Market,* Author: Bob Steiner, Markets International Ltd.
Federal Reserve Board, *Trading and Capital-Markets Activities Manual, Repurchase Agreements,* April 2001

initial seller. The security serves as collateral against the obligation of the borrower and does not actually become the property of the lender. Given the short time element of a typical repo and the need to make proper custody arrangements for the securities involved, operational issues are important to the proper management of repo transactions.

A reverse repo is the same arrangement viewed from the other party's perspective. The deal is generally a repo if it is initiated by the party borrowing the money and lending the security and a reverse repo if it is initiated by the party borrowing the security and lending the money.

The security involved will often be of high credit quality, such as a government bond. Most repos are conducted with US Treasury or agency securities as collateral. Repos can be conducted on an overnight basis, for a longer fixed term, or on an open-account basis. Overnight repos or one-day transactions represent approximately 80% of all repo transactions. In general, repos are attractive to a variety of market participants as:
1. low cost source of short-term funding for borrowers and;
2. an asset with high credit quality regardless of the counterparty for suppliers of funds.

Repos can be used to finance long positions in dealers' portfolios by short-term borrowing. The repo market is a highly liquid and is an efficient market for funding dealers' bond inventory at a short-term rate of interest. Dealers may also use repos to speculate on future levels of interest rates.

Eurocurrency
Eurocurrency is a currency that's borrowed and lent outside it's country of origin. The most used currency in the Eurocurrency market is the USD.

Eurodollar Certificate of Deposit[6]
A Eurodollar certificate of deposit (CD) is a negotiable dollar-denominated time deposit issued by a US bank outside the US or by a foreign bank located abroad. Eurodollar deposits are generally free from domestic (US) regulation and reserve requirements and are not subject to other fees. Most Eurodollar CDs are issued in denominations over $ 1 million. The maturity must be at least 7 days and most CDs are issued for three-to six months. There is no upward limit on the term. Eurodollar CDs are quoted and sold on an interest-bearing basis on an actual 360-day basis. The bid/offer quotes are measured in 16ths. The quotes directly translate to rates on the given Eurodollar CD.

---

[6]Federal Reserve Board, *Trading and Capital-Markets Activities Manual, Eurodollar Certificate of Deposit,* April 2001

Euro time deposit

The interest on a Euro time deposit can be based on LIBOR (British Bankers Association) or Euribor offered rate (European Bankers Federations).

Derivative markets

Futures[7]
Futures on short-term instruments such as Eurodollar deposits and Treasury bills trade on the IMM of CME. The fed fund futures is traded on the Chicago Board of Trade. The Euribor future (3-months) is traded on Eurex and on LIFFE.

Interest rate swaps
See the chapter 9, part Swaps. The product is the same, only the timeframe is short-term.

Options
There are options available on Eurodollar futures, LIBOR futures and Euribor futures.

---

[7]Federal Reserve Board, *Trading and Capital-Markets Activities Manual, Financial Futurest,* April 2001

Production plan

The Production plan describes everything that's needed to sell the products mentioned in the product plan.
1. MARKET
2. KNOWLEDGE TO UNDERSTAND THE MARKETS
3. INFORMATION SYSTEMS

Money Supply

Money Supply US
Since mid 1996, the US monetary-base growth rallied 1.9% to a high of 12.2% in June 2001. The Fed cut interest rates 450bps (including 6th of November) in 2001, helping the monetary base growth to pick up[8].

Money Supply Eurozone[9]
The ECB keeps a close eye on the M3 concerning inflation pressures.

Table 10.4.2: 1999 M3 annual growth rates. Source: Bloomberg + ECB

	Jan	Feb	Mar	Apr	May	Jun	Jul	Aug	Sep	Oct	Nov	Dec
US	10.3	10.4	9.2	9.9	9.8	9.6	9.8	9.8	8.4	8.2	8.4	8.7
EU	6.0	5.3	5.5	5.3	5.6	5.6	6.0	5.8	6.1	5.8	6.2	6.1

Table 10.4.3: 2000 M3 annual growth rates. Source: Bloomberg + ECB

	Jan	Feb	Mar	Apr	May	Jun	Jul	Aug	Sep	Oct	Nov	Dec
US	8.4	7.9	9.0	9.2	9.0	9.2	9.5	10.0	9.5	10.0	9.1	8.9
EU	5.2	6.2	6.6	6.7	6.0	5.3	5.1	5.5	5.0	4.9	4.7	4.9

Table 10.4.4: 2001 M3 annual growth rates. Source: Bloomberg + ECB

	Jan	Feb	Mar	Apr	May	Jun	Jul	Aug	Sep	Oct
US	9.7	10.2	10.0	10.9	11.6	12.0	11.8	10.9	12.3	12.9
EU	4.5	4.4	4.6	4.8	5.3	6.3	6.4	6.6	7.0	7.3

Money Market

Treasury bills
In the secondary markets, Treasury bills are traded on a straight discount basis. Further, the issuance of Treasury bills affects the money supply.

---

[8]Deutsche Bank
[9]ECB, *Montly Monetary Developments in Euro area*

Commercial Paper
US CP[10]
CP issued in maturities which range anywhere from a few days to 270 days depending on the funding needs of the issuer. The SEC does not generally require registration of securities due in less than 270 days. Most issuers need ongoing financing and roll the CP over at maturity, using the new proceeds to pay off the maturing CP. The minimum round-lot transaction is $100,000. CP is typically issued in bearer form, but may also be issued in registered form.

Credit ratings are crucial to the CP market because most investors restrict their CP investments to high-quality CP or will only buy rated CP.

Issuers of CP include industrial companies such as manufacturers, public utilities and retailers and financial institutions such as banks and leasing companies. Bank holding companies are active issuers of CP. The money raised is often used to fund nonbank activities in areas such as leasing and credit cards to fund offshore branches.

The primary market consists of CP sold directly by issuers or sold through a dealer acting as principal (dealer paper) Dealer paper accounts for most of the market. Dealers are mostly large investment banks and commercial banks. The secondary market is only moderate active. Most investors have purchased CP tailored to their short-term investment needs and hold it to maturity.

ECP[11]
The Euro Commercial Paper market has demonstrated significant growth in recent years. The current amount outstanding is about US $251.4 billion, up 43% since the start of 1999. This means that the ECP market has a volume of around 15% of the US CP market. Most growth is coming from EUR denominated CP. Expectations for further growth are strong, especially given the developments of the European Monetary Union, the growth rates of Money Market Funds and the growing integration of short-term interest rate markets around the world. The USD remains the most important currency in the CP with 50% of the total and the EUR is second with 31%. In ECP, financial institutional borrowers (and not corporates) are responsible for more than 60% of the total outstanding.

Table 10.4.5

Relations between long-term ratings and short-term ratings			
Short-term S&P	Long-term S&P	Short-term Moody	Long-term Moody
A1+	AAA, AA+, AA, AA-	P1	Aaa, Aa1, Aa2, Aa3
A1	A+, A, A-	P1	A1, A2, A3
A2	A, A- BBB+, BBB	P2	A2, A3, Baa1, Baa2
A3	BBB, BBB-	P3	Baa2, Baa3
B	BB+, BB, BB-	B	Ba1, Ba2, Ba3

---
[10] Federal Reserve Board, *Trading and Capital-Markets Activities Manual, Commercial Paper*, April 2001
[11] Mechteld van Gastel, CP desk, ABN AMRO Bank Amsterdam, presentation

Repo[12]
The repo market began in the US where it has grown into by far the largest domestic repo market in the world. The volume of repo trading worldwide has grown dramatically since the early 1990s. The US repo market, which still accounts for over half the total market, probably turns over more than USD $1,000 billion per day, with the European domestic and international markets rapidly catching up to this total. The rapid growth in the market has been fueled by a series of factors:
- The growth in the securities markets, creating the need for dealers to use repo to fund their positions.
- The growing need to be able to take and hedge short positions in capital and derivative markets.
- Growing concern over counterparty credit risk among both banks and investors.
- Investors' search for greater yields and wider choice of risk/return profiles.
- The favorable capital adequacy treatment given to repos.
- Investors' growing awareness of the opportunities offered by the specials markets.

By Krishnamurthy[13]
"Repos are used in a wide range of circumstances linked to the bond and derivative markets. In particular, the existence of a strong repo market helps to provide liquidity and depth to markets by allowing dealers to take short positions.
In US Treasury bonds, the repo market is an active market. An important aspect of the repo market is market-wide limitations on the aggregate shorts established in a particular bond. Because of the fact that every short has to be matched by a borrowing of the bond in the repo market, the shorts are tied to the quantity of bonds available for borrowing. The theoretical maximum number of bonds that can be borrowed is equal to the issued amount of bonds. In practice there are two considerations that affect this constraint. First, it is actually tighter, as only a fraction of outstanding bonds is available for lending in the repo market. Second, the repo market actually clears throughout the day so that this smaller float can service a larger number of shorts. When a bond goes special, the owner becomes entitled to an additional benefit of ownership (lower repo rate). Only bonds that are in high demand in the repo market will have repo rates below overnight risk-less rates. So a high demand for a bond has the result that it goes special – meaning the repo rate drops below overnight risk-less rates".

Eurocurrency
The easiest way to explain it is by examples. A corporate in the UK takes a loan in USD or investor in the US is lending in EUR.

---

[12]Steiner, R., *MASTERING REPO MARKETS,* Copyright © 1997. Reprinted by permission of Pearson Education, Inc., Upper Saddle River, New Jersey.
[13]A. Krishnamurthy, *The Bond/Old-Bond Spread, February 11,* 2001

Derivative Market

Futures market
Treasury bill futures(CME)[14]

Contract size	$1,000,000
Quotations	Index points
Tick value	$12.50/contract
Contract months	March, June, September, December and 2 serial months
Regular trading hours	7:20 a.m. – 2:00 p.m.
GLOBEX	2:10 p.m. – 7:05 a.m. On Sunday trading begins at 5:30 p.m.
Last trading day	12:00 p.m. Chicago time on the day of the 91-day T-bill auction occurring in the week of the third Wednesday of the contract month.

Eurodollar futures(CME)[15]

Contract size	$1,000,000
Quotations	Index points
Tick value	$6.25/contract for spot-month contract $12.50/contract for all other contracts
Contract months	March, June, September, December and 4 serial months
Regular trading hours	7:20 a.m. – 2:00 p.m.
GLOBEX	4:30 p.m. – 4:00 p.m. the following day; On Sunday trading begins at 5:30 p.m.
Last trading day	11:00 a.m. London time on the second London bank business day immediately preceding the third Wednesday on the contract month.
Finanl settlement	Based of the British Bankers' Association Interest Settlement Rate.

---

[14] www.cme.com/products/interest_rate
[15] www.cme.com/products/interest_rate

DIVISION V SHORT-TERM-INTEREST-RATE MARKET

One-month LIBOR futures[16]

Contract size	$3,000,000
Quotations	Index points
Tick value	$6.25/contract for spot-month contract
	$12.50/contract for all other contracts
Contract months	All 12 calendar months
Regular trading hours	7:20 a.m. – 2:00 p.m.
GLOBEX	2:10 p.m. – 7:05 a.m.
	On Sunday trading begins at 5:30 p.m.
Last trading day	11:00 a.m. London time on the second London bank business day immediately preceding the third Wednesday on the contract month.
Final settlement	Based of the British Bankers' Association Interest Settlement Rate.

Euribor futures[17]

Unit of trading	Euro time deposits of 1,000,000
Delivery months	March, June, September, December.
Delivery day	First business day after the last Trading Day.
Last trading day	10.00 - two business days prior to the third Wednesday of the delivery month.
Quotation	100.00 minus the rate of interest.
Minimum price move	0.005 representing EUR 12.50
Settlement	Cash settlement, payable on the first exchange trading day immediately following the last trading day.

The Eurodollar and Euribor futures contracts are heavily traded contracts. They are frequently used to trade the short end of the yield curve. The Eurodollar, LIBOR and Euribor do cash settlement. The quoted price is 100 minus the annualized yield.

Options
Eurodollar futures option
Options on Eurodollar futures are based on the quoted Eurodollar futures. Like the underlying future, the size of the contract is $1 million each and each 0.01 change in the price carries a value of $25. The option premium is quoted in terms of basis points.

---

[16] www.cme.com/products/interest_rate
[17] www.liffe.com/products/stirs/specs/euribor.htm
 www.eurechange.com/marketplace/products_specification_feu3_en.html

Euribor futures option[18]:

Contract standard	Three-month Euribor futures
Unit of trading	One futures contract
Expiration months	March, June, September, December. Options contracts are available with a duration of 3, 6, 9 and 12 months.
Exercise period	American style. An option can be exercised up to the end of the Post-Trading period on any exchange trading day during the life of the option.
Exercise prices	Options have exercise prices with gradations of 0.10 of a point. Twenty-one exercise prices are introduced for each contract month.
Last trading day	Two exchange trading days prior to the third Wednesday of the respective settlement month. Trading in the settling contract cases at 11.00 a.m. CET.
Quotation	In points, carried out to three decimal places.
Minimum price move	0.005 percent, representing a value of EUR 12.50
Settlement	The exercise of a Three-month Euribor futures option results in the creation of a corresponding Three-month Euribor futures position for the purchaser as well as the seller to whom the exercise is assigned. The position is established immediately following the Post-Trading Period of the exercise day, and is based on the agreed-upon exercise price.

---

[18] www.eurechange.com/marketplace/products_specification_oeu3_en.html

Marketing plan

The marketing plan will give answers on the following questions
1. WHO ARE THE CLIENTS?
2. WHAT IS THE SCALE OF THE MARKET?
3. WHO ARE THE MAIN COMPETITORS?
4. WHAT IS THE MARKET SHARE?

Clients and Market

Bond dealers[19]
Bond dealers use repos to fund a long position or to cover a short position in a bond. Further, they use the other short-term interest products to play the curve or to partly hedge their positions.

Investors[20]
A repo offers the unique credit enhancement for investors provided by the double security of its structure. Investors can look to the credit standing of both the counterparty and the issuer of the collateral. It also has the advantage that investors can determine both the exact maturity and the exact amount of the investment.
The investors use the other products to hedge their position and to play the yield curve based on the interest rate view.

Fundmanagers[21]
Fundmanagers, who do not need funds, but own a security in demand, can use the special (very high demand for this bond) to repo in cash, which they can then reverse out again against general collateral. Further, they do the same as investors concerning the other products.

Hedge funds[22]
Hedge fund managers can leverage their portfolios through repo by using their existing holdings as collateral to repo in more cash, which they then invest in new securities. The process can be repeated to leverage as far as prudence and margin requirements allow.

---

[19]Steiner, R., *MASTERING REPO MARKETS*, Copyright © 1997. Reprinted by permission of Pearson Education, Inc., Upper Saddle River, New Jersey.
[20]Steiner, R., *MASTERING REPO MARKETS*, Copyright © 1997. Reprinted by permission of Pearson Education, Inc., Upper Saddle River, New Jersey.
[21]Steiner, R., *MASTERING REPO MARKETS*, Copyright © 1997. Reprinted by permission of Pearson Education, Inc., Upper Saddle River, New Jersey.
[22]Steiner, R., *MASTERING REPO MARKETS*, Copyright © 1997. Reprinted by permission of Pearson Education, Inc., Upper Saddle River, New Jersey.

Investment companies and commercial bank trust departments[23]

Investment companies, especially money funds, are the largest investors in the CP market. Other significant investors include the trust departments of banks.

Central banks
US[24]

Open market operations are the Federal Reserve's principal tool for implementing monetary policy. These purchases and sales of US Treasury and federal agency securities largely determine the federal funds rate – the interest rate at which depository institutions lend balances at the Federal Reserve to other depository institutions overnight. Open market operations are arranged by the Domestic Trading Desk at the Federal Reserve Bank of New York under authorization from the FMOC, which was created by statute to direct open market operations. Open market operations are a powerful tool in implementing monetary policy because of their connection with the total supply of balances at the Federal Reserve and the federal funds rate. Many depository institutions maintain accounts at Federal Reserves Banks that they use to make payments on behalf of their customers or themselves. They use the end-of-day balances in these accounts to meet reserve and other balance requirements. Each depository institution must hold a percentage of certain of its deposit liabilities as reserves.

The discount window credit makes up a relatively small portion of the total domestic financial assets held by the Federal Reserve. Much of this credit is seasonal borrowing, which behaviorally is more akin to an autonomous factor in terms of its implications for open market operations. Adjustment credit is typically quite small , but the existence of the adjustment credit facility is an important part of monetary policy implementation framework. It acts as a stabilizer, moderating the upward movements in the federal funds rate in the event a shortage of Fed balances leaves a bank overdrawn on its Fed account at the end of any day or deficient in meeting its requirements on a maintenance period settlement day.

Eurozone[25]

The ESCB uses three types of instruments: reserve requirements, standing facilities and open market operations (OMOs). The choice among them depends, to a large extent, on the views regarding the respective roles of the central bank (see below) and the markets in stabilizing the system. Reserve requirements are deposits that banks are required to hold with the central bank to back their own deposit liabilities. Reserve requirements fulfill two monetary functions: monetary control and money market management. Standing facilities are central bank financing facilities for commercial

---

[23]Federal Reserve Board, *Trading and Capital-Markets Activities Manual,Commercial Paper,* April 2001
[24]www.e-analytics.com/bonds/fed12.htm
[25]C. Enoch & Marc Quintyn, *European Monetary Union: Operating Monetary Policy,* Interanational Monetary Fund

banks that can be activated at their discretion. There are three types: marginal lending facilities (a Lombard facility) at above market rates; lending (discount) facilities close to or below market rates; and deposit facilities. Changes in the rates on the standing facilities would generally signal a substantive policy change, while changes in interest rates deriving from OMOs might rather reflect day-to-day developments. OMOs are to be the key instrument in steering day-to-day developments in the money markets. They are seen as the main instrument for providing or withdrawing liquidity, steering interest rates and, if needed, performing signaling functions.

Central banks are traditionally strong buyers of sovereign and supranational ECP (they own 20% of it)[26].

Private clients

Individuals are large indirect investors in CP through MMFs and trusts. Further, private clients place a lot of deposits.

---

[26] Mechteld van Gastel, CP desk, ABN AMRO Bank Amsterdam, presentation

Outcome Business Plan

Table 10.4.6 Business Plan

Business Plan	Questions	Answers
Product plan	Products?	Money supply
		Treasury bills
		CP
		Eurocurrency
		Repo
		Derivatives
Production plan	What's needed?	Market
		Knowledge
		Information systems
Marketing plan	Clients?	Bond dealers
		Investors and fund managers
		Hedge funds
		Corporates
		Private clients
	Competitors?	Division I (FX Option Market)
		Division II (Commodity Market)
		Division III (Equity Market)
		Division IV (International Debt Market)

Strategy:
Division V (S-T-I-R Market) offers its clients a variety of products to use for hedging or speculative use. To understand the different products, a certain amount of knowledge is necessary.

DESIGN APPROACH II: SWOT ANALYSIS

S-T-I-R Market as driver of EUR/USD Interbank Market

Strengths

US Debt growth by sector

Table 10.5.1: US Debt growth by Sector, in percent

	Households	Business	EUR/$ Open	EUR/$ High	EUR/$ Low	EUR/$ Close
1999 Q1	9.2	13.2	1.1670	1.1906	1.0674	1.0765
1999 Q2	8.2	8.3	1.0771	1.0883	1.0254	1.0352
1999 Q3	9.1	10.7	1.0359	1.0826	1.0104	1.0682
1999 Q4	7.6	9.8	1.0676	1.0911	0.9986	1.0070
2000 Q1	7.9	10.4	1.0050	1.0414	0.9390	0.9560
2000 Q2	9.5	11.8	0.9560	0.9750	0.8843	0.9523
2000 Q3	8.0	6.4	0.9522	0.9597	0.8437	0.8837
2000 Q4	8.1	8.5	0.8840	0.9425	0.8225	0.9422
2001 Q1	7.8	5.1	0.9423	0.9595	0.8748	0.8774
2001 Q2	9.2	7.2	0.8742	0.9091	0.8408	0.8495

Source: Federal Reserve statistical release, Flow of Funds Accounts of the US, September 18, 2001, Reuters daily & weekly data

In the second quarter of 1999 the Debt growth of the Business sector decreases from +13.2 % to +8.3% and the EUR/USD moved from 1.0771 to 1.0352. The changes in the Debt growth explain, in six of the ten quarters, the movements in the EUR/USD.

So what happened in 1999-2001?
In the beginning of 1999 the stock markets were overshooting (going above their real value). The demand for stocks (technology) was not based on fundamentals but on Market Psychology. Market players were afraid of missing the boat and didn't listen to warning signals. The market was driven by greed and the greed was highly leveraged. When the bubble burst the market became the Movie Theater with one emergency exit. Market participants needed to sell their stocks to payoff their loans. A lot of capital was destroyed with the sell-off of the NASDAQ and other stock markets. The strange thing was that the USD was not affected by it. One of the reasons is that everyone was facing a liquidity squeeze. The US has the highest rate of participation of households in the equity markets. So when a liquidity squeeze is started, dollars are needed more than ever. This happened in the third quarter of 2000 and the first quarter of 2001, when the debt growth for households and businesses decreased.

Changes in outstanding US CP

Table 10.5.2[27]

		Commercial Paper outstanding (mln of dollars)		EUR/USD	
		CP	Change %	Open	Close
1999	Jan	1,178,168.00	0.01%	1.1670	1.1355
	Feb	1,178,303.00	2.23%	1.1355	1.0921
	Mar	1,204,627.00	1.26%	1.0921	1.0765
	Apr	1,219,789.00	0.84%	1.0771	1.0565
	May	1,230,009.00	-0.73%	1.0586	1.0420
	Jun	1,221,020.00	1.73%	1.0426	1.0352
	Jul	1,242,107.00	1.25%	1.0359	1.0705
	Aug	1,257,658.00	1.36%	1.0680	1.0562
	Sep	1,274,726.00	3.64%	1.0564	1.0682
	Oct	1,321,163.00	3.63%	1.0676	1.0548
	Nov	1,369,100.00	2.48%	1.0548	1.0089
	Dec	1,403,023.00	0.34%	1.0091	1.0070
2000	Jan	1,407,789.00	1.48%	1.0050	0.9693
	Feb	1,428,605.00	1.44%	0.9701	0.9646
	Mar	1,449,143.00	1.14%	0.9643	0.9560
	Apr	1,465,697.00	2.18%	0.9560	0.9120
	May	1,497,712.00	1.23%	0.9118	0.9377
	Jun	1,516,205.00	2.34%	0.9369	0.9523
	Jul	1,551,668.00	0.48%	0.9522	0.9259
	Aug	1,559,054.00	-0.09%	0.9263	0.8886
	Sep	1,557,700.00	1.92%	0.8885	0.8837
	Oct	1,587,591.00	2.32%	0.8840	0.8490
	Nov	1,624,421.00	-0.56%	0.8484	0.8722
	Dec	1,615,341.00	-3.04%	0.8722	0.9422
2001	Jan	1,566,104.00	-1.37%	0.9423	0.9362
	Feb	1,544,572.00	-2.15%	0.9370	0.9230
	Mar	1,511,354.00	0.54%	0.9235	0.8774
	Apr	1,519,528.00	-1.21%	0.8742	0.8888
	May	1,501,113.00	-2.14%	0.8888	0.8456
	June	1,468,919.00	1.03%	0.8446	0.8495
	July	1,453,770.00	1.34%	0.8495	0.8761
	Aug	1,434,238.00	-0.78%	0.8761	0.9122
	Sep	1,423,004.00	0.93%	0.9123	0.9098
	Oct	1,436,254.00		0.9100	0.8995

Source: Federal Reserve, Reuters daily data

The correlation between the change in the outstanding US CP and the change in the EUR/USD is –0.33 for the period January 1999 to October 2001. An increase in outstanding US CP means an increase in USD demand.

---

[27] www.federalreserve.gov/releases/cp/histouts.txt

By Sutton (BIS)[28]
"In the fourth quarter of 2000 the decline of issuance in the long-term debt market segment was more than offset by the surge of a large net issuance in the money market to $82 billion, more than five times as much as during the previous quarter. Issuers favor the USD over the EUR as the currency-denomination.

In the first quarter of 2001, net issuance of money market instruments in the international debt securities market fell from an unusually large $46 billion to $15 billion, with that of commercial paper, the largest component of money market instruments, decreasing from $25 billion to $16 billion. After several years of rapid growth, net domestic issuance in the three largest markets (US, Japan and Canada) turned sharply negative during the first quarter of 2001. Contributing factors to the slowdown in net CP issuance were a number of credit downgrades and the reduced willingness of banks to underwrite new issues. Money market funds are the main purchasers of CP, and the amount of lower-rated CP that they can hold is limited by SEC regulations. Credit downgrades below a given threshold can therefore severely curtail the demand for a particular issuer's CP".

By Gadanecz (BIS)[29]
"An important factor behind the overall slowdown in activity in the first quarter was the more than moderate pace of lending to telecommunications companies. Massive sums had been arranged for Telecoms in the second half of 2000, but this activity dropped off in the first quarter of 2001. Telecoms instead tapped the bond market".

So there was a shift from the S-T-I-R Market to the International Debt Market. Many of the Telecoms facilities arranged in 2000 were short-term and consequently will need to be refinanced.

---

[28] G.D. Sutton, *The International Debt Securities Market*, BIS Quarterly Review, March-June 2001
[29] B. Gadanecz, *The International Banking Market*, BIS Quarterly Review, June 2001

Table 10.5.3: in billions, inflows Eurozone (+); outflows (-)

		Portfolio investment	EUR/USD	
		MM instruments	Open	Close
1999	Jan	-0.7	1.1670	1.1355
	Feb	7.3	1.1355	1.0921
	Mar	6.8	1.0921	1.0765
	Apr	4.2	1.0771	1.0565
	May	8.9	1.0586	1.0420
	Jun	-1.5	1.0426	1.0352
	Jul	6.0	1.0359	1.0705
	Aug	7.0	1.0680	1.0562
	Sep	-2.2	1.0564	1.0682
	Oct	-10.7	1.0676	1.0548
	Nov	1.3	1.0548	1.0089
	Dec	13.2	1.0091	1.0070
2000	Jan	6.2	1.0050	0.9693
	Feb	11.3	0.9701	0.9646
	Mar	4.3	0.9643	0.9560
	Apr	10.7	0.9560	0.9120
	May	-0.3	0.9118	0.9377
	Jun	14.9	0.9369	0.9523
	Jul	-9.8	0.9522	0.9259
	Aug	-2.3	0.9263	0.8886
	Sep	-4.9	0.8885	0.8837
	Oct	-7.6	0.8840	0.8490
	Nov	-5.2	0.8484	0.8722
	Dec	3.2	0.8722	0.9422
2001	Jan	-5.7	0.9423	0.9362
	Feb	-2.0	0.9370	0.9230
	Mar	-7.7	0.9235	0.8774
	Apr	-1.3	0.8742	0.8888
	May	-1.8	0.8888	0.8456
	June	3.8	0.8446	0.8495
	July	2.1	0.8495	0.8761
	Aug	2.0	0.8761	0.9122
	Sep	-2.0	0.9123	0.9098
	Oct		0.9100	0.8995

Source: ECB Monthly Bulletin various issues, Reuters daily & weekly data

3 months interest rate spread Eurozone versus US

Table 10.5.4: 3 months spread

Year	Month	Euro area 3-months deposit	US 3-months deposit	Spread	EUR/USD Open	EUR/USD Close
1999	Jan	3.13	4.99	-1.86	1.1670	1.1355
	Feb	3.09	5.00	-1.91	1.1355	1.0921
	Mar	3.05	4.99	-1.94	1.0921	1.0765
	Apr	2.70	4.97	-2.27	1.0771	1.0565
	May	2.58	4.98	-2.40	1.0586	1.0420
	Jun	2.63	5.17	-2.54	1.0426	1.0352
	Jul	2.68	5.30	-2.62	1.0359	1.0705
	Aug	2.70	5.46	-2.76	1.0680	1.0562
	Sept	2.73	5.56	-2.83	1.0564	1.0682
	Oct	3.38	6.20	-2.82	1.0676	1.0548
	Nov	3.47	6.09	-2.62	1.0548	1.0089
	Dec	3.44	6.15	-2.71	1.0091	1.0070
2000	Jan	3.34	6.04	-2.70	1.0050	0.9693
	Feb	3.54	6.10	-2.56	0.9701	0.9646
	Mar	3.75	6.20	-2.45	0.9643	0.9560
	Apr	3.93	6.31	-2.38	0.9560	0.9120
	May	4.35	6.75	-2.40	0.9118	0.9377
	Jun	4.50	6.79	-2.29	0.9369	0.9523
	Jul	4.58	6.73	-2.15	0.9522	0.9259
	Aug	4.78	6.69	-1.91	0.9263	0.8886
	Sept	4.85	6.67	-1.82	0.8885	0.8837
	Oct	5.04	6.78	-1.74	0.8840	0.8490
	Nov	5.09	6.75	-1.66	0.8484	0.8722
	Dec	4.93	6.54	-1.61	0.8722	0.9422
2001	Jan	4.77	5.73	-0.96	0.9423	0.9362
	Feb	4.76	5.35	-0.59	0.9370	0.9230
	Mar	4.71	4.96	-0.25	0.9235	0.8774
	Apr	4.69	4.63	0.06	0.8742	0.8888
	May	4.64	4.11	0.53	0.8888	0.8456
	Jun	4.45	3.83	0.62	0.8446	0.8495
	Jul	4.47	3.75	0.72	0.8495	0.8761
	Aug	4.35	3.56	0.79	0.8761	0.9122
	Sept	3.98	3.03	0.95	0.9123	0.9098
	Oct	3.60	2.40	1.20	0.9100	0.8995

Source: ECB Monthly bulletin, various issues, Reuters daily data

The correlation between the EUR/USD movements and the 3-months Eurozone/US money market spread is 0.14 for the period January 1999 to October 2001. This means that an interest rate spread in favor of the Eurozone will give some support to the EUR/USD.

The correlation between the 3-month eurodollar future and EUR/USD is -0.45 (20 August 1999 – 31 October 2001). This can be explained from the turnover point of view. A decrease in US interest rates caused a higher demand of US interest rate derivative contracts. The correlation between the 3-months Euribor and EUR/USD is also negative, −0.35 (20 August 1999 − 31 October 2001). This negative correlation can be explained from the interest rate point of view. Lower Euro rates lower EUR/USD. So the two interest rate futures contracts have both a negative correlation with EUR/USD, which are based on two different explanations.

Increase turnover in US money market contracts

By Jeanneau (BIS)[30]
"In the second quarter of 2001 the turnover on exchange-traded derivatives markets reached a new high. Monetary policy easing appears to have been an important element in the high turnover of interest rate instruments. However, the changes in risk management practices may also have played a role. The ongoing strength of the turnover in the US money market contracts seems to have been related to attempts to hedge or take positions ahead of further US monetary easing. The sharp increase in the turnover of US money market contracts since the beginning of the year may also have reflected other underlying factors. The first two quarters witnessed high levels of gross issuance of dollar-denominated corporate and agency debt. This generated activity in the interest swap market and in turn, in the eurodollar futures, since such instruments are commonly used in the hedging of swaps. Activity may also have benefited from a broader movement of hedgers and traders away from the US Treasury yield curve and towards the LIBOR-based swap curve. Indeed, the higher turnover in eurodollar futures and options was accompanied by an even more rapid expansion of shorter-maturity contracts.

In the first quarter of 2001, exchange traded Interest rate contracts grew by 55%, to $124.8 trillion. Developments in short-term interest rate markets took center stage, with the turnover of money market contracts rising by 61%, to $107.3 trillion. Activity was particularly buoyant on the short-term US dollar rates (up by 76%) and on the Euribor (by 50%). The surge in short-term contracts seems to have been primarily related to the surprise 50bp inter-meeting cut in the federal funds target rate in early January and by the possibility of further monetary easing. In the case of Europe, the Eurosystem did not reverse its tightening stance of the first half of 2000, but market participants' expectations of lower short-term rates appear to have supported turnover in Euribor contracts. Activity in short-term contracts may have received an additional boost from second-round effects working through the other market segments. The increase in swap transactions, as a result of the sharp recovery in dollar-denominated corporate debt, may in turn have been associated with more active money market business, particularly in the eurodollar futures, since such instruments are commonly used in the hedging of swaps".

---

[30]S. Jeanneau, *Derivative Markets*, BIS Quarterly Review, June 2001, pp.28-37-September 2001, pp.29-33

DIVISION V SHORT-TERM-INTEREST-RATE MARKET

Weaknesses

M3 growth difference US/Eurozone

Table 10.5.5[31]

		M3 Growth				EUR/USD	
		US		Eurozone			
		Growth %	Change of growth %	Growth %	Change of growth %	Open	Close
1999	Jan	10.27	1.46	6.00	-11.67	1.1670	1.1355
	Feb	10.42	-12.00	5.30	3.77	1.1355	1.0921
	Mar	9.17	8.29	5.50	-3.64	1.0921	1.0765
	Apr	9.93	-1.41	5.30	5.66	1.0771	1.0565
	May	9.79	-2.04	5.60	0.00	1.0586	1.0420
	Jun	9.59	1.67	5.60	7.14	1.0426	1.0352
	Jul	9.75	0.51	6.00	-3.33	1.0359	1.0705
	Aug	9.80	-14.49	5.80	5.17	1.0680	1.0562
	Sep	8.38	-2.63	6.10	-4.92	1.0564	1.0682
	Oct	8.16	2.94	5.80	6.90	1.0676	1.0548
	Nov	8.40	3.93	6.20	-1.61	1.0548	1.0089
	Dec	8.73	-4.12	6.10	-14.75	1.0091	1.0070
2000	Jan	8.37	-5.50	5.20	19.23	1.0050	0.9693
	Feb	7.91	13.27	6.20	6.45	0.9701	0.9646
	Mar	8.96	2.34	6.60	1.52	0.9643	0.9560
	Apr	9.17	-1.64	6.70	-10.45	0.9560	0.9120
	May	9.02	2.11	6.00	-11.67	0.9118	0.9377
	Jun	9.21	2.71	5.30	-3.77	0.9369	0.9523
	Jul	9.46	6.13	5.10	7.84	0.9522	0.9259
	Aug	10.04	-5.38	5.50	-9.09	0.9263	0.8886
	Sep	9.50	5.26	5.00	-2.00	0.8885	0.8837
	Oct	10.00	-9.00	4.90	-4.08	0.8840	0.8490
	Nov	9.10	-2.20	4.70	4.26	0.8484	0.8722
	Dec	8.90	8.99	4.90	-8.16	0.8722	0.9422
2001	Jan	9.70	5.15	4.50	-2.22	0.9423	0.9362
	Feb	10.20	-1.96	4.40	4.55	0.9370	0.9230
	Mar	10.00	9.00	4.60	4.35	0.9235	0.8774
	Apr	10.90	6.42	4.80	10.42	0.8742	0.8888
	May	11.60	3.45	5.30	18.87	0.8888	0.8456
	June	12.00	-1.67	6.30	1.59	0.8446	0.8495
	Jul	11.80	-7.63	6.40	3.12	0.8495	0.8761
	Aug	10.90	12.84	6.60	6.06	0.8761	0.9122
	Sep	12.30	4.88	7.00	4.29	0.9123	0.9098
	Oct	12.90		7.30		0.9100	0.8995

Source: Reuters daily data, Bloomberg, ECB

---

[31] The idea to use the monetary base growth is from Deutsche Bank, however I use the relative M3 growth Eurozone divided by US

The period 1999-October 2001 shows a correlation between the change in the EUR/USD and US M3 growth % divided by Eurozone M3 growth % of -0.01 The means that a relative increase of the US M3 growth % is small but negative for the movements in EUR/USD. The relative M3 growth differential provides very limited or no explanation for movements in EUR/USD.

Lagging data

The ECB balance of payments data have a time lag of around two months. These data give good information as to what happened at that time. However, they are historical data, and don't give any explanations about what's driving EUR/USD at the moment.

Opportunity

Since April of this year the short-term interest rate spread moved from in favor for the US to in favor for the Eurozone. The real short-term interest rates in the US are well below the real short-term interest rates in Euroland for the first time since 1994. In the past, a significant move toward lower real short-term interest rates in the US would have been dollar negative. However, so far the USD has not been hurt by the negative interest-rate differential. One of the reasons is that the longer-term interest rate spread between the US and the Eurozone is around zero. A large change in this interest rate spread is needed before the EUR can profit from a relatively higher interest rate.

Threats

The main threats are Division I (FX Option Market), Division II (Commodity Market). Division III (Equity Market) and Division IV (International Debt Market). The first two market entities have already proved their influence on the EUR/USD. Division III (Equity Market) was surpassed in 2000 by Division IV (International Debt Market) because of the poor market performance of the Equity Markets. Up to November/December, in a low growth and low inflation environment, the bond markets have rallied. However, the recovery scenario of the US economy in 2002 made a partial shift of power back to the Equity Markets possible. The beginning of 2001, the S-T-I-R Market was able to gain some market share from the International Debt Market, because of market expectations of lower short-term interest rates. The International Debt Market regained this market share from the S-T-I-R Market as result of: 1) credit downgrades and, 2) being close to the easing cycle of the Fed.

Outcome SWOT Analysis

Table 10.5.6: SWOT Analysis

Strengths	Weaknesses
US Debt growth	Lagging flow data
Change outstanding US CP	Low correlation relative M3 growth
3-months interest rate spread Eurozone/US	
Increase turnover US money market contracts.	

Opportunities	Threats
Interest rate differential	FX Option, Commodity, Equity, Fixed-Income and Market

The strategy resulting from this SWOT Analysis is the following:
Use the strengths to explain movements in the EUR/USD. Keep an eye on the US Debt growth, and the outstanding US CP and 3-months interest rate spread between the Eurozone and the US.

10.6 POSITIONING APPROACH I

Let's view the position of this division compared to the other divisions in the EUR/USD Interbank Market Organization. The key question is:
Is this division able to explain the movements in the EUR/USD Interbank Market and how is this compared to the competitors?

Potential entrants:
The potential entrants are low since almost all the financial markets are defined as a division in the EUR/USD Interbank Market Organization. The only market left is the real-estate market including the funds operating in this market.

Intensity of rivalry among existing competitors:
The competitors of this division are:
- FX Option Market Division
- Commodity Market Division
- Equity Market Division
- International Debt Market Division

Division V (Short-Term Interest Rate, S-T-I-R, Market) is the fifth and last division in the EUR/USD Interbank Market organization. Division III (Equity Market) and Division IV (International Debt Market) are focused on a longer time horizon than this division. Both divisions have already proved that they provide explanations for the movements in EUR/USD. Flows continuously switch from the International Debt Market to S-T-I-R Market and vice versa.

Bargaining power of buyers:
The buyers are the funds, bond traders, investors, corporates and private clients. The buying power is high because they have the power to switch easily into other products such as Equity Market and International Debt Market products depending on the sentiment in the market.

Bargaining power of suppliers:
The suppliers in this market are Treasury, central banks (money supply), banks, corporates, the brokers, the providers of the trading system/pricing system/booking systems and information systems and the providers of specialized courses and seminars. The economic fundamentals are also part of the supply side. The suppliers are important in financial markets however the buyers have more power.

Pressure from substitute products:
The substitute products are the products offered by the other divisions in the EUR/USD Interbank Market Organization.
- FX Options
- Commodities Oil and Gold
- Equity Market products
- International Debt Market products.

Especially the Equity Market and International Debt Market products are good substitutes for the S-T-I-R Market products depending on the market sentiment.

10.7 THE POSITIONING APPROACH II:

Division V (S-T-I-R Market) is based on the industry evolution perspective, because the industry is complex, with a number of forces interacting simultaneously. In this industry the products are specialized and there are different levels of knowledge interacting with each other. It's necessary to understand all the levels of knowledge before it's clear what's driving this industry. This industry is in a maturity phase.

Buyer and Buyer Behavior
Investors usually have part of their funds invested in short-term deposits or other short-term money markets products. When the interest is very low they try to find alternatives to invest their money.

Products and products change
The quality is high in terms of pricing and information and there are independent rating agencies (CP issue). The standardization is seen in information and pricing.

Marketing
There is market segmentation towards small investors, bond traders, fund managers and hedge funds. Bond traders, fund managers and hedge funds have high knowledge and use it to get the highest quality available. The packaging is important, more tailor-made approach towards clients and information.

Manufacturing and Distribution
There is some overcapacity of short-term-interest-rate traders and trading desks are centralized.

Overall Strategy
In the market shares are more or less set. The strategy to increase market share is buying another company or merging with another company.

Competition
The competition among banks is fierce, and the sale people try to differentiate by combining information and traders' views with the product.

Margins and profits
The tight spreads means low prices. It is almost impossible to make money on the spread. There is an increased stability of market shares and price structures.

For more details about the concepts of industry evolution see "Competitive Strategy" by Michael Porter (1980).

SUMMARY 10

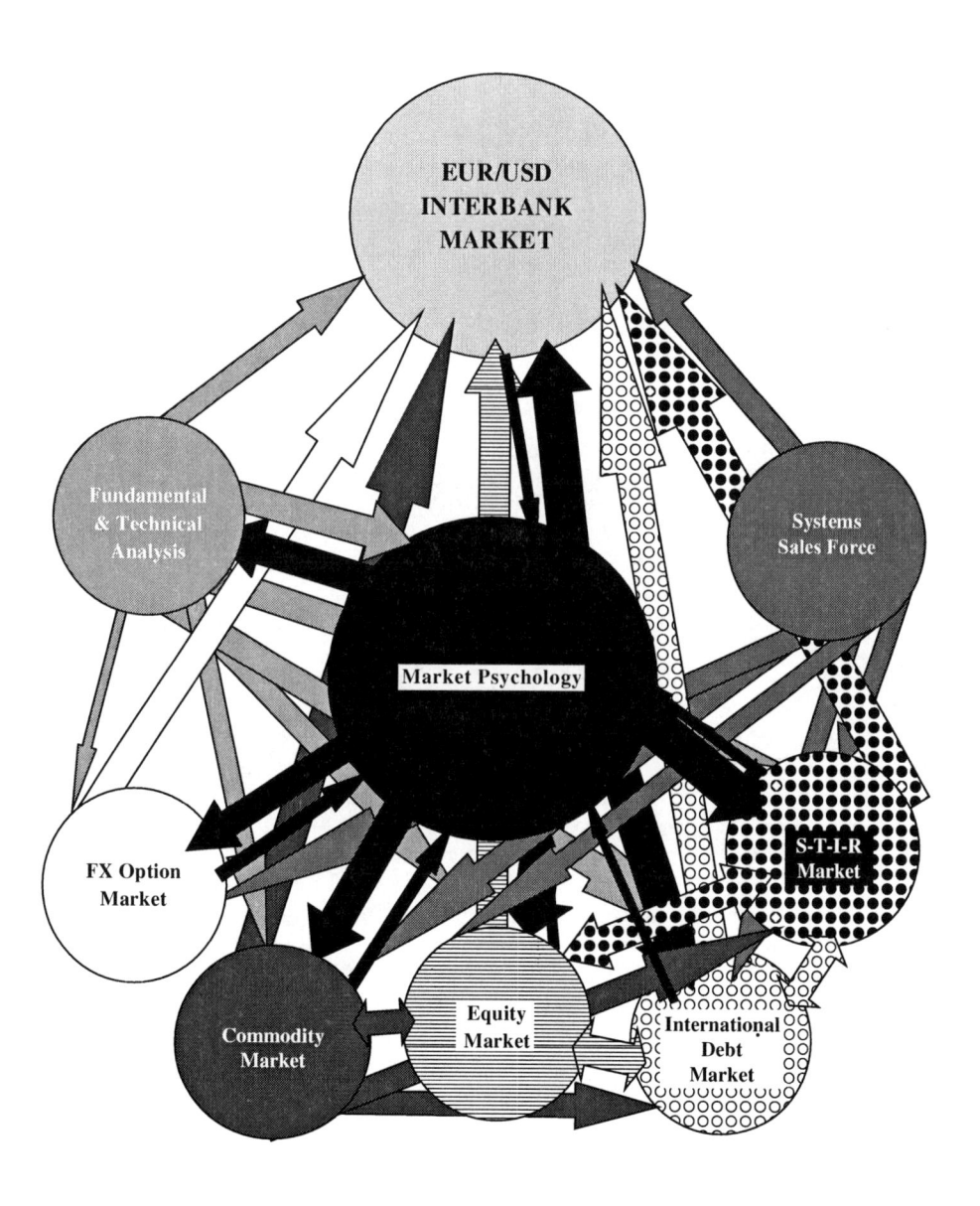

CHAPTER 10

➡

Market Psychology has a very high influence:
1. EUR/USD Interbank Market (Diversified Organization)
2. FX Option Market (Division I)
3. Commodity Market (Division II)
4. Equity Market (Division III)
5. International Debt Market (Division IV)
6. Short-Term-Interest-Rate Market (Division V)
7. Fundamental & Technical Analysis (Techno Structure) => for example cognitive dissonance

➡

When the market participants decide to widely use Behavioral Finance then the small arrow will become larger.

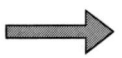

⇨

The systems are very important for EUR/USD Interbank Market and the other markets because without them the market we know now would not function well. The sales force is the crucial link between the products of the organization(s) and the clients.

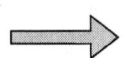

⇨

Market participants use widely fundamental and technical analysis. One participant might favor more fundamental analysis and another might favor a more technical analysis. Market participants in the FX Option Market are less frequent users of fundamental and technical analysis, because the highly specialized environment demands from the participants to do their own analysis. Fundamental and technical analysis have a large influence on Market Psychology:
– A panic reaction due to new information/news in the market
– The break of an important technical level.

⇨

The high influence of the FX Option Market on the EUR/USD Interbank Market in situations of:
1. Spot close large expirations.
2. High volatility in the market.
3. Extreme levels for risk reversals.
4. Spot close barrier levels or binary option level.
5. High demand for out-of-the-money options.

→

The Commodity Market has a high influence on the EUR/USD Interbank Market. **Gold/Oil ratio has a correlation of 0.65 with EUR/USD.** The Commodity Market also has a high influence on the Equity Market, International Debt Market and Short-Term-Interest-Rate Market. High oil prices will increase the change of higher interest rates, which would be negative for the equities, long-term, and short-term debt (the existing debt paper is worth less when interest rates increase).

↔

Uncertainty in equity markets such as accountancy problems & earnings uncertainty cause investors to switch out of equities into gold (Jan 2002 up to June 2002).

⇒

The Equity Market has a high influence on the EUR/USD Interbank Market in the following environments:
1. High GDP growth with low inflation.
2. Increasing GDP growth with low inflation.

In these environments the confidence in the economy is high and has as results:
 – Rallying equity markets
 – High M&A activity
 – High economic activity.

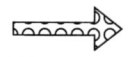

⇒

The International Debt Market has a high influence on the EUR/USD Interbank Market in the following environment: **Economic slowdown or recession with low inflation.**

⇒

The Short-Term Interest Rate Market has a moderate influence on the EUR/USD Interbank Market in the following environment: **Highly uncertain environments (credit downgrades and emerging markets turmoil) combined with a starting or ongoing (for that moment) easing cycle.**

Chapter 10

⇔

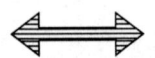

The Equity Market has a high influence on the International Debt Market and vise versa for the following reasons:
1. A sell-off in equities would cause investors to migrate from equities into bonds.
2. A sell-off in equities would cause the shift to an alternative financing method than IPO in M&A deals.
3. The fear of deterioration of the economic environment follows an interest easing cycle, which generally portends a good future for bonds.
4. Any expectations of an economic recovery would cause investors to migrate back from bonds into equities.

⇔

The International Debt Market has a high influence on the Short-Term-Interest-Rate Market and vise versa for the following reasons:
1. Borrowers would attract short-term debt when lower interest rates are expected.
2. Commercial Paper (CP) issue combined with a bridge loan will be favored over a bond issue when lower interest rates are expected.
3. When close to the end of an easing cycle, borrowers would move out of short-term debt into long-term debt, while investors would invest their money only short-term.
4. In an environment with credit downgrades and a reduced willingness of banks to underwrite new CP issue, issuers are forced to use the bond market to attract funds instead of the CP market.
5. When close to the end of a tightening cycle, investors would fix their investments for long-term maturities.

⇔

The Short-Term-Interest-Rate Market has a high influence on the Equity Market and vice versa for the following reasons:
1. In a high uncertain environment (sell-off equities, emerging markets turmoil, September 11 attacks) investors move their money out of equities into short-term deposits. This behavior would increase the M3 money supply.
2. When the environment becomes more stable again, the money comes slowly back in equities again.

REFERENCES

Enoch, C. and M. Quintyn. "European Monetary Union: Operating Monetary Policy", International Monetary Fund
Federal Reserve Board (2001). "Trading and Capital-Markets Activities Manual: Eurodollar Certificate of Deposit".
Federal Reserve Board (2001). "Trading and Capital-Markets Activities Manual: Commercial Paper".
Federal Reserve Board (2001). "Trading and Capital-Markets Activities Manual: Repurchase Agreements".
Federal Reserve Board (2002). "Trading and Capital-Markets Activities Manual: US Treasury Bills, Notes, and Bonds".
Federal Reserve Board (1998). "Trading and Capital-Markets Activities Manual: Financial Futures".
Jeanneau, S. "Derivative Markets", BIS Quarterly Review, June-September 2001
JP Morgan (1996), "Global Data Watch Handbook", New York
Gadanecz, B. "The International Banking Market", BIS Quarterly Review, June 2001
Krishnamurthy, A. (2001). "The Bond/Old Bond Spread".
Mintzberg, H., *STRUCTURES IN FIVES: Designing Effective Organizations*, Copyright © 1993. Reprinted by permission of Pearson Education, Inc., Upper Saddle River, New Jersey.
Mintzberg, H., B. Ahlstrand, J. Lampel, *STRATEGY SAFARI: The complete guide through the wilds of strategic management*, Copyright © 1998. Reprinted by permission of Pearson Education Ltd, 128 LongAcre, London WC2E 9AN
COMPETITIVE STRATEGY: Techniques for Analyzing Industries and Competitors by Michael E. Porter. Copyright © 1980, 1998 by The Free Press, an imprint of Simon & Schuster Adult Publishing Group. Reprinted with permission of the publisher.
Steiner, B. "The Money Market", Markets International Ltd, ACI Diploma study material.
Steiner, R., "MASTERING REPO MARKETS", Copyright © 1997. Reprinted by permission of Pearson Education, Inc., Upper Saddle River, New Jersey.
Sutton, G.D. "International Debt Market Securities", BIS Quarterly Review, March-June 2001

RECOMMENDED BOOKS

Fabozzi, F.J. (2001). "The Handbook of Fixed Income Securities", Mc-Graw-Hill, 6th edition.
Jones, F.J. and R.J. Teweles (1999). "The Futures Game: Who wins, Who loses & Why", Mc-Graw-Hill.

---

[47] S. Jeanneau, *Derivative markets*, BIS Quarterly Review, June 2001, pp.29-30

GLOSSARY

American style	The option can be exercised at any time up to and including its expiration date.
Asset swap	Usually the fixed-income arbitrageur purchases a bond and simultaneously swaps the bond's fixed-rate cash flows for floating rate cash of another security.
ATM	At-the-money. An option is ATM if its strike price is the same as the current market price for the underlying financial instrument.
ATS	Austrian Schilling
AUD	Australian Dollar
Average down	You buy the underlying and buy more when the price goes lower to make your average price more attractive. It is a trading strategy.
Average up	You sell the underlying and sell more when the price goes higher to make your average price more attractive. It is a trading strategy.
Barrier	A general term for a family of path-dependent options, which are either canceled or activated if the underlying price reaches a pre-determined level.
Base currency	**EUR**/USD, **USD**/JPY, **USD**/CHF, **GBP**/USD, **EUR**/GBP
BEF	Belgium Franc
Behavioral Finance	Behavioral Finance investigates the cognitive factors and emotional issues that influence on the decision-making processes of individuals, groups and organizations.
Bid	The price at which the trader buys when trader makes the quote.
"Big" figure	100 pips EUR/USD 0.8980, USD/JPY 131.10
Binary options	The principle is that the payout is either on or off, like a light switch.
BIS	Bank for International Settlements
Bobl	5-year German federal notes
BoE	Bank of England
Bunds	German government bonds
Butterfly spread	A butterfly spread is to purchase an out-off–the money strangle and simultaneously sell an at-the-money straddle.
CAD	Canadian Dollar
Callable	The call option gives the issuer (bond) the right to buy back the issue prior to the stated maturity.
Call option	A call option gives the holder the right to buy the underlying at a pre-determined exchange rate (strike = X) at a specific date in the future.
CAPM	Capital Asset Pricing Model
CBOT	Chicago Board of Trade
CD	Certificate of Deposit
CHF	Swiss Franc
CME	Chicago Mercantile Exchange
CMO	Collateralized Mortgage Obligations
COMEX	New York Commodity Exchange
Contango	Forward price (in futures market) is higher than the spot price.
Convergence criteria	Inflation, interest rate, exchange rate and finance policy criterion.
Covered call/put	A covered call or put arises when the writer has an offsetting position in the underlying.
CP	Commercial Paper
CPI	Consumer Price Index
Delta	Change in Price of the option for a change in spot
DEM	Deutsche Mark
Digital option	See binary option.
DJ	Dow Jones

DKK	Danish Kroner
EBS	Electronic Brokerage System, trading system for traders
ECB	European Central Bank
Econometrics	The field of economics that concerns itself with the application of mathematical statistics and the tools of statistical inference to the empirical measurement of relationship postulated by economic theory.
European style	The option can be exercised only on its expiration date.
Equity swap	A loan with equity as collateral.
ESCB	European System of Central Banks
EMI	European Monetary Institute
EMS	European Monetary System
ERM	**Exchange Rate Mechanism**
ESIN	**EU Economic Sentiment Indicator**
ESP	**Spanish Peseta**
EU	European Union
Euro fixings rates	Fixed rates against the Euro of DEM, FRF, NLG, ITL, PTE, ESP, ATS, LUF, BEF, FIM, IEP, GRD
EUR	Euro
Exercise price	See strike.
Exotic options	These are complicated derivatives with bizarre names.
Expiration date	The date on which the option ends.
Extrinsic value	The extrinsic value is the additional value above the intrinsic value (=optionality).
Fannie Mae	US Federal National Mortgage Association
Fed Beige Book	Sum of commentary on current conditions by the Federal Reserve Districts.
FIM	Finnish Markka
FOMC	Federal Open Market Committee (US)
Freddie Mac	US Federal Home Loan Mortgage Corporation
FRF	French Franc
FX	Foreign Exchange
FX Option	An FX Option gives the owner the right but not the obligation to exchange one pre-determined currency for another at a pre-determined exchange rate at a specific date in the future
Gamma	Change in delta for a change in spot.
GBP	Great Britain Pound
GDP	Gross Domestic Product
Ginnie Mae	US Government National Mortgage Association
GNP	Gross National Product
GRD	Greece Drachma
Quoted currency	EUR/**USD**, USD/**JPY**, USD/**CHF**, GBP/**USD**, EUR/**GBP**
Hedge	Make the position/exposure risk neutral.
Hedge funds	These are investment companies with legal and organizational structures conducive to an aggressive investment style.
HICP	Harmonized Indices Consumer Prices.
Holder	Option buyer.
HUD	US Department of Housing and Urban Development
IEP	Irish Punt
IFO	Institute of economic research in Germany.
IMF	International Monetary Fund
IMM	International Monetary Market (future exchange)
Interbank market	The market between market parties such as banks.
Intrinsic value	The intrinsic value is the difference between strike price and forward.
IPE	International Petroleum Exchange
IRS	Interest Rate Swap
ITL	Italian Lira
ITM	In-the-money.

GLOSSARY

JPY	Japanese Yen
Knock-in	A barrier option that becomes active if the underlying hits or crosses the barrier price.
Knock-out	A barrier option that dies if the underlying hits or crosses the barrier price.
LIBID	London interbank bid rate
LIBOR	London interbank offered rate, the rate at which banks are willing to lend to other banks of top creditworthiness.
LIFFE	London International Financial Futures and Options Exchange
LIMEAN	The average between LIBID and LIBOR.
Liquidity	The ease with which an operator can enter and exit the market for a given block of securities.
Liquidity hole	This is a temporary event in the market that suspends the regular mechanism of equilibrium attainment.
Long	You bought the underlying.
LUF	Luxembourg Franc
M&A	Merger and acquisition
MBS	Mortgage backed security
MBS arbitrage	Hedge fund strategy.
Mine	You bought the base currency on the trader's offer.
Mine 10	You bought 10 million of the base currency on the trader's offer.
MMF	Market Mutual Fund
Moments of an option	This represent the sensitivity to some order of change in the underlying security.
MSCI	Morgan Stanley Capital International
MSCI ACWI	MSCI All Country World Index
MTN	Medium-Term Notes
Naked option	The sell of a call or put without any underlying exposure.
NAPM (now ISM)	National Purchasing Managers Survey
NCBs	National Central Banks
NLG	Dutch Guilder
NOK	Norwegian Krone
NYMEX	New York Mercantile Exchange
NZD	New Zealand Dollar
Offer	The price at which the trader sells when trader makes the quote.
OMO	Open Market Operation
OPEC	Organization of Petroleum Exporting Countries.
Open interest	Open interest is the number of unliquidated or open contracts in a given futures market.
OTC	Over-the-counter
OTM	Out-of-the-money.
Outright	A FX deal with any value date different than spot
Payroll	The establishment survey records the number of employees on nonargricultural payrolls, the length of the average workweek.
Pfandbriefe	These are standardized German law debt instruments that are strictly regulated by the Mortgage Bank Act and reviewed by the Federal Banking Supervisory Authority.
Pip	1/10,000 except in JPY 1/100 EUR/USD 0.898**0**, USD/JPY 131.1**0**
PMI	Producer Manufacturing Index
PPI	Producer Price Index
PTE	Portuguese Escudo
Put option	A put option gives its holder the right to sell the underlying at a pre-determined exchange rate (strike = X) at a specific date in the future.
Regular barrier	A barrier option that dies out-of-the money.
Repo	Repurchase agreement
Resistance	The opposite of support and represents a price level or area over the market where selling pressure overcomes buying pressure and a price advance is turned back.

GLOSSARY

Reverse barrier	A barrier option that dies in –the-money.
Rho	Rho is the sensitiveness for domestic interest.
Risk reversals	An option strategy in which you buy the call option and sell the put option or vice versa.
Quote	Two-way price, bid and offer
Sallie Mae	Student Loan Marketing Association
SEK	Swedish Krona
SIMEX	Singapore International Monetary Exchange
Single currency	Euro
Short	You sold the underlying
Skew	Third moment, the delta of the gamma.
SNB	Swiss National Bank
Slippage	A practitioner's measurement for liquidity.
Spread	1. Difference between bid and offer. EUR/USD 0.8910-12 => 2 pips spread 2. Trading strategy 3. Difference in prices (or rates) of two financial securities
Spot	Deal (FX) for value two working days
Sticky strikes	These are OTC or listed strikes in which the buildup of a large open interest alters the behavior of the market around the strike price near expiration.
S-T-I-R Market	Short-Term-Interest-Rate Market
Straddle	An option strategy; the buy of both put and call and the same strike price.
Strangle	A straddle with both strikes out-of-the-money.
Strike	The pre-determined exchange rate at which the owner of the option can buy in case of a call option or sell in case of a put option is the strike price or strike.
SWOT Analysis	Strength, Weakness, Opportunity and Threat Analysis
Theta	Time decay of the option.
TVA	Tennessee Valley Authority
Unities	German Unity Fund bonds
U-Schatze	**Zero-coupon German Treasury notes**
USD	**United States Dollar**
Vega	**Change in Price of the option for a change in vol.**
Volatility	**Volatility measures the speed of the market by calculating the standard deviation of the return.**
Volume	**Volume is the number of futures contracts traded during a given time period which is usually a day.**
Writer	Option seller
Yours	You sold the base currency on the trader's bid
Yours 10	You sold 10 million of the base currency on the trader's bid

INDEX

Adhocracy, 4
American style, 152, 154,155, 338
Anchoring, 46, 73
ATM, 154, 159, 161
ATS, 19
AUD, 74
Barrier, 24, 46, 50, 56, 143, 152, 162, 163, 165, 168, 171, 175, 180, 356
Base currency, 19, 20, 21
BEF, 19
Behavioral Finance, 28, 29, 50, 51, 56, 58, 60, 61, 62, 79, 80, 109, 129, 130, 356
Bid, 289, 296, 297, 331
Binary options, 152, 153
Binomial trees, 158
BIS, 40, 174, 244, 245, 246, 263, 270, 292, 293, 295, 298, 309, 312-315, 345, 348,
Black & Scholes, 157, 160, 161
Bobl, 285, 286, 297, 300, 301, 302, 314
Bunds, 285, 296
Business Plan, 15, 31, 44, 55, 147, 164, 180, 205, 211, 232, 239, 260, 276, 284, 305, 321, 329, 342
CAD, 74
Call, 23, 37, 147-151, 154, 158, 159, 161, 172
Call option, 147, 149, 151-153
CAPM, 66
CBOT, 66
CD, 331
CHF, 23, 24, 32-35, 37, 52, 74, 215, 266
Cognitive approach, 9, 28-30, 51, 55, 56, 58
Cognitive dissonance, 28, 46, 69, 356
COMEX, 208
Commercial Paper, 293, 294, 329, 330, 334, 344, 345, 358
Commodity, 14, 26, 27, 28, 33, 46, 49, 50, 55, 56, 173, 182, 208, 251
Commodity Market, 4, 6, 10, 14, 26, 27, 46, 49, 50, 55, 56, 164, 176, 180, 183, 194, 195, 196, 205, 212, 215, 218, 220, 232, 235, 260, 271, 272, 273, 276, 280, 305, 308, 317, 318, 321, 342, 350, 351, 352, 355-357
Configuration, 2, 4, 13, 27, 55, 145, 195, 232, 237, 282, 327
Configuration approach, 4, 15, 25, 30, 51, 55, 140, 143, 144, 180, 183, 194, 232, 235, 236, 276, 280, 281, 321, 325, 326
Consolidation, 40, 42, 246, 315
Contamination principle, 162
Contango, 209
Convertible arbitrage, 246
Convexity, 161
Coordination mechanism, 4, 5, 6 , 8, 25, 27, 126, 145, 195, 237, 282, 327
Covered, 149, 163
Covertible bond arbitrage, 303
CP, 22, 47, 48, 50, 56, 247, 248, 313, 325-327, 330, 334, 340-342, 344, 345, 351, 358
CPI, 18, 75, 87, 93, 100, 107, 114, 115, 250, 251, 252, 308

Credit arbitrage, 299
Cross currency swap, 299, 315
Culture, 26, 27, 58, 145, 195, 237, 282, 327
Decentralization, 4, 6, 8, 27, 145, 195, 237, 282, 327
Delta, 154, 158-160, 174
DEM, 19, 20, 21
Derivative market, 238, 239, 248, 249, 254, 258, 260, 270, 272, 276, 281, 283, 284, 290, 299, 317, 321, 328, 329, 335, 336, 348
Derivatives, 173-175, 236, 254-256, 270, 303, 305, 321, 325, 326, 335, 342
Design approach, 10, 30, 31, 42, 45, 51, 55, 140, 143, 147, 165, 180, 205, 212, 232, 235, 239, 261, 280, 284, 306, 321, 325, 329, 343
Digital, 152, 153
Disjunction effect, 46, 75
Disposition effect, 64
Distressed Securitied, 257
Diversified, 4, 8, 9, 14, 15, 27, 30, 53, 237, 249, 312, 327, 356
Diversified configuration, 4, 8, 27, 55, 237, 276, 282, 327
DJ, 186, 187, 188, 223, 224, 225, 226, 227, 228, 229, 230, 231
DKK, 74
Dow Jones, 239, 240, 241, 258
Dynamic hedging, 154, 161, 162, 164, 171, 180
EBS, 37, 40, 52
ECB, 18, 19, 21, 23, 104, 106, 108, 113, 114, 115, 116, 124, 125, 126, 127, 192, 193, 203, 235, 268, 271, 272, 306, 307, 308, 310, 316, 317, 321, 333, 346, 347, 350
Econometrics, 249, 254
Economic exposure, 36
EMI, 17, 193
EMS, 15, 16, 17, 18
Entrepreneurial, 2, 4
Entrepreneurial approach, 9, 13, 28, 29, 30, 55, 140, 143, 146, 180, 196, 232, 235, 238, 276, 280, 283, 321, 325, 328
Equity Index arbitrage, 257
Equity Market, 14, 24, 26, 28, 47, 49, 50, 55, 56, 164, 176, 180, 183, 210, 211, 218, 220, 232, 234, 235, 236, 237, 238, 239, 257, 260, 261, 272, 273-276, 280, 304, 305, 317-319, 320, 321, 325, 342, 350, 351-353, 355-358
Equity swap, 237, 254, 255
ERM, 16, 17, 18
ESCB, 18, 21, 192, 340
ESIN, 107
ESP, 19
EU, 17, 86, 106, 107, 193, 287, 294, 333
Eurex, 300, 301, 302, 309, 314, 315, 332
Euro STOXX, 240, 241, 271
Eurocurrency, 326, 329, 331, 335, 342
Event-Driven, 245, 246, 257
Exchange rate criterion, 18
Exotic options, 43, 144, 146, 147, 152, 163-165, 171, 172, 178-180

364

INDEX

Expiration, 46, 50, 56, 143, 146, 154, 155, 163, 164, 165, 167, 168, 171, 172, 175, 180, 330, 338, 356, 360
Extrinsic value, 154, 156, 164, 180
Fed Beige Book, 71, 94
FIM, 19
Fixed-income arbitrage, 303
FOMC, 75, 94
FRF, 19
Fundamental, 14, 25, 27, 55, 130, 139, 244, 249, 253, 260, 273, 276, 345
Fundamental analysis, 82, 144, 145, 194, 195, 236, 237, 249, 253, 281, 282, 319, 326, 327, 355, 356
FX, 143, 147, 148, 173, 174, 178, 221, 268, 274
FX Option Market, 2, 7, 10, 14, 26, 27, 36, 46, 48, 55, 56, 140, 142-145, 147, 165, 166, 171, 176, 178, 180, 183, 210, 211, 218, 220, 232, 235, 260, 271-273, 276, 280, 305, 317, 318, 321, 342, 350-352, 355, 356
Gambling, 46, 76
Gamma, 159, 160
GBP, 17, 32, 34, 35, 40, 74, 190, 266, 269
GDP, 18, 47, 48, 50, 56, 75, 83, 84, 85, 86, 88, 91, 92, 93, 96, 97, 98, 102, 103, 104, 107, 110, 114, 115, 118, 119, 127, 235, 250, 251, 261, 263, 272, 276, 329, 357
GNP, 84
Gold, 23, 24, 33, 46, 48, 49, 50, 56, 182, 183, 189-196, 201, 202-211, 215-220, 222, 232, 274, 319, 353, 357
Gold lease, 207-209, 211, 217, 232
Government bonds, 281, 282, 284, 285, 297, 301, 303, 305, 321
GRD, 19
Greeks, 154, 159, 164, 180
Hedge, 32, 36, 37, 39, 151, 152, 159, 160, 162, 171, 174, 208, 209, 217, 256, 259, 270, 288, 300, 308, 315, 335, 339, 348
Hedge fund, 19, 39, 41, 163, 164, 180, 236, 237, 244, 245, 246, 254, 256, 258-260, 269, 275, 276, 282, 303, 304, 305, 320, 321, 339, 342, 354
Hedge fund strategies, 236, 239, 244, 256, 257, 260, 298
HICP, 107, 114, 115
Holder, 147, 148, 154, 190, 192
IEP, 19
IFO, 106, 107, 108, 117, 127
IMF, 71, 190, 191, 192, 202
IMM, 155
Inflation criterion, 18
Interbank, 2, 9, 10, 11, 14, 15, 19, 21, 25-30, 32, 39, 40, 46, 49, 52, 53, 55, 56, 74, 79, 82, 132, 143, 144, 165, 175, 176, 178, 183, 194, 212, 220, 221, 235, 236, 261, 273, 274, 280, 284, 292, 297, 303, 305, 306, 318, 319, 321, 325, 326, 343, 352, 353, 355-357
Interest rate criterion, 18

International bond market, 281, 283-285, 295, 304, 312-314
International Debt Market, 14, 26-28, 39, 47, 49, 50, 55, 56, 164, 176, 177, 180, 211, 218, 220, 232, 235, 248, 260, 261, 267, 271-274, 276, 279-284, 304, 305, 306, 313, 316-318, 321, 325, 342, 345, 350, 352, 353, 355-358
International loan market, 282-284, 292
Intrinsic value, 154, 156,164, 180
Irrelevance of history, 46, 77
IRS, 290
ITL, 19
ITM, 154, 159, 160, 162
JPY, 32, 33, 34, 35, 40, 49, 50, 51, 56, 74
Knock-in, 152, 168, 172
Knock-out, 152, 153, 172
Leverage, 245, 254, 257, 270, 339, 343
LIBOR, 332, 348
LIFFE, 155, 300, 301, 302, 309, 332
Liquidity, 67, 143, 162, 165, 171, 208, 217, 244, 253, 256, 259, 288, 289, 296, 303, 304, 309, 314, 315, 316, 335, 341, 343
Long, 20, 21, 147-151, 159, 160, 163, 245, 246, 257, 298
Loss aversion, 66
Loss realization aversion, 64
LUF, 19
M&A, 22, 23, 47, 50, 56, 235, 236, 239, 246, 247, 248, 256, 258, 260, 264, 265, 266, 267, 268, 271, 272, 276, 284, 293, 294, 357, 358
Maastricht Treaty, 15, 17
Machine, 4, 5, 6, 183, 195, 232
Magical, 46, 78
Market Neutral, 245, 257
Market Psychology, 26, 27, 29, 46, 49, 58, 61, 62, 79, 80, 109, 129, 145, 195, 237, 282, 327, 343, 356
MBS, 282
Mental compartments, 46, 74
Merger arbitrage, 47, 50, 56, 235, 258, 269, 272, 276
Middle line, 4, 5, 6, 8, 26, 27, 55, 144, 145, 194, 195, 236, 237, 281, 282, 326, 327
MSCI, 22, 47, 50, 56, 235, 241, 242, 243, 244, 246, 256, 267, 269, 272, 276
MTN, 282
Naked option, 149
NAPM, 89, 90, 105, 113, 127
NASDAQ, 240, 270, 343
NCBs, 18
NLG, 19
NOK, 74
NYMEX, 186, 187, 188, 225, 226, 227, 229, 230, 231
NZD, 74
Offer, 37

365

INDEX

Oil, 22, 23, 28, 33, 46, 50, 56, 182-188, 194-196-200, 205, 207, 210-215, 218-232, 246, 250, 274, 292, 308, 316-319, 321, 353 357
OPEC, 184-188, 196-200, 222, 223, 225-232 292
Operating core, 4, 5, 6, 7, 8, 26, 27, 55, 145, 194, 195, 236, 237, 281, 282, 326, 327
Option, 14, 50, 56, 145-155, 157-159, 163, 164, 171, 172, 174-176, 178, 179, 183, 194, 195, 203, 205, 207, 239, 248, 256, 257, 259, 270, 272, 276, 282, 288, 291, 302, 313, 327, 351
OTC, 154, 155, 163, 164, 174, 180, 245, 255, 288, 290, 297
OTM, 46, 50, 56, 154, 159, 160, 162, 165, 172, 175, 180
Outright, 37
Overconfidence, 46, 70, 77
Overreaction & underreaction, 46, 71
Payroll, 71, 91, 121
Pfandbrief, 281, 287, 288, 298, 315
Phi, 159, 160
Planning approach, 10, 30, 51, 196
PMI, 105, 113
Portfolio construction, 252
Positioning approach, 11, 13, 30, 51, 52, 53, 176, 178, 180, 220, 222, 232, 235, 273, 275, 276, 318, 320, 325, 352, 354
PPI, 75, 86, 87, 114
Pricing models, 154, 155, 157, 164, 180
Professional, 4, 6, 7, 145, 180
Prospect theory, 46, 63, 66, 70
PTE, 19
Put, 23, 37, 147, 148, 149, 150, 151, 154, 158, 159, 161, 166, 168, 169, 172,
Put option, 148, 150, 151, 154
Put/call relationship, 158
Quoted currency, 20
Rating, 290, 320, 330, 334, 354
Regret, 46, 68
Repo, 288, 289, 326, 327, 329-331, 335, 339, 342
Reverse barrier, 152, 153
Rho, 159, 160
Risk reversal, 46, 50, 56, 143, 151, 155, 156, 160, 161, 165, 166, 168-170, 175, 180, 356
S&P, 240, 246, 271
Sector approach, 240, 250
SEK, 74
Short, 20, 22, 148, 149, 151, 159, 160, 162, 244, 246, 257, 269, 298, 299, 301, 304, 335
Slippage, 162
Snake, 15, 16, 17
SNB, 33
Spot, 42, 143, 146, 160-162, 165, 166, 171, 172, 176, 185, 208, 209, 356
Spread, 150, 151, 287-289, 297-299, 304, 307, 325, 326, 335, 347, 350, 351, 354
Sticky strikes, 162
S-T-I-R Market, 9, 26, 27, 28, 47, 49, 50, 55, 56, 112, 176, 177, 180, 210, 211, 218, 220, 232, 235, 260, 267, 272-274, 276, 314, 317- 319,
321, 324, 325, 326, 327, 328, 329, 342, 343, 345, 350, 352-358
Stock index, 237, 239, 240, 248, 272
Stock indices, 49, 50, 56, 236, 237, 239, 256, 260, 269-272, 276
Stock swap, 247, 266, 272, 276
STOXX 50, 118-126, 240, 241
Straddle, 150, 151, 161
Strangle, 151, 161
Strategic apex, 4, 5, 6, 8, 25, 27, 55, 144, 145, 194, 195, 236, 237, 281, 282, 326, 327
Strategy, 2, 3, 6, 8, 9, 11, 27-29, 31, 45, 51, 53, 150, 151, 164, 175, 179, 209, 211, 219, 222, 237, 238, 260, 272, 275, 281-283, 305, 317, 327, 342, 351
Strike, 147, 148, 150, 151, 153, 154, 156, 157, 159, 162, 164, 168, 172, 180
Structure, 4, 6, 8, 11, 25, 31, 163, 183, 194, 236, 281, 326, 339
Support staff, 4, 5, 6, 8, 25, 27, 55, 144, 145, 194, 195, 236, 237, 281, 282, 326, 327
Swapnote, 300, 301, 302
SWOT Analysis, 10, 15, 30, 45, 50, 56, 143, 175, 180, 183, 212, 218, 232, 235, 261, 272, 276, 280, 306, 317, 321, 325, 343, 351
Syndicated loans, 284, 292, 294, 305, 321
Synthetic forwards, 158
Technical analysis, 14, 25, 27, 55, 130, 132, 133, 137, 138, 140, 145, 236, 237, 253, 281, 282, 326, 327, 355, 356
Techno structure, 4, 5, 6, 8, 25, 27, 55, 82, 132, 144, 145, 194, 195, 236, 237, 281, 282, 326, 327, 356
Theta, 159, 160
Transaction exposure, 36
Translating exposure, 36
Treasury bills, 285, 326, 329, 330, 332, 333, 336, 342
Treasury bonds, 285, 300, 303, 306, 307, 311, 335
Treasury notes, 285, 296, 300
Unities, 286
U-Schatze, 285, 286
Vega, 158, 159
Volatility, 48, 50, 56, 67, 70, 75, 133, 146, 150, 151, 154-161, 164-166, 175, 180, 254, 267, 270, 288, 306, 356
Volatility smile, 154, 161, 164, 180
Volume, 40, 42, 64, 70, 75, 139, 208, 268, 289, 298, 301, 334, 335
Washington Agreement, 192, 203, 220, 222
Writer, 149
Zurich Gold Pool, 208